ANNUAL EDIT

CW00351024

Human Sexuality

Thirtieth Edition

EDITOR

Susan J. Bunting

Lincoln College

Susan Bunting is a child, adolescent, and family therapist at Chestnut Health Systems, a consultant for Chestnut Global Partners, and an instructor in sociology and psychology at Lincoln College in Illinois. Dr. Bunting received her B.S. and M.S. in sociology and her Ed.D. in curriculum and instruction from Illinois State University. She has taught, counseled, trained, and developed curriculum in human sexuality, sexual abuse, substance abuse, domestic violence, self-esteem, child and human development, learning disabilities, behavior change, family, and intimate relationships. Dr. Bunting publishes pamphlets, instructional materials, articles, and books in these areas.

Contemporary Learning Series

2460 Kerper Blvd., Dubuque, IA 52001

Visit us on the Internet
http://www.mhcls.com

Credits

1. **Sexuality and Society**
   Unit photo—Rubber Ball Productions/Getty Images
2. **Sexual Biology, Behavior, and Orientation**
   Unit photo—Thinkstock
3. **Interpersonal Relationships**
   Unit photo—Royalty-Free/CORBIS
4. **Reproduction**
   Unit photo—Photodisc Collection/Getty Images
5. **Sexuality Through the Life Cycle**
   Unit photo—Digital Vision
6. **Old/New Sexual Concerns**
   Unit photo—The McGraw-Hill Companies, Inc./John Flournoy

Copyright

Cataloging in Publication Data
Main entry under title: Annual Editions: Human Sexuality. 30th Edition.
1. Sexual Behavior—Periodicals. 2. Sexual hygiene—Periodicals. 3. Sex education—Periodicals.
4. Human relations—Periodicals. I. Bunting, Susan J. *comp. II.* Title: Human Sexuality.
ISBN-13: 978–0–07–351618–9   ISBN-10: 0–07–351618–X   658'.05   ISSN 1091–9961

Thirtieth Edition

Cover image Photos.com and Image 100/PunchStock
Printed in the United States of America   1234567890QPDQPD9876   Printed on Recycled Paper

Editors/Advisory Board

Members of the Advisory Board are instrumental in the final selection of articles for each edition of ANNUAL EDITIONS. Their review of articles for content, level, currentness, and appropriateness provides critical direction to the editor and staff. We think that you will find their careful consideration well reflected in this volume.

Preface

In publishing ANNUAL EDITIONS we recognize the enormous role played by the magazines, newspapers, and journals of the public press in providing current, first-rate educational information in a broad spectrum of interest areas. Many of these articles are appropriate for students, researchers, and professionals seeking accurate, current material to help bridge the gap between principles and theories and the real world. These articles, however, become more useful for study when those of lasting value are carefully collected, organized, indexed, and reproduced in a low-cost format, which provides easy and permanent access when the material is needed. That is the role played by ANNUAL EDITIONS.

"Sex lies at the root of life and we can never learn to reverence life until we know how to understand sex."

The above quote represents a core belief of Havelock Ellis, a late nineteenth century sexologist. Some things haven't changed, but some things clearly have. In the 20 years that I have been involved with compiling the *Annual Editions: Human Sexuality*, one of the most remarkable changes has been in the amount and breadth of coverage sexuality-related topics and issues have received in the media. It is therefore likely that you, as students reading this edition, have already been exposed to far more discussion and information about sexuality than students of previous decades.

Despite this greater inclusion of sex and sexuality in the media and in social life, in general it is clear to experts in the fields of human sexuality and human relationships that the goal of most collegiate courses in human sexuality has not yet been accomplished. As you begin your examination of human sexuality in the first decade of the twenty-first century, try to remember that some things have changed, some things will change, and many things are likely to stay much the same. Maybe that's why it's important to emphasize the *human* in human sexuality.

Annual Editions: Human Sexuality is organized into six sections. *Sexuality and Society* notes historical and cross-cultural views and analyzes our constantly changing society and sexuality. *Sexual Biology, Behavior, and Orientation* explains the functioning and responses of the human body and contains expanded sections on sexual hygiene, diseases, and conditions affecting sexuality and functioning, and guides to preventive and ongoing sexual health care. *Interpersonal Relationships* provides suggestions for establishing and maintaining intimate, responsible, quality relationships. *Reproduction* discusses some recent trends related to pregnancy and childbearing and deals with reproductive topics including conception, infertility, contraception, and abortion. *Sexuality Through the Life Cycle* looks at what happens sexually throughout one's lifetime—from childhood to the later years. Finally, *Old/New Sexual Concerns* deals with such topics as sexual abuse, rape, sexual harassment, and legal and ethical issues regarding sexual behavior.

Also, in this edition of *Annual Editions: Human Sexuality* are selected *Internet References* that can be used to further explore the topics. These sites will be cross-referenced by number in the *topic guide*.

The articles have been carefully reviewed and selected for their quality, readability, currency, and interest. They present a variety of viewpoints. Some you will agree with, some you will not, but we hope you will learn from all of them.

Appreciation and thanks go to Loree Adams for her suggestions and expertise; to Cathy Ahart, Michael Fatten, Sue LeSeure, Marian Micke, Al Sodetz, and Joe Strano for their willingness to act as two-way sounding boards; to Mary Roy for her organization and assistance, to Ollie Pocs for inspiration, and to those who have submitted articles for this anthology or reviewed articles from previous editions. We feel that *Annual Editions: Human Sexuality* is one of the most useful and up-to-date books available. Please return the postage-paid article rating form on the last page of this book with your suggestions and comments. Any book can be improved. This one will continue to be—annually.

Susan J. Bunting
Editor

Contents

UNIT 1
Sexuality and Society

The concepts in bold italics are developed in the article. For further expansion, please refer to the Topic Guide and the Index.

UNIT 2
Sexual Biology, Behavior, and Orientation

The concepts in bold italics are developed in the article. For further expansion, please refer to the Topic Guide and the Index.

UNIT 3
Interpersonal Relationships

The concepts in bold italics are developed in the article. For further expansion, please refer to the Topic Guide and the Index.

The concepts in bold italics are developed in the article. For further expansion, please refer to the Topic Guide and the Index.

UNIT 4
Reproduction

The concepts in bold italics are developed in the article. For further expansion, please refer to the Topic Guide and the Index.

UNIT 5
Sexuality Through the Life Cycle

The concepts in bold italics are developed in the article. For further expansion, please refer to the Topic Guide and the Index.

UNIT 6
Old/New Sexual Concerns

The concepts in bold italics are developed in the article. For further expansion, please refer to the Topic Guide and the Index.

Part C.   Focus: Valuing Sexuality

The concepts in bold italics are developed in the article. For further expansion, please refer to the Topic Guide and the Index.

Topic Guide

This topic guide suggests how the selections in this book relate to the subjects covered in your course. You may want to use the topics listed on these pages to search the Web more easily.

On the following pages a number of Web sites have been gathered specifically for this book. They are arranged to reflect the units of this *Annual Edition*. You can link to these sites by going to the student online support site at *http://www.mhcls.com/online/*.

ALL THE ARTICLES THAT RELATE TO EACH TOPIC ARE LISTED BELOW THE BOLD-FACED TERM.

Internet References

The following Internet sites have been carefully researched and selected to support the articles found in this reader. The easiest way to access these selected sites is to go to our student online support site at *http://www.mhcls.com/online/*.

AE: Human Sexuality, 30/e

The following sites were available at the time of publication. Visit our Web site—we update our student online support site regularly to reflect any changes.

General Sources

National Institutes of Health (NIH)
http://www.nih.gov

Consult this site for links to extensive health information and scientific resources. The NIH is one of eight health agencies of the Public Health Service, which in turn is part of the U.S. Department of Health and Human Services.

SIECUS
http://www.siecus.org

Visit the Sexuality Information and Education Council of the United States (SIECUS) home page to learn about the organization, to find news of its educational programs and activities, and to access links to resources in sexuality education.

UNIT 1: Sexuality and Society

Department of State: Human Rights
http://www.state.gov/g/drl/hr/

The U.S. State Department's Web page for human rights includes country reports, fact sheets, reports on discrimination and violations of human rights, plus the latest news covering human rights issues from around the world.

SocioSite: Feminism and Women's Issues
http://www.pscw.uva.nl/sociosite/TOPICS/Women.html

Open this University of Amsterdam Sociology Department's site to gain insights into a number of issues that affect both men and women. It provides biographies of women in history, an international network for women in the workplace, links to family and children's issues, and more.

Woman in Islam: Sex and Society
http://www.jamaat.org/islam/WomanSociety.html

This Web site is sponsored by the secretary general of Pakistan offering objective analysis and explanations regarding a woman's role in Islamic society. Topics include marriage, family matters, and sex within Islamic society.

Women's Human Rights Resources
http://www.law-lib.utoronto.ca/Diana/

This list of international women's human rights Web sites provides interesting resources on marriage and the family; rights of girls; sexual orientation; slavery, trafficking, and prostitution; and violence against women.

UNIT 2: Sexual Biology, Behavior, and Orientation

The Body: A Multimedia AIDS/HIV Information Resource
http://www.thebody.com/cgi-bin/body.cgi

On this site you can find the basics about AIDS/HIV, learn about treatments, exchange information in forums, and gain insight from experts.

Healthy Way
http://www.ab.sympatico.ca/Contents/health/

This Canadian site, which is directed toward consumers, will lead you to many links related to sexual orientation. It also addresses aspects of human sexuality over the life span, general health, and reproductive health.

Hispanic Sexual Behavior and Gender Roles
http://www.caps.ucsf.edu/hispnews.html

This research report from the University of California at San Francisco Center for AIDS Prevention Studies describes and analyzes Hispanic sexual behavior and gender roles, particularly as regards prevention of STDs and HIV/AIDS.

Johan's Guide to Aphrodisiacs
http://www.santesson.com/aphrodis/aphrhome.htm

"The Aphrodisiac Home Page" provides links to information about a multitude of substances that some believe arouse or increase sexual response or cause or increase sexual desire. Skepticism about aphrodisiacs is also discussed.

Site of Parents, Familes, and Friends of Lesbians and Gays
http://www.pflag.org

This is the site of a national non-profit organization. Information and downloadable pamphlets with information and support on a variety of topics including "coming out" can be found here.

UNIT 3: Interpersonal Relationships

American Psychological Association
http://www.apa.org/topics/homepage.html

By exploring the APA's "PsycNET," you will be able to find links to an abundance of articles and other resources related to interpersonal relationships throughout the life span.

Bonobos Sex and Society
http://songweaver.com/info/bonobos.html

This site, accessed through Carnegie Mellon University, includes an article explaining how a primate's behavior challenges traditional assumptions about male supremacy in human evolution.

The Celibate FAQ
http://www.glandscape.com/celibate.html

Martin Poulter's definitions, thoughts, and suggested resources on celibacy were created, he says, "in response to the lack of celibate stuff (outside of religious contexts) on the Internet," and his perception of the Net's bias against celibacy can be found on this site.

Go Ask Alice
http://www.goaskalice.columbia.edu

This interactive site provided by Healthwise, a division of Columbia University Health Services, includes discussion and insight into a number of personal issues of interest to college-age people—and those younger and older. Many questions about physical and emotional health and well-being in the modern world are answered.

UNIT 4: Reproduction

Ask NOAH About Pregnancy: Fertility & Infertility
http://www.noah-health.org/en/search/health.html

New York Online Access to Health (NOAH) seeks to provide relevant, timely, and unbiased health information for consumers. At this site, the organization presents extensive links to a variety of resources about infertility treatments and issues.

Childbirth.Org
http://www.childbirth.org

This interactive site about childbirth options is from an organization that aims to educate consumers to know their options and provide themselves with the best possible care to ensure healthy pregnancies and deliveries. The site and its links address a myriad of topics, from episiotomy to water birth.

Planned Parenthood
http://www.plannedparenthood.org

Visit this well-known organization's home page for links to information on the various kinds of contraceptives (including outercourse and abstinence) and to discussions of other topics related to sexual and reproductive health.

UNIT 5: Sexuality Through the Life Cycle

American Association of Retired Persons (AARP)
http://www.aarp.org

The AARP, a major advocacy group for older people, includes among its many resources suggested readings and Internet links to organizations that deal with the health and social issues that may affect one's sexuality as one ages.

National Institute on Aging (NIA)
http://www.nih.gov/nia/

The NIA, one of the institutes of the National Institutes of Health, presents this home page to lead you to a variety of resources on health and lifestyle issues that are of interest to people as they grow older.

Teacher Talk
http://education.indiana.edu/cas/tt/tthmpg.html

This home page of the publication *Teacher Talk* from the Indiana University School of Education Center for Adolescent Studies will lead you to many interesting teacher comments, suggestions, and ideas regarding sexuality education and how to deal with sex issues in the classroom.

World Association for Sexology

http://www.tc.umn.edu/nlhome/m201/colem001/was/wasindex.htm

The World Association for Sexology works to further the understanding and development of sexology throughout the world. Access this site to explore a number of issues and links related to sexuality throughout life.

UNIT 6: Old/New Sexual Concerns

The Child Rights Information Network (CRIN)

http://www.crin.org

The Child Rights Information Network (CRIN) is a global network that disseminates information about the Convention on the Rights of the Child and child rights among nongovernmental organizations (NGOs), United Nations agencies, intergovernmental organizations (IGOs), educational institutions, and other child rights experts.

Infertility Resources

http://www.ihr.com/infertility/index.html

This site includes links to the Oregon Health Sciences University Fertility Program and the Center for Reproductive Growth in Nashville, Tennessee. Ethical, legal, financial, psychological, and social issues are discussed.

Third Age: Love and Sex

http://www.thirdage.com/romance/

This interactive site explores a current topic: relationships forged on the Internet. Browse here to hear various viewpoints on the issue. Advice columnists and psychologists add their perspectives.

We highly recommend that you review our Web site for expanded information and our other product lines. We are continually updating and adding links to our Web site in order to offer you the most usable and useful information that will support and expand the value of your Annual Editions. You can reach us at: *http://www.mhcls.com/annualeditions/*.

UNIT 1
Sexuality and Society

Unit Selections

Key Points to Consider

- Many people, both within and outside the American culture, have judged its beliefs and values about sex as unhealthy and/or problematic. What do you think?

- Have you ever spoken to a young person from another culture/country about sexuality-related ideas, norms, education, or behavior? If so, what surprised you? What did you think about their perspective or ways?

- Do you feel the American culture is too permissive or too rigid with respect to sexual norms, expectations, and laws? Why? Do we talk too much or too little about sex? Why?

- What do you think can and should be done about HIV/AIDS, child sexual abuse, and prostitution in developing countries?

- In what ways does it matter whether the source of gender differences is biological or cultural? Do you feel that either gender has a "better" sex role or a wider range of acceptable behaviors? If so, which?

Student Web Site

www.mhcls.com/online

Internet References

Further information regarding these Web sites may be found in this book's preface or online.

Department of State: Human Rights
http://www.state.gov/g/drl/hr/
SocioSite: Feminism and Women's Issues
http://www.pscw.uva.nl/sociosite/TOPICS/Women.html
Woman in Islam: Sex and Society
http://www.jamaat.org/islam/WomanSociety.html
Women's Human Rights Resources
http://www.law-lib.utoronto.ca/Diana/

People of different civilizations in different historical periods have engaged in a variety of modes of sexual expression and behavior. Despite this cultural and historical diversity, it is clear that human sexuality is a dynamic and complex force that involves psychological and sociocultural, as well as physiological facets. Our sexuality includes our whole body and personality, while we learn what it means to be sexual and to behave sexually within the structure and parameters of our era through our family, social group, and society. By studying varying cultures and eras we see more clearly the interplay between the biological, psychological, and sociocultural, as well as between the person, generation, and society.

For several centuries, Western civilization, especially Western European and, in turn, American cultures, has been characterized by an "antisex ethic." This belief system includes a variety of negative views and norms about sex and sexuality, including denial, fear, restriction, and the detachment of sexual feelings and behavior from the wholeness of personhood or humanity. Indeed, it has only been in the last 50 years that the antisex proscriptions against knowing or learning about sex have lost their stranglehold so that people can find accurate information about their sexual health, sexual functioning, and birth control without fear of stigma or even incarceration. In fact, many Americans and others have become increasingly concerned in recent years about the ways in which sex and sexual topics have

been discussed and written about in various media formats. On the surface it might seem that the "antisex ethic" no longer reigns. However, it is still active but now co-exists with an in-your-face, commercialized and also negative view of sex.

One generalization on which sociologists and others who study human behavior anywhere in the world can agree on is that social change in beliefs, norms, or behavior—sexual or otherwise—is not easily accomplished. When it does occur, it is linked to significant changes in the social environment and usually happens as a result of interest groups that move society to confront and question existing beliefs, norms, and behavior. Changes in the social environment that have been most often linked to changes in sexuality and its expression include the invention of the car, the liberation of women from the kitchen, changes in the legality and availability of birth control, the reconsideration of democratic values of individual freedom and the pursuit of happiness, demographic shifts where particular (or different) age groups predominate, the growth of mass media, and the coming of the computer age and related technologies. The social groups that have been involved in the process of this sexual/social change have also been far-reaching. In the United States they include the earliest feminists, the suffragettes; Margaret Sanger, the mother of the birth control movement; mainstream religious groups that insist that "sexuality is a good gift from God"; publishers of sex education curricula for youth; pioneering researchers like Alfred Kinsey, Havelock Ellis, William Masters, Virginia Johnson, and others; and a panorama of interest groups who have advocated changes, demanded rights, or both.

Many events, people, and perspectives have played a role in sexuality beliefs and behaviors today. One of the most dramatic is from the "don't-talk-about-it" to an "everyone's-talking-about-it" communication norm. Current examples range from baby-boomer women about menopause and hormone replacement therapy, to prominent politicians, athletes, or entertainment celebrities about erectile dysfunction, sexually transmitted diseases, breast or prostate cancer, to public service and paid advertisements on television, radio, and the Internet for contraceptives, erectile dysfunction medications, and sexual lubricants. However, it is also clear that some things have not changed as much as we might expect given the increased talk, information, and availability of birth control and other sexual health products and services. It is not characteristic for the majority of people of any age to feel comfortable with and communicate about sexual feelings, fears, needs, and desires. Negotiating, even understanding, consent and responsibility seems even harder today than when we were not talking. The incidence of unplanned, unwed, and teenage pregnancies, sexually transmitted diseases (some life-threatening), molestation, incest, rape, and sexual harassment continue to be troubling, especially because rates of these sexuality-related problems are not lowest in what we perceive as the "most developed" or enlightened country, the United States. At the same time, despite more knowledge than ever before and the efforts of many in the educational, medical, and political spheres, the dream of healthy, positive, and fulfilling sexuality still eludes many individuals and society as a whole.

This unit overviews historical, cross-cultural, and current issues and trends in order to illustrate the connectedness of our values, practices, and experiences of sexuality. In so doing it is meant to challenge readers to adopt a very broad perspective through which their examination of today's sexuality, and their experience of it, can be more meaningful. Only in so doing can we hope to avoid a fear-based return to the "antisex ethic" of the past while striving to evaluate the impact and value of the social changes that have so profoundly affected sexuality at the dawn of the twenty-first century.

Vox Populi: Sex, Lies, and Blood Sport

Gossip in the glory days of Rome was just like ours—but written in stone

HEATHER PRINGLE

P liny the Elder, the Roman savant who compiled the eclectic 37-book encyclopedia *Historia Naturalis* nearly 2,000 years ago, was obsessed with the written word. He pored over countless Greek and Latin texts, instructing his personal secretary to read aloud to him even while he was dining or soaking in the bath. And when he traveled the streets of Rome, he insisted upon being carried everywhere by slaves so he could continue reading. To Pliny, books were the ultimate repository of knowledge. "Our civilization—or at any rate our written records—depends especially on the use of paper," he wrote in *Historia Naturalis*.

Pliny was largely blind, however, to another vast treasury of knowledge, much of it literally written in stone by ordinary Romans. Employing sharp styli generally reserved for writing on wax tablets, some Romans scratched graffiti into the plastered walls of private residences. Others hired professional stonecutters to engrave their ramblings on tombs and city walls. Collectively, they left behind an astonishing trove of pop culture—advertisements, gambling forms, official proclamations, birth announcements, magical spells, declarations of love, dedications to gods, obituaries, playbills, complaints, and epigrams. "Oh, wall," noted one citizen of Pompeii, "I am surprised that you have not collapsed and fallen, seeing that you support the loathsome scribblings of so many writers."

More than 180,000 of these inscriptions are now cataloged in the *Corpus Inscriptionum Latinarum,* a mammoth scientific database maintained by the Berlin-Brandenburg Academy of Sciences and Humanities. The *Corpus* throws open a large window on Roman society and reveals the ragged edges of ordinary life—from the grief of parents over the loss of a child to the prices prostitutes charged clients. Moreover, the inscriptions span the length and breadth of the empire, from the Atlantic coast of Spain to the desert towns of Iraq, from the garrisons of Britain to the temples of Egypt. "It would be impossible to do most of Roman history without them," says Michael Crawford, a classicist at University College London.

The *Corpus* was conceived in 1853 by Theodor Mommsen, a German historian who dispatched a small army of epigraphists to peruse Roman ruins, inspect museum collections, and ferret out inscribed slabs of marble or limestone wherever they had been recycled, including the tops of medieval bell towers and the undersides of toilet seats. Working largely in obscurity, Mommsen's legions and their successors measured, sketched, and squeezed wet paper into crevices. Currently, *Corpus* researchers add as many as 500 inscriptions each year to the collection, mostly from Spain and other popular tourist destinations in the Mediterranean where excavations for hotel and restaurant foundations reveal new epigraphic treasures.

Packed with surprising details, the *Corpus* offers scholars a remarkable picture of everyday life: the tumult of the teeming streets in Rome, the clamor of commerce in the provinces, and the hopes and dreams of thousands of ordinary Romans—innkeepers, ointment sellers, pastrycooks, prostitutes, weavers, and wine sellers. The world revealed is at once tantalizingly, achingly familiar, yet strangely alien, a society that both closely parallels our own in its heedless pursuit of pleasure and yet remains starkly at odds with our cherished values of human rights and dignity.

The Gift of Bacchus

To most Romans, civilization was simply untenable without the pleasures of the grape. Inscriptions confirm that wine was quaffed by everyone from the wealthy patrician in his painted villa to soldiers and sailors in the roughest provincial inns. And although overconsumption no doubt took a toll, wine was far safer than water: The acid and alcohol in wine curbed the growth of dangerous pathogens.

Epicures took particular delight in a costly white wine known as Falernian, produced from Aminean grapes grown on mountain slopes south of modern-day Naples. To improve the flavor, Roman vintners aged the wine in large clay amphorae for at least a decade until it turned a delicate amber. Premium vintages—some as much as 160 years old—were reserved for the emperor and were served in fine crystal goblets. Roman oenophiles, however, could purchase younger vintages of Falernian, and they clearly delighted in bragging of its expense. "In the grave I lie," notes the tombstone of one wine lover, "who was once well known as Primus. I lived on Lucrine oysters, often drank Falernian wine. The pleasures of bathing, wine, and love aged with me over the years."

Estate owners coveted their own vineyards and inscribed heartfelt praises for "nectar-sweet juices" and "the gift of Bacchus" on their winepresses. Innkeepers marked their walls with wine lists and prices. Most Romans preferred their wine diluted with water, perhaps because they drank so much of it, but they complained bitterly when servers tried to give them less than they bargained for. "May cheating like this trip you up, bartender," noted the graffito of one disgruntled customer. "You sell water and yourself drink undiluted wine."

So steeped was Roman culture in wine that its citizens often rated its pleasures above nearly all else. In the fashionable resort town of Tibur, just outside Rome, the tomb inscription of one bon vivant counseled others to follow his own example. "Flavius Agricola [was] my name. . . . Friends who read this listen to my advice: Mix wine, tie the garlands around your head, drink deep. And do not deny pretty girls the sweets of love."

Pleasures of Venus

Literary scholars such as C. S. Lewis (who wrote, among many other things, *The Chronicles of Narnia*) have often suggested that romantic love is a relatively recent invention, first surfacing in the poems of wandering French and Italian troubadours in the 11th and 12th centuries. Before then, goes the argument, couples did not know or express to one another a passionate attachment, and therefore left no oral or written record of such relationships. Surviving inscriptions from the Roman Empire paint a very different portrait, revealing just how much Romans delighted in matters of the heart and how tolerant they were of the love struck. As one nameless writer observed, "Lovers, like bees, lead a honeyed life."

Many of the infatuated sound remarkably like their counterparts today. "Girl," reads an inscription found in a Pompeian bedroom, "you're beautiful! I've been sent to you by one who is yours." Other graffiti are infused with yearning that transcends time and place. "Vibius Restitutus slept here alone, longing for his Urbana," wrote a traveler in a Roman inn. Some capture impatience. "Driver," confides one, "if you could only feel the fires of love, you would hurry more to enjoy the pleasures of Venus. I love a young charmer, please spur on the horses, let's get on."

Often, men boasted publicly about their amorous adventures. In bathhouses and other public buildings, they carved frank descriptions of their encounters, sometimes scrawling them near the very spot where the acts took place. The language is graphic and bawdy, and the messages brim with detail about Roman sexual attitudes and practices. Many authors, for example, name both themselves and their partners. In Rome, men who preferred other men instead of women felt no pressure to hide it.

A large and lucrative sex trade flourished in Roman cities, and prostitutes often advertised their services in short inscriptions. One of the stranger aspects of Roman life is that many wealthy families rented out small rooms in their homes as miniature brothels, known as *cellae meretriciae*. Such businesses subsidized the lavish lifestyles of the owners. At the other end of the sex trade were elegant Roman courtesans. In Nuceria, near present-day Naples, at least two inscriptions describe Novelli Primigenia, who lived and worked in the "Venus Quarter." So besotted was one of her clients that he carved: "Greetings to you, Primigenia of Nuceria. Would that I were the gemstone (of the signet ring I gave you), if only for one single hour, so that, when you moisten it with your lips to seal a letter, I can give you all the kisses that I have pressed on it."

Most Roman citizens married, and some clearly enjoyed remarkably happy unions. One inscription unearthed just outside Rome records an epitaph for a particularly impressive woman, composed by her adoring husband. Classicists have fervently debated the identity of this matron, for the epitaph recalls the story of Turia, who helped her husband escape execution during civil unrest in the first century B.C. The inscription has crumbled into fragments, however, and the section containing the name of the woman has been lost, but it is clear her cleverness and audacity saved the day for her spouse. "You furnished most ample means for my escape," reads the inscription, elegantly carved by a stonecutter. "With your jewels you aided me when you took off all the gold and pearls from your person, and handed them over to me, and promptly, with slaves, money, and provisions, having cleverly deceived the enemies' guards, you enriched my absence."

Little Darlings

A prominent French historian, Philippe Ariès, has theorized that it was not until the beginning of industrialization—which boosted the standard of living in Europe during the 18th and 19th centuries—that parents began bonding deeply with their babies. In earlier times, infant mortality rates were staggering, leading parents to distance themselves emotionally from babies who might perish from malnutrition or infection before learning to walk.

Intriguingly, studies of Roman tomb inscriptions lend credence to Ariès's idea. The British classicist Keith Hopkins has estimated, based on comparative demographic data, that 28 percent of all Roman children died before reaching 12 months of age. Yet epigraphists have found relatively few inscribed tombs for Roman infants in Italy: Just 1.3 percent of all funerary stones mark such burials. The statistical discrepancy suggests to many classicists that parents in ancient Rome refrained from raising an expensive marble monument for a child, unwilling to mourn publicly or privately.

Some Romans, however, could not and did not repress the love they felt for their infants. As many graffiti reveal, they celebrated a baby's birth in an openly sentimental manner recognizable to parents today. "Cornelius Sabinus has been born," announced a family in a message carved in a residential entranceway, a spot where neighbors and passersby could easily see it. Others went further, jubilantly inscribing the equivalent of baby pictures. "Iuvenilla is born on Saturday the 2nd of August, in the second hour of the evening," reads one such announcement; nearby, someone sketched in charcoal a picture of a newborn.

The epitaphs composed for infant tombs also disclose a great deal about the intense grief some parents suffered. One inscription describes a baby whose brief life consisted of just "nine sighs," as if the parents had tenderly counted each breath their newborn had taken. Another funerary inscription describes in poignant detail a father's grief. "My baby Acerva," he wrote, "was snatched away to live in Hades before she had her fill of the sweet light of life. She was beautiful and charming, a little darling as if from heaven. Her father weeps for her and, because he is her father, asks that the earth may rest lightly on her forever."

Other carved messages supply details about schooling. As children learned to write, local walls served as giant exercise books where they could practice their alphabets. On one, a young student scrawled what seems to be a language arts drill, interlacing the opening letters of the Roman alphabet with its final ones—A X B V C T. In another inscription, a Roman couple marveled at the eloquence of their 11-year-old son, who had entered a major adult competition for Greek poetry. The boy took his place, they noted, "among 52 Greek poets in the third lustrum of the contest, [and] by his talent brought to admiration the sympathy that he had roused because of his tender age, and he came away with honor." The young poet died shortly after his performance.

The Sporting Life

The Romans loved to be entertained, and few things riveted them more than the spectacle of gladiatorial combat. Sports fans fervently tracked the career records of the most skilled gladiators and laid wagers on their survival, while well-to-do female admirers stole into gladiator barracks by night, prompting one combatant, Celadus, to boast in an inscription that he was "the girls' desire." That most gladiators were slaves forced to fight to the death for an afternoon's entertainment of the public did not trouble most Romans: They believed that a demonstration of bravery in the arena brought nobility to even the lowliest slave and that the price—death—was worth it.

So ingrained were gladiatorial games in Roman culture that senior government officials dug into their own pockets and emptied public purses to stage them. To pack an arena, the sponsor often advertised the games with an *edicta munerum,* an inscription painted by teams of professional artists on walls near the local amphitheater. One surviving poster describes how Decimus Lucretius Satrius Valeris, a priest of Nero, and another prominent Roman sponsored a major event in Pompeii spanning five consecutive days before the ides of April. The expensive attractions included 20 pairs of gladiators, the "customary [wild] beast hunt," and "awnings" to shade spectators against the summer sun.

The gladiators steeled themselves for the battle ahead, practicing their deadly swordplay. The devout among them prayed to gods for a victory. In a North African barrack, Manuetus the Provocator, a gladiator who fought with a short, straight sword, made a last vow, promising to "bring Venus the gift of a shield if victorious." Outside the gladiators' barracks, scribes painted walls with announcements and programs for the upcoming event, listing the combatants' names and career records.

On the day of the games, raucous and bloodthirsty crowds flooded the arena. At Rome's Colosseum, each spectator held a tessera, a ticket corresponding to a number inscribed on one of the building's 80 arcades. Each arcade then led ticket holders to a staircase and a specific section of seating. As spectators waited for the bloody combat matches to begin, they snacked on bread or cakes purchased from stalls outside the arena. Local chefs baked breads especially for the games, employing molds bearing designs of dueling gladiators and the name of the baker.

At the end of each fatal match, stretcher bearers hustled out on the floor of the arena to collect the fallen gladiator and carry his body to a nearby morgue, or *spoliarium.* There officials slit the man's throat to ensure that he was truly dead: Roman bettors despised fixed matches. Friends and family members then claimed the body and, if they possessed sufficient funds, raised a tomb in his memory. "To the reverend spirits of the Dead," inscribed one grieving widow. "Glauca was born at Mutina, fought seven times, died in the eighth. He lived 23 years, 5 days. Aurelia set this up to her well-deserving husband, together with those who loved him. My advice to you is to find your own star. Don't trust Nemesis [patroness of gladiators]; that is how I was deceived. Hail and Farewell."

As studies of epitaphs show, skilled gladiators rarely survived more than 10 matches, dying on average at the age of 27.

Ancient Pipe Dreams

Some of the humblest inscriptions shed surprising light on one of the glories of Roman technology, revealing just how close ancient metalworkers came to a major coup—the invention of printing. In the Roman waterworks, messages were raised in relief on the lead pipes that fed fountains, baths, and private homes. As a rule, these short texts recorded the name of the emperor or the municipal official who had ordered and paid for the expansion of the water system.

To form these inscriptions, workers first created small individual molds for each letter in the Latin alphabet. They then spelled out the name of the emperor or official by selecting the appropriate letter molds, placing them into a carved slot in a stone slab. Ensuring that the molds lay flush with the surface of the stone, they locked the type into place and laid the stone slab on a large flat tray. Then they poured molten lead across slab and tray, forming a large metal sheet. Once cooled, the sheet could be rolled into a cylinder and soldered at the seam. On the pipe's contour, the emperor's name appeared in elevated letters.

5

The pipemakers' ingenuity in using movable type to form a line of text is eerily similar to the method used by Johannes Gutenberg and other European printers more than 1,000 years later. As Canadian classicist A. Trevor Hodge has noted, this overlooked Roman technology "tempts one into speculating how close the ancient world was to making the full-scale break-through into printing." But the Romans failed to capitalize on this remarkable invention.

Perhaps they were simply too immersed in the culture of carved and painted words to see the future of print—the real writing on the wall.

Women's Ideal Bodies Then & Now

Just 100 years ago, the Chinese worshipped a woman's round belly as a symbol of fertility and sexual desire. Today, they strive for a flat, Westernized ideal. And in South Africa, women's once-revered big hips have given way to skin and bones. Every day, TV, the Internet, and the inevitable creep of modernization force women around the globe to abandon their unique body ideals. *Marie Claire* investigates the changing shape of women

JULIA SAVACOOL

China

China 1900 Slim Body, Soft Belly

THEN For centuries in China, the most desirable women were slim by Western standards with "a modest touch of fullness" in their midsection (the Chinese actually had a term for it: *feng man*). This body ideal was related to traditional Chinese-medicine principles that said a woman's *qi*, or vital energy, has its central reservoir in the abdomen. "For the Chinese, a rounded belly translated into a woman of sexual desire, fertility, and strength," says anthropologist Susan Brownell, Ph.D., an expert on Chinese culture at the University of Missouri-St. Louis.

China 2004 Thin Body, Flat Belly

NOW The thin are getting thinner! According to a recent study, up to 70 percent of Chinese college women now think they're too fat, even though their weight is normal. And Dr. Sing Lee, director of the Hong Kong Eating Disorders Clinic, says he sees 25 to 50 times as many patients as he did 15 years ago. "Fatness is subjective in these women's minds," Dr. Lee explains. "In one study we did, more than half the women were at normal or below-normal weight, but they were all trying to lose at least 10 pounds." The growing Chinese fixation on skinniness is apparent in the proliferating weight-loss ads in their women's magazines—as many as one in every two ads is for diet products, pills, or teas.

The decline of *feng man* can be traced directly to the 1966 Cultural Revolution and the influence of communism. "With the rise of communism, femininity and softness were discouraged," Dr. Brownell explains. "A masculine ideal was associated with revolutionary fervor and was emulated because it is also associated with hard work, a communist ideal." And China's strict one-child policy today means that women's bodies are less appreciated as fertility symbols. "In China, thinness and a flat belly are in," says Dr. Brownell.

Fiji

Then, Fat

THEN When Harvard Medical School anthropologist/psychiatrist Anne Becker, M.D., Ph.D., was studying the women of Fiji in the 1980s, she found that two-thirds of the population were overweight or obese. Amazingly, almost one in five obese women surveyed said they wished to gain even more weight. "In Fiji, social position was partly determined by how well you were fed. At any meal, you were supposed to eat beyond the point of fullness." In particular, large calves were a mark of attractiveness. "Thick calves were equated with a woman's ability to do work—a valued attribute," explains Dr. Becker. "Calling someone 'skinny legs' was the ultimate insult."

Now, Slim

NOW When Dr. Becker visited the villagers in 1988, eating disorders were unfamiliar, and women laughed at her description of the Western world's quest for thinness. But today, being thin is the goal of many young women on the island. "The change in women's thinking about their bodies has been remarkable," says Dr. Becker.

So what happened? In a word: television. In 1995, TV came to the rural island villages, and young women started spending hours watching soaps and sitcoms. The quality of life portrayed in these shows far surpassed the Fijians' own, says Dr. Becker, and native women equated those higher living standards with the willowy look of the Western actresses—an ideal they began to emulate. Thirty-eight months after TV's arrival, 15 percent of girls surveyed had vomited to control their weight. "Fijians are leaping from an isolated agricultural society into the information age," says Dr. Becker, "and the psychological impact has been immense."

Jamaica

Then, Coca Cola-Bottle Shape

THEN "In my mother's generation, proper proportion was king," says Gail Marcia Anderson, M.A., the Jamaican co-author of a new study in the *Journal of Cross-Cultural Psychology* that compares body-image attitudes of white American and black Jamaican youth. "It was believed that the bust should be moderate, the waist smaller, the hips larger—all in proportion, like an old-fashioned Coca-Cola bottle." Moreover, says Anderson, it has always been more attractive for a Jamaican woman to be 10 pounds overweight than 10 pounds underweight: "Jamaicans have traditionally valued the curvy, voluptuous figures of women."

Now, Large Butts

NOW Voluptuousness is still valued, but today, big butts are emphasized— and proper proportion is a thing of the past. In pursuit of a supersize rear, some women even risk their health by taking animal-hormone pills, used by farmers to fatten chickens, in a misguided attempt to "grow" a larger butt. (There's no scientific evidence that it works.) "These pills are extremely dangerous," says Dr. Manuel Peña, representative of Jamaica's Pan American Health Organization. "They are not meant for humans. Taking them can have severe health implications, including high blood pressure and metabolic problems."

A driving factor behind Jamaica's big-bottom fascination comes from the rise in popularity of Jamaican "dancehall" music, which exploded with the current generation, says Anderson. "In dancehall, most dance moves center around the hips and buttocks."

"There's even a popular song that explicitly celebrates '*mampi*-size' women—a colloquialism for the big-bodied female," adds Carolyn Cooper, Ph.D., a professor of literary and cultural studies at the University of the West Indies in Jamaica and author of *Sound Clash: Jamaican Dancehall Culture*. "Some foolhardy women are taking chicken pills in an attempt to give themselves the full figure celebrated in dancehall lyrics."

Reinforcing the image of voluptuous hips are the super-curvy "dancehall queens"—women who win the annual dance contests and wow the crowds with their overtly sexual gyrations. "These women sit at the pinnacle of what most young Jamaicans want their bodies to look like," says Anderson. "In previous generations, women covered up their bodies out of modesty; their figures were less on display. Today, dancehall queens are just about showing it all." She adds, "Women in Jamaica have always liked curves; it's just that the type of curve has changed."

Mongolia

Then, Plump and Short

THEN "Mongolians traditionally described the ideal woman as plump enough and short enough to 'fill your eyes' when you look at her," says Naidan Tsogzolmaa, a native Mongolian guide and program director for Nomadic Expeditions. This body ideal was suited to the harsh way of life of Mongolia's nomadic horseback riders—extra flesh is imperative for survival in a country where temperatures drop to negative-26 degrees Fahrenheit at night. "Skinny women will not survive the extreme Mongolian winters, and tall women will not fit on the native horses, which are quite small," says Tsogzolmaa. "And, because nomadic Mongolians are so isolated, husband and wife must depend on each other for keeping the family healthy and fed. A man would not want a wife who looks like she might not be strong enough to carry her share of the work." Moreover, high-fat horses' milk and cheese have long been dietary staples for nomadic Mongolians, encouraging their rounder physiques.

Now, Thin and Tall

NOW Among nomadic tribeswomen, plump and short is still considered ideal, but the nomadic population itself is in decline. More than 50 percent of Mongolians now live in urban centers (a 20-percent increase over the past two decades), where the physical ideal closely resembles that of Western culture. In Ulaanbaatar—Mongolia's capital city, where nearly one-third of the country's people live—tall and thin is in vogue.

The influence of Western culture can actually be traced back to the 1930s, when "young, affluent girls were sent to Russia and Germany to study," says Tsogzolmaa. "They brought back with them a certain notion of body shape, which has grown stronger over time. Now Ulaanbaatar women are striving to get that slim shape you see in the West."

Better infrastructure and jobs have also lured more Mongolians to urban centers. And modern amenities have negated nomadic concerns about surviving long, cold winters, while giving women instant access to global trends. "We have the same technology in our cities as every other city in the world," says Tsogzolmaa. "So Ulaanbaatar women see images of Western models in the media." Dieting is very popular, she notes, and fitness centers, which didn't even exist here 10 years ago, are now starting to take off.

South Africa

Then, Big Legs and Hips

THEN For centuries, large lower bodies were the mark of sexiness for South Africa's indigenous women. In fact, women of the Ndebele—one of the largest native populations—wore large, beaded waist and leg hoops called golwani, stuffed with rubber to produce a larger-than-life bottom half. These padded costumes symbolized rolls of body fat, considered marks of beauty. The Zulu, another South African tribe, created rituals to highlight women's hips and legs. "Among black natives, large buttocks and thighs were considered signs of womanliness," says anthropologist Carolyn Martin Shaw, Ph.D., of the University of California Santa Cruz. "Large buttocks were the focal point of celebratory dances that required women to turn their backsides to the audience and show off fantastic muscle control by contracting their buttocks to the music."

Now, Slim All Over

NOW All-around thin is in. A new study reports that Zulu women have the fastest-growing rate of eating disorders of any group in the country. "In our study of black female university students in a rural area, 45 percent had some form of disordered eating," says researcher Julie Seed, senior lecturer in psychology at Northumbria University in the U.K. "Considering that bigness has traditionally been seen as a sign of wealth and beauty, this was a shock."

"Thin" has even become a political statement. "Prior to the end of apartheid in 1995, there were no documented cases of eating disorders among blacks in South Africa," says Seed. "But today, women in the black community equate 'thin' with being educated and having rights—in other words, being more like a white person. Younger black women don't want to look big, because big symbolizes their past, and their past has not been particularly rosy." Seed and her colleagues' study also reveals that some Zulu and Ndebele women feel being thin will improve their job prospects.

Kenya: The Last Holdout
Then and Now

The Maasai are one of the last global cultures to remain true to their natural look (long and lanky). Why are they holding on to their body ideal? For one, their shape is already similar to the Western ideal that other countries are importing. But lifestyle also plays an important role: The nomadic Maasai, who often walk dozens of miles a day, expend a tremendous amount of energy. Meanwhile, their food sources are poor: The traditional diet consists of milk, cow's blood, and meat on special occasions. And finally, the warrior Maasai (who also inhabit parts of Tanzania) have enormous pride in their culture. Their coming-of-age rituals strengthen the ties of women to their community, and language barriers limit their contact with outsiders.

Sex Around the World

***More* takes a revealing look at the intimate lives of women in seven countries. When we dispatched our foreign correspondents around the globe, even they didn't know if women in traditional societies would talk about sex and love. They did—in detail. Here are their true confessions**

SHARLENE K. JOHNSON

Italy

Love, Italian Style

MARA MEMO, 53
A divorced professor of urban sociology at the University of Rome, she has two daughters, 23 and 12, by two different men. She has managed to carve out both a career and what she calls a "joyous existence."

Beautiful Beginning "I was almost eighteen, and he was my first great love. We were in an alpine field full of flowers, and we took off our clothes and made love on the grass—the first time for both of us. Afterward, I said, 'How marvelous!'"

Today "Sex is a wonder—the most joyous thing. If it's missing from my life, I feel sad, depressed, nervous, like a lion in a cage. It's not enough to have children or work. I want to be cuddled, embraced and caressed, and to reciprocate. I can make love two or three times a night, as many as five times a week, with my current partner."

Improvising "I like variety: making love on the ground, on the table, wherever."

Looking Good "I'm proud of my legs. When I'm ninety, I'll still pinch men's bottoms and wear miniskirts."

Younger Lovers "I've often been with younger men—once a twenty-three-year-old when I was forty-four. They are more open to playing soccer or taking a walk at one in the morning."

The Main Attraction "He has to be a great lover. Attractiveness is second."

Mother Knew Best "When I lived with my first daughter's father without marrying him, my mother said, 'People will think you're a whore.' I told her that was silly; we're no longer in the nineteenth century. But she was right: People did think that, and I was really hurt."

Surviving Heartache "When a great love ends, it's painful, but you pick yourself up and discover that you can be lighthearted once more. You can fall in love again and again."
—*Elisabetta Povoledo*

ITALY: "I'm Proud of my legs. When I'm ninety, I'll still pinch men's bottoms and wear miniskirts."

EGYPT: "I like being on top best. Here, women call the missionary position 'the roach,' because the woman is on the bottom with her legs and arms flailing."

EGYPT

From Desert to Oasis

HALA, 40-something
A career woman and veiled Muslim with two school-age children, she divorced her first husband a few months after their arranged marriage. Several years later, she married for love. She asked that neither her full name nor her photo be published.

A Bad Start "My first time was at the hotel after my first wedding. I was tense. I didn't know him well. I didn't love him. I thought afterward, 'Sex isn't romantic, it's animalistic.'"

The Bloody Sheet "His family wanted to be reassured about my virginity. My husband's sister asked him, 'Is everything okay? Is she good?' Sometimes the husband's female relatives want to see the "blood on the sheet."

Not a Virgin "In the villages, if the girl is found not to be a virgin, I hear they may kill her—even nowadays."

No Foreplay "My first husband would just come and then finish. After sex with him, I would go to the bathroom and cry. I heard from friends that they enjoyed sex, but I was in pain."

A Second Chance "It's about feelings, not just sex. My second husband wants me to enjoy intercourse as well. We try everything. He tells me, 'I've taught you fifty positions. During our lifetime, I'll teach you ninety-nine.' I like being on top best. Here, women call the missionary position 'the roach,' because the woman is on the bottom with her legs and arms flailing."

Changing Times "I never spoke to my mother about sex—not when I got my period, not on the day of my wedding, not to this day. Now, my daughter has sex education at school, and I talk to her, too. I tell her not to have intimate relations before marriage. When she is older, I will talk to her about sex itself and tell her not to be passive."

Female Circumcision "I wasn't circumcised, but all my aunts were. It was common in the villages until recently; girls were thought to be excitable, so their clitorises were cut. It's not a religious idea. It's for men's benefit. It's bad, because it makes a woman cold sexually."

Religion and Sex "The Koran says that sex is important within marriage, because from it comes life."

—*Sarah Gauch*

Mexico
Sex as the Spice of Life

ALEJANDRA ALLEN MAGANA, 41
Magana, an advertising sales executive, lost her virginity at 16 to a rapist and then had an unsatisfying marriage. The widowed mother of two teenage boys now still has an adventurous sexual relationship with her boyfriend.

First Things First "You can't have sex without love."

The Calm and the Storm "I can guarantee you that my mother has never had an orgasm in her life. Furthermore, my father left my mother years ago, and she never had another relationship. She has passed the time so calmly. I would go crazy after one month. When I have sex, all my problems dissipate, and I feel so good."

Times Have Changed "I tell my two sons that sex is a very important and beautiful part of life, but that they need to be careful to avoid STDs."

Favorite Position "I could be making love in all sorts of positions with my partner, but if I don't have the last orgasm on top, I don't feel satisfied."

Faking It "When I was married, I followed the lead of Donna Summer—I copied her ahs, ohs and ooohs. But I didn't feel anything. Now I scream, cry, kick, and it's all real."

Cultural Norms "Most women are not open about sex; many don't have orgasms. I tell girlfriends how wonderful it feels, and they say, 'He lets me know when it's over.' That's not worth it."

Self-Gratification "It's considered normal for men to masturbate, but not for women to do so."

Rape "Rapes occur on the streets, but I think they also happen within the family. A single woman might invite a boyfriend to live with her, and he turns around and rapes her daughter."

Sexual Goal "Sex is more important for me today than ever before. I want to reach menopause feeling that I have the same satisfying sex life that I do now."

—*Eliza Hughes*

Sweden
Northern Lights Shine On

GUN MARIANNE KRISTOFFERSSON, 57
Kristoffersson, a translator in Stockholm, has a "cozy relationship" with the man she has been dating for three years. Never married, she says she has had her most intense sexual experiences in the years since she turned 40.

Her First Time "Just before I turned twenty-two, I looked for a 'deflowerer.' I had never dated and thought my virginity was embarrassing. It was a blood-bath and didn't feel good in any way, but I was glad to have it over with."

SWEDEN: "I never longed for marriage and children and had scores of lovers. I always do what I want and fulfill my dreams."

INDIA: "I had a very close friend with whom I talked about many things. We were closer than if we had had sex. He died and I've never found that tremendous bond again."

Single by Choice "I'm very unusual, almost unique, because I've never longed for marriage and children and had scores of lovers. I always do what I want and fulfill my dreams. I do love, but I also fear becoming dependent and vulnerable."

Being the Other Woman "I've often had relationships with married men, and was smitten with a few of them. I thought they suited my way of life—the silver lining without the everyday nagging."

Is Love Necessary? "No. I might be a virgin if that were the case."

Pillow Talk "It turns me on to talk in bed about what you're going to do. But my current partner is a bit shy about this, and I have to accept it."

Taboo "Anal intercourse."

Generation Gap "Miles wide. My mother didn't know how her body worked. She thought she menstruated and ovulated at the same time. We never, ever talked about sex. My generation is the first to be able to make decisions about our bodies and our lives. Friends my age who have daughters are very open with them."

Homosexuality "Sweden is pretty free of prejudice. Homosexuals are allowed to marry, through so-called registered partnerships. I think that sexual preference is a private matter."

Changing Priorities "Earlier in my life, I chose men for their physical attractiveness and was disappointed and hurt. Those men conquer woman after woman. Now, I'm mature enough to choose a warm and loving man whom I can trust."

—*Anna Pandolfi*

India

Love Lost, Twice Over

RENU BHASIN, 55

Defying her parents and India's rigid social norms, Bhasin married for love 33 years ago. At first, she enjoyed an active sex life with her husband, a businessman in New Delhi. But as she became busy with their daughters, now 25 and 28, and he with his career, they grew apart. Five years ago, he took a mistress. Bhasin asked that her face not be shown.

Wedding Night "I was nervous. My first night was not as exciting as succeeding ones, because I got more and more comfortable."

Mother and Daughter "My mother never talked to me about sex. What little I knew was from discussions with friends. With my daughters, I let them know that they could say what they wanted to me about the subject. There is nothing wrong with sex."

The Other Woman "I don't know what he sees in her, and I cannot see where I was lacking."

His Punishment "I say I'm tired, and I think he understands what I'm saying. This is the only way I can pay him back. Having a sexual relationship with him just doesn't make me feel comfortable these days."

Her Temptation "I had a very close friend, with whom I talked a lot. We were closer than if we had had sex. It was more satisfying, because sex is a one-time thing, and then it's finished. Our relationship was an ongoing process. He died, and I've never found that tremendous bond again."

Why She Stays "I'm over fifty. It's too late for me to start earning a living. And why should I? He married me, so he has to take care of me. It's my birthright. If he's been indiscreet, let him live with it."

Bottom Line "Today, I find that I can dictate my own terms—even though there is something missing in my life. Still, I have no regrets."

—*Martha Ann Overland*

Brazil

The Girl from San Paulo

CACILDA CAMARGO, 45

An accomplished ceramicist with her own studio, Camargo lives with her husband of 23 years, their 22-year-old daughter Gabriela and Gabriela's boyfriend. Deeply involved in spiritualism, Camargo spends hours on the Internet, meeting like-minded people.

First and Forever "The first person I had sex with was my husband, right after he asked me to marry him. I was nineteen. It was during Carnival, and we were at a farmhouse. Our friends threw us together in a room. I thought we were just going to sleep."

Motel Sex "When we were dating, we'd go to motels. We'd schedule a wake-up call for about four o'clock, so we could get home before sunrise. My mother and my mother-in-law still think I was a virgin bride. After we got married, we kept going to motels for the big beds, hot tubs and mirrors."

The More Things Change "My daughter is embarrassed to talk about all the things that my mother couldn't tell me about. I don't know if my daughter has a good sex life, but I prefer that she have sex here in the house, rather than sneak around."

Total Trust "Sometimes I go out dancing with a group from my ceramics class. I'm not interested in having affairs, and my husband knows that. He trusts me. I know a lot of couples who could never have the open relationship that we have."

Brazilian Culture "Until recently, women weren't thought of as having orgasms. That's changing now. Women talk about multiple orgasms. Men talk about impotence and sexual dysfunction. That was taboo for a long time."

Difference of Opinion "Men here love the rear-entry position, and most women don't like it at all."

Advanced Lessons "I've been reading a lot lately about techniques to strengthen the vaginal muscles. A woman who perfects that will keep her man forever."

Adult Toys "There is no reason why an old married couple can't have their toys. Why not improve your sexual performance?"

—*Jennifer L. Rich*

BRAZIL: "I've been reading a lot lately about techniques to strengthen the vaginal muscles. A woman who perfects that will keep her man forever."

JAPAN: "I envy the younger generations freedom. My daughter says she'll live with boyfriends before marrying. If I had wanted that, my mother would have disowned me."

Japan
Looking Back, and Forward

MIDORI SEKIYAMA, 49

With five kids between 7 and 21 and a busy architect husband, this Tokyo public-health worker says her sex life has deteriorated. She allots time weekly to go a movie or take a day trip— unusual for a married woman in Japan.

A Good Start "To me, sex is spiritual and physical. That is why I had no sex with my boyfriends until, at twenty-one, I met the man who would become my husband. After we got married, we enjoyed sex and experimented a lot—having intercourse anywhere and often."

Baby Talk "Things changed after I devoted my time to our first child and was usually tired. My husband woke up early for work, so we often slept in separate rooms. Sex became routine."

Different Priorities "I want to have a satisfying sex life that expresses my love for my husband. But he believes his work is most important. To him, I am just the children's mother; he does not expect me to be attractive. We have intercourse once or twice a month. I keep quiet and pretend to be a good wife."

An Affair to Remember "I had a lover for about two years. It was so romantic. I was happy to be cared for by him. Then his wife found out, and our affair ended. I was heartbroken."

Silence "Affairs are not common among married women my age, so I would never talk to my friends about my lover."

Her Lifeline "My children."

Her Mother's Way "My mother and I never discussed sex. I suspect her marriage was not entirely happy—which did not stop her from being a loyal wife and devoted mother."

New Freedoms "I envy the younger generation's freedom. My daughter says she'll live with boyfriends before marrying. If I had wanted that, my mother would have disowned me."

—Suvendrini Kakuchi

The Beauty Pageant Prevails

As snow flickers across the bleak, colorless Moscow sky, eight young women walk into a Soviet-era building that houses a cramped indoor firing range. They're all very dewy and innocent-looking, so the military-style fatigues they're wearing seem more like a fashion statement than a uniform. But the women are here today for a shooting contest that's part of the newest Russian beauty pageant; Miss Ugolovno-Ispol'nitel'naya Sistema or, literally translated, Miss Criminal Execution System.

Less literally, I suppose, you'd call it Miss Bureau of Prisons. Its youngest contestant, 17-year-old Katya Zagrebina, is studying to be a criminal lawyer at the Ministry of Justice's Pskov Law Institute. Katya has a gorgeous smile, and her sleek body ripples with muscles. When it's her turn, she slowly holds the gun out in her right hand, aims and makes me go deaf as the gunpowder spark flashes. No shaking, no hesitation. After her target is brought forward, we can see that all of her shots were accurate, with one dead-on in the bull's eye, giving her a top rating of five out of five points. She'll make a perfect employee one day.

Katya tells me she learned all about guns at the institute, "I like shooting," she says through a translator, smiling. "I especially love Kalashnikovs." When I ask why she would want to enter such a contest, she says that all 15 of the women (with 400 men) in her school were "strongly encouraged" to take part in the two earlier regional contests. Still, Katya says she hopes to become the first Miss Bureau of Prisons (M-BOP? Ha). Yesterday there was a short swimming competition, and today they get to show off their abilities to accurately shoot a target and run 1,000 meters before indulging in the standard beauty-pageant fare: talent show, etiquette, diplomacy and evening gowns. The winner gets a crown with precious stones and may get to travel to Western Europe with the Minister of Justice.

Half of the women display various hues of red dye in their dark hair, ranging from fire-engine to maroon, but despite that, they're all very attractive. I'm slightly disappointed that none of the contestants is six feet tall, 250 pounds or wearing head-to-toe gray, because that's what I picture when I think of Russian women working in prisons (a random stereotype I've never really pondered before this instant). Russia has the second-highest incarceration rate in the world, behind the U.S.—partially because of the high amount of crime after the country switched over to capitalism, partially from civil unrest and partially because the government will still lock you up at the drop of a hat. Actually, I guess I'm not the only one who thinks badly of prison employees. That's sort of why they decided to have this pageant in the first place.

"We are reforming the bureau of prisons. We are trying to be more humanitarian, more liberal," says Alexander Juravski, the Ministry of Justice Cultural Center employee who masterminded this event. "Many people have the opinion that those who work in the corrections facilities break rules, that they're rude, vulgar, impolite and mean. But it's not really like that. There are around 400,000 workers, about one-third women, in the Russian corrections system. A great majority of them are educated, cultured, goodwilled, well-meaning, good workers." And they look hot in ball gowns.

We all squish into the tiny firing range for the contest. One of the coordinators asks the women if they've shot guns before, and they laugh and say, "Yes, of course." None of them has had to shoot her gun on the job, they tell me later, but most are required to practice at least once a month.

The women, who represent different regions of the country, look delicate and sweet even as they raise their guns. But each of their targets has at least one puncture wound in the bull's-eye or in the first ring. Don't mess with these chicks.

In the U.S., we're used to hearing about tiny pageants at every county fair and shopping mall across the nation—Ms. Wheelchair, Most Glamorous Grandmother, Miss Hell Hole Swamp. But apparently, Colombia, known as the "country of queens," is giving us a run for our money. Colombia has hundreds of pageants year-round crowning queens of everything from cattle to coal. And each November, various surgically enhanced women from every region compete in a 17-day extravaganza called the National Beauty Contest to try to become Miss Colombia, who goes on to compete in the Miss Universe pageant. Last year, one of the judges was a plastic surgeon. In this country, where the daily headlines are filled with stories about drug deals, murders, massacres and brutal kidnappings, the citizens seem to look to the beauty queens for inspiration and hope for a better future. The contestants are considered heroes, ideal citizens who are not only beautiful and elegant but who also do good deeds—last year, the queens released endangered turtles into the ocean and visited developmentally disabled children during the pageant. Celebrities, entrepreneurs and politicians show up at the daily festivities, which are broadcast throughout the country via every type of media outlet. This is by far the biggest event of the year for Colombians.

Now we're inside an impressive track-and-field facility in northeastern Moscow. About 25 young, fine-looking, non-smiling male and female athletes-apparently Olympic hopefuls—are pole-vaulting, jumping hurdles, lifting weights and sprinting. They seem annoyed that they have to put their sports on hold for five minutes while the M-BOP ladies run 1,000 meters. One sprinter nearly knocks me down when we all step onto the track. To lend importance to our little event, the organizers have invited four old guys clad in dozens of shiny medals to be guests of honor: legendary Soviet-era Olympic athletes. "I've run 6,900 miles in my lifetime!" one boasts to me, awards clanging.

As the girls change into their Nike and Adidas gear, I speak with Marina Kibenko, a stylish blond instructor from the law institute who is here to support Katya. Her answers sound like propaganda: "This contest is good for the girls because this will help them succeed! This will increase the prestige of the employees of the penal system!"

The announcer interrupts. "We welcome you to participate in a fair and uncompromised race," he says. The athletes totally ignore us. "Please cheer on these beauties!"

The eight girls begin running, and Katya takes the lead. The rest don't look so happy. The announcer yells, "You're doing well, you only have three laps to go—no big deal!" A few minutes later Katya wins, and a purplish-haired woman named Irina Kolchina, 30, sputters over the finish line last.

I turn back to Marina and ask if she enjoys working for the prison system. "I have a very specific job," she says carefully. "You have to get used to it, and you have to love it."

"So *do* you love it?" I ask. She squirms.

"I'm trying to avoid the question," she says, smiling and looking away. "I've spent my life teaching. I'm doing what I love. It's difficult to work here. You have to be a very strong woman. A weak woman wouldn't survive in this system."

During Colombia's National Beauty Contest, a much smaller local one also takes place. It's called the Popular Beauty Contest, and it's where the less affluent, mainly black contestants go from the local barrios to be crowned the Popular Queen. And even though it would make sense that the winner would automatically go on to compete in the national pageant, this traditionally has not been the case. Instead, Cartagena's official contestant has historically been chosen by a special committee, which generally picks someone who is much whiter and wealthier and willing to have plastic surgery if deemed necessary. But this past year, the mayor of Cartagena stepped in and appointed the winner of the Popular Beauty Contest, who was black and from a humble background, to be the local rep. Jeymmy Paola Vargas Gomez went on to place second in the big pageant, a prestigious position known as Vice Queen, and Cartagena's masses went crazy for her, like she was royalty they could relate to. Like she could take away some of their problems for a while.

An instrumental version of "Nights in White Satin" is playing over the PA system in the theater at the Ministry of Justice building on the morning after the running event. Onstage, some very girly young men are escorting the contestants in a dress rehearsal. One of the guys keeps leaping spontaneously, while a big screen above him displays dreary aerial shots of the contestants' hometowns and on-the-job photos involving rifles, barbed wire and modest smiles.

I ask Alexander why he decided to include ballroom dancing and an etiquette contest in the grand finale, which will be the next day. "My belief is that there is a movement in music, movies and the press which idealizes crime and rape, sex, blood, murder. And we are trying to go against that," he answers. "The challenge at the top is to develop a high-quality culture among the workers and to raise their moral system. We want to show our employees as role models, saying, 'There's another way of life, in which people love one another and have sincere friendships that say nice words to one another and smile and do good deeds.' And we are inviting everyone to this kind of life-including you!" he says, motioning to me. I beam at him.

"The miss bureau of prisons winner will increase the prestige of the penal system!" says Marina, a government employee.

Then I get it together. "But if the general public sees how beautiful the women are, do you think they'll commit more crimes just to be near them?" I ask.

He laughs. "I think there are more interesting ways to meet these girls. Legal ways without complications and headaches."

In 2002, the first Miss Tibet pageant was supposed to "highlight the Tibetan identity," according to its organizers, and bring a little glitz to the lives of those who want more attention for their cause of independence from China. Thirty women registered for the pageant, which included a controversial swimsuit competition. But there was such an uproar in Dharamsala, the Indian city where the pageant was to be held, that only four women showed up. Many exiled Tibetan locals there, who favor long skirts and long-sleeved shirts to cover their bodies, said it trivialized their cause and was "un-Tibetan." Then last year, only one registered. The ceremony still took place, in a modified form: After they re-capped the accomplishments of the previous Miss Tibet, showcased a musical act and gave a speech about freedom, 20-year-old Tsering Kyi was crowned the new Miss Tibet and given a $2,000 scholarship. Shortly after she was crowned, she met Prince Charles. Which all makes me wonder what's more disturbing: when society dictates that females are most valued if they're wearing revealing clothes, or when women are ostracized if they actually choose to take part in a swimsuit competition.

Now I'm backstage, interviewing the women who have put on their evening gowns for the Miss Bureau of Prisons dress rehearsal. The Tom Jones song "Sex Bomb" is playing loudly and Alyona Kazlova, the pageant's artistic director, is telling the girls to really feel the music. They start to shake their hips more, and some flick their skirts and throw their hair around their shoulders. They're finally relaxing.

I corner Irina when she walks offstage. "This pageant shows that we're able to be different, strong, sexy and beautiful," she says enthusiastically. Irina is responsible for safety in one of the bureau of prison departments. Like the other women I interview, she seems to find no hypocrisy in this contest. Irina says she thoroughly enjoys her job and has never felt discriminated against. Quite the opposite. "I like working there because I'm the only woman in a group of men. The men in our system are very controlled, self-possessed and cultured," she says. "I like the discipline ... and I like the uniform."

Contestant Marina Kulkova, 21, also mentions the uniform as one of the perks of her job figuring out pensions for inmates. "With this pageant we will not only discover our hidden talents, but we will prove to others that the penal system has many pretty girls in it," she points out. "A girl with a gun is always scary. No one would expect anything good to come out of it. But we want to show that's not true."

Irina heads onstage to practice for the talent competition dressed in a bondage-like outfit-fake leather, gold belt and slimming stilettos. She sings a song interspersed with spoken-word bits extolling the virtues of Russia over an instrumental version of "Pretty Woman." After that, the professional dancers do a modern-ballet-type routine to a brass version of "Power of Love." By the end, it's late and the ladies are tired, so we say good night.

Why do American pageants seem so much cheesier and less meaningful, even when they're giving out pro-woman scholarships? Maybe it's because they appear to benefit only the beauty queen who wins and the advertisers who bought time slots during the event, instead of giving the nation any sort of hope. Still, I just wonder when all these countries will find more direct ways to affect society—say, if the Colombian government were to set aside some of the money it normally spends on the National Beauty Contest and put it toward microcredit loans for women. Because attempting to create social change via human Barbie dolls? That's not going to get anybody very far.

To show off their talents, a Russian contestant did a Geisha-style dance, and in Tibet, a woman sang Celine Dion's "my heart will go on."

Which brings us back to Moscow. I wake up on the last morning eager to watch the pageant's grand finale. Then I turn on the news and see pictures of bloody people being carried on stretchers out of a Moscow subway station. A terrorist—presumably a Chechen rebel—set oft a bomb in one of the cars, and at least 39 people are dead, 130 wounded. The Chechens want to secede from Russia to have their own autonomous state and, with the presidential elections coming up, this was maybe a good time to get attention.

The locals I encounter don't seem afraid so much as resigned to the fact that nothing can really be done to stop such acts of violence. Suddenly, I get a phone call from one of the pageant's coordinators. "We're postponing the pageant and sending the girls home," she says. "It doesn't seem right to celebrate now."

How AIDS Changed America

The plague years: It brought out the worst in us at first, but ultimately it brought out the best, and transformed the nation. The story of a disease that left an indelible mark on our history, our culture and our souls.

DAVID JEFFERSON

Jeanne White-Ginder sits at home, assembling a scrapbook about her son, Ryan. She pastes in newspaper stories about his fight to return to the Indiana middle school that barred him in 1985 for having AIDS. She sorts through photos of Ryan with Elton John, Greg Louganis and others who championed his cause. She organizes mementos from his PBS special, "I Have AIDS: A Teenager's Story." "I just got done with his funeral. Eight pages. That was very hard," says White-Ginder, who buried her 18-year-old son in 1991, seven years after he was diagnosed with the disease, which he contracted through a blood product used to treat hemophiliacs. The scrapbook, along with Ryan's bedroom, the way his mother left it when he died, will be part of an exhibit at the Children's Museum of Indianapolis on three children who changed history: Anne Frank. Ruby Bridges. And Ryan White. "He put a face to the epidemic, so people could care about people with AIDS," his mother says.

At a time when the mere threat of avian flu or SARS can set off a coast-to-coast panic—and prompt the federal government to draw up contingency plans and stockpile medicines—it's hard to imagine that the national response to the emergence of AIDS ranged from indifference to hostility. But that's exactly what happened when gay men in 1981 began dying of a strange array of opportunistic infections. President Ronald Reagan didn't discuss AIDS in a public forum until a press conference four years into the epidemic, by which time more than 12,000 Americans had already died. (He didn't publicly utter the term "AIDS" until 1987.) People with the disease were routinely evicted from their homes, fired from jobs and denied health insurance. Gays were demonized by the extreme right wing: Reagan adviser Pat Buchanan editorialized in 1983, "The poor homosexuals—they have declared war against nature, and now nature is exacting an awful retribution." In much of the rest of the culture, AIDS was simply treated as the punch line to a tasteless joke: "I just heard the Statue of Liberty has AIDS," Bob Hope quipped during the rededication ceremony of the statue in 1986. "Nobody knows if she got it from the mouth of the Hudson or the Staten Island Fairy." Across the river in Manhattan, a generation of young adults was attending more funerals than weddings.

> **In 1995, Americans regarded HIV/AIDS as the nation's most urgent health problem. Today, only 17% rank it as the top concern.**
>
> All poll results are from the Kaiser family foundation's 2006 "Survey of Americans on HIV/AIDS," conducted among 2,517 Americans nationwide.

As AIDS made its death march across the nation, killing more Americans than every conflict from World War II through Iraq, it left an indelible mark on our history and culture. It changed so many things in so many ways, from how the media portray homosexuality to how cancer patients deal with their disease. At the same time, AIDS itself changed, from a disease that killed gay men and drug addicts to a global scourge that has decimated the African continent, cut a large swath through black America and infected almost as many women as men worldwide. The death toll to date: 25 million and counting. Through the crucible of AIDS, America was forced to face its fears and prejudices—fears that denied Ryan White a seat in school for a year and a half, prejudices that had customers boycotting restaurants with gay chefs. "At first, a ton of people said that whoever gets AIDS deserves to have AIDS, deserves to literally suffer all the physical pain that the virus carries with it," says Tom Hanks, who won an Oscar for playing a gay lawyer dying of the disease in 1993's "Philadelphia." "But that didn't hold." Watching a generation of gay men wither and die, the nation came to acknowledge the humanity of a community it had mostly ignored and reviled. "AIDS was the great unifier," says Craig Thompson, executive director of AIDS Project Los Angeles and HIV-positive for 25 years.

Without AIDS, and the activism and consciousness-raising that accompanied it, would gay marriage even be up for debate

17

today? Would we be welcoming "Will & Grace" into our living rooms or weeping over "Brokeback Mountain"? Without red ribbons, first worn in 1991 to promote AIDS awareness, would we be donning rubber yellow bracelets to show our support for cancer research? And without the experience of battling AIDS, would scientists have the strategies and technologies to develop the antiviral drugs we'll need to battle microbial killers yet to emerge?

AIDS, of course, did happen. "Don't you dare tell me there's any good news in this," says Larry Kramer, who has been raging against the disease—and those who let it spread unchecked—since it was first identified in 1981. "We should be having a national day of mourning!" True. But as we try to comprehend the carnage, it's impossible not to acknowledge the displays of strength, compassion and, yes, love, that were a direct result of all that pain and loss. Without AIDS, we wouldn't have the degree of patient activism we see today among people with breast cancer, lymphoma, ALS and other life-threatening diseases. It was Kramer, after all, who organized 10,000 frustrated AIDS patients into ACT UP, a street army chanting "Silence equals death" that marched on the White House and shut down Wall Street, demanding more government funding for research and quicker access to drugs that might save lives. "The only thing that makes people fight is fear. That's what we discovered about AIDS activism," Kramer says.

Fear can mobilize, but it can also paralyze—which is what AIDS did when it first appeared. And no one—not the government, not the media, not the gay community itself—reacted fast enough to head off disaster. In the fiscally and socially conservative climate of Reagan's America, politicians were loath to fund research into a new pathogen that was killing mostly gay men and intravenous drug users. "In the first years of AIDS, I imagine we felt like the folks on the rooftops during Katrina, waiting for help," says Dr. Michael Gottlieb, the Los Angeles immunologist credited as the first doctor to recognize the looming epidemic. When epidemiologist Donald Francis of the federal Centers for Disease Control in Atlanta tried to get $30 million in funding for an AIDS-prevention campaign, "it went up to Washington and they said f--- off," says Francis, who quit the CDC soon after, defeated.

"Gay Cancer," as it was referred to at the time, wasn't a story the press wanted to cover—especially since it required a discussion of gay sex. While the media had a field day with Legionnaire's disease, toxic shock syndrome and the Tylenol scare, few outlets paid much attention to the new syndrome, even after scores of people had died. The New York Times ran fewer than a dozen stories about the new killer in 1981 and 1982, almost all of them buried inside the paper. (NEWSWEEK, for that matter, didn't run its first cover story on what "may be the public-health threat of the century" until April 1983.) The Wall Street Journal first reported on the disease only after it had spread to heterosexuals: NEW, OFTEN-FATAL ILLNESS IN HOMOSEXUALS TURNS UP IN WOMEN, HETEROSEXUAL MALES, read the February 1982 headline. Even the gay press missed the story at first: afraid of alarming the community and inflaming antigay forces, editors at the New York Native slapped the headline DISEASE RUMORS LARGELY UNFOUNDED

atop the very first press report about the syndrome, which ran May 18, 1981. There were a few notable exceptions, particularly the work of the late Randy Shilts, an openly gay journalist who convinced his editors at the San Francisco Chronicle to let him cover AIDS as a full-time beat: that reporting led to the landmark 1987 book "And the Band Played On," a detailed account of how the nation's failure to take AIDS seriously allowed the disease to spread exponentially in the early '80s.

Many gay men were slow to recognize the time bomb in their midst, even as people around them were being hospitalized with strange, purplish skin cancers and life-threatening pneumonia. Kramer and his friends tried to raise money for research during the 1981 Labor Day weekend in The Pines, a popular gay vacation spot on New York's Fire Island. "When we opened the collection boxes, we could not believe how truly awful the results were," says Kramer. The total? $769.55. "People thought we were a bunch of creeps with our GIVE TO GAY CANCER signs, raining on the parade of Pines' holiday festivities." The denial in some corners of the gay community would continue for years. Many were reluctant to give up the sexual liberation they believed they'd earned: as late as 1984, the community was bitterly debating whether to close San Francisco's gay bathhouses, where men were having unprotected sex with any number of partners in a single night.

With death a constant companion, the gay community sobered up from the party that was the '70s and rose to meet the unprecedented challenge of AIDS. There was no other choice, really: they had been abandoned by the nation, left to fend for themselves. "It's important to remember that there was a time when people did not want to use the same bathroom as a person with AIDS, when cabdrivers didn't want to pick up patients who had the disease, when hospitals put signs on patients' doors that said WARNING. DO NOT ENTER," recalls Marjorie Hill, executive director of Gay Men's Health Crisis in New York. Organizations like GMHC sprang up around the country to provide HIV patients with everything from medical care to counseling to food and housing. "Out of whole cloth, and without experience, we built a healthcare system that was affordable, effective and humane," says Darrel Cummings, chief of staff of the Los Angeles Gay & Lesbian Center. "I can't believe our community did what it did while so many people were dying." Patients took a hands-on approach to managing their disease, learning the intricacies of T-cell counts and grilling their doctors about treatment options. And they shared what they learned with one another. "There's something that a person with a disease can only get from another person with that disease. It's support and information and inspiration," says Sean Strub, who founded the magazine Poz for HIV-positive readers.

It took a movie star to get the rest of the nation's attention. In the summer of 1985, the world learned that Rock Hudson—the romantic leading man who'd been a symbol of American virility—was not only gay, but had full-blown AIDS. "It was a bombshell event," says Gottlieb, who remembers standing on the helipad at UCLA Medical Center, waiting for his celebrity patient to arrive, as news helicopters circled overhead. "For many Americans, it was their first awareness at all of AIDS. This prominent man had been diagnosed, and the image of him looking as sick as he did really stuck." Six years later, basketball legend Magic Johnson announced he was HIV-positive, and the shock waves were even bigger. A straight, healthy-looking superstar athlete had contracted the "gay" disease. "It can happen to anybody, even me, Magic Johnson," the 32-year-old announced to a stunned nation, as he urged Americans to practice safe sex.

Given the tremendous stigma, most well-known public figures with AIDS tried to keep their condition a secret. Actor Brad Davis, the star of "Midnight Express," kept his diagnosis hidden for six years, until he died in 1991. "He assumed, and I think rightly so, that he wouldn't be able to find work," says his widow, Susan Bluestein, a Hollywood casting director. After Davis died, rumors flew that he must have been secretly gay. "That part of the gossip mill was the most hurtful to me and my daughter," says Bluestein, who acknowledges in her book "After Midnight" that her husband was a drug addict and unfaithful—but not gay.

With the disease afflicting so many of their own, celebrities were quick to lend support and raise money. Elizabeth Taylor was among the first, taking her friend Rock Hudson's hand in public, before the TV cameras and the world, to dispel the notion that AIDS was something you could catch through casual contact. Her gesture seems quaint today, but in 1985—when the tabloids were awash with speculation that Hudson could have infected actress Linda Evans by simply kissing her during a love scene in "Dynasty"—Taylor's gesture was revolutionary. She became the celebrity face of the American Foundation for AIDS Research. "I've lost so many friends," Taylor says. "I have so many friends who are HIV-positive and you just wonder how long it's going to be. And it breaks your heart."

Behind the scenes, Hollywood wasn't nearly as progressive as it likes to appear. John Erman recalls the uphill battle getting the 1985 AIDS drama, "An Early Frost," on TV. "The meetings we had with NBC's Standards and Practices [the network's censors] were absolutely medieval," says Erman. One of the censors' demands: that the boyfriend of the main character be portrayed as "a bad guy" for infecting him: "They did not want to show a positive gay relationship," Erman recalls. Ultimately, with the support of the late NBC Entertainment president Brandon Tartikoff, Erman got to make the picture he wanted—though major advertisers refused to buy commercial time during the broadcast. Within a decade, AIDS had changed the face of television. In 1991, "thirtysomething" featured a gay character who'd contracted the disease. And in 1994, on MTV's "The Real World," 23-year-old Pedro Zamora, who died later that same year, taught a generation of young people what it meant to be HIV-positive.

If TV was slow to deal with AIDS, cinema was downright glacial. "Longtime Companion," the first feature film about the disease, didn't make it to the screen until 1990, nine years into the epidemic. "There was a lot of talk before the movie came out about how this was going to hurt my career, the same way there was talk about Heath Ledger in 'Brokeback Mountain'," says Bruce Davison, who received an Oscar nomination for his

role. As for "Philadelphia," Hanks is the first to admit " it was late to the game."

Broadway was the major exception when it came to taking on AIDS as subject matter—in part because so many early casualties came from the world of theater. "I remember in 1982 sitting in a restaurant with seven friends of mine. All were gay men either working or looking to work in the theater, and we were talking about AIDS," recalls Tom Viola, executive director of Broadway Cares/Equity Fights AIDS. "Of those eight guys, four are dead, and two, including myself, are HIV-positive." By the time Tony Kushner's Pulitzer Prize-winning "Angels in America" made its Broadway debut in 1993, some 60 plays about the disease had opened in New York. Producer Jeffrey Seller remembers how he was told he "could never do a show on Broadway that's about, quote unquote, AIDS, homosexuality and drug addiction." He's talking about "Rent," which a decade later still draws capacity crowds.

The world of "Rent" is something of an artifact now. Just before it hit Broadway in 1996, scientists introduced the antiretroviral drug cocktails that have gone on to extend the lives of millions of patients with HIV. Since then, the urgency that once surrounded the AIDS fight in the United States has ebbed, as HIV has come to be seen as a chronic, rather than fatal, condition. But the drugs aren't a panacea—despite the fact that many people too young to remember the funerals of the '80s think the new medications have made it safe to be unsafe. "Everywhere I go, I'm meeting young people who've just found out they've been infected, many with drug-resistant strains of the virus," says Cleve Jones, who two decades ago decided to start stitching a quilt to honor a friend who had died of AIDS. That quilt grew to become an iconic patchwork of more than 40,000 panels, each one the size of a grave, handmade by loved ones to honor their dead. Ever-expanding, it was displayed several times in Washington, transforming the National Mall into what Jones had always intended: a colorful cemetery that would force the country to acknowledge the toll of AIDS. "If I'd have known 20 years ago that in 2006 I'd be watching a whole new generation facing this tragedy, I don't think I would have had the strength to continue," says Jones, whose own HIV infection has grown resistant to treatment.

Inner strength is what has allowed people living with HIV to persevere. "They think I'm gonna die. You know what, they better not hold their breath," Ryan White once told his mother. Though given six months to live when he was diagnosed with HIV, Ryan lived five and a half years, long enough to prod a nation into joining the fight against AIDS. When he died in 1990 at the age of 18, Congress named a new comprehensive AIDS funding act after him. But the real tribute to Ryan has been the ongoing efforts of his mother. "I think the hostility around the epidemic is still there. And because of religious and moral issues, it's been really hard to educate people about this disease and be explicit," says White-Ginder, who continues to give speeches about watching her son live and die of AIDS. "We should not still be facing this disease." Sadly, we are.

Remembering Bayard Rustin

JOHN D'EMILIO

In her 2004 Presidential address to the Organization of American Historians, Jacquelyn Dowd Hail described history, the stories about the past that we remember, as "always a form of forgetting." Scrutinizing what she called the "dominant narrative" of the civil rights movement— a triumphal story that begins with the *Brown* decision and the Montgomery bus boycott in the mid-1950s and ends with the Civil Rights and Voting Rights Acts a decade later—Hall argued that it "distorts and suppresses as much as it reveals."[1]

If one bad to choose a single event to illustrate both the standard interpretation of the civil rights movement and Hall's caution about it. It would be the March on Washington. More than four decades later, the March has come down to us as a moment of hope, unity, inspiration, and vision. Standing in front of the Lincoln Memorial before a peaceful crowd of 250,000 Americans, black and white, young and old. male and female, the Reverend Martin Luther King Jr. delivered an oration that high school students now memorize for speech contests, its central recurring line—"I have a dream"—has become as well recognized and as thoroughly American as "We hold these truths to be self-evident."

Standing in the background as King intoned these words was Bayard Rustin, another civil rights activist. Barely known today beyond circles of professional historians, Rustin was the man who, more than anyone, made the March on Washington happen. When the *Washington Post* profiled Rustin two weeks before the demonstration, it closed its article with the comment "He's Mr. March himself." After the event, *Life* magazine featured Rustin on its cover.[2] How could he have figured so prominently at the time and yet be so peripheral to historical memory today? Why have we forgotten Bayard Rustin? And what do we suppress when we forget him?

Of Rustin's importance to the African American freedom struggle there can be no doubt. He was one of the moving forces behind the Congress of Racial Equality (CORE), a key organization in the civil rights movement. Founded in 1942, CORE pioneered in the use of Gandhian nonviolence to challenge racial injustice. Throughout the 1940s, Rustin trained and led groups of nonviolent protesters in actions against segregated restaurants, movie theaters, barber shops, amusement parks, and department stores. In 1947, be spearheaded an interracial team of activists who traveled into the South to test continuing segregation in interstate bus travel despite a Supreme Court decision

against the practice. A year later, Rustin led a campaign of nonviolent resistance against racial segregation in the armed forces. Throughout these years, he traveled incessantly, lecturing to audiences across the country and inspiring countless numbers of young men and women to take action on behalf of social justice. "I was transformed listening to him," one young pacifist recalled. "I was absolutely hypnotized."[3]

In February 1956, in the early stages of the Montgomery bus boycott, Rustin journeyed there to offer his services to the boycott leaders. He made contact with the young Martin Luther King Jr., and the two men quickly formed a deep bond of trust and respect. Rustin offered to the inexperienced King a wealth of practical knowledge about how to use nonviolence effectively. Over the next few years Rustin functioned as a key adviser and mentor to King. He put him in touch with men like A. Philip Randolph, perhaps the senior statesman among African American activists at the time. He mobilized support among progressive union leaders for King and the Southern freedom movement. He persuaded King of the need to form an organization to carry on the struggle beyond Montgomery, and he drew up the outline of what became the Southern Christian Leadership Conference. In the late 1950s, Rustin proposed, planned, and organized demonstrations in Washington that gave King a national platform from which to project his message of resistance to racial injustice. Together with Randolph, in 1963 Rustin pushed and prodded other civil rights leaders to support a national March on Washington. No wonder that, when the time came, Rustin was the man who organized it.

And organize it he did! In just seven short weeks he set up an office and put together a skilled and energetic staff. He negotiated with federal officials to secure legal permission for the March and rally, fashioned a set of demands around which all civil rights organizations could unite, and drew national religious and labor organizations into the coalition Lewis, a militant young activist who had gained fame as a Freedom Rider in 1961, visited the office that summer and saw Rustin at work. "This was Bayard at his best," he later recollected.[4]

With a resume like this, how can we all **not** know who Bayard Rustin is? What stands between his profound contributions to the African American civil rights movement and historical memory? Rustin had three liabilities—three strikes against him, if you will—that have made it difficult to incorporate him into a simple narrative that most Americans can applaud of progress toward equality and justice.

First of all, Rustin had been a Communist. He joined the Young Communist League in the 1930s, attracted by its militant approach to fighting against the suffering caused by the Great Depression and the violence that African Americans faced in the South. Tens of thousands of other Americans of conscience made the same decision that he did during those years. Communists seemed to have answers to problems that neither Democrats nor Republicans could solve. Although Rustin did not remain a Communist for long (he broke decisively with the Communist Party in 1941), he never disavowed the value of the experience for him. "I'm happy I had it," he once reminisced. "It taught me a great deal, and I presume that if I had to do it over again, I'd do the same thing."[5] Though no longer connected to the party, for the rest of his days Rustin remained critical of the inequalities that capitalism produced and embraced a political philosophy of democratic socialism.

During the long decades of the cold war nothing marked someone as so beyond the boundaries of Americanism as did involvement with the communist movement. Communists were dangerous and menacing; they were disloyal and subversive. In the eyes of J. Edgar Hoover, the long-time director of the Federal Bureau of Investigation (FBI), once someone had been a Communist, he or she was always considered a threat. Rustin's communist past justified government surveillance of his activities. For many years the FBI tapped his home telephone, and agents of the Bureau secretly disrupted his work. How could a Communist be a civil rights hero? How could someone so critical of American free enterprise be central to the struggle for black freedom in the United States?

In Rustin's eyes, racial justice would never come to a world in which one nation fought to dominate another.

Rustin was also a pacifist, another identity difficult to incorporate into notions of American heroism. The Revolutionary War created the nation, and the Civil War saved and improved it. For more than two centuries, American men conducted war against the native peoples of the continent, allowing the United States to spread from the Atlantic to the Pacific. In the 1940s, the nation fought—and won—a world war, and in the 1950s and 1960s it waged a global cold war against the Soviet Union and communism.

Rustin said "no" to this history of violence. The same moral values that made him adapt Gandhian nonviolence to the struggle for racial equality in the United States made him refuse induction into the armed forces during World War II. While millions of Americans were fighting overseas, Rustin was serving a term in federal prison. The same moral values that allowed him to face down segregationist mobs nonviolently made him protest against the Korean War and demonstrate against the nuclear arms race. Rustin's moral economy led him to reject the rabid cold war rhetoric that justified the militarization of American society during these years. "We are living in 'an iron lung of militarism,'" he wrote during the Korean War. "Let us resist with our whole beings!"[6]

Rustin was true to his word. He was arrested for protesting outside draft boards after the federal government instituted peacetime conscription. In 1955, the same year that the Montgomery bus boycott started, he was part of a band of pacifists who disrupted tests of a civilian defense system in the United States. Rustin took his protests against war and nuclear weapons to Western and Eastern Europe and to Africa as well.

In Rustin's view, war would never bring peace, and violence would never bring justice. To him, nationalism and imperialism were destructive forces in the world. He saw the African's struggle for independence from European colonialism and the Southern Negro's struggle for full citizenship in the United States as two sides of the same coin. In Rustin's eyes, racial justice would never come to a world in which one nation fought to dominate another.

Finally, Rustin was a gay man. Today, in the first decade of the twenty-first century, gay things often seem everywhere. We see gay characters on network television and in Hollywood movies. Issues like same-sex marriage and the rights of gay men and lesbians to serve openly in the armed forces are discussed in our daily newspapers. Legislators debate whether to protect gay people from job discrimination, and all over the country teenagers form gay/straight alliances in their high schools. Though same-sex love and relationships remain hotly contested subjects, the presence of gay men and lesbians in American society is an acknowledged fact of life.

This was not so in Rustin's day. Between the 1930s, when he came into adulthood, and the early 1960s, when he was most influential in the black freedom movement, homosexuality was roundly condemned, harshly punished, and pushed out of sight. Every state had sodomy laws that criminalized homosexual behavior. Every religious faith damned it as sinful. The medical profession classified a homosexual orientation as a form of mental illness. In the 1950s, the federal government prohibited the employment of gay men and lesbians, and the military even excluded those with homosexual tendencies. Local police forces felt free to raid gay and lesbian bars and other meeting places, and they routinely arrested people en masse for holding hands, for dancing together, for inviting someone to come home with them for the evening. The morning newspaper often printed the names and addresses of those arrested, and men and women lost jobs as a result.

To be gay in these decades meant living with an almost constant awareness of vulnerability, and most men and women responded by staying deep in the closet. Many married. Many others told no one but their closest friends. They dissembled with their family and at work, creating a facade of heterosexuality to protect themselves from exposure and trouble.

Rustin was not "out of the closet in the way that phrase has meaning today, but neither did he attempt to deny his attractions to men. Davis Platt, one of his intimates from the 1940s, recalled that "I never had any sense at all that Bayard felt any shame or guilt about his homosexuality. That was rare in those days. Rare."[7] Yet his openness only made him more vulnerable. His willingness to go in search of sexual partners put him in the path of police officers looking to make arrests, and more than once Rustin found himself hauled into court on gay-related charges. In 1953, he was convicted in Los Angeles County under California's lewd-vagrancy law, and he served a sixty day sentence.

Rustin's homosexuality and the trouble it brought him created an endless series of difficulties for him. In the Christian pacifist world in which he toiled, it made him appear morally suspect. He worked as if on probation, always in danger of losing his place in the movement. In the South, where white segregationists seized any opportunity to discredit the black freedom struggle, Rustin's sexuality was potentially a liability of great consequence. It meant that he had to work one step removed from Martin Luther King, so that neither King nor the Southern Christian Leadership Conference could be tainted by Rustin's identity.

Throughout the 1950s and 1960s concerns about Rustin's sexuality rippled through the movement for racial justice. Sometimes the concerns came from friends and allies, as when activists in 1956 urged him to leave Montgomery as quickly as possible in order not to give enemies of the bus boycott a weapon to attack it. Sometimes rivals within the movement used it to limit Rustin's influence. In 1960, Adam Clayton Powell, a black member of Congress from the Harlem section of New York, threatened to spread scurrilous rumors about Rustin unless he was removed from a political project. Enemies of everything Rustin fought for often broadcast his homosexuality as a way of discrediting him and his causes. In 1958, an American Legion chapter in Montana publicized his conviction in Pasadena, California, in an effort to have his lectures in the state cancelled. The most dramatic example of these attacks came in August 1963, in the weeks before the March on Washington. Strom Thurmond, a white supremacist senator from South Carolina, inserted into the *Congressional Record* information not only about Rustin's left-wing past, but about his homosexuality, too.

Put all of these liabilities together—a communist past in cold war America, a pacifist in an armed-to-the-teeth national security state, and a homosexual during the years that one historian has labeled "the lavender scare"[8]—and one can understand why Rustin would have developed a style of leadership that tended to keep him out of the public eye. But historians have an obligation to look beyond the surface of things, beyond the strategies that historical actors devise to disguise their role in events. We are expected to dig through the sources until we can piece together as truthful a reconstruction of the past as possible.

So let me rephrase slightly the questions I posed at the beginning: What would happen if we inserted Rustin fully into the popular narrative of the civil rights movement? We might have

to acknowledge that the vision and the energy and the skills of radicals were essential to its success, that agitation for racial justice was often most likely to come from those who stood far outside mainstream assumptions in the United States. We might have to acknowledge that the fight for civil rights drew strength and resources from other movements of dissent and that a belief in racial equality often lived alongside a commitment to peace and to the redistribution of wealth in America. We might also have to acknowledge that the distinction Americans like to draw between the private sphere and the public, between matters like sex and matters like politics, is a fragile one. We might have to acknowledge the complicated intersections between race and sexuality and recognize how love and intimacy become excuses for oppression that crush human lives no less than other forms of injustice. We might, in short, find ourselves with a more truthful version of a vital part of America's past.

Endnotes

1. Jacquelyn Dowd Hall, "The Long Civil Rights Movement and the Political Uses of the *Past," Journal of American History* 91 (March 2005): 1233.
2. *Washington Post,* August 11, 1963, A, 6; *Life,* September 6, 1963.
3. Details about Rustin's career in this and the following paragraphs come from my biography of Rustin, *Lost Prophet: The life and Times of Bayard Rustin* (New York: Free Press, 2003). The quotation comes from my interview with David McReynolds, now on deposit at the Swarthmore College Peace Collection.
4. John Lewis with Michael D'Orso, *Walking with the Wind: A Memoir of the Movement* (New York: Simon & Schuster, 1998), 217.
5. The Reminiscences of Bayard Rustin, Oral History Collection of Columbia University.
6. Quoted in *Lost Prophet,* 180.
7. Ibid., 71.
8. David K. Johnson, *The Lavender Scare: The Cold War Persecution of Gays and Lesbians in the Federal Government* (Chicago: University of Chicago Press, 2004).

JOHN D'EMILIO *is a professor of history and of gender & women's studies at the University of Illinois at Chicago. Among his several publications are* Sexual Politics, Sexual Communities: The Making of a Homosexual Minority in the United States *(1983), and, with Estelle Freedman,* Intimate Matters: A History of Sexuality in America *(1988). His most recent book,* Lost Prophet: The Life and Times of Bayard Rustin *(2003), was a finalist for the National Book Award, winner of the Stonewall Award from the American Library Association, and a* New York Times *Notable Book of the year.*

The Magdalene Mystique

Why her archetype matters

LILA SOPHIA TRESEMER (WITH DAVID TRESEMER)

Never before has a thriller hit the reading market like Dan Brown's 2003 book, *The Da Vinci Code*. Millions of readers rushed to buy the novel, debates raged about its authenticity, the Louvre and other museums used the story to sell tickets, cults of followers took tours that explained how "the code" was cracked.

At the center of all the debate and mystery is Mary Magdalene, who traveled with Jesus and is now considered a saint by major religions. Magdalene has come to the forefront of people's consciousness for a reason—not because of Brown, but because her archetype is re-emerging. Brown captured the attention of millions through good storytelling, and to some extent, her voice came through.

Still, the story of Magdalene and all she represents is far from settled. There are many questions that may never be answered. Was she the lover and wife of Yeshua Ben Joseph (Jesus)? One first-century text observes that the two of them used to kiss frequently. There are many hints in Gnostic texts that she and Yeshua had an intimate connection. Perhaps the wedding at Cana was their wedding; perhaps they had a daughter named Sarah. Perhaps Magdalene was an initiate of the Egyptian mysteries and a priestess. We think this part is true. But . . . perhaps not.

One thing is certain. Mary Magdalene—her life and her archetype—are resonating, especially with women. Her archetype is an essential one, which the modern-day feminine needs to reclaim, rediscover, and re-engage.

Several years ago, before *The Da Vinci Code*, my husband, David, and I traveled deep into Israel and France to "track down Magdalene." We wrote a play about what we found, and made a video. Our work was stimulated by a dream I had while I was sleeping near the Sea of Galilee, in which "She" directed me: "Tell my story." I've spent a lot of time reviewing the materials and meditating, and I've come up with this personal interpretation of Magdalene and her life:

A beautiful woman lives in the early first century at the time of a great teacher, and she travels with him and his disciples. She doesn't accept the roles assigned to women and is not about to meekly accept her place as defined by the spiritual and cultural authorities. She is intimate with the teacher, and he respects and encourages her intellect as well as her spiritual process. He calls her koinonos, *which means companion or partner. She asks insightful questions of the spiritual teacher, and she is familiar enough with the Egyptian mysteries to know when and how to anoint the "King," seven times in all. She witnesses her beloved teacher and friend die a brutal death, while most of the men disappear out of terror. She is the first person to witness his successful initiation rite, the rising from the tomb. At that time, she receives a teaching from him in his "light body," or his resurrected form. When she returns to report on this encounter, some of the male disciples scorn and belittle her, jealous of her close relationship with the teacher. By tradition, she would be the first apostle and the recipient of the mantle of the spiritual teacher; but alas, she is mocked and ostracized. Later she is named a prostitute. She, who was deeply loved by the anointed one, has no more place in the community he founded. But she leaves a trail of mystery, some bread crumbs along the way, so that perhaps at another time, when women are more independent and empowered, they might discover her trail. They might find that there is a root to Western mysticism that has the face of a beautiful and powerful woman.*

If this is true, one of the most enlightened individuals of all history loved and honored a woman. If this is true, their partnership was at the core of a dominant religion for the past 2000 years. Maybe celibacy and sin are not as important as we think. Maybe partnership is the central tenet of Christianity. This aspect of partnership is what has captured the collective imagination. Yeshua and Magdalene loved one another, regardless of the nature of that love. They were, in my opinion, intimate. Intimacy doesn't need to be sexual; it implies that two people are close, and honor deeply the gifts of the other.

Looking back to Leonardo da Vinci's depiction of the Last Supper, scholars and historians have asked, "Is that figure on the left John the Beloved, or Mary Magdalene?" The bigger question might be: "Is there a place at that table for a woman, for the feminine?" Accepting that Magdalene was part of Jesus' inner circle could make a significant difference to us now, at a time when people need to know that powerful, capable women are essential to solving the world's problems. As I watch women rediscover Mary Magdalene as an archetype, I see them wake up to feisty spirit and boldness. I witness them standing up and facing discrimination, not violently or reactively, but with grace and dignity. I also see that they are able to look back at the story, the myth, of Christianity and claim something as their own: another archetype besides Virgin, Mother, and Whore.

Another world is not only possible, she is on her way. On a quiet day, I can hear her breathing.

—Arundhati Roy
*From a speech given at the World Social Forum,
Porte Alegre, Brazil, in 2003*

If women can believe this, they change their roles: They can accept that women have a place at the table. They can claim the teacher who, at the core, accepted a woman who burned a wilder fire than was acceptable, and loved her. He saw her. He honored her.

This is her time to be remembered. And as this memory fires up the passion of women and men, may we find the way to respect the feminine and let its power lead the way to healthy living for all.

To find Lila and David Tresemer's DVD *Re-Discovering Mary Malagdalene: The Making of a Mythic Drama* (Cancom, 2001), go to www.pathoftheceremonialarts.org.

The Manliness of Men

Harvey Mansfield

Today the very word "manliness" seems obsolete. There are other words, such as "courage," "frankness," or "confidence," that convey the good side of manliness without naming a sex. But to use them in place of "manliness" begs the question of whether moral or psychological qualities specific to each sex exist. Our society today denies that such differences are real, and seeks to abolish all signs of such qualities in our language. To the extent that feminism recognizes gender differences at all, it presents them as bad, and as the fault of men.

The women's revolution has succeeded to an amazing degree. Our society has adopted, quite without realizing the magnitude of the change, a practice of equality between the sexes never before known in human history. My intent is not to stand in the way of this change. Women are not going to be herded back into the kitchen by men. But we need to recognize that there have been both gains and losses in this revolution.

Manliness can be heroic. But it can also be vainly boastful, prone to meaningless scuffling, and unfriendly. It jeers at those who do not seem to measure up, and asks men to continually prove themselves. It defines turf and fights for it—sometimes to defend precious rights, sometimes for no good reason. Manliness has always been under a cloud of doubt—raised by men who may not have the time or taste for it.

But such doubts about manliness can hardly be found in today's feminism. Contemporary feminists, and the women they influence, have essentially a single problem with manliness: that it excludes women. Betty Friedan's feminist classic *The Feminine Mystique* is not an attack on manliness, but on femininity. It insists women should be strong and aggressive—like men.

Though the word is scarce in use, there is an abundance of manliness in action in America today. Young males still pick fights, often with deadly weapons. What we suffer from today, is a lack of intelligent *criticism* of manliness. Feminism has undermined, if not destroyed, the counterpart to manliness—femininity—and with it the basis on which half the population could be skeptical of the excesses of manliness.

Of course, women are still women. While they want men to be sensitive to women, they don't necessarily want them to be sensitive in general. That's why the traditional manly male—who is protective of women, but a sorry flop when it comes to sensitivity—is far from a disappearing species.

The manly male protects women, but is a sorry flop when it comes to sensitivity.

Manliness offers gallantry to women. But is gallantry fundamentally insincere because it always contains an element of disdain? The man who opens a door for a woman makes a show of being stronger than she, one could say. At the same time, the woman does go first. Manly men are romantic about women; unmanly men are sympathetic. Which is better for women?

The "sensitive male" who mimics many female emotions and interests, while discarding the small favors men have traditionally done for women, is mostly just a creation of contemporary feminists who are irritated with the ways of men, no longer tolerant of their foibles, and demanding new behavior that would pave the way for ambitious women. Feminists insist that men must work harder to appreciate women. Yet they never ask women to be more understanding of men.

Manliness is a quality that causes individuals to stand up for something. It is a quality that calls private persons into public life. In the past such people have been predominantly male, and it is no accident that those who possess this quality have often ended up as political rulers and leaders.

Manly men defend their turf, just as other male mammals do. The analogy to animals obviously suggests something animalistic about manliness. But manliness is specifically human as well. Manly men defend not just their turf but their country. Manliness is best shown in war, the defense of one's country at its most difficult and dangerous. In Greek, the word for manliness, *andreia*, is also the word for courage.

For good and for ill, males impelled by their manliness have dominated all politics of which we know. Is there something inevitable about this domination or are we free to depart from it? With more and more countries moving toward democracy and peace, perhaps manliness will become less necessary.

Yet there might also be a democratic manliness. In democracies, Tocqueville said, a manly frankness prevails—an open and fearless stance of "man to man" in which all are equal. Does democracy, then, tend to produce, and require, manliness?

Feminists find all sexual roles objectionable. They are insulted by the idea that nature has determined different social parts and purposes for the sexes. They have largely forced the abandonment of any idea of sexual nature in favor of the feminist notion of "choice." A woman today has the choice of every occupation that used to be reserved for men, *plus* traditional women's roles. Inevitably, "choice" for women opens up choices for men too. What happens when men are no longer pressed to face the duties that used to go with being a man? Traditionally, the performance of a man's duties has required him to protect and support his family. To be a man means to support dependents, not merely yourself.

But the modern woman above all does not want to be a dependent. She may not have thought about what her independence does to the manliness of men (it might make men more selfish). And she may not have considered carefully whether the protection she does without will be replaced by sensitivity, or by neglect. The statistics on male abandonment of their children in our day are not heart-warming.

According to feminists, any traditional notion that the different sexes complement each other serves merely to justify the inferiority of women. On its face, complementarity suggests real equality—each sex is superior in its place. But if you are sure that the best positions have been the men's, and that women have been the "second sex," then in order to achieve equality

you must go for full interchangeability of the sexes. You must deny any natural preponderance of one quality or another in men and women.

Do men and women have different natures that justify different social roles? Or are these natures just "socially constructed"? If women can conclude that their roles have been designed artificially by society, then they are free to remake themselves without constraint. But the latest science suggests that being a man or a woman is much more than having certain bodily equipment. Perhaps men and women are characterized more by how they think than by their sexual organs.

While maleness is partly just a fact of biology, in humans it is linked to thinking and reason in ways that make manliness something much more than mere aggression. In humans, masculinity is more than just defense of one's own; it has been extended to require noble sacrifice for a cause beyond oneself.

Certainly, women reason and sacrifice too, and they are not devoid of aggressiveness. But their participation in these things is not "equal." As Aristotle said, men find it easier to be courageous—and women find it easier to be moderate. Of course, you cannot avoid Aristotle's qualifier, "for the most part."

For the most part, men will always have more manliness than women have, and it is up to both sexes to fashion this fact into something good.

HARVEY MANSFIELD is professor of government at Harvard University.

The Trouble with Boys

**They're kinetic, maddening and failing at school.
Now educators are trying new ways to help them succeed.**

PEG TYRE

Spend a few minutes on the phone with Danny Frankhuizen and you come away thinking, "What a *nice* boy." He's thoughtful, articulate, bright. He has a good relationship with his mom, goes to church every Sunday, loves the rock band Phish and spends hours each day practicing his guitar. But once he's inside his large public Salt Lake City high school, everything seems to go wrong. He's 16, but he can't stay organized. He finishes his homework and then can't find it in his backpack. He loses focus in class, and his teachers, with 40 kids to wrangle, aren't much help. "If I miss a concept, they tell me, 'Figure it out yourself'," says Danny. Last year Danny's grades dropped from B's to D's and F's. The sophomore, who once dreamed of Stanford, is pulling his grades up but worries that "I won't even get accepted at community college."

44%—The number of male undergraduates on college campuses; 30 years ago, the number was 58%.

His mother, Susie Malcom, a math teacher who is divorced, says it's been wrenching to watch Danny stumble. "I tell myself he's going to make something good out of himself," she says. "But it's hard to see doors close and opportunities fall away."

What's wrong with Danny? By almost every benchmark, boys across the nation and in every demographic group are falling behind. In elementary school, boys are two times more likely than girls to be diagnosed with learning disabilities and twice as likely to be placed in special-education classes. High-school boys are losing ground to girls on standardized writing tests. The number of boys who said they didn't like school rose 71 percent between 1980 and 2001, according to a University of Michigan study. Nowhere is the shift more evident than on college campuses. Thirty years ago men represented 58 percent of the undergraduate student body. Now they're a minority at 44 percent. This widening achievement gap, says Margaret Spellings, U.S. Secretary of Education, "has profound implications for the economy, society, families and democracy."

With millions of parents wringing their hands, educators are searching for new tools to help tackle the problem of boys.

Books including Michael Thompson's best seller "Raising Cain" (recently made into a PBS documentary) and Harvard psychologist William Pollack's definitive work "Real Boys" have become must-reads in the teachers' lounge. The Gurian Institute, founded in 1997 by family therapist Michael Gurian to help the people on the front lines help boys, has enrolled 15,000 teachers in its seminars. Even the Gates Foundation, which in the last five years has given away nearly a billion dollars to innovative high schools, is making boys a big priority. "Helping underperforming boys," says Jim Shelton, the foundation's education director, "has become part of our core mission."

The problem won't be solved overnight. In the last two decades, the education system has become obsessed with a quantifiable and narrowly defined kind of academic success, these experts say, and that myopic view is harming boys. Boys are biologically, developmentally and psychologically different from girls—and teachers need to learn how to bring out the best in every one. "Very well-meaning people," says Dr. Bruce Perry, a Houston neurologist who advocates for troubled kids, "have created a biologically disrespectful model of education."

Thirty years ago it was girls, not boys, who were lagging. The 1972 federal law Title IX forced schools to provide equal opportunities for girls in the classroom and on the playing field. Over the next two decades, billions of dollars were funneled into finding new ways to help girls achieve. In 1992, the American Association of University Women issued a report claiming that the work of Title IX was not done—girls still fell behind in math and science; by the mid-1990s, girls had reduced the gap in math and more girls than boys were taking high-school-level biology and chemistry.

'Often boys are treated like defective girls,' says Thompson.

Some scholars, notably Christina Hoff Sommers, a fellow at the American Enterprise Institute, charge that misguided feminism is what's been hurting boys. In the 1990s, she says, girls were making strong, steady progress toward parity in schools,

27

Elementary School

Boys start off with lower literacy skills than girls, and are less often encouraged to read, which only widens the gap.

- Girls ages 3 to 5 are **5%** more likely than boys to be read to at home at least three times a week.

- Girls are **10%** more likely than boys to recognize words by sight by the spring of first grade.

- Boys ages 5 to 12 are **60%** more likely than girls to have repeated at least one grade.

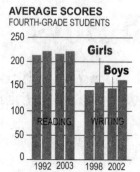

AVERAGE SCORES
FOURTH-GRADE STUDENTS

Girls

Boys

READING   WRITING

1992 2003   1998 2002

SOURCES: U.S. DEPARTMENT OF EDUCATION, CENTERS FOR DISEASE CONTROL

- Girls' reading scores improve **6%** more than boys' between kindergarten and third grade.

- First- to fifth-grade boys are **47%** more likely than girls to have disabilities such as emotional disturbances, learning problems or speech impediments.

- Fourth-grade girls score **3%** higher on standardized reading tests than boys.

- Fourth-grade girls score **12%** higher on writing tests than boys.

but feminist educators portrayed them as disadvantaged and lavished them with support and attention. Boys, meanwhile, whose rates of achievement had begun to falter, were ignored and their problems allowed to fester.

Standardized tests have become common for kids as young as 6.

Boys have always been boys, but the expectations for how they're supposed to act and learn in school have changed. In the last 10 years, thanks in part to activist parents concerned about their children's success, school performance has been measured in two simple ways: how many students are enrolled in accelerated courses and whether test scores stay high. Standardized assessments have become commonplace for kids as young as 6. Curricula have become more rigid. Instead of allowing teachers to instruct kids in the manner and pace that suit each class, some states now tell teachers what, when and how to teach. At the same time, student-teacher ratios have risen, physical education and sports programs have been cut and recess is a distant memory. These new pressures are undermining the strengths and underscoring the limitations of what psychologists call the "boy brain"—the kinetic, disorganized, maddening and sometimes brilliant behaviors that scientists now believe are not learned but hard-wired.

When Cris Messler of Mountainside, N.J., brought her 3-year-old son Sam to a pediatrician to get him checked for ADHD, she was acknowledging the desperation parents can feel. He's a high-energy kid, and Messler found herself hoping for a positive diagnosis. "If I could get a diagnosis from the doctor, I could get him on medicine," she says. The doctor said Sam is a normal boy. School has been tough, though. Sam's reading teacher said he was hopeless. His first-grade teacher complains he's antsy, and Sam, now 7, has been referring to himself as "stupid." Messler's glad her son doesn't need medication, but what, she wonders, can she do now to help her boy in school?

For many boys, the trouble starts as young as 5, when they bring to kindergarten a set of physical and mental abilities very different from girls'. As almost any parent knows, most 5-year-old girls are more fluent than boys and can sight-read more words. Boys tend to have better hand-eye coordination, but their fine motor skills are less developed, making it a struggle for some to control a pencil or a paintbrush. Boys are more impulsive than girls; even if they can sit still, many prefer not to—at least not for long.

Thirty years ago feminists argued that classic "boy" behaviors were a result of socialization, but these days scientists believe they are an expression of male brain chemistry. Sometime in the first trimester, a boy fetus begins producing male sex hormones that bathe his brain in testosterone for the rest of his gestation. "That exposure wires the male brain differently," says Arthur Arnold, professor of physiological science at UCLA. How? Scientists aren't exactly sure. New studies show that prenatal exposure to male sex hormones directly affects the way children play. Girls whose mothers have high levels of testosterone during pregnancy are more likely to prefer playing with trucks to playing with dolls. There are also clues that hormones influence the way we learn all through life. In a Dutch study published in 1994, doctors found that when males were given female hormones, their spatial skills dropped but their verbal skills improved.

In elementary-school classrooms—where teachers increasingly put an emphasis on language and a premium on sitting quietly and speaking in turn—the mismatch between boys and school can become painfully obvious. "Girl behavior becomes the gold standard," says "Raising Cain" coauthor Thompson. "Boys are treated like defective girls."

Two years ago Kelley King, principal of Douglass Elementary School in Boulder, Colo., looked at the gap between boys and girls and decided to take action. Boys were lagging 10 points behind girls in reading and 14 points in writing. Many more boys—than girls were being labeled as learning disabled, too. So King asked her teachers to buy copies of Gurian's book "The Minds of Boys," on boy-friendly classrooms, and in the fall of 2004 she launched a bold experiment. Whenever possi-

Middle School

Coming of age in a culture that discourages bookishness, boys are more likely to fall victim to drugs and violence.

- Eighth-grade girls score an average of **11 points** higher than eighth-grade boys on standardized reading tests.
- Eighth-grade girls score **21 points** higher than boys on standardized writing tests.
- Between 1993 and 2003, the number of ninth-grade

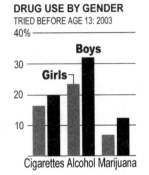

DRUG USE BY GENDER
TRIED BEFORE AGE 13: 2003

boys who skipped school at least once a month because they didn't feel safe increased **22%**.

- Boys between the ages of 5 and 14 are **200%** more likely to commit suicide than girls.
- Ninth-grade boys are **78%** more likely than girls to get injured in a fight at least once a year.
- Between the ages of 5 and 14, boys are **36%** more likely to die than their female counterparts.

ble, teachers replaced lecture time with fast-moving lessons that all kids could enjoy. Three weeks ago, instead of discussing the book "The View From Saturday," teacher Pam Unrau divided her third graders into small groups, and one student in each group pretended to be a character from the book. Classes are noisier, Unrau says, but the boys are closing the gap. Last spring, Douglass girls scored an average of 106 on state writing tests, while boys got a respectable 101.

Boys love video-games because when they lose, the defeat is private.

Primatologists have long observed that juvenile male chimps battle each other not just for food and females, but to establish and maintain their place in the hierarchy of the tribe. Primates face off against each other rather than appear weak. That same evolutionary imperative, psychologists say, can make it hard for boys to thrive in middle school—and difficult for boys who are failing to accept the help they need. The transition to middle school is rarely easy, but like the juvenile primates they are, middle-school boys will do almost anything to avoid admitting that they're overwhelmed. "Boys measure everything they do or say by a single yardstick: does this make me look weak?" says Thompson. "And if it does, he isn't going to do it." That's part of the reason that videogames have such a powerful hold on boys: the action is constant, they can calibrate just how hard the challenges will be and, when they lose, the defeat is private.

When Brian Johns hit seventh grade, he never admitted how vulnerable it made him feel. "I got behind and never caught up," says Brian, now 17 and a senior at Grand River Academy, an Ohio boarding school. When his parents tried to help, he rebuffed them. When his mother, Anita, tried to help him organize his assignment book, he grew evasive about when his homework was due. Anita didn't know where to turn. Brian's school had a program for gifted kids, and support for ones with special needs. But what, Anita asked his teachers, do they do about kids like her son who are in the middle and struggling? Those kids,

one of Brian's teachers told Anita, "are the ones who fall through the cracks."

It's easy for middle-school boys to feel outgunned. Girls reach sexual maturity two years ahead of boys, but other, less visible differences put boys at a disadvantage, too. The prefrontal cortex is a knobby region of the brain directly behind the forehead that scientists believe helps humans organize complex thoughts, control their impulses and understand the consequences of their own behavior. In the last five years, Dr. Jay Giedd, an expert in brain development at the National Institutes of Health, has used brain scans to show that in girls, it reaches its maximum thickness by the age of 11 and, for the next decade or more, continues to mature. In boys, this process is delayed by 18 months.

Middle-school boys may use their brains less efficiently than girls.

Middle-school boys may use their brains less efficiently, too. Using a type of MRI that traces activity in the brain, Deborah Yurgelun-Todd, director of the cognitive neuroimaging laboratory at McLean Hospital in Belmont, Mass., tested the activity patterns in the prefrontal cortex of children between the ages of 11 and 18. When shown pictures of fearful faces, adolescent girls registered activity on the right side of the prefrontal cortex, similar to an adult. Adolescent boys used both sides—a less mature pattern of brain activity. Teenage girls can process information faster, too. In a study about to be published in the journal Intelligence, researchers at Vanderbilt University administered timed tests—picking similar objects and matching groups of numbers—to 8,000 boys and girls between the ages of 5 and 18. In kindergarten, boys and girls processed information at about the same speeds. In early adolescence, girls finished faster and got more right. By 18, boys and girls were processing with the same speed and accuracy.

Scientists caution that brain research doesn't tell the whole story: temperament, family background and environment play

29

High School and Beyond

Many boys continue to fall behind girls in reading and writing proficiency, and fewer are going to college.

- Boys are **33%** more likely than girls to drop out of high school.

- Twelfth-grade girls score **16 points** higher than boys on standardized reading tests.

- High-school boys are **30%** more likely to use cocaine than high-school girls.

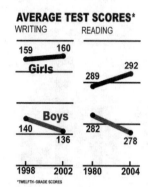

AVERAGE TEST SCORES*

WRITING   READING

159   160
Girls   289   292

Boys   282
140   278
136

1998   2002   1980   2004

*TWELFTH-GRADE SCORES

- Twelfth-grade girls score **24 points** higher than boys on standardized writing tests.

- High-school girls are **36%** more likely to take Advanced Placement or honors biology than high-school boys.

- **22%** more high-school girls are planning to go to college than boys.

- The percentage of male undergraduates dropped **24%** from 1970 to 2000.

---

big roles, too. Some boys are every bit as organized and assertive as the highest-achieving girls. All kids can be scarred by violence, alcohol or drugs in the family. But if your brain hasn't reached maturity yet, says Yurgelun-Todd, "it's not going to be able to do its job optimally."

Across the nation, educators are reviving an old idea: separate the girls from the boys—and at Roncalli Middle School, in Pueblo, Colo., administrators say, it's helping kids of both genders. This past fall, with the blessing of parents, school guidance counselor Mike Horton assigned a random group of 50 sixth graders to single-sex classes in core subjects. These days, when sixth-grade science teacher Pat Farrell assigns an earth-science lab on measuring crystals, the girls collect their materials—a Bunsen burner, a beaker of phenyl salicylate and a spoon. Then they read the directions and follow the sequence from beginning to end. The first things boys do is ask, "Can we eat this?" They're less organized, Farrell notes, but sometimes, "they're willing to go beyond what the lab asks them to do." With this in mind, he hands out written instructions to both classes but now goes over them step by step for the boys. Although it's too soon to declare victory, there are some positive signs: the shyest boys are participating more. This fall, the all-girl class did best in math, English and science, followed by the all-boy class and then coed classes.

One of the most reliable predictors of whether a boy will succeed or fail in high school rests on a single question: does he have a man in his life to look up to? Too often, the answer is no. High rates of divorce and single motherhood have created a generation of fatherless boys. In every kind of neighborhood, rich or poor, an increasing number of boys—now a startling 40 percent—are being raised without their biological dads.

Psychologists say that grandfathers and uncles can help, but emphasize that an adolescent boy without a father figure is like an explorer without a map. And that is especially true for poor boys and boys who are struggling in school. Older males, says Gurian, model self-restraint and solid work habits for younger ones. And whether they're breathing down their necks about grades or admonishing them to show up for school on time, "an older man reminds a boy in a million different ways that school is crucial to their mission in life."

A boy without a father figure is like an explorer without a map.

In the past, boys had many opportunities to learn from older men. They might have been paired with a tutor, apprenticed to a master or put to work in the family store. High schools offered boys a rich array of roles in which to exercise leadership skills—class officer, yearbook editor or a place on the debate team. These days, with the exception of sports, more girls than boys are involved in those activities.

In neighborhoods where fathers are most scarce, the high-school dropout rates are shocking: more than half of African-American boys who start high school don't finish. David Banks, principal of the Eagle Academy for Young Men, one of four all-boy public high schools in the New York City system, wants each of his 180 students not only to graduate from high school but to enroll in college. And he's leaving nothing to chance. Almost every Eagle Academy boy has a male mentor—a lawyer, a police officer or an entrepreneur from the school's South Bronx neighborhood. The impact of the mentoring program, says Banks, has been "beyond profound." Tenth grader Rafael Mendez is unequivocal: his mentor "is the best thing that ever happened to me." Before Rafael came to Eagle Academy, he dreamed about playing pro baseball, but his mentor, Bronx Assistant District Attorney Rafael Curbelo, has shown him another way to succeed: Mendez is thinking about attending college in order to study forensic science.

'An older man reminds a boy that school is crucial to life,' says Gurian.

Colleges would welcome more applications from young men like Rafael Mendez. At many state universities the gender balance is already tilting 60-40 toward women. Primary and secondary schools are going to have to make some major changes, says Ange Peterson, president-elect of the American Association of Collegiate Registrars and Admissions Officers, to restore the gender balance. "There's a whole group of men we're losing in education completely," says Peterson.

For Nikolas Arnold, 15, a sophomore at a public high school in Santa Monica, Calif., college is a distant dream. Nikolas is smart: he's got an encyclopedic knowledge of weaponry and war. When he was in first grade, his principal told his mother he was too immature and needed ADHD drugs. His mother balked. "Too immature?" says Diane Arnold, a widow. "He was six and a half!" He's always been an advanced reader, but his grades are erratic. Last semester, when his English teacher assigned two girls' favorites—"Memoirs of a Geisha" and "The Secret Life of Bees" Nikolas got a D. But lately, he has a math teacher he likes and is getting excited about numbers. He's reserved in class sometimes. But now that he's more engaged, his grades are improving slightly and his mother, who's pushing college, is hopeful he will begin to hit his stride. Girls get A's and B's on their report cards, she tells him, but that doesn't mean boys can't do it, too.

With Andrew Murr, Vanessa Juarez,
Anne Underwood, Karen Springen and Pat Wingert

The Gender Quotient Test

We all have both feminine and masculine traits. Some of us are mostly balanced, and some of us tip to one side or the other. Where do you fit? We asked author and spiritual thinker David Deida to develop a quiz to test your "gender genius." Take the test quickly, without thinking about it. Scoring—always optional—is at the end.

DAVID DEIDA

KNOW THE MASCULINE, KEEP TO THE FEMININE.

—Lao Tzu

1. I am ...

A. happy to relate warmly and humorously with my male and female colleagues while simultaneously focusing on project deadlines.

B. hard-pressed to understand why people can't leave me alone when it's clear that I need to attend to pressing business.

2. I feel ...

A. natural and comfortable in motion and emotion, both calm and chaotic.

B. uneasy when people change plans at the last minute; schedules and routines are the most efficient way I know to accomplish my goals.

3. I can and do ...

A. enjoy extreme intensity in many dimensions, including sexually, intellectually, and socially.

B. contain any overexuberance. Strong emotions have their place, but I usually prefer peace and harmony to wild abandon.

4. I don't ...

A. ignore my love of life for the sake of accomplishing a project or meeting the bottom line.

B. lose track of my commitments. I am very trustworthy, since I do what I say I will without changing my mind or getting distracted.

5. I consider myself ...

A. a practiced artist of the earth's elements, sensual skills, and beautiful adornment.

B. a practical and effective person; I tend to concern myself more with function than form.

6. I ...

A. may get frazzled, but I am at home in the always unpredictable ups and downs, of birth, life, and death.

B. lose my patience with the endless drama around people's lives, so I choose to focus on achievable goals.

7. I am driven ...

A. to create real love and cooperation in the world more strongly than to achieve a specific set of quantifiable goals.

B. to make the most of my capacities and create something great, or die trying.

8. The bittersweet heartache of yearning (rather than the desire for accomplishment) is the bodily source of my passion and creativity.

A. Exactly!
B. What, exactly, does this mean?

9. Although I may enjoy ...

A. silence, solitude, and meditation, my soul is most often healed by sharing laughter and love with my friends, talking, dancing, and celebrating our precious life together on earth.

B. spending time with friends and family, my soul is most healed and inspired by solitude, intentional austerity, and extreme challenge.

10. I'm happy ...

A. to multitask. I can talk on the phone with a disgruntled employee, hug my lover, and write a business proposal at the same time.

B. when I get a solid block of time to work on one thing and get it done so I am free to move on to the next thing.

Scoring: Give yourself a feminine point for every A answer and a masculine point for every B answer. Not all of us have equal access to our inner masculine and feminine genius. Don't try to balance yourself. Instead, compassionately embrace all your qualities and team up with others who complement you, while cultivating your natural strengths as you give your true gifts to the world.

FLUID HARDENS TO SOLID, SOLID RUSHES TO FLUID. THERE IS NO WHOLLY MASCULINE MAN, NO PURELY FEMININE WOMAN.
—Margaret Fuller, *Woman in the Nineteenth Century,* 1845

Spiritual teacher and best-selling author **DAVID DEIDA** writes about the ties between sexuality and spirituality in his many books, including *Blue Truth* and *The Way of the Superior Man*. A founding member of Integral Institute, a nonprofit organization that takes a holistic approach to psychology, business, politics, education, and other disciplines, Deida has taught and conducted research at the University of California Medical School at San Diego and the Ecole Polytechnique in Paris; he holds workshops worldwide that aim to awaken and transform the mind, body, and heart. (see www.deida .info).

UNIT 2

Sexual Biology, Behavior, and Orientation

Unit Selections

Key Points to Consider

- How have (or would) you react if a friend confided in you that he or she was having sexual functioning problems, for example erections or painful intercourse problems? What if the person confiding in you was a co-worker? A stranger? Your mother or your grandfather? Who would you talk to if it were you with the problem, and what response would you want from the other person?

- Let's assume you were shown research that predicted that behaviors you currently engage in could cause you to have serious health problems in the future. What likelihood of future problems and what nature of problems would make you change the behaviors in question?

- It is rare for people to wonder why someone is heterosexual in the same ways as we wonder why someone is homosexual or bisexual. What do you think contributes to a person's sexual orientation? Do you think it is possible for people not to feel threatened by sexual orientations different from their own? Why or why not?

Student Web Site

www.mhcls.com/online

Internet References

Further information regarding these Web sites may be found in this book's preface or online.

The Body: A Multimedia AIDS/HIV Information Resource
  http://www.thebody.com/cgi-bin/body.cgi

Healthy Way
  http://www.ab.sympatico.ca/Contents/health/

Hispanic Sexual Behavior and Gender Roles
  http://www.caps.ucsf.edu/hispnews.html

Johan's Guide to Aphrodisiacs
  http://www.santesson.com/aphrodis/aphrhome.htm

Site of Parents, Familes, and Friends of Lesbians and Gays
  http://www.pflag.org

Human bodies are miraculous things. Most of us, however, have less than a complete understanding of how they work. This is especially true of our bodily responses and functioning during sexual activity. Efforts to develop a healthy sexual awareness are severely hindered by misconceptions and lack of quality information about physiology. The first portion of this unit directs attention to the development of a clearer understanding and appreciation of the workings of the human body.

Over the past decade and a half, the general public's awareness of, and interest and involvement in, their own health care has dramatically increased. We want to stay healthy and live longer, and we know that to do so, we must know more about our bodies, including how to prevent problems, recognize danger signs, and find the most effective treatments. By the same token, if we want to stay sexually fit—from robust youth through a healthy, happy, sexy old age—we must be knowledgeable about sexual health care.

As you read through the articles in this section, you will be able to see more clearly that matters of sexual biology and behavior are not merely physiological in origin. The articles included clearly demonstrate the psychological, social, and cultural origins of sexual behavior as well.

Why we humans feel, react, respond, and behave sexually can be quite complex. This is especially true regarding the issue of sexual orientation. Perhaps no other area of sexual behavior is as misunderstood as this one. Although experts do not agree about what causes our sexual orientation—homosexual, heterosexual, bisexual, or ambisexual—growing evidence suggests a complex interaction of biological or genetic determination, environmental or sociocultural influence, and free choice. In the early 1900s sexologist Alfred Kinsey introduced his seven-point continuum of sexual orientation. It placed exclusive heterosexual orientation at one end, exclusive homosexual orientation at the other, and identified the middle range as where most people would fall if society and culture were unprejudiced. Since Kinsey, many others have added their research findings and theories to what is known about sexual orientation including some apparent differences in relative contribution of biological, psychological, environmental, and cultural factors for males versus females and sexual orientation. In addition, further elaboration of the "middle" on the Kinsey scale has included some distinction between bisexuality—the attraction to males and females—and ambisexuality—representing individuals for whom gender is no more relevant than any other personal characteristic, such as height, hair color, right- or left-handedness—with respect to sexual attraction and/or orientation. A final addition to our understanding of sexuality and sexual orientation comes from Anne Fausto-Sterling, a professor of biology and women's studies at Brown University, who has become the leading advocate for in-

tersexuals, people who are not clearly male or female by anatomy or behavior. As a result of these and other findings about sexual orientation, leaders in the field now recommend that we pluralize our terms in this area: human sexualities and orientations.

The fact that the previous paragraph may have been upsetting, even distasteful, to some readers emphasizes the connectedness of psychological, social, and cultural issues with those of sexuality. Human sexuality is biology, behavior, and much, much more. Our sexual beliefs, behaviors, choices, even feelings and comfort levels are profoundly affected by what our culture prescribes and proscribes, which has been transmitted to us by the full range of social institutions and processes. This section begins our attempt to address these interrelationships and their impact on human sexuality.

The New Sex Scorecard

Talking openly about sex differences is no longer an exercise in political incorrectness; it is a necessity in fighting disease and forging successful relationships. At 109 and counting, *PT* examines the tally.

Hara Estroff Marano

Get out the spittoon. Men produce twice as much saliva as women. Women, for their part, learn to speak earlier, know more words, recall them better, pause less and glide through tongue twisters.

Put aside Simone de Beauvoir's famous dictum, "One is not born a woman but rather becomes one." Science suggests otherwise, and it's driving a whole new view of who and what we are. Males and females, it turns out, are different from the moment of conception, and the difference shows itself in every system of body and brain.

It's safe to talk about sex differences again. Of course, it's the oldest story in the world. And the newest. But for a while it was also the most treacherous. Now it may be the most urgent. The next stage of progress against disorders as disabling as depression and heart disease rests on cracking the binary code of biology. Most common conditions are marked by pronounced gender differences in incidence or appearance.

Although sex differences in brain and body take their inspiration from the central agenda of reproduction, they don't end there. "We've practiced medicine as though only a woman's breasts, uterus and ovaries made her unique—and as though her heart, brain and every other part of her body were identical to those of a man," says Marianne J. Legato, M.D., a cardiologist at Columbia University who spearheads the new push on gender differences. Legato notes that women live longer but break down more.

Do we need to explain that difference doesn't imply superiority or inferiority? Although sex differences may provide ammunition for David Letterman or the Simpsons, they unfold in the most private recesses of our lives, surreptitiously molding our responses to everything from stress to space to speech. Yet there are some ways the sexes are becoming more alike—they are now both engaging in the same kind of infidelity, one that is equally threatening to their marriages.

Everyone gains from the new imperative to explore sex differences. When we know why depression favors women two to one, or why the symptoms of heart disease literally hit women in the gut, it will change our understanding of how our bodies and our minds work.

The Gene Scene

Whatever sets men and women apart, it all starts with a single chromosome: the male-making Y, a puny thread bearing a paltry 25 genes, compared with the lavish female X, studded with 1,000 to 1,500 genes. But the Y guy trumps. He has a gene dubbed Sry, which, if all goes well, instigates an Olympic relay of development. It commands primitive fetal tissue to become testes, and they then spread word of masculinity out to the provinces via their chief product, testosterone. The circulating hormone not only masculinizes the body but affects the developing brain, influencing the size of specific structures and the wiring of nerve cells.

25% of females experience daytime sleepiness, versus 18% of males

But sex genes themselves don't cede everything to hormones. Over the past few years, scientists have come to believe that they too play ongoing roles in gender-flavoring the brain and behavior.

Females, it turns out, appear to have backup genes that protect their brains from big trouble. To level the genetic playing field between men and women, nature normally shuts off one of the two X chromosomes in every cell in females. But about 19 percent of genes escape inactivation; cells get a double dose of some X genes. Having fall-back genes may explain why females are far less subject than males to mental disorders from autism to schizophrenia.

What's more, which X gene of a pair is inactivated makes a difference in the way female and male brains respond to things, says neurophysiologist Arthur P. Arnold, Ph.D., of the University of California at Los Angeles. In some cases, the X gene donated by Dad is nullified; in other cases it's the X from Mom. The parent from whom a woman gets her working genes determines how robust her genes are. Paternal genes ramp up the genetic volume, maternal genes tune it down. This is known as genomic imprinting of the chromosome.

For many functions, it doesn't matter which sex genes you have or from whom you get them. But the Y chromosome itself spurs the brain to grow extra dopamine neurons, Arnold says. These nerve cells are involved in reward and motivation, and dopamine release underlies the pleasure of addiction and novelty seeking. Dopamine neurons also affect motor skills and go awry in Parkinson's disease, a disorder that afflicts twice as many males as females.

XY makeup also boosts the density of vasopressin fibers in the brain. Vasopressin is a hormone that both abets and minimizes sex differences; in some circuits it fosters parental behavior in males; in others it may spur aggression.

Sex on the Brain

Ruben Gur, Ph.D., always wanted to do the kind of psychological research that when he found something new, no one could say his grandmother already knew it. Well, "My grandmother couldn't tell you that women have a higher percentage of gray matter in their brains," he says. Nor could she explain how that discovery resolves a long-standing puzzle.

99% of girls play with dolls at age 6, versus 17% of boys

Gur's discovery that females have about 15 to 20 percent more gray matter than males suddenly made sense of another major sex difference: Men, overall, have larger brains than women (their heads and bodies are larger), but the sexes score equally well on tests of intelligence.

Gray matter, made up of the bodies of nerve cells and their connecting dendrites, is where the brain's heavy lifting is done. The female brain is more densely packed with neurons and dendrites, providing concentrated processing power—and more thought-linking capability.

The larger male cranium is filled with more white matter and cerebrospinal fluid. "That fluid is probably helpful," says Gur, director of the Brain Behavior Laboratory at the University of Pennsylvania. "It cushions the brain, and men are more likely to get their heads banged about."

White matter, made of the long arms of neurons encased in a protective film of fat, helps distribute processing throughout the brain. It gives males superiority at spatial reasoning. White matter also carries fibers that inhibit "information spread" in the cortex. That allows a single-mindedness that spatial problems require, especially difficult ones. The harder a spatial task, Gur finds, the more circumscribed the right-sided brain activation in males, but not in females. The white matter advantage of males, he believes, suppresses activation of areas that could interfere with work.

The white matter in women's brains is concentrated in the corpus callosum, which links the brain's hemispheres, and enables the right side of the brain to pitch in on language tasks. The more difficult the verbal task, the more global the neural participation required—a response that's stronger in females.

Women have another heady advantage—faster blood flow to the brain, which offsets the cognitive effects of aging. Men lose more brain tissue with age, especially in the left frontal cortex, the part of the brain that thinks about consequences and provides self-control.

"You can see the tissue loss by age 45, and that may explain why midlife crisis is harder on men," says Gur. "Men have the same impulses but they lose the ability to consider long-term consequences." Now, there's a fact someone's grandmother may have figured out already.

Minds of Their Own

The difference between the sexes may boil down to this: dividing the tasks of processing experience. Male and female minds are innately drawn to different aspects of the world around them. And there's new evidence that testosterone may be calling some surprising shots.

Women's perceptual skills are oriented to quick—call it intuitive—people reading. Females are gifted at detecting the feelings and thoughts of others, inferring intentions, absorbing contextual clues and responding in emotionally appropriate ways. They empathize. Tuned to others, they more readily see alternate sides of an argument. Such empathy fosters communication and primes females for attachment.

Women, in other words, seem to be hard-wired for a top-down, big-picture take. Men might be programmed to look at things from the bottom up (no surprise there).

Men focus first on minute detail, and operate most easily with a certain detachment. They construct rules-based analyses of the natural world, inanimate objects and events. In the coinage of Cambridge University psychologist Simon Baron-Cohen, Ph.D., they systemize.

The superiority of males at spatial cognition and females' talent for language probably subserve the more basic difference of systemizing versus empathizing. The two mental styles manifest in the toys kids prefer (humanlike dolls versus mechanical trucks); verbal impatience in males (ordering rather than negotiating); and navigation (women personalize space by finding landmarks; men see a geometric system, taking directional cues in the layout of routes).

26% of males say they have extramarital sex without being emotionally involved, versus 3% of females

Almost everyone has some mix of both types of skills, although males and females differ in the degree to which one set predominates, contends Baron-Cohen. In his work as director of Cambridge's Autism Research Centre, he finds that children and adults with autism, and its less severe variant Asperger syndrome, are unusual in both dimensions of perception. Its victims are "mindblind," unable to recognize people's feelings. They also have a peculiar talent for systemizing, obsessively focusing on, say, light switches or sink faucets.

Autism overwhelmingly strikes males; the ratio is ten to one for Asperger. In his new book, *The Essential Difference: The Truth About the Male and Female Brain*, Baron-Cohen argues that autism is a magnifying mirror of maleness.

The brain basis of empathizing and systemizing is not well understood, although there seems to be a "social brain," nerve circuitry dedicated to person perception. Its key components lie on the left side of the brain, along with language centers generally more developed in females.

Baron-Cohen's work supports a view that neuroscientists have flirted with for years: Early in development, the male hormone testosterone slows the growth of the brain's left hemisphere and accelerates growth of the right.

Testosterone may even have a profound influence on eye contact. Baron-Cohen's team filmed year-old children at play and measured the amount of eye contact they made with their mothers, all of whom had undergone amniocentesis during pregnancy. The researchers looked at various social factors—birth order, parental education, among others—as well as the level of testosterone the child had been exposed to in fetal life.

Baron-Cohen was "bowled over" by the results. The more testosterone the children had been exposed to in the womb, the less able they were to make eye contact at 1 year of age. "Who would have thought that a behavior like eye contact, which is so intrinsically social, could be in part shaped by a biological factor?" he asks. What's more, the testosterone level during fetal life also influenced language skills. The higher the prenatal testosterone level, the smaller a child's vocabulary at 18 months and again at 24 months.

Lack of eye contact and poor language aptitude are early hallmarks of autism. "Being strongly attracted to systems, together with a lack of empathy, may be the core characteristics of individuals on the autistic spectrum," says Baron-Cohen. "Maybe testosterone does more than affect spatial ability and language. Maybe it also affects social ability." And perhaps autism represents an "extreme form" of the male brain.

Depression: Pink—and Blue, Blue, Blue

This year, 19 million Americans will suffer a serious depression. Two out of three will be female. Over the course of their lives, 21.3 percent of women and 12.7 percent of men experience at least one bout of major depression.

The female preponderance in depression is virtually universal. And it's specific to unipolar depression. Males and females suffer equally from bipolar, or manic, depression. However, once depression occurs, the clinical course is identical in men and women.

The gender difference in susceptibility to depression emerges at 13. Before that age, boys, if anything, are a bit more likely than girls to be depressed. The gender difference seems to wind down four decades later, making depression mostly a disorder of women in the child-bearing years.

As director of the Virginia Institute for Psychiatric and Behavioral Genetics at Virginia Commonwealth University,

Kenneth S. Kendler, M.D., presides over "the best natural experiment that God has given us to study gender differences"—thousands of pairs of opposite-sex twins. He finds a significant difference between men and women in their response to low levels of adversity. He says, "Women have the capacity to be precipitated into depressive episodes at lower levels of stress."

Adding injury to insult, women's bodies respond to stress differently than do men's. They pour out higher levels of stress hormones and fail to shut off production readily. The female sex hormone progesterone blocks the normal ability of the stress hormone system to turn itself off. Sustained exposure to stress hormones kills brain cells, especially in the hippocampus, which is crucial to memory.

It's bad enough that females are set up biologically to internally amplify their negative life experiences. They are prone to it psychologically as well, finds University of Michigan psychologist Susan Nolen-Hoeksema, Ph.D.

Women ruminate over upsetting situations, going over and over negative thoughts and feelings, especially if they have to do with relationships. Too often they get caught in downward spirals of hopelessness and despair.

It's entirely possible that women are biologically primed to be highly sensitive to relationships. Eons ago it might have helped alert them to the possibility of abandonment while they were busy raising the children. Today, however, there's a clear downside. Ruminators are unpleasant to be around, with their oversize need for reassurance. Of course, men have their own ways of inadvertently fending off people. As pronounced as the female tilt to depression is the male excess of alcoholism, drug abuse and antisocial behaviors.

The Incredible Shrinking Double Standard

Nothing unites men and women better than sex. Yet nothing divides us more either. Males and females differ most in mating psychology because our minds are shaped by and for our reproductive mandates. That sets up men for sex on the side and a more casual attitude toward it.

Twenty-five percent of wives and 44 percent of husbands have had extramarital intercourse, reports Baltimore psychologist Shirley Glass, Ph.D. Traditionally for men, love is one thing and sex is . . . well, sex.

90% of males and females agree that infidelity is always wrong, 20–25% of all marital fights are about jealousy

In what may be a shift of epic proportions, sexual infidelity is mutating before our very eyes. Increasingly, men as well as women are forming deep emotional attachments before they even slip into an extramarital bed together. It often happens as they work long hours together in the office.

"The sex differences in infidelity are disappearing," says Glass, the doyenne of infidelity research. "In my original 1980 study, there was a high proportion of men who had intercourse with almost no emotional involvement at all—nonrelational sex. Today, more men are getting emotionally involved."

One consequence of the growing parity in affairs is greater devastation of the betrayed spouse. The old-style strictly sexual affair never impacted men's marital satisfaction. "You could be in a good marriage and still cheat," reports Glass.

Liaisons born of the new infidelity are much more disruptive—much more likely to end in divorce. "You can move away from just a sexual relationship but it's very difficult to break an attachment," says Rutgers University anthropologist Helen Fisher, Ph.D. "The betrayed partner can probably provide more exciting sex but not a different kind of friendship."

It's not that today's adulterers start out unhappy or looking for love. Says Glass: "The work relationship becomes so rich and the stuff at home is pressurized and child-centered. People get involved insidiously without planning to betray."

Any way it happens, the combined sexual-emotional affair delivers a fatal blow not just to marriages but to the traditional male code. "The double standard for adultery is disappearing," Fisher emphasizes. "It's been around for 5,000 years and it's changing in our lifetime. It's quite striking. Men used to feel that they had the right. They don't feel that anymore."

LEARN MORE ABOUT IT:

Eve's Rib: The New Science of Gender-Specific Medicine and How It Can Save Your Life. Marianne J. Legato, M.D. (*Harmony Books, 2002*).

Not "Just Friends": Protect Your Relationship from Infidelity and Heal the Trauma of Betrayal. Shirley P. Glass, Ph.D. (*The Free Press, 2003*).

Male, Female: The Evolution of Human Sex Differences. David C. Geary, Ph.D. (*American Psychological Association, 1998*).

Sudden Infertility

If your periods become irregular in your 30s, don't delay in seeing your doctor. You might be one of a disturbing number of women who suffer from sudden infertility.

KAREN BRUNO

Kristin Rhodes's life was on track. At 32, she had finished graduate school, and she and her husband had booked a vacation to Europe, where they hoped to conceive their first child. Rhodes, a nurse-practitioner, had gone off birth control pills to prepare. At a routine gynecological exam before the trip, a nurse told her she was pregnant. Rhodes was thrilled. But the next day, she learned there had been a mistake. She wasn't pregnant; she appeared to be in menopause.

"I didn't want it to be true," she says. Then she recalled that her menstrual cycle had recently gone from 36 to 112 days. She also felt overheated whenever she curled up with her husband to watch television. "I blamed it on our new velour couch," says Rhodes, now 38. "I now realize I was having hot flashes."

A Cruel Condition

Previously referred to as "early menopause," premature ovarian failure (POF) affects up to 10 percent of women under 40, a lot more than the 1 percent usually cited by the medical literature. "This disorder is not as uncommon as we thought," says Michelle Warren, MD, director of the Center for Menopause, Hormonal Disorders, and Women's Health at Columbia–Presbyterian/Eastside, a medical facility in New York City. Spontaneous POF—meaning it's not caused by surgical removal of the ovaries, radiation, or chemotherapy—is the main reason young women stop having periods. It strikes women during their prime reproductive years—the average age of spontaneous POF is 31.

Doctors aren't sure what triggers POF. It might occur because a woman is born with fewer egg follicles than normal, or because the ones she has don't work properly. About 4 percent of women with POF may have an autoimmune problem in which their bodies "attack" the follicles. Whatever the cause, the toll is high. Women must cope with a low libido and hot flashes, as well as osteoporosis; they also feel as though they have been robbed of their womanhood. Tara MacDonald, 26, of Honolulu, says she felt "like a fake woman" when she was diagnosed at 21. Not surprisingly, women frequently plunge into depression. "It was like watching a train wreck and not being able to do anything," says Rhodes's husband, Dave, about her diagnosis. Rhodes says she collapsed into "gut-wrenching" sobs in the months following it.

Delays in Diagnosis

Most women learn they have POF after years of puzzling symptoms and frustrating doctors' visits. Up to one-fourth of women aren't diagnosed for five years after the start of menstrual irregularities. When a young, healthy woman complains of irregular periods, hot flashes, low libido, fuzzy thinking, and heart palpitations—classic menopausal symptoms—doctors often attribute them to stress and tell them to relax. But "even one missed period can signal POF," says Lawrence N. Nelson, MD, principal investigator for a research project on POF at the National Institutes of Health (NIH), in Bethesda, Maryland, who maintains that doctors and patients need to put POF on their radar. A delay in diagnosis can lead to osteopenia—low bone density—and eventually osteoporosis. Neither Tara MacDonald nor her identical twin, Colleen, who also has POF, had had periods from their early teens on. Tara's doctor blamed it on an active lifestyle, while Colleen's doctor attributed it to low body fat.

Researchers are working to reverse some types of POF so that women might be able to conceive

Both women paid the price. When Tara fell while hiking at 20, her doctor was astounded by her X-ray: Her hand was riddled with fractures, a sign of severe osteoporosis. It turned out her levels of follicle-stimulating hormone, or FSH (they rise as the pituitary gland works overtime to get the ovaries to work), were sky-high: She had POF. At the same time, the broken wrist Colleen had sustained at age 20 still hadn't healed. When she stopped the birth control pill and had her FSH measured (easier to do if a woman isn't using an oral contraceptive), she learned hers had also soared.

Though Colleen, of Laurel, Maryland, was on the pill to prevent pregnancy, women are often prescribed the pill to regulate their cycles. "It isn't until they go off it that they are diagnosed with POF," says Michael Heard, MD, a New Jersey-based reproductive endocrinologist.

No Easy Solution

Although about 5 percent to 10 percent of women with spontaneous POF become pregnant without medical intervention, sometimes as much as a decade after their diagnosis, there is no way to predict which women will. Currently there is no cure for POF. To replenish a young woman's estrogen levels, keep her from losing bone, and alleviate menopausal symptoms, most doctors prescribe hormone replacement therapy, a combination of estrogen and progestin. Long-term HRT is controversial for women who enter menopause at the normal age—from about 40 to 55—but an accepted protocol for women with POF. Some women with POF are also given testosterone, which is produced by the ovaries in small quantities and may improve cognitive and sexual functioning.

There is hope. Scientists recently identified a gene that may lead to a screening test for POF. At the NIH, Dr. Nelson is trying to "reverse" autoimmune POF so that some of the women might be able to conceive. In the meantime, Dr. Heard advises women to research their family trees. In 10 to 30 percent of cases, a woman with POF has a female relative with the condition. Knowing you're at risk should prompt you to have your FSH levels regularly checked. If they're creeping up, you may decide to have children sooner rather than later, and take steps to slow bone loss.

Awareness is essential. Many women don't view a change in their menstrual patterns as important, so they may not mention it to their doctors. "There is a devastating level of suffering associated with this diagnosis, since it's so final," says Nanette Santoro, MD, director of reproductive endocrinology at Albert Einstein College of Medicine, in New York City. "Since there is such a narrow window of opportunity to help these women get pregnant, doctors should check for POF sooner than they do."

Kristin Rhodes and the MacDonald twins eventually came to terms with their condition, although it took several years and lots of tears. Rhodes, who felt less alone after joining an online support group for women with POF, (www.pofsupport.org), occasionally lectures about menstrual health at a local college. The twins recently participated in NIH research investigating treatments for POF patients and whether women who have the autoimmune form of the disorder can eventually get pregnant. All three women are considering other ways to become parents, including adoption. Says Tara, "I would give anything to have kids."

Battling a Black Epidemic

AIDS now threatens tens of thousands of African-Americans, many of them women, in big cities and small towns alike. A community in peril tries to save itself.

CLAUDIA KALB AND ANDREW MURR

It's a warm spring morning, and two dozen African-American women are gathered around a conference table at the Women's Collective in Washington, D.C. Easter is just a few days away, but nobody is thinking about painted eggs and bunny rabbits. The collective, less than two miles north of the White House, is a haven for HIV-positive women, and on this day the focus is on sex, condoms and prevention. "Our responsibility," says one woman in a rousing voice, "is to tell the truth!" Together, the women are on a mission to educate, empower themselves and stop the spread of the virus. Patricia Nalls, the collective's founder and executive director, asks the group to read a fact sheet about HIV and AIDS, a staggering array of statistics documenting the impact of the disease in the United States. "So now we know what's happening to us," says Nalls.

What's happening is an epidemic among black women, their husbands, boyfriends, brothers, sisters, sons and daughters. Twenty-five years after the virus was first documented in gay white men, HIV has increasingly become a disease of color, with blacks bearing the heaviest burden by far. African-Americans make up just 13 percent of the U.S. population but account for an astounding 51 percent of new HIV diagnoses. Black men are diagnosed at more than seven times the rate of white men, black females at 20 times the rate of white women.

Anxiety about HIV/AIDS is highest among African-Americans—39% see it as the nations top health problem.

Decades into the epidemic, scientists have made enormous strides in unlocking the disease at the molecular level. Understanding why HIV has taken hold of black America and how to prevent its spread has proved to be no less daunting a challenge. The root of the problem is poverty and the neglect that comes with it—inadequate health care and a dearth of information about safe sex. IV drug use, sexually transmitted diseases and high-risk sex (marked by multiple partners and no protection) have fueled transmission; homophobia and religious leaders steeped in moralistic doctrine have suppressed honest conversations about how to stop it. All the while, much of black leadership has been slow in responding, only recently mobilizing to protect its community. HIV, says Cathy Cohen, a political scientist at the University of Chicago and author of a book about blacks and AIDS, "is one of the greatest crises threatening the black community. It's the life and death of black people."

The crisis plays out in inner cities and rural towns alike, where money, education and access to good medical care are limited. Protecting against HIV isn't necessarily priority No. 1 among the poor. "If you're focused on day-to-day survival, you're not thinking about where to get condoms," says Marjorie Hill, of the Gay Men's Health Crisis in New York City. Alijah Burwell, 39, lives in a rundown 110-year-old clapboard house with seven family members in Oxford, N.C. Burwell, who was diagnosed with HIV eight years ago and has long had sex with both men and women, doesn't know which of his partners made him sick. "I had one too many" is all he'll say. But for several years after he was diagnosed, Burwell says, he continued to have sex, often unprotected. And he didn't tell the women that he was sleeping with men too. He also smoked crack and drank a lot. And though he sought treatment for HIV, he wasn't vigilant about taking his medication, spiking his viral load, which made him a greater threat to his partners.

The virus once referred to as "gay-related immunodeficiency disease" has become increasingly gender-blind, especially in the black community, where heterosexual transmission accounts for 25 percent of male infections and 78 percent of female infections. Men who have sex with men still account for almost half of all male cases, and last week the Centers for Disease Control and Prevention published data pinpointing two key risk factors for transmission: STDs—which facilitate infection—and low levels of testing among black men. STDs are a menace for both African-American men and women: gonorrhea rates, for example, are 26 times higher in black men than white men and 15 times higher in black females. Testing takes initiative, time and a willingness to overlook stigma on the part of both sexes.

Even 25 years on, that stigma is powerful. The AIDS and STD clinic in rural Henderson, N.C., is tucked away near the back of a one-story medical building. A small sign next to the door says NORTHERN OUTREACH CLINIC. Only inside, where HIV posters adorn the walls, is the clinic's mission clear. "No one wants anyone else to know they're infected," says Dr. Michelle Collins Ogle, who treats more than 200 men and women, mostly black and poor, ranging in age from 18 (a young woman who contracted HIV as a sexually active 10-year-old) to 79 (a widower who appears to have been infected by a young girl who traded sex for his financial support). Before funerals, family members will hint to Ogle that the presence of the woman known as "the AIDS doctor" would be embarrassing. Especially when they've told other loved ones that the cause of death was cancer.

Such denial is hardly uncommon. With powerful drugs saving lives, some African-Americans believe the threat is either over or limited to gay white men. Distrust of the medical establishment has never fully waned since the Tuskegee syphilis experiment, launched in the 1930s; in a 2005 poll, 27 percent of black Americans said they thought "AIDS was produced in a government laboratory." Every day, such wariness and misinformation breed new infections. In a recent five-city study of more than 2,000 gay and bisexual men, researchers found that nearly half of black men tested positive for HIV—and of those, an astounding two thirds did not know their status.

Among African-Americans, 63% say they personally know someone who has died of AIDS or is living with HIV.

Burwell learned that he was positive after being tested while serving a drug sentence in prison—a hotbed for HIV, with a disproportionately high population of blacks. According to a new government study, the vast majority of HIV-positive inmates contract the virus before they enter prison. But some men become infected inside. Harold Atkins, 30, spent just over five years in San Quentin State Prison in California, where he was a peer educator for Centerforce, a group that provides HIV education to inmates. "There was a lot of sex happening in prison," says Atkins. There was not a lot of clarity about sexuality, however. "The same individual who had unprotected sex with males on the inside Monday through Friday would be in the visiting room with his wife and kids on Saturday and Sunday," says Atkins, who himself is HIV-negative. The men, who engaged in what Atkins calls "survival sex," did not consider themselves homosexual, and they didn't tell anybody on the outside what they were doing. "They'd say, 'I have sex with men. I'm not gay, they're gay'."

Driving this sexual ambiguity is homophobia in the black community. The prototypical black male role model is big, strong and masculine; being gay or bisexual is weak. It's also a sin. "The church has caused people to go underground" about their sexuality, says the Rev. Charles Straight, who helped launch an AIDS ministry in 1984 and is now an assistant pastor at Wesley United Methodist Church in Chicago. "People are afraid to be who they are." That fear has driven some men to have sex with men "on the down-low": secretly indulging in homosexual behavior while keeping up the appearance of being straight—and sleeping with their girlfriends and wives without protection.

Is the DL contributing to the spread of HIV among blacks? There are no scientific data to support the hypothesis. And the phenomenon has caused consternation in the black community, where men already battle stereotypes about sexuality. But women who've fallen victim say people need to know that it happens. Margot, now 52, learned she was HIV-positive when she was pregnant in October 1991. Margot says she was never promiscuous and never used drugs. "My fault was that I slept with my husband," she says. Margot says her now ex-husband never discussed his sexuality, but through conversations with his family and her doctor, it became clear that he was having sex with a man, most likely a buddy from work. In January 1992, Margot's baby was born HIV-positive. In March 1994, she died. "It's so horrible," says Margot, "every day knowing you had to bury a child as a result of lies, mistrust and misdeeds."

The DL has made Oprah-esque headlines, but there are far less sinister factors involved in the spread of HIV. Dr. Donna Futterman, director of the Adolescent AIDS Program at the Children's Hospital at Montefiore Medical Center in the Bronx, N.Y., says about half of the young women she sees have had only one sex partner and don't consider themselves at risk. "They say, 'I can look into his eyes and know. He looks fine, he looks clean, he told me he loves me'," she says. Women, young and old, enter into or stay in risky relationships because they're desperate for financial security. They're also eager to be loved. Diane Campbell, 50, tested positive after she and her boyfriend stopped using condoms. Low self-esteem, says Campbell, played a major role: "I let my guard down with the wrong person." Women can infect men, too. Ricky Allen, 45, who is straight, believes he contracted HIV from his late wife, who infected their baby daughter. Both have since died.

Activists are determined to stop the dying, neighborhood by neighborhood. In Henderson, N.C., Ogle coordinates a team of outreach workers who preach safe sex and hand out condoms and dental dams, even in areas where crack is rampant and often traded for sex. Every week, the Center for Health Justice in Los Angeles distributes condoms to inmates in L.A. County jails, and at the Falkenberg Road Jail in Tampa, Fla., prisoners are given rapid HIV tests so they know their status before release. In New York, GMHC's Women's Institute sends Laverne Patent, a 54-year-old HIV-positive woman, to beauty salons; one recent Saturday morning, she gave out "pussy packs" containing condoms to clients at Hair Players 2000 in Brooklyn.

The Women's Collective, operating at an epicenter of the epidemic—the nation's capital has one of the highest rates of AIDS cases in the country—provides services and builds self-esteem even as it, and similar groups nationwide, battle debilitating cuts in funding. Black Entertainment Television, partnering with the Kaiser Family Foundation, spent $15 million in donated air time last year to run public-service announcements encouraging teens to "Rap It Up" and get tested—a potential inoculation against the nonstop bombardment of sexual music and videos. And the CDC, which devotes 43 percent of its $650 million HIV budget to the black community, is exploring new testing and prevention programs, like North Carolina's "d-Up," aimed at educating men at black bars and clubs, says Dr. Kevin Fenton, CDC's AIDS chief.

Nowhere is the need for change greater than in the black church. "It is the center of turning this crisis around," says Pernessa Seele, founder of the Balm in Gilead, which began mobilizing clergy in Harlem in 1989 and now works with 15,000 churches nationwide. The challenge is getting church leaders to acknowledge sexuality, not preach against it. "Too many pastors are still stuck on theological doctrine. They have not been able to see the suffering," says Seele. Progress is being made little by little. The Rev. Doris Green, of the AIDS Foundation of Chicago, has been pounding on pulpits for years. Some churches have shut their doors; others have braved the challenge. One even "did a condom demonstration in the church with a dildo!" says Green. "That blessed my heart."

The future of HIV in the black community is in the hands of young warriors like Marvelyn Brown and Shelton Jackson. Brown, who just turned 22, tested positive in 2003, the victim of unprotected sex with a guy she thought was her soulmate. News of her diagnosis "spread like death" in her hometown of Nashville, but Brown has refused to stay silent. She went public in a local paper in 2004 and is now working with Kaiser to get the message out. Last month Brown toured college campuses with Hope's Voice, a prevention outreach group aimed at young adults. At Brown University, after another speaker pointed out that kissing isn't a risk factor for HIV transmission, Brown quickly interjected: "It depends on what you kiss."

Jackson, 28 and HIV-positive, was on tour that day, too. An openly gay student at Morgan State University in Baltimore, Jackson watched his partner die of AIDS in 2002. Today, he's eager to break the stigma and dispel the myths. He says he'll talk to people about HIV "anywhere they will listen." His hope: if one man acts up, others may follow.

With Sarah Childress, Mary Carmichael and Catharine Skipp

Positive Thinking

Twenty-five years after the first reported cases of AIDS and ten years after her own diagnosis, Regan Hofmann speaks out about what it's like to be a young, single, straight woman with HIV.

REGAN HOFMANN

For ten years, I have lived a double life. Until recently, very few people knew that I, a woman from Princeton, New Jersey, who went to prep school, spent her junior year of college abroad, summered in the Hamptons, and rode Thoroughbred horses, am HIV positive. Thanks to medications that have turned what was once considered a death sentence into a manageable, chronic illness, I have been able to conceal my fight with a disease many erroneously consider to be the exclusive property of gay men, IV-drug users, and sex workers.

I contracted HIV from my boyfriend when I was 28. He was the kind of man I'd happily seat beside my mother at Thanksgiving. He was romantic and sensitive and sweet to animals, and the last thing I ever thought he'd give me was HIV. We'd known each other for just over a year when I found out. When I told him of my diagnosis, he seemed shocked; I am almost certain that he didn't know he had the virus (he claimed not to know). I never knew how he got it. We stayed together for a short while longer, but we weren't meant to marry, and it seemed wrong to be artificially bound by a biological agent.

In the beginning, I told no one except a therapist and the group of gay HIV-positive men she sent me to for emotional support. The news that I was positive completely undid me. I'd been so careful about protecting myself sexually, it seemed like I was stuck in someone else's reality. I tried to face what had happened, but each time I thought about the fact that I could never go back to a life without HIV, my mind retreated to denial. I felt so isolated; in 1996, it was hard to find other heterosexual women with HIV. Today nearly 50 percent of people currently infected with HIV/AIDS globally are women, and women are 27 percent of those infected in the U.S. Seventy percent of all new infections among American women are the result of unprotected heterosexual sex. Part of the reason that so many women continue to get infected is that AIDS has fallen off the radar; we're no longer talking about the disease.

While the virus battled it out daily with the cells of my immune system, I went about my life as if nothing had changed. The only side effects that I experienced from the handfuls of pills I secretly popped three times a day worked to my advan-

tage as far as my physique went. I dropped from a size 8 to a 4. People inquired about my diet and my workout regimen. "Oh, you know, high stress, low fat, tons of sugar and caffeine, and no sleep," I'd joke.

As much as I wanted to tell the truth—that the meds killed my appetite, made me nauseated, and caused metabolic changes that eroded my lean muscle mass and melted away my subcutaneous fat—I couldn't. While people admired my svelte arms, I lived in terror that my body would continue to shrink. At five feet nine and 120 pounds, I was already pushing the limits of "healthy skinny." So when I dropped my towel poolside at the country club, I smiled gratefully at people's appreciative and sometimes envious glances at my flat stomach and prayed that other physical changes wouldn't take place that would out my HIV-positive status. I worried that if people knew my secret they'd assume I'd used drugs or been promiscuous. Most of all, I didn't want everyone to flee the pool when I took a dip.

I turned to my new gay friends for support. I thought the differences in our lifestyle might prevent them from offering relevant advice, but they turned out to be incredibly helpful and pulled me out of the depression that came with the news. We talked about whether and how to tell our families. Where I come from, no matter what happens, the family holiday letter contains only rosy news. If we don't acknowledge problems, the logic goes, they might just disappear. One man in my support group said that his parents, part of the Old Guard in Baton Rouge, had been wonderfully supportive. Or so he thought until he returned to the house 20 minutes after leaving (he'd forgotten his bag) and found his mother burning his sheets and his portion of the family silver (a knife, a fork, and a spoon) in an oil drum in the backyard.

I spent the first three months after my diagnosis imagining every horrific scenario that might unfold when I told my mom and dad that despite their loving parenting I'd contracted the worst STD in the history of copulation. Eventually the pain of trying to face the disease without them was too much. I told my family. And they were great. My father stoically told me that I wasn't going to die (not from this) and said he would do everything and anything to save me. My mother never once let me see the fears she certainly had and immediately set out to find the best doctors in America. And after I told my one sibling, my younger sister, Tracy, that I was HIV positive, she made a point of dipping her French fries in my ketchup without hesitation.

I remember first learning about HIV as a freshman in high school. I volunteered at Planned Parenthood and talked openly with my friends about protecting ourselves from pregnancy and STDs. Though we thought of HIV as primarily a "gay disease," I was scared like everyone else that it would eventually find its way into the non-IV-drug-using, heterosexual crowd. I regularly used a condom and always asked my dates whether they'd engaged in risky behavior and if they'd recently been tested. At one point, I even insisted that my boyfriends get tested before I slept with them. But once in my late 20s, I lowered my guard. I was on birth control and didn't feel I needed to worry about any other kind of protection. That's when the virus set up camp in my bloodstream.

After I told my sister, Tracy, that I was HIV positive, she made a point of dipping her French fries in my ketchup without hesitation

When I first contracted HIV, they told me I had two years to live. Initially, I figured I'd be celibate. Finding a husband, or even a willing sex partner, seemed the least of my concerns. And having a child wasn't an option at that time (the risk of transmission was too high). But soon after my diagnosis, medical progress allowed people with HIV to plan for a future. New medicines meant there was no reason I couldn't see 75. Or even 100. Today there's a 98 percent chance I can have an HIV-negative baby. With some difficulty I went from believing I'd die young and alone to thinking about dating, even getting married and having a child.

I went out with two men who seemed like great prospects, but I just couldn't tell them. After several dates with each of them I went AWOL rather than divulge my secret and risk social suicide. I gave up thinking that I could tell a potential partner until a year later when I met a certain Canadian man on a weekend trip to a friend's polo farm in Aiken, South Carolina. I was so completely enamored of him, I decided he was worth the risk of rejection.

The hardest part about telling someone you're HIV positive is picking the right time. Tell them before they know you enough to see that you are worth the risks and they're likely to vanish without giving you a chance to educate them about the reality of HIV. Tell them too late and they may be upset with you for withholding such a critical bit of information.

I shared the fact that I was HIV positive with my Canadian friend after a few very intense conversations. We were sitting beside a campfire, and he was so open about his life, I felt confident that he'd at least hear me out. At first he seemed OK. We spent the weekend together talking about his fears and clarifying his misperceptions about how you can, and can't, contract the virus. It seemed promising. But three weeks later, his nightly phone call didn't come, and when I finally got him on the phone, he muttered that he'd gotten back together with his ex-girlfriend. I wasn't mad; I understood his trepidation. I tried to put myself in his shoes and wondered whether I'd want to risk being with someone who might get sick and die. But all the rationalizing in the world didn't stop me from feeling like my heart had been cleaved in two by an ice ax. It was then that I realized that even with all the medical advances, I was going to have to adjust to a new set of relationship rules and dynamics.

Too afraid to try to date again, I took a break from men. I decided to retrench and focus on my body. As a way of testing my physical strength, I accepted a job as a horse trainer. I'd get up at five in the morning, work on the farm all day, and pass out at nine at night, seven days a week. I left myself no time or energy to think about men or sex. I was encouraged that my body withstood the heavy labor without weakening, and my mind began to strengthen as well.

I felt confident enough to broach the topic with my female friends. I first told a woman whom I'd known a long time who had risen above some incredible adversity herself, so I figured she'd be able to handle the news. She took it in stride, but seeing the pain and fear on her face, I knew I'd have to bolster my resilience before facing multiple conversations like the one we had. In the end, telling her and others over time led to a feeling of relief. To my surprise, the only negative reactions were from friends who wished I had told them sooner. Each person who heard my story without abandoning me brought me closer to the world I thought I'd left behind for good.

Still, I couldn't stop feeling that I had to be extraordinary for a man to want to be with me. I fought a nasty battle with self-esteem, pulling apart my physical and emotional qualities, trying to determine what self-improvements would make myself worth the added complications. Even though I knew no one would be jeopardizing his life—I would always use protection—that's how others saw it. I realized that I didn't have to change myself; I had to alter how people viewed HIV. Part of that was education, and part of that was undoing the stigma.

It occurred to me that I might be reinforcing people's negative perceptions about HIV by telegraphing the shame that has surrounded the disease since it was identified 25 years ago. So rather than relaying the news apologetically and with great embarrassment, I tried presenting it as a simple fact of my life. I went armed into the Discussion, as I called disclosure (my family politely referred to HIV as the Situation), with printouts of medical stats from Web sites, pamphlets from my doctor, and 800-numbers of HIV-info lines. I promised myself that the next man that I told would not run away—at least not before he'd heard all the facts.

The next man I told became my husband. He came as a guest to a dinner party I hosted. We'd known of each other since high school; his brother had died of a heart attack at fourteen. I was right when I sensed that he could face the potential for loss. Together we worked through his fears, and we had a relationship that had nothing to do with the virus.

Though my marriage lasted only a year and a half, it wasn't HIV that drove us apart. The stress of keeping up with our jobs, paying the mortgage, and running a farm finally took its toll. After our divorce, I tried dating again, this time with a little more confidence that there might be men out there strong and brave enough to deal with HIV.

I thought about some of the promising men I'd passed up in the early days of my diagnosis, thinking that my newfound faith in the power of others to accept the disease might allow me to divulge to them. I randomly ran into one of them shortly after deciding to look him up. We were at a party and the conversation turned to HIV. Perfect, I thought. I'll be able to discern his predisposition before potentially exposing myself and my status. "I think HIV is nature's way of getting rid of those with unnatural behavior," he said. "Think about it: It gets rids of the homos and the druggies and the whores. Oh, and those that are overpopulating areas that can't support them, like the Africans, the Indians, and the Chinese."

HIV serves as the ultimate litmus test. The thing that I worried was keeping me from the right men was also protecting me from the wrong ones

His comment made me see something I'd never considered before: HIV could serve as the ultimate litmus test for a person's character. Ironically, the thing that I worried was keeping me from the right men was also protecting me from the wrong ones.

I am glad for the insight, empowerment, and courage I now have when it comes to bedroom politics. I wish I'd known a long time ago what I know now about how to talk to a man about sex and health. Don't get me wrong. There's not a day that I don't wish I (and everyone else with the disease) didn't have HIV. But I have learned to live with it.

I am now dating a wonderful man who has faced HIV with me every day for fifteen months. We have talked about a future together and having children. Who knows whether we'll marry or have kids, but if we don't, it won't be because I have HIV. He has stood by me, not only after hearing that I have the disease but also through my recent decision to tell the world. In January, I took the editor-in-chief position at *POZ*, a monthly magazine for those with the disease and those who support them. I put my face on the cover of the April issue, above the words "I HAVE HIV." It wasn't the magazine cover I dreamed of gracing when I was a little girl, but I am glad nonetheless. I am tired of living behind a veil of shame and secrecy. And I am not alone.

Prison Outbreak: An Epidemic of Hepatitis C

KAI WRIGHT

odger Anstett's death in 2003 was neither sudden nor inevitable. The symptoms started back in 1998: the abdominal pain around his kidneys' and liver, the achy joints, the debilitating fatigue. Blood tests later that year showed that his liver enzymes were far above normal—one of them was eight times higher than it should have been. It all pointed to advanced hepatitis C infection, but Anstett's doctor waited another two full years before giving him a test to confirm the presence of the disease. It was another year before the doctors for Oregon's corrections system, where Anstett had been locked up for twelve years, finally treated him, just a month before his release. At that point, his liver was far too damaged for the drugs to do much good, and he died a year and a half later.

Thousands of hepatitis C-positive prisoners around the country are today facing Anstett's dilemma—barreling towards a preventable death because they are at the mercy of corrections health systems that are refusing to treat them. Moreover, say an increasing number of public health watchers, the unchecked hepatitis C epidemic inside the nation's prisons is undermining efforts to bring it under control in the broader community.

"No matter what you're in prison for," says Rodney Anstett, who watched his brother Rodger wither away from liver failure, "you deserve basic human rights." Rodger was the lead plaintiff in a lawsuit making just that assertion. Two days before his death, Anstett recorded a deposition for a case that would be the first successful class-action challenge to a state prison system's hepatitis C treatment policies. Last year, the state settled the suit, agreeing to open up treatment, and a federal judge is now monitoring its compliance with that settlement.

But Oregon's case is unique only in that the courts have intervened. Hepatitis C infection rates in some incarcerated populations are as high as 42 percent, according to an article in the *Clinical Infectious Diseases* journal, and anywhere from 15 to 30 percent of all prisoners are believed to carry the blood-borne virus. More precise counts are unavailable because few systems have come up with effective ways to screen for it—indeed, few even tried until federal health officials prodded them into action in recent years.

"Most prison systems are purposely not testing for hep C," charges civil rights lawyer Michelle Burrows, who led the Oregon lawsuit, "so they can say 'we don't know who's got it,' and don't have to treat it."

cience didn't identify hepatitis C until 1989, and it has been over-shadowed by its more prominent viral sister, HIV. But the U.S. Centers for Disease Control and Prevention (CDC) estimates at least three million people nationwide now have chronic hepatitis C infections—triple the HIV caseload. Most are injection drug users, since unlike HIV the hepatitis C virus spreads less easily through sex than through direct blood-to-blood contact—which explains the epidemic's intensity among people who cycle through prison.

Hepatitis C is emerging as a leading cause of death in several state prison systems, according to Scott Allen, the medical director of Rhode Island's corrections department. It's also the number one reason for liver transplants in America. The disease has overwhelmed the market, creating a waiting list of more than 15,000 people.

As with most diseases, early treatment separates the well from the ill. But hepatitis C-positive prisoners around the country testify that prison health care providers are delaying treatment as long as possible.

Many prisons insist that anyone with a history of drug or alcohol use—no matter how long ago—complete a rehab course before beginning treatment. And they usually add a requirement that inmates be far enough away from any potential release date to guarantee that they will complete the year-long treatment regimen while still locked up. Finally, many systems also bar anyone with potential mental health problems from getting care. Oregon denied Anstett's repeated requests for treatment based on his need for a psych evaluation, which he never got, and the requirement that he take a drug abuse class, which, he testified, he had previously completed.

There are few national or even state-by-state numbers on how many prisoners actually get medical care under these policies. But Oregon had treated just a dozen of its at least 3,500 hepatitis C-positive inmates when Burrows filed suit.

A Justice Department census in 2000 tried to uncover how many inmates are tested and treated nationwide. It found that around 57,000 hepatitis C tests were conducted in the preceding year (a quarter of which were in California), and a whopping 31 percent came back positive. But of these nearly 18,000 people, only 4,750 were being treated (and 40 percent of those were in California alone). In New York State, which has about 10,000 hepatitis C-positive inmates, the highest in the nation, only about 300 were being treated, according to the Justice Department's census.

In August, New York civil rights lawyers filed a class-action suit challenging that system's policy. The lead plaintiff, Robert Hilton, had begun treatment at a New York City public hospital for his hepatitis C and subsequent liver disease in 2002. A few months after starting, he became homeless, and his treatment was interrupted. In August of 2004, Hilton was incarcerated on a parole violation and, after a few days in a downtown holding cell, shipped to a facility upstate. Upon intake there, he underwent a routine exam, and he told doctors about his infection, his liver disease, and his treatment history. Court records show that the doctors received copies of a May 2004 medical record confirming Hilton's report and recommending that his treatment resume.

But the medical staff allegedly waited two months to conduct its own screening, and a full seven months to recommend him for treatment—a process that would have taken weeks at best on the outside. By May 2005, an outside specialist had also recommended treatment for him, he'd been cleared by a mental health evaluation, and he'd signed the necessary consent form. Then, according to the suit, state Chief Medical Officer Lester Wright stepped in and shut the process down by demanding Hilton first take drug addiction classes, even though no previous doctor inside or out of the system had suggested it, and even though Hilton professed to not having used drugs in thirteen years.

Wanting his treatment resumed, Hilton acquiesced and signed up for the class—only to be put on a lengthy waiting list, since the facility at which he was incarcerated didn't have enough classes to accommodate the demand. He was then transferred to another facility, where counseling staff again tried to enroll him in a drug addiction class. This time, his enrollment was denied because he would be eligible for parole before the class finished. "As antiretroviral treatment continues to be denied on the basis of this Catch-22," the class action complaint notes, "Mr. Hilton's liver continues to deteriorate."

The state declined to comment on this and other suits it now faces related to its treatment policy. It did, however, file court papers in November asking that the suit be dismissed because, it said, it had just changed its treatment policy to ensure that "programmatic needs for alcohol and substance abuse treatment do not interfere with medical requirement" for hepatitis C treatment.

But Alex Reinert, who is representing the plaintiffs for the firm Koob & Magoolaghan, charges that he has already received at least one complaint from a prisoner who says he was denied treatment for not going to rehab, even though that policy was supposedly repealed.

"What Dr. Wright is saying is, 'Trust us, you don't have to be involved anymore,'" Reinert says. "But our experience is, the only time an individual gets treated is when an attorney has stepped in."

Coincidentally or not, treating hepatitis C is one of the more expensive tasks in medicine. Unlike HIV, doctors believe it can be permanently eradicated from a patient's body. But doing so can cost as much as $35,000 per person. Even evaluation can be an expensive process. Corrections officials around the country, however, say they're just following federal health agencies' guidelines. In 2002 and 2003, in response to growing concern about the hepatitis C epidemic, the National Institutes of Health (NIH) and the CDC each issued recommendations for treating the virus. Around that time, state correctional officials gathered in San Antonio to share their experiences and compare ideas. They came away agreeing that each system should come up with firm criteria for both screening and treatment decisions, according to people in attendance. The rehab, time-remaining-on-sentence, and psych evaluation requirements fast became national standards.

Corrections health officials do face a complicated set of considerations. Because hepatitis C is a slow-progressing virus and because medicine is still learning how it works, just how fatal it is remains unclear.

Currently, the CDC estimates that 5 percent to 20 percent of those infected with hepatitis C might develop cirrhosis over two or three decades. When and how to treat those who may not progress to that stage is a difficult question, and not just because of the costs. Hepatitis C treatment is brutal. Even the most advanced therapies involve regular injections. Side effects include psychiatric problems, particularly depression, and flu-like symptoms similar to heroin withdrawal—taxing circumstances for someone trying to stay sober. Both the CDC and NIH guidelines urge caution in treating active users, because failed adherence can jeopardize treatment success.

But the prison systems' policies are far inferior to the standard of care on the outside. Both the CDC and NIH stress that even active drug use should not automatically rule someone out for treatment. And at least one study—conducted by Rhode Island's corrections department—found that preexisting mental health problems don't get in the way of treatment. As a result, class-action suits have been lodged in at least four states since 2001.

Oregon's case has been the most watched. The settlement was unprecedented. Outside specialists crafted a treatment policy that Burrows calls "the Cadillac standard." Doctors can still demand drug rehab classes and delay treatment if there's not enough time left on the sentence to finish a course of medicines, but those judgments must be made case by case, and everyone who tests positive must get at least a full medical workup to determine whether immediate treatment is needed.

Since the agreement, Burrows estimates, the state has begun treatment on around 1,000 inmates. But the legal fight continues, as several inmates and families—including the Anstetts—filed a wrongful death and damage civil claim in May. A spokesperson for the Oregon Department of Corrections declined to comment on the case or the department's hepatitis C treatment policies.

While states are failing to provide adequate treatment for hepatitis C-positive inmates, they are doing even less to prevent further spread of the disease. In many places, prisoners receive no information whatsoever about how to live healthy lives with the virus and how to prevent passing it on.

Prisoners nationwide testify that the sorts of behaviors hepatitis C thrives upon are widespread behind bars. While locked-up users more often sniff or smoke heroin than shoot it, plenty inject it as well. Some fish used syringes out of hazardous waste buckets in the infirmary and sell them on the black market. Others fashion makeshift "works" out of an eyedropper and a needle.

"I actually made a syringe out of a Bic pen," says Greg, who spent seventeen years in New Jersey prisons and requested anonymity. "If you get one set of works, the whole wing's using it. And that's how HIV and hepatitis C are spread. That's where I believe I got it."

New Jersey faces at least one lawsuit challenging its hepatitis C treatment policy. New Jersey Department of Corrections spokesperson Matthew Schuman refuses to comment on the case or the states hepatitis C policies. While he acknowledges that injection drug use through shared syringes takes place, he stresses the department has a "zero tolerance" policy and has made strides cutting out drugs of all sorts in recent years. "When you're dealing with inmates," he says, "it's always going to be a cat and mouse game."

Widespread tattooing inside prison offers a similarly efficient way to contract hepatitis C. Tattoo machines are as easy to make as syringes—just pull a motor out of an old Walkman and hook it up to anything sharpened into a point. The problem is the ink, which prisons ban. So jailhouse artists shave down lead pencils or burn checkers and use the ash. Because they go to such extremes to get this valuable commodity, the artists do not dream of making a new pool each time they have a new customer, as those on the outside do. Hepatitis C can live for a few days outside the body.

And then there's sex. In an informal survey by the Latino Commission on AIDS of just over 100 New York State prisoners and ex-offenders in 1999, 63 percent of respondents reported having witnessed other inmates having sex. Nearly a fifth acknowledged having had sex themselves. And more than 30 percent said they knew someone who had contracted HIV while in prison due to unprotected sex.

"They figure we're criminals, so we're going to die anyway one way or the other."

University of North Carolina researcher James Thomas says all of this raises questions about the relationship between the hepatitis C and HIV epidemics in prisons and in neighborhoods—particularly African American ones. His research suggests "incarceration is leading to STDs," he says, adding that there appears to be a dynamic interaction between sexually transmitted disease patterns in the street and in the jailhouse. An estimated 1.4 million hepatitis C-positive inmates are released from America's prisons and jails each year, according to the *Clinical Infectious Diseases* journal.

Greg doesn't know if he infected his wife or not. She left him after his last prison term and now refuses to tell him if she's hep C- or HIV-positive. But the possibility that he brought the virus outside the prison walls is one that America's corrections health care system doesn't seem to grasp.

"They really don't care," scoffs Greg. "They figure we're criminals, so we're going to die anyway one way or the other."

KAI WRIGHT is a writer in Brooklyn, New York, and editor of BlackAIDS.org. You can read more of his work at KaiWright.com.

When Sex Hurts

If lovemaking is more agony than ecstasy, the problem may be medical. Now there's help.

LISA COLLIER COOL

Thanks to recent advances, doctors have more effective treatments than ever for sexual pain. But zeroing in on the right diagnosis may be tricky, says Susan McSherry, M.D., who is affiliated with Tulane Medical School, in New Orleans. "If the first treatment doesn't help, keep working with your doctor. Painful sex isn't something you have to grit your teeth and tolerate. It's usually very treatable." Below are some common problems—and solutions.

Infections

Vaginal infections (collectively known as vaginitis) are so common that more than 75 percent of women can expect to develop at least one during their lifetime. The usual culprits are bacteria (bacterial vaginosis), yeast, and *Trichomonas* microorganisms, which are responsible for trichomoniasis, a sexually transmitted infection.

Symptoms With some infections, you may have an unpleasant-smelling discharge, painful urination, and, in some cases, lower abdominal discomfort—plus itching and burning of the vagina and outer labia. But with other forms of vaginitis, there may be no special symptoms, says Erica V. Breneman, M.D., an obstetrician-gynecologist at Kaiser Permanente in Oakland, California.

During sex The irritation may worsen when you're having intercourse or afterward.

Diagnosis If itching is your main symptom and you have been diagnosed with a yeast infection in the past, try an over-the-counter medication. But if the problem doesn't clear up in a few days, see a gynecologist; left untreated, some forms of vaginitis can lead to more serious problems, including infertility. Your doctor will do a pelvic exam and examine your vaginal fluid for microorganisms.

Treatment Depending on the cause, antibiotics, antifungal drugs, or medicated vaginal creams or suppositories. (For some infections, both partners need to be treated.) Symptoms should clear up—and sex should be comfortable—within several days.

Endometriosis

This disorder occurs when cells from the uterine lining (the endometrium) migrate to other parts of the abdomen, then swell and bleed during your period but aren't discharged as the uterine lining is. Over time, this misplaced tissue often causes chronic inflammation, scars, and weblike adhesions, most commonly on the ovaries or fallopian tubes, on the outer surface of the uterus, or on the internal area between your vagina and rectum.

Symptoms Pain in the abdomen or lower back, severe menstrual cramps, fatigue, diarrhea, and/or painful bowel movements during your period.

During sex Often there is deep, burning pain in the pelvis, abdomen, or lower back.

Diagnosis In a procedure called laparoscopy, a gynecologist examines your pelvic organs using a lighted tube inserted through a small incision in your abdomen. Small lesions can usually be removed during the same procedure.

Treatment For mild or moderate endometriosis, pain medication may be enough. But if you have severe cramping, or if the condition is interfering with your ability to become pregnant, or in order to suppress further growth of the lesions, you may need surgery or hormone treatment that temporarily stops your period. Neither of these is a cure, but two thirds of women improve after surgery; for the hormone treatment, the rate is a little more than half.

As for sex, you may find it's more comfortable during the week or two after your period rather than later in your cycle. And choosing a position that avoids deep penetration—side by side, for example, or with the woman on top—may help too.

"Painful sex isn't something you have to grit your teeth and tolerate," says one expert.

Fibroids

An estimated 20 to 30 percent of American women are affected by these noncancerous masses of muscle and fibrous tissue that grow inside the uterus (or, occasionally, outside). No one knows why some women are more prone, but a report from the National Institute of Child Health and Development shows that women who have had two or more children are far less likely to develop fibroids than those who have never given birth.

Symptoms Some women are never bothered by their fibroids. But others may have heavy and painful periods, midmonth bleeding, a feeling of fullness in the lower abdomen, frequent urination, constipation, bloating, and lower back pain.

During sex Your husband's thrusting can set off deep pelvic pain, due to pressure on your uterus.

Diagnosis A routine pelvic exam. If a fibroid is detected, your doctor may use ultrasound or magnetic resonance imaging to check its size and location.

Treatment For mild or occasional pelvic pain—including during sex—ibuprofen or other analgesics may be enough. If your fibroids need to be treated, there are several surgical approaches, as well as a new nonsurgical technique called fibroid embolization.

Interstitial Cystitis (IC)

Unlike "regular" cystitis, which is caused by a bacterial infection, the cause of IC is a mystery. This chronic inflammation of the bladder wall strikes women almost exclusively.

Symptoms Very frequent urination (up to 30 times a day) and/or burning and pressure before urination; chronic lower abdominal pain that may intensify before your period.

During sex Intercourse frequently triggers painful flare-ups, "like a severe headache all over your pelvis," says Dr. McSherry. Some women also have vaginal spasms, lower back pain, or pain that radiates down the thighs.

Diagnosis First, your doctor will rule out other causes. Then she'll perform a test called cystoscopy—in which the bladder is filled with fluid and examined for tiny hemorrhages (a telltale sign of IC).

Treatment Elmiron is the only oral medication specifically approved for IC. But many other drugs are available to relieve symptoms: Some women are helped by certain antidepressants that have pain-blocking effects (such as Elavil) or anti-inflammatory drugs that are inserted into the bladder. The good news is that 85 percent of patients can be successfully treated with one or more of these therapies, says Dr. McSherry. As for sex, women may find it's more comfortable side by side and when they're fully aroused.

Vaginal Dryness

The most common reason for this annoying (though not medically serious) problem is the drop in estrogen that takes place at

A Mysterious Disorder

Imagine pain so piercing you can't even tolerate pantyhose rubbing against your genitals, much less sex. That's what vulvodynia can feel like, say sufferers, who may seek help from doctor after doctor, only to be dismissed as hypochondriacs. Part of the problem is that everything usually looks normal; women have no symptoms beyond persistent pain in the vulva, the skin folds around the vagina. (In a few cases, however, there may be inflammation.)

Experts don't know for sure what causes vulvodynia, though they theorize that nerve injury may play a role. Interestingly, over-the-counter products can trigger the condition in women who are pre-disposed, says Howard Glazer, Ph.D., associate professor in the department of obstetrics and gynecology at Cornell University Medical Center in New York City and codirector of the New York Center for Vulvovaginal Pain. "Some 85 percent of my patients tell me they treated what they thought was a yeast infection with an OTC cream or douche—and then developed pain that never went away." It may be they're re-acting to an irritant in the cream, Glazer suggests.

To diagnose the condition, your doctor may do what's called a Q-Tip Test, in which a cotton swab is used to gently check the vulva and the vaginal entrance for areas of pain and hypersensitivity. You may be able to relieve symptoms with medication (antidepressants, nerve blocks, or anticonvulsant drugs that also combat pain) or with biofeedback. In severe cases, surgery to remove the affected tissue may help.

menopause or during perimenopause—the three to six years before your periods actually stop. Some women also experience a decrease in lubrication after having a baby or while breastfeeding. Allergies, too, can trigger dryness. Soap is probably the biggest offender, but laundry detergent, fabric softeners, bubble bath, vaginal-hygiene products, and spermicidal creams or foams can all be culprits as well.

Symptoms Chafing, irritation, and itching. At menopause, falling estrogen levels also cause the walls of your vagina to become thinner and less elastic.

During sex Friction may leave you quite sore. Discomfort may occur only at penetration or during thrusting.

Diagnosis Fairly self-evident, but check with your doctor if you suspect an allergy.

Treatment Over-the-counter lubricants, such as Replens or Astroglide. At menopause, talk to your gynecologist about hormone replacement therapy or estrogen cream. For allergic dryness, try using mild liquid bath soaps and fragrance-free or hypoallergenic brands of laundry and cosmetic products. Try different brands of spermicides until you find a nonirritating one. And ask your doctor about taking antihistamines: That might be wise until you figure out what you are allergic to.

Pelvic Congestion Syndrome (PCS)

There's some controversy about this syndrome: Not all doctors are convinced that it is a cause of pain during sex. Those who believe it is say that the disorder is triggered by varicose veins in the pelvis, a condition similar to varicose veins in the legs (and, indeed, about half the women with PCS also have the leg problem). In both cases, valves that normally keep the blood moving forward become leaky, allowing blood to flow backward and pool. As a result of the pressure, veins become large and bulgy. Most women develop the disorder after pregnancy, says Luis Navarro, M.D., director of The Vein Treatment Center, in New York City.

Symptoms Aching, heaviness, pressure, or throbbing in the pelvis; sometimes visibly protruding veins in the genital area.

During sex The discomfort intensifies during or after intercourse (as well as before or during your menstrual period).

Diagnosis Several noninvasive tests, including the recently developed venography. During this procedure, a thin catheter is used to inject special dye into the pelvic veins, allowing the doctor to map blood flow with X rays.

Treatment Tiny metal coils or a gluelike liquid are used to block off the affected area. The procedure has a success rate of 80 to 90 percent, says Dr. Navarro. But it can take a couple of weeks for symptoms to clear up.

From *Good Housekeeping*, March 2003, pp. 67–68, 71. Copyright © 2003 by Lisa Collier Cool. Reprinted by permission of the author.

Everyone's Queer

Leila J. Rupp

When I was growing up, one of my Quaker mother's favorite expressions was "Everyone's queer except thee and me, and sometimes I think thee is a little queer, too." Even as a child, I loved both the sentiment and the language, and then later I got a special kick out of the possibilities of the word "queer." But until I sat down to write this piece, I had never thought about how appropriate the saying is to a consideration of the history of sexuality. For the most striking thing about the literature is that the vast majority of what we know about sexuality in the past is about what is "queer," in the sense of nonnormative. We assume that "normative" describes most of what happened sexually in the past, but we know very little about that. Except what the history of nonnormative sexuality—same-sex, commercial, non- or extra-marital, or in some other way deemed inappropriate—can tell us. And that, it turns out, is quite a lot.

Like motherhood or childhood, sexuality, we once assumed, had no history. Now we know better.

Like motherhood or childhood, sexuality, we once assumed, had no history. Now we know better. Sexuality, consisting of, among other elements, sexual desires, sexual acts, love, sexual identities, and sexual communities, has not been fixed over time and differs from place to place. That is, whether and how people act on their desires, what kinds of acts they engage in and with whom, what kinds of meanings they attribute to those desires and acts, whether they think love can be sexual, whether they think of sexuality as having meaning for identities, whether they form communities with people with like desires—all of this is shaped by the societies in which people live. On the streets of New York at the turn of the nineteenth century, men engaged in sexual acts with other men without any bearing on their identity as heterosexual, as long as they took what they thought of as the "male part." Women embraced their women friends, pledged their undying love, and slept with each other without necessarily interfering with their married lives. Knowing these patterns, it begins to make more sense that Jonathan Katz wrote a wonderfully titled book. *The Invention of Heterosexuality* (1995). for it was only when certain acts and feelings came to be identified as the characteristics of a new type of

person, "the homosexual." that people began to think of "heterosexuals".[1] And what defined a heterosexual? Someone who did not, under any (or almost any) circumstances, engage in same-sex love or intimacy or sex. That this never became a hard and fast rule throughout U.S. society is suggested by the recent attention to life on "the down low," the practice of some black men who secretly engage in sex with other men but live in heterosexual relationships, or to patterns of sexuality among Latino men.[2] But the important point here is that normative heterosexuality—what scholars sometimes call "heteronormativity— can only be defined in contrast to what it is not. Which is why the history of nonnormative sexuality and the concept of "queer" is so important.

So how did people come to think of themselves as homosexual or bisexual or heterosexual or transsexual? That is one of the interesting questions that historians have explored. We now know a great deal about the development of the concepts by the sexologists, scientists, and social scientists who studied sexual behavior, but we also are learning more about the complex relationship between scientific definitions (and, in the case of transsexuality, medical techniques) and the desires and identities of individuals.[3] For example, Lisa Duggan, in her book *Sapphic Slashers* (2000), details the ways that publicity about a notorious lesbian murder in Memphis in the late nineteenth century both fed on and fed into such diverse genres as scientific case studies and French novels.[4] In his work on New York, George Chauncey opens the curtains on an early twentieth-century world in which men were not homosexual or heterosexual, despite the categorizations of the sexologists, but instead fairies or pansies, wolves or husbands, queers or "normal" men depending on their class position, ethnicity, and sexual role (the part one plays in a sexual act—generally penetrator or encloser).[5] And Joanne Meyerowitz, in *How Sex Changed* (2002), reveals that even before the publicity about Christine Jorgensen's sex-change surgery hit American newsstands, individual men and women wrote of their longings to change sex and bombarded physicians with questions and demands.[6] That is, we do not have the doctors and scientists to thank for our identities; their definitions sometimes enabled people to come to an understanding of their feelings and actions, sometimes to reject the definitions. But it was observation of individuals and communities that led the sexologists to their thinking about categories in the first place. We, as homosexuals and heterosexuals and bisexuals, were not created out of thin air.

Identities—and by identities I mean not just homosexual or gay or lesbian, but all their elaborate manifestations such as fairy, faggot, pogue, lamb, bulldagger, ladylover, butch, stud, fem—have a complex relationship to behavior, as the contemporary case of life on the down low makes clear. Over time, the sexologists came to define homosexuality not as gender inversion—effeminacy in men and masculinity in women—but as desire for someone of the same sex. By extension, heterosexuals felt no such desire. But how to explain men who identified as heterosexual but had (appropriately masculine-defined—that is, insertive rather than receptive) sex with other men? Or, in the case of women who came to be known as "political lesbians" in 1970s lesbian feminist communities, women who identified as lesbians but didn't have sex with women?[7] Identity and behavior are not always a neat fit, as the revelations of widespread same-sex sexual interactions in the famous Kinsey studies of male and female sexuality made clear to a stunned American public in the postwar decades. In response to his findings, based on interviews with individuals about their sexual behavior, Kinsey developed a scale to position people in terms of their behavior on a spectrum from exclusively heterosexual to exclusively homosexual.[8]

Another aspect of the relationship of identity to behavior is suggested by some of the labels people claimed for themselves, for many of them referred to a preference for specific kinds of sexual acts, sexual roles, or sexual partners. George Chauncey's research on the Naval investigation into "perversion" in Newport, Rhode Island, in the second decade of the twentieth century revealed the very specific terms used for those who preferred particular acts and roles.[9] In his study of the Pacific Northwest, Peter Boag describes a preference for anal or interfemoral intercourse in the intergenerational relationships between "wolves" and "punks" among transient laborers.[10] Liz Kennedy and Madeleine Davis's study of the working-class lesbian bar community in Buffalo, New York, in the 1940s and 1950s makes clear how central sexual roles were, at least in theory, to the making of butches and fems.[11] One identity, that of "stone butch," was defined by what a woman did not do, in this case desire and/or allow her lover to make love to her.

One of the things that historians' uncovering of the sexual acts that took place between people of the same sex reveals is how these changed over time. Sharon Ullman's research shows that oral sex between men was considered something new in the early twentieth century. When the police in Long Beach, California, broke up a "society of queers," they were confounded to discover that they were having oral rather than anal sex and concluded that that didn't really count as homosexual sex. The men themselves dubbed oral sex "the twentieth-century way".[12] Likewise, Kennedy and Davis found that butches and fems in Buffalo did not engage in oral sex. We know, or should know, that cultures in different times and places foster different kinds of sexual acts. Kissing, for example, is a relatively recent Western innovation as something erotic. But on the whole, as Heather Miller has pointed out, historians of sexuality have paid very little attention to the actual sexual acts in which people—and especially heterosexual people—engage.[13] One of the things that nonnormative sexuality can tell us about heteronormativity is what kinds of sexual acts are acceptable. We know, for example, that heterosexual oral sex was something confined to prostitution— at least in theory—until the early twentieth century. What prostitutes, both male and female, were willing to do, especially for increased fees, tells us something about what "respectable" women were probably not.

In addition to interest in desire, love, sexual acts, and identities—and the complex relationships among them—historians of sexuality have concentrated on the building of communities and on struggles to make the world a better place. Martin Meeker, in his book *Contacts Desired* (2006), uncovers the communications networks that made same-sex sexuality visible and both resulted from and contributed to the building of communities and the homophile movement in the post-Second World War decades.[14] His concentration on a wide variety of media adds to incredibly rich research on different communities. In addition to Chauncey on New York, Kennedy and Davis on Buffalo, and Boag on Portland, there's Esther Newton on Cherry Grove, telling the story of the creation of a gay resort.[15] In the same vein, Karen Krahulik has detailed the ways that Provincetown became "Cape Queer".[16] Marc Stein, in *City of Sisterly and Brotherly Loves* (2000), uses the history of Philadelphia to detail, among other things, the relationship between lesbian and gay worlds in the city and in the movement.[17] Nan Alamilla Boyd, in her study of San Francisco, shows not only how the city by the Bay became a gay mecca (something Meeker addresses as well from a different perspective), but also how queer culture and the homophile movement had a more symbiotic relationship than we had thought.[18] A collection of articles on different communities, *Creating a Place for Ourselves* (1997), provides even more geographical diversity, as does John Howard's work on the vibrant networks gay men fashioned in the rural South.[19]

> We know that, without the concept of homosexuality, there would be no heterosexuality. Without knowing which sexual desires and acts are deemed deviant, we would not know which ones passed muster. Knowing how identities are created, institutions established, communities built, and movements mobilized, we learn from the margins what the center looks like.

What these studies collectively reveal is the way economic, political, and social forces, especially in the years since the Second World War, enhanced the possibilities for individuals with same-sex desires to find others like themselves, to build institutions and communities, to elaborate identities, and to organize in order to win basic rights: to gather, work, play, and live. This despite the crackdown following the war, which David Johnson argues in *The Lavender Scare* (2004) was more intense and long lasting than the effort to root Communists out of government.[20] These works on diverse communities have also fleshed out the story John D'Emilio tells of the rise of the homophile movement in his classic *Sexual Politics, Sexual Communities* (1983) and responded to the question of how the war shaped the experiences of gay men and women first told by Allan Bérubé in his 1990 book *Coming Out Under fire.*[21]

Increasingly, research on same-sex sexuality and other forms of nonnormative sexuality has attended to the relationship of sexual desires and identities to gender, class, race, and ethnicity. Lisa Duggan's *Sapphic Slashers,* for example, tells the story of white middle-class Alice Mitchell's murder of her lover Freda Ward intertwined with the Memphis lynching that drove Ida B. Wells from her hometown and into her anti-lynching crusade. Judy Wu and Nayan Shah attend to how ethnicity shaped sexuality in the Chinese American community.[22] John D'Emilio's biography of Bayard Rustin makes his identity as a black gay man inseparable from considering his role in the civil rights movement.[23] George Chauncey and Peter Boag detail different ways that class distinctions emerged in forms of male same-sex sexuality on opposite sides of the continent. Karen Krahulik makes ethnicity and class central to the story of the coexistence, sometimes peaceful and sometimes not, of gay and lesbian pioneers and Portuguese fishermen in Provincetown. And Kevin Mumford, in *Interzones* (1997), argues for the centrality of the areas of New York and Chicago in which racial mixing and all sorts of nonnormative sexuality took place for the shaping of both mainstream and gay culture.[24]

Which brings us back to the notion of the queerness of us all. We know that, without the concept of homosexuality, there would be no heterosexuality. Without knowing which sexual desires and acts are deemed deviant, we would not know which ones passed muster. Knowing how identities are created, institutions established, communities built, and movements mobilized, we learn from the margins what the center looks like.

What we do know more directly about normative sexuality tends to be about prescription, and we know that directives about how to act are not necessary if everyone is behaving properly. So Marilyn Hegarty has shown how the forces of government, the military, and medicine cooperated and competed both to mobilize and contain women's sexuality in the interests of victory during the Second World War.[25] Carolyn Lewis's forthcoming work on the premarital pelvic exam in the 1950s reveals the cold war anxieties that lay behind the initiative to teach women how to enjoy and reach orgasm through heterosexual vaginal intercourse.[26] To take another example, in her forthcoming book, Susan Freeman explores sex education directed at girls in the 1950s and 1960s, revealing, among other things, the ways that girls pushed to learn what they needed to know.[27] These contributions—examples from my own students or former students—add to what we know about heteronormativity from scholars such as Sharon Ullman, Beth Bailey, David Allyn, and Jeffrey Moran.[28]

So my mother was right, except she didn't go far enough. As Dennis Altman pointed out in arguing for the "homosexualization of America," and as my own work with Verta Taylor on drag queens and the responses they evoke in audience members reveals, in a wide variety of ways, from what we desire to how we love to how we make love to how we play, we are all a little queer.[29] And we have a lot to learn from the history of nonnormative sexualities.

Endnotes

1. Jonathan Ned Katz, *The Invention of Heterosexuality* (New York: Dutton, 1995).
2. See, for example, J. L. King, On *the Down Low: A Journey Into the Lives of "Straight" Black Men Who Sleep with Men* (New York: Broadway Books, 2004); Tomás Almaguer, "Chicano Men: A Cartography of Homosexual Identity and Behavior," *differences: A Journal of Feminist Cultural Studies* 3 (Summer 1991): 75–100; Don Kulick, *Travesti: Sex, Gender, and Culture among Brazilian Transgendered Prostitutes* (Chicago: University of Chicago Press, 1998); Annick Prieur, *Mema's House, Mexico City. On Transvestites, Queens, and Machos* (Chicago: University of Chicago Press, 1998); Claibome Smith, "Gay Caballeros: Inside the Secret World of Dallas' *Mayates,*" *Dallas Observer* (January 13, 2005).
3. On sexology, see Jennifer Terry, *An American Obsession: Science, Medicine, and Homosexuality in Modern Society* (Chicago: University of Chicago Press, 1999).
4. Lisa Duggan, *Sapphic Slashers: Sex, Violence, and American Modernity* (Durham, NC: Duke University Press, 2000).
5. George Chauncey, *Gay New York: Gender, Urban Culture, and the Making of the Gay Male World,* 1590–1940 (New York: Basic Books, 1994),
6. Joanne Meyerowitz, *How Sex Changed: A History of Transsexuality in the United States* (Cambridge, MA: Harvard University Press, 2002).
7. See Arlene Stein, *Sex and Sensibility: Stories of a Lesbian Generation* (Berkeley: University of California Press, 1997).
8. Alfred Kinsey et al., *Sexual Behavior in the Human Male* (Philadelphia: W.B. Saunders Col, 1948); Kinsey et al., *Sexual Behavior in the Human Female* (Philadelphia: W.B. Sanders Co., 1953).
9. George Chauncey Jr., "Christian Brotherhood or Sexual Perversion? Homosexual Identities and the Construction of Sexual Boundaries in the World War I Era," *Journal of Social History* 19 (1985): 189–212.
10. Peter Boag, *Same-Sex Affairs: Constructing and Controlling Homosexuality in the Pacific Northwest* (Berkeley: University of California Press. 2003).
11. Elizabeth Lapovsky Kennedy and Madeline D. Davis, *Boots of Leather, Slippers of Gold: The History of a Lesbian Community* (New York: Routledge, 1993).
12. Sharon Ullman, "'The Twentieth Century Way:' Female Impersonation and Sexual Practice in Turn-of-the-Century America," *Journal of the History of Sexuality* 5 (1995): 573–600.
13. Heather Lee Miller, "The Teeming Brothel: Sex Acts, Desires, and Sexual Identities in the United States, 1870–1940" (Ph.D. diss., Ohio State University, 2002).
14. Martin Meeker, *Contacts Desired: Gay and Lesbian Communications and Community,* 1940s–1970s (Chicago: University of Chicago Press, 2006).
15. Esther Newton, *Cherry Grove, Fire Island: Sixty Years in America's First Gay and Lesbian Town* (Boston: Beacon Press, 1993).
16. Karen Christel Krahulik, *Provincetown: From Pilgrim Landing to Gay Resort* (New York: New York University Press, 2005).

17. Marc Stein, *City of Sisterly and Brotherly Loves: Lesbian and Gay Philadelphia,* 1945–1972 (Chicago: University of Chicago Press, 2000).

18. Nan Alamilla Boyd, *Wide Open Town: A History of Queer San Francisco to 1965* (Berkeley: University of California Press, 2003).

19. Brett Beemyn, ed., *Creating a Place for Ourselves: Lesbian, Gay, and Bisexual Community Histories* (New York: Routledge, 1997); John Howard, ed., *Carryin' on in the Lesbian and Gay South* (New York: New York University Press, 1997); and Howard, *Men Like That: A Southern Queer History* (Chicago: University of Chicago Press, 1999).

20. David K. Johnson, *The Lavender Scare: The Cold War Persecution of Gays and Lesbians in the Federal Government* (Chicago: University of Chicago Press, 2004).

21. John D'Emilio, *Sexual Politics, Sexual Communities: The Making of a Homosexual Minority in the United States,* 1940–1970 (Chicago: University of Chicago Press, 1983); Allan Bérubé, *Coming Out Under Fire: The History of Gay Men and Women in World War II* (New York: Free Press, 1990).

22. Judy Tzu-Chun Wu, *Doctor Mom Chung of the Fair-Haired Bastards: The Life of a Wartime Celebrity* (Berkeley: University of California Press, 2005); Nayan Shah, *Contagious Divides: Epidemics and Race in San Francisco's Chinatown* (Berkeley: University of California Press, 2001).

23. John D'Emilio, *Lost Prophet: The Life and Times of Bayard Rustin* (New York: Free Press, 2003).

24. Kevin J. Mumford, *Interzones: Black/White Sex Districts in Chicago and New York in the Early Twentieth Century* (New York: Columbia University Press, 1997).

25. Marilyn Elizabeth Hegarty, "Patriots, Prostitutes, Patriotutes: The Mobilization and Control of Female Sexuality in the United States during World War II" (Ph.D. diss., Ohio State University, 1998). Revised version forthcoming from the University of California Press.

26. Carolyn Herbst Lewis, "Waking Sleeping Beauty: The Pelvic Exam, Heterosexuality and National Security in the Cold War," *Journal of Women's History* 17 (2005): 86–110.

27. Susan Kathleen Freeman, "Making Sense of Sex: Adolescent Girls and Sex Education in the United States, 1940–1960" (Ph. D, diss., Ohio State University, 2002). Revised version to be published by the University of Illinois Press.

28. Sharon R. Ullman, *Sex Seen: The Emergence of Modern Sexuality in America* (Berkeley; University of California Press, 1997); Beth Bailey, *Sex in the Heartland,* 1st paperback ed. (Cambridge, MA: Harvard University Press, 2002); David Allyn, *Make Love, Not War. The Sexual Revolution, An Unfettered History,* 1st paperback ed. (New York: Routledge, 2001); Jeffrey P. Moran, *Teaching Sex: The Shaping of Adolescence in the 20th Century* (Cambridge, MA: Harvard University Press, 2000).

29. Dennis Altman, *The Homosexualization of America* (New York: St. Martin's Press, 1982); Leila J. Rupp and Verta Taylor, *Drag Queens at the 801 Cabaret* (Chicago: University of Chicago Press, 2003).

LEILA J. RUPP is Professor and Chair of Women's Studies at the University of California, Santa Barbara. She is the author of *A Desired Past: A Short History of Same-Sex Love in America (1999)* and coauthor, with Verta Taylor, of *Drag Queens at the 801 Cabaret (2003).* She is currently working on a book called "Sapphistries."

From *OAH Magazine of History*, March 2006, pp. 8-10. Copyright © 2006 by Organization of American Historians. http://www.oah.org Reprinted by permission.

Why Are We Gay?

Everybody has an idea: It's genetics—we're born that way. It's our mothers and testosterone in the womb. It's the environment as we were growing up. One thing we know for sure: The possible explanations raise as many questions as they answer, particularly: What would happen if we found the one true answer? and, Would we change if we could?

MUBARAK DAHIR

Mark Stoner pins it on the clarinet.

Ever since Stoner, a 41-year-old creative director for an advertising agency in Lancaster, Pa., realized that three out of four of his childhood friends who played the clarinet grew up to be gay, he has taken note of who among his adult gay friends once played the instrument. What he calls an "exhaustive but unscientific" survey covering two decades indicates that "there is an extremely high correlation between playing the clarinet and being gay," he says.

> **"The question of whether or not gayness is immutable is rather crucial in the political arena. The American public will have a different attitude toward gay rights depending on whether they believe being gay is a matter of choice or not."**
> —Neuroscientist Simon LeVay,
> who found differences in the brain

"My theory is that most boys want to play the trumpet," the former woodwind player says, only partly in jest. "But the more sensitive boys wind up with the clarinet, and we're the ones who turn out gay."

Stoner's theory, of course, is offered tongue-in-cheek. But in the past decade or so, researchers from disparate fields spanning genetics, audiology, and behavioral science have amassed bits and pieces of evidence that they believe indicate what may determine sexual orientation. If they're right, our sexual orientation may well be fixed long before any maestro blows his first note.

But despite some compelling studies that indicate that the propensity to be gay or lesbian is determined before birth—either genetically or through biological processes in the womb—most researchers today agree a complex combination of genetics, biology, and environmental influences work together to make the determination. Just how much is predetermined by the forces of genes and how much is shaped by influences such as society and culture remain unclear—and hotly debated. So too does the corollary question of whether sexual orientation is somehow an innate

All the Science So Far
Here's What Researchers Have Reported in Their Search for the "Cause"

- Lesbians' ring fingers tend to be longer than their index fingers, whereas straight women's ring fingers tend to be the same length as their index fingers.
- Boys who show "pervasive and persistently" effeminate behavior have about a 75% chance of growing up gay.
- A person with a gay identical twin is at least 10 times more likely to be gay than a person without one.
- There is about a 2% chance that a firstborn male will grow up gay. That chance grows to at least 6% for males with four or more older brothers.

- Gay men and lesbians are more likely to be left-handed.
- Gay men have smaller hypothalamuses than straight men.
- A man is more likely to be gay if there are gay men on his mother's side of the family.
- Lesbians' inner ears tend to react to sounds more like men's inner ears than like straight women's.
- Gay men have more testosterone and larger genitalia than straight men.

Is It Genetic?

Nick Velasquez

Stats: Student, 21, California native
Gay relatives: "My dad was gay. He died of AIDS in 1991 at 34 years old. Also on my dad's side I have two distant cousins, both lesbian."
Why are you gay? "I identify as bisexual, actually. I think it's very limiting, the notion that people can't love both [sexes], that it is one way or the other—it's on a continuum. I've always felt different, that there was something that separated me from other people, a different outlook on life; even when I was so young, [it was] in a nonsexual way."

Deborah Reece

Stats: Security guard and student, 45, California native
Gay relatives: "I have a gay grandmother, a bisexual aunt, and at least two gay nephews. Half my family is gay!"
Why are you gay? "That's the million-dollar question. And if I knew the answer, I'd be a millionaire! I am who I am. I've known since I was 4. It's natural to me. My mother told me [I was gay]. She used to tell me, 'Don't bother with those guys.'"

Danny Lemos

Stats: TV writer, 44, California native
Gay relatives: "Three gay brothers, including my twin, who died of AIDS."
Why are you gay? "Destiny. Some people are meant to be doctors, artists. I was meant to be gay, out, expressive. I served as a role model, especially to my younger brothers. If there's a God, I think he picks it. If it's science, that's what picks it. I've never had a moment where I didn't know who I was."

Kate Nielsen

Stats: Writer, 41, Colorado native
Gay relatives: None
Why are you gay? "I think you're born into it, just like some people are born left-handed. It's just what you're dealt. I was 6, I went to see *The Sound of Music*, and I wanted to be Christopher Plummer because I wanted to be with Julie Andrews."

trait and thus fixed for life or whether it is malleable and thus changeable over time.

More than scientific curiosity hangs in the balance. For years the gay and lesbian political establishment has leaned, at least to some degree, on the argument that sexual orientation is inborn and permanent and thus should not be a basis for discrimination. The tactic has proved incredibly successful. Polls repeatedly indicate that Americans who believe sexual orientation is either genetic or biological are much more likely to support gay and lesbian civil rights than those who believe it is determined primarily by environmental influences.

In a Gallup Poll conducted in May, half of those surveyed said they believe homosexuality is genetic, and half said it is environmental. In a 1977 Gallup Poll, respondents pointed to the environment over genetics by more than a 4-to-1 ratio. The poll calls this shift in perception "one of the more significant changes in American public opinion on gay and lesbian issues." It is clearly accompanied by increasing tolerance toward gays and lesbians. In May, 52% of Gallup respondents said homosexuality is an "acceptable alternative lifestyle," compared with 38% in 1977. And a majority, 54%, agreed that "homosexual relations between consenting adults should be legal," compared with 43% in 1977.

"The question of whether or not gayness is immutable is rather crucial in the political arena," says Simon LeVay, a neuroscientist who in 1991 found structural differences between the brains of gay men and heterosexual men. "The American public will have a different attitude toward gay rights depending on whether they believe being gay is a matter of choice or not. You can argue all you want that it shouldn't be that way, but that's the fact. If science can show sexual orientation is a deep

aspect of a person's being, there is potential for immense good. But it does mean the science gets politicized."

Politics aside, scientists insist there is commanding research to show that sexual orientation is largely influenced by genetics. "There's no debate on that from any reasonable scientist. The evidence for it stands fast," says Dean Hamer, a molecular biologist at the National Institutes of Health and an early pioneer in research linking sexual orientation to genes. In 1993, Hamer was the first to report finding a specific slice of DNA that could be linked to homosexuality.

He first studied the family histories of 114 gay men and discovered that many male relatives on the mother's side of the family were also gay. Since men always inherit an X chromosome from their mothers, the study suggested a genetic link between the X chromosome and homosexuality. Hamer then scrutinized the DNA for 40 pairs of gay brothers and found that 33 of them shared a specific region on a portion of the X chromosome.

His work supported earlier evidence pointing to a genetic link to homosexuality. In 1991, J. Michael Bailey, a psychology professor at Northwestern University, and Richard Pillard, a psychiatrist at Boston University School of Medicine, examined a group of gay men, 56 of whom had an identical twin, 54 of whom had a fraternal twin brother, and 57 of whom had a brother by adoption. Among those with an identical twin, in 52% of the cases the twin was also gay. Among fraternal twin bothers, in 22% of cases both twins were gay. Just 11% of those who had a brother by adoption reported that the brother was gay. Another study by Bailey and Pillard found similar patterns in lesbians.

Overall, a person with a gay identical twin is at least 10 times more likely to be gay. A man with a gay brother is anywhere from three to seven times more likely to also be gay. And a

Advocate Readers Weigh In

We asked our online visitors to tell us *their* stories about why they're gay. Here are some of their responses.

Genetics

No doubt about it in my family: God made us the way we are—genetically. I suspect that my grandfather was gay for many reasons. His second son, my uncle, came out to the entire family at my parents' 50th wedding anniversary party—he was 70 at the time! His son, my cousin, is gay. I am gay. Pretty sound evidence, considering we were all born in different decades, in different places, and were raised in totally different environments.—*W.Z., Indianapolis, Ind.*

I don't have a history of abuse, and I didn't just wake up one morning and decide to be lesbian. Also, I don't think it was anything my mom did while she was pregnant with me, as she often laments. I am this way. I must have been born this way. When I was growing up, The *Dukes of Hazard* was popular. I watched it every night, religiously. Daisy stirred something in me that I couldn't explain. I was 8 or 9 then.—*T.M., Indiana*

I am sure I was born gay. I used to steal dolls and jump ropes from girls then hide them, knowing that I would get into *big* trouble if I didn't like "boy things." Luckily I learned to "pass for a boy," so I didn't get bullied too often, but I did bear witness to the horrors bestowed upon more fey-type males.—*A.S., via the Internet*

Clearly genetic. No straight person I know can tell me the date, time, and even when they "decided" they were straight—so this notion of "choice" is pure crap. It can't be a gift—it would be one that most people would return. But to where and to whom? Is there a customer service line for this? It's not a "choice" and it is not a "lifestyle"—it's a genetic "orientation." It was an initially unwelcome visitor... now [it] gives me comfort as well as challenges me every day.—*E.B., Chicago, Ill.*

Environment

I was raised in the archetypal situation for being a gay man: with a chronically overbearing, fiercely possessive mother; a weak, quiet, completely uncommunicative father; and a thorough disinterest in violent sports! I, like many, many thousands of other gay men of my generation (I was born in 1950, in a tiny town), went through absolute hell growing up "hiding." Growing up "gay" (never liked that word—there's nothing "gay" about being gay!) nearly destroyed my life! Frankly, I wish to God (or whoever or whatever is out there) that I had *never* been homosexual!—*M.D., San Francisco, Calif.*

I think genes are passed on with neutral sexual orientation. To me, homosexuality or heterosexuality is totally due to the environment in which we are raised. In a nutshell, I believe a male who stays bonded with his mother is usually homosexual. A female who bonds more strongly with the father is usually homosexual. A male and a female who bond about equally with the mother and the father are more likely to be bisexual.

My mother died when I was 8 months old. My father remarried when I was 1 year old. His new wife did not want him to have much to do with his first children. I had five older brothers and three older sisters. My brothers did not want to have much to do with me. My three sisters adored me, so I spent most of my time with them. The sisters painted my deceased mother as being almost a saint. I think I naturally identified with my sisters' values and the values of my mother, which they told me about in detail. This included their sexual orientation.

We all inherit certain physical characteristics from our parents and we can inherit certain abstract characteristics such as temperament. I do not think that these genetically inherited qualities lead to homosexuality.—*J.D., via the Internet*

God

I personally believe I am gay because God made me such. I believe it is a gift and that he has a special reason for creating me as a lesbian. It doesn't matter if I was created this way biologically or if circumstances in my life molded me; this is who I am meant to be. I am proud to be a lesbian and at peace.—*D.S., Poland, Ohio*

I embrace the gift God gave me. I believe God chose each and every gay, lesbian, bi, and transgendered individual to teach others about love, tolerance, and acceptance. So I remind all my gay brothers and sisters: Don't worry. God did not make a mistake. He has a plan and a reason for your existence.—*A.G., Oxnard, Calif.*

Before I met Mary-love and fell in love with her, I never told myself I wanted to be a lesbian. The thought never crossed my mind. After a few bad relationships with guys, I guess falling in love with Mary-love after two years and four months of a friendship was bound to happen—it was a destiny I believe God gave to me.—*E.D., via the Internet*

It's a Choice

Although I have been married and have two sons, I was a late bloomer and decided in my late 20s or early 30s that being a lesbian was OK and that, for me, it is a choice.—*J.L., via the Internet*

As a graduate clinician in speech-language pathology, I find it difficult to deny that there is a genetic propensity to homosexuality, just as there is to stuttering. However, the choice to act upon the drive is entirely a symbol of our humanity. The degree to which we embrace our genetic predisposition is the degree to which we marry our understanding of our physical self and our identity. —*T.A., Boston. Mass.*

It is always a choice whether to be completely honest with yourself and admit you are not in the majority and are attracted to the same sex. I wasn't able to admit this to myself until a few weeks before my 28th birthday. The *choice* is to live your life as best as you can. The question "Why are you gay or lesbian?" is a small part of a much bigger question: "Why are you You?"—*C.F., Louisville, Ky.*

woman with a lesbian sister is anywhere from four to eight times more likely to also be lesbian. "All this shows that sexual orientation is largely genetic," Pillard says.

Hamer says genes provide about 50% of the influence on sexual orientation. Pillard wouldn't give a fixed percentage, although he said he believes it is "substantially" greater than 50%. Other scientists have estimated the genetic contribution could be as high as 70%.

However strong the influence of genes, it is not 100%. "We're never going to find the 'gay gene'" Hamer says. "There's no switch that turns it on or off. It's not that simple."

Was It Our Parents?

Susan Dost

Stats: Owner of an assisted-living company, 36, Michigan native
Gay relatives: "There seems to be a lineage of women in my family who end up 'single.'"
Why are you gay? "I believe that is the way the universe intended for me [to be]. I don't think I have a choice in the way I am. I think it's biological."

Haines Wilkerson

Stats: Magazine creative director, 46, California native
Gay relatives: "One, but not out."
Why are you gay? "I didn't have any choice in the matter whatsoever. It's completely genetic. Environment modifies a gay person's behavior, but it doesn't cause it. I tried to impose straight attributes for my life. They never stuck."

Chuck Kim

Stats: Reporter and comic book writer, 29, New York native
Gay relatives: None
Why are you gay? "I just remember always wanting to be around guys. I think being gay is a combination of environment and genetics—something that may act as a catalyst, activating that potential."

Claudia Sanchez

Stats: Educator, personal chef, 26, California native
Gay relatives: None
Why are you gay? "All my physical and emotional attractions have been to women. It wasn't really a choice, just something I've always had. Men just never attracted me. Being a lesbian is my reality."

By Choice?

John Strauss

Stats: Retired motion picture music editor, 81, New York native
Gay relatives: None
Why are you gay? "Because I'm gay. I was an overprotected child, a sissy boy, and felt uncomfortable with my surroundings. My mother was very protective. My first awareness that I had a sexuality at all was when I was 12 or 13. It developed in an instance when I saw my roommate at camp undressed, and there was a voice in my head that said, *Oh, my God, I'm gay*. Only we didn't call it that at the time; we called it *homosexual*."

Tony Roman

Stats: CyberCenter coordinator, Los Angeles Gay and Lesbian Center, 56, New York native
Gay relatives: "I had a gay cousin, who died of AIDS."
Why are you gay? "Nature and God just made me that way. At first I blamed my upbringing for it. I was raised by my mom and stepdad; my father died when I was young. It was a strict Catholic upbringing, [which] had a lot to do with the guilt and suppressing these feelings. I have no kind words for churches. I did a lot of drinking. After I sobered up, I realized I had no one to blame. I am who I am."

—Profiles reported by Alexander Cho

"There is a small minority of people in which sexual orientation is malleable. It would seem that reparative therapy is sometimes successful. I talked to 200 people on the phone. Some may be exaggerating their changes, but I can't believe the whole thing is just made up."

—Psychiatrist Robert Spitzer, who found that gay people can change their sexual orientation if they are "highly motivated"

He an other researchers agree that the remaining influences are a complex mixture of biological developments and environmental stimuli. But how much power each wields is as yet unknown.

Evidence is mounting, however, for the argument that much of the remaining influence comes from prenatal biological phenomena. LeVay, for example, found a size difference between gay men's and straight men's hypothalamuses—a part of the brain believed to affect sexual behavior. His "hunch," he says, is that gay men's brains develop differently than straight men's because they are exposed to higher levels of testosterone during pregnancy.

"There's a growing evidence to support the idea that biological and developmental factors before birth exert a strong influence on sexual orientation," LeVay says.

A host of biological indicators of homosexuality boost the theory. For example, research from the University of Liverpool in England has shown that gay men and lesbians are more likely than straights to be left-handed and that lesbians have hand patterns that resemble a man's more than a straight female's. Dennis McFadden, a scientist at the University of Texas at Austin, has reported that lesbians' auditory systems seem to develop somewhere between what is typical for heterosexual men and women. According to studies done by Marc Breedlove, a psychologist at the University of California, Berkeley, there is a direct correlation between the lengths of some fingers of the hand and gayness. An what gay man doesn't relish the study that found that gay men tend to be better endowed than their straight counterparts?

The common thread in many of these findings is the belief that differences in prenatal development are responsible for the variances in anatomy—and in sexual orientation as well. Like LeVay, Breedlove attributes his finding of finger-length differences between gay and straight men to the level of fetal exposure

Why Are We Gay?

Jessica Mendieta

Stats: hairdresser, 31, Ohio native
Gay relatives: "I have a gay nephew and at least four gay cousins."
Why are you gay? "I was born gay. I was always attracted to women. My best friends all through junior high and high school were all women. I had my first lover when I was 19. When I met her it was like, *Bang! I definitely love women.*"

Joshua Ewing

Stats: Student, 18, California native
Gay relatives: None
Why are you gay? "I think it's most definitely genetics. I grew up with my mom and step-dad, and in high school moved in with my biological father. My dad thinks it's a choice, but I knew all along that I wasn't like the other boys, chasing girls. I was doing it, but more to fit in, to conceal my true identity of being homosexual. There are people out there who say they choose, and that's OK. But I didn't have a choice. Everyone is different."

Michael King

Stats: Editor-designer, 28, West Virginia native
Gay relatives: "I don't know of any concretely, but there are a few that I suspect."
Why are you gay? "It's just who I am. I grew up in the Bible Belt; I played football. I am the perfect example of why environment *doesn't* cause you to be gay, because being gay in West Virginia is not even an option."

Lionel Friedman

Stats: Retired from the entertainment industry, 69, Missouri native
Gay relatives: "My younger brother is gay."
Why are you gay? "It's always been there. I just like men. I absolutely feel like I was born with it. I came out at a very young age, 13. My dad was very supportive. My mother wasn't."

Alexander Cho

Stats: Intern at *The Advocate*, 20, California native
Gay relatives: None

Why are you gay? "I have no clue. I grew up in a conventional home, and [being gay] has been with me as long as I can remember, so I'd probably say I was born with it. It was certainly not a choice, although I did choose to suppress it for a long time. I was filled with a lot of self-hate when I realized [I was gay], and it's something that I'm just now beginning the process of getting over."

Mercedes Salas

Stats: Waitress, 24, native of the Dominican Republic
Gay relatives: "I have two bisexual cousins, both female."
Why are you gay? "I just feel it. I feel no sexual attraction to men. Instead, I feel attraction to women. Even when I didn't know the concept, the feeling was always there. It was at age 16, when I was reading about it, I came to know that people were 'gay.' Women weren't as badly treated [as gay men], so that made me feel more comfortable asking questions."

to testosterone. "There is a growing body of research to support the theory that different hormone levels can cause the brain to differentiate one way or the other—to be straight or gay," LeVay adds.

But it remains murky just how much and just how strongly these biological factors shape sexual orientation. "I honestly can't be sure how to interpret the differences I found in brain structure." LeVay says.

Which leaves open the final, and most controversial, possibility: How much is sexual orientation determined by a person's environment?

Even the most ardent geneticists and biologists aren't willing to discount a role for external stimuli. "I certainly wouldn't rule out that life experiences can play a role in sexual orientation." LeVay says.

Historically, determining the "causes" of homosexuality was left entirely to the domain of psychology, which attempted to explain homosexuality with theories of mental maladjustment. Perhaps ironically, today it is often psychologists and psychiatrists who argue most arduously against the environmental influence on gayness.

"I've spent 30 years studying psychology, and I don't see any environmental differences that affect a person's sexual ori-

entation," says Richard Isay, a psychiatry professor at Cornell University and author of the book *Becoming Gay*.

Psychiatrist Richard Pillard agrees. "I strongly believe that at birth the wiring in the brain tells us if we are gay or straight," he says.

Isay says that "all the tired old postulations"—that homosexuality is caused by, for instance, an overprotective mother, a distant father, or a sexual molestation or trauma in childhood—have been "completely discredited" by the mental health profession. What the environment affects, he says, is "how you express your sexuality. Very, very few mental health professionals hold on to the notion that environment molds sexual orientation, and there's just no real evidence to support that."

However, numerous researchers point to what LeVay categorizes as the "oodles of data" that sexuality appears to be more fluid in women than in men, suggesting that, for some people at least, sexual orientation may not be genetically or biologically predetermined but heavily influenced by factors such as culture, customs, politics, and religion.

It's no secret why the long-standing debate over environmental influences is so critical and so contentious: If environmental stimuli can "make" us gay, can't other stimuli then "make" us straight?

Commentaries: "Why?" Is The Wrong Question

Being gay or lesbian is a blessing, says spiritual writer **Christian De la Huerta**. The best use of that gift is not to seek its cause or try to change it but to use it to find our true purpose

Part of me would be fascinated to know what makes me gay. My earliest sexual fantasies—before I knew what sex was—were always about men. Interestingly, my earliest romantic fantasies—those involving kissing, holding hands, etc.—were about women. The heterosexist cultural conditioning had already begun.

Though we may never know for sure, I suspect that gayness results from a combination of genetic and environmental factors. Ultimately, however, does it really matter? Nature or nurture, genetics or the environment, choice or not, so what? Knowing what makes us gay might be interesting, might help take the discussion out of religious and moral arenas, but it won't change who we are or the fact that we are here and always have been.

Clearly, evolution, in its mysterious and inexorable wisdom, would long ago have handled the situation if queer folk did not serve some kind of purpose. It may be more useful, then, to ask a different question: What are we going to do with the reality of our existence? If, in fact, we serve a purpose, what might that be? What contributions do we make? How do we make a difference in the world?

In contrast to what "ex-gay" ad campaigns would have us believe, far from needing to "recover" from homosexuality in order to have spiritual grace, it appears that throughout history and across different cultures queer people have not only been spiritually inclined but have actually been respected and revered for assuming roles of spiritual leadership. Many enact those same roles today. Mediators, scouts of consciousness, keepers of beauty, healers, teachers, caregivers, sacred clowns, shamans, priests—these are roles to which we have gravitated, for which we have exhibited a propensity, and which we have filled in disproportionate numbers.

Our outsider status gives us a special sense of perspective—our ability to see the forest *and* the trees.

Because we stand outside the mainstream in one area, we are not as rigidly bound by its rules in other areas. Although this may be stressful and cause pain, loneliness, and alienation at some points in our lives, it also creates the opportunity to live by our own rules. We are privy to a more honest process of enlightenment than blind acceptance of tired rules handed down to us by past generations.

Countless people have suppressed their sexual feelings—with varying degrees of success and failure—throughout history and continue to do so. But modifying or suppressing sexual behavior is one thing; changing a person's fundamental orientation is quite another. Far from being an effort to be more "natural," the attempt to change such a fundamental characteristic is an *affront* to what is natural.

One year after I came out to my father, a Catholic psychiatrist, I understood what is often meant by *choice*. After kindly reassuring me that I would always be his son and that he and my mother would always love me, my father proceeded to advise that I choose another lifestyle. He said that it is a very difficult life, that he knew because he had treated many homosexuals, even "curing" some. What my father didn't know, however, is that at least two of those he'd "cured" I'd slept with postcure. I know because after we did our thing, they asked if I was related to so-and-so. When I answered that he was my father, they said "Oh, I used to go to him."

Sexuality, like everything else, including matter, is a form of energy. Though it can be transmuted, energy cannot be destroyed. What is suppressed in one place will inevitably surface elsewhere. And when the suppressed energy of sexuality reemerges elsewhere, it too often does so in ugly and unhealthy forms.

For me, repressing such an intrinsic part of myself was no longer an option. It's been a very long and arduous journey, but I have come to such a profound place of acceptance that I actually live in a state of gratitude for being gay.

I look forward to the day when sexual orientation will be a nonissue, and perhaps all the energy now spent on trying to figure out why we're here could be redirected toward maximizing our unique potential. More and more people are beginning to realize that queers add value to our collective human existence, and given the desperate state of our world, we need all the help we can get—whatever the source.

Being gay is an advantage. It is a gift, a blessing, a privilege. In many ways it frees us up to discover who we really are. And who we are goes far beyond our sexual practices or the people with whom we tend to make romantic and emotional connections.

Had there been a way to alter my sexual orientation when I was growing up—and barely surviving the long, existential depression of my adolescence—what would I have done? I don't know, but now the answer is clear. To even consider the possibility of changing is ludicrous to me. Sure, life is still much easier for heteros. I still experience self-consciousness—truth be told, fear—in certain situations. Recently, at a national park, the guy I was with reached out and held my hand while a group of tourists approached. I felt tension. I felt fear. I pulled my hand away.

But would I change? Not a chance! I love being who I am and what I am. I love being gay. I love the sense of perspective, the freedom from societal rules, the generally more fun and open outlook on life. These blessings don't tell me *why* I'm gay, but they make me understand that "Why?" is not a question I need to ask.

De la Huerta is the founder of QSpirit and the author of Coming Out Spiritually *and* Coming Out Spiritually: The Next Step.

Commentaries: "Why?" Is The Wrong Question

As a gay rights battle cry, "it's not our fault" shortchanges our humanity, argues Rebecca Isaacs. What's more, the fluidity of sexuality makes hard-and-fast definitions poor political tools.

Whatever we know about the origins of sexual orientation, we know that it is a complex and fascinating topic that will remain unresolved and controversial for the foreseeable future. Many discussions of sexual orientation's causes have subtext of the search for responsibility, even blame. But we need to attach blame only if we accept our opponents' premise that homosexuality is bad. The major point for me as we continue this discussion of the interplay between nature and nurture is that we need to affirm a basic premise: *Gay is good*. As a parent of a 6-year-old daughter, imparting a sense of pride in her family is critical to her well-being. Vanessa, my partner of 11 years, and I want Rachel to know that the most important value of our family is that we love and care for each other. She has learned from an early age about the importance of validating and believing in herself and her family.

From my perspective, the question is not so much "Where does homosexuality come from?" but "Why are we so concerned about knowing the 'cause'?" In the political arena, as in our daily lives, we need to assert the validity of our sexuality and our humanity as lesbian, gay, bisexual, and transgendered people *without* the need for caveats or explanations. After all, there is little discussion about the origins of *hetero*sexuality.

It's ironic that while heterosexuality is so entrenched and unquestioned, the right wing continues to paint marriage and heterosexuality as being in a constant state of instability and crisis, with alternative sexualities as a principal threat. Rightwing ideology puts forward the premise that homosexuality is an enticing disease that people will catch if exposed, that it's a choice or temporary mental condition that must be overcome by counseling, prayer, coercion, abstinence, repression or electroshock therapy.

The counterassertion, that sexual orientation is a fixed and immutable characteristic, has also long been a part of the legal and political arguments we make for equal rights.

If sexual orientation is fixed, the argument goes, then we are not responsible for being gay and are therefore worthy of protection from discrimination. Yet a definitive answer to "Why are we gay?"—even if it were found—would not resolve our quest for equal rights, because those who would block our rights would continue to oppose us on other grounds.

I think that most people extrapolate a universal homosexual-origin story from their own personal experience. If they remember feeling different, feeling attraction to the same sex at an early age, they tend to think that sexual orientation is fixed from birth. Yet many people, women in particular, experience sexual orientation as more fluid than fixed. We need to be open to the range of personal, scientific, and social science theories that analyze sexuality in all its manifestations. Sexual orientation is not fixed in the same way for all people.

We know, for example, that there is a range to when people identify their sexual orientation. Many recognize same-sex attraction from an early age, but others come out later in life, in a particular context, with a particular person. Because we must embrace these differences, it also becomes more difficult to embrace a unified theory of sexuality's origins.

It is very hard to know what sexuality would look like freed from the dominance of heterosexuality. What if there were no stigma attached to being gay, lesbian, or bisexual? What if being gay didn't correlate to isolation, violence, rejection, and limited horizons for many teens? What if the strong arm of normative heterosexuality didn't force all of us into a separate and unequal box? What if sexual orientation truly were a part of each person's journey of self-discovery?

In my own experience I came to lesbianism through feminism, both personally and politically. Ti-Grace Atkinson said, "Feminism is the theory, lesbianism is the practice." I truly believed that, and I was in college in the 1970s at a time and in an environment where the heavy curtain of heterosexuality was momentarily lifted. My friends and I came out during that time of openness. Life after the lesbian nirvana, when we left our created community, was not so open. The pressures of dominant structures like heterosexual marriage reappeared. Today, some of us are still lesbians, some became straight-identified, and some identify as bisexual. I don't believe we each followed our one true, essential path or that there was only one path for each of us. A confluence of societal and personal experiences shaped our identities. Explaining that away with a scientific theory of sexual orientation seems unnecessary and indeed impossible.

I really do believe that for many people, sexuality involves acting on a range of feelings, behaviors, and opportunities. And I also believe that in a society that exacts a toll on people open to same-sex desire, options are more limited than they should be. We have learned from the bisexual movement that there is a range of sexual orientations and that desire is much more complicated than the identity categories we have set up. We box ourselves into a corner when we let others set the agenda and narrow the possibilities of expression.

Those who oppose our equal status politically and socially do so to deny our validity as human beings. Proving a biological or genetic basis will now sway them from that goal. The burden of equal treatment is on a society that discriminates, not on those who experience discrimination, coercion, and physical violence. We must show that the toll on a society that tolerates homophobia is great, that all of us suffer when any one group is targeted for discrimination and harassment. Each of us has a unique origin story that must be embraced. Our rights and freedoms depend not on what causes our sexuality but on our common humanity.

Isaacs is a director of policy and public affairs at the Los Angeles Gay and Lesbian Center.

It's All About Choices
Notes from a Blond Bruce Vilanch

You can't blame straight people for being confused. Not only do we want to get married, have children, and serve in the military—three things they would cheerfully be rid of, given the chance—but just when they have decided that we are fundamentally OK, a doctor comes along on CNN and tells them that a lot of us would rather be straight. And it wasn't even Dr. Laura. His name is Spitzer, and he's gotten some mileage recently out of a survey he did that seemed to say it is easy for gays to convert. His subjects turned out mostly to be the product of "ex-gay" ministries, so his entire study would appear to be statistically flawed, but that didn't stop the networks from pouncing on him as catnip for the evening news.

Hot on the heels of this pronouncement, the folks at the Gallup Poll revealed that, at long last, a majority of Americans seem to accept homosexuality as "an alternative lifestyle" and don't register any major disapproval of us per se, even though we appear to register it about ourselves. Gallup probably didn't use the same phone book as Spitzer.

But straight people, who want to know as much about us as they want to know about plumbing, can be forgiven for shaking their heads in disbelief. If a straight majority thinks homosexuality is OK, why are homosexuals turning away from it? If homosexuality is as wicked as it is painted, why are so many gay people at KFC buying the family pack? Why do so many gay men spend so much time making women look pretty? How can

people decide their sexuality anyway, and at so many different times of life? Is the closet we come out of stacked full of discarded ballots with dimpled chads from previous votes when we decided *not* to come out?

Just get me a beer and the remote and let somebody else work on it.

> That's when you begin to understand what choice is about. It's denial. We come out when we are finished denying our true natures.

Part of the confusion stems from the notion of choice, of choosing to be gay. Since one thing science won't agree on is the genetic explanation of sexuality and since people keep tromping onto *Jenny* and *Jerry* and *Oprah* and *Ricki* to announce they have decided they are gay, it's difficult for the unknowing to dismiss the idea of choice.

It always amazes me when people who see me on *Hollywood Squares* ask me if I am really gay, as casually as they ask if I'm really blond. Why would I make this up? I like being blond because I like the look, but that's not why I'm gay. "Well," they say, "it works so well for you. It's your shtick, you know, like Dean Martin was drunk." But guess what? Dean Martin *was* drunk. I drank with Dean Martin. He didn't knock back a pitcher of lemonade before he staggered onto the stage. It was part of who he was. Cheech

and Chong didn't hire a roomful of stoners and take notes. Besides, if I were going to choose a comic shtick, why would I choose one that would leave me open to so much potential hostility? Couldn't I just be a jovial fat guy?

The fact that sexuality is a part of who you are has been a very difficult concept for Americans to swallow, from Kinsey on down. Even prominent black civil rights leaders have had a difficult time when we try to position ourselves as an oppressed minority like theirs. We have a choice, they say. They have to be black, but we can be invisible. And that's when you begin to understand what choice is about. It's denial. We come out when we are finished denying our true natures. When we have had enough of paying the emotional price of passing for, I don't know, call it white. No one suddenly chooses to be gay. Even Anne Heche, at the height of her whirlwind ride on the gay roller coaster, didn't claim to be a lesbian. She just claimed to be in love.

No one chooses to be gay. But they do choose to be straight. They are comfortable enough in their lives, if not in their skin. They choose not to jeopardize their lives and instead do damage to their souls. Eventually, the gnawing within becomes too painful, and they can't stand it. They no longer have a choice. And that, the right wing will tell you, is when we choose to be gay. But we know different. It's when we choose to be free.

The latest firebomb thrown into this discussion is the now highly contested report by Columbia University psychiatrist Robert Spitzer, who in May disclosed results of a study in which he claimed that 66% of the gay male participants and 44% of the lesbians who were "highly motivated" could change not just their sexual behavior but their sexual orientation. The study has come under harsh criticism from psychologists and psychiatrists for its methodology, particularly for relying on data provided solely by phone-interviewed subjects recruited primarily from religiously biased "ex-gay" organizations.

"There's no question in my mind that what Spitzer reported was not a change in sexual orientation but simply a change in sexual behavior," Isay says.

But Spitzer is sticking to his guns. While he admits that "the kinds of changes my subjects reported are highly unlikely to be available to the vast majority" of gay men and lesbians, "there is a small minority of people in which sexual orientation is malleable." He estimates that perhaps 3% of gays and lesbians can change their sexual orientation. "It would seem that reparative therapy is sometimes successful," he says. He brushes aside questions about his methodology of relying too heavily on the self-reporting of obviously self-interested parties. "I talked to 200 people on the phone. Some may be exaggerating [their changes], but I can't believe the whole thing is just made up."

Spitzer, who was among those who worked to get homosexuality removed as a mental disorder from the American Psychiatric Association in 1973 and who has long been a supporter of gay rights, says his work has come under attack "because it challenges both the mental health professionals and the gay activists on their party line. I would hope my work causes people in both camps to rethink their dogma."

Spitzer also acknowledges that his research is being "twisted by the Christian right" for political purposes and says that was never the intention of his work. But science, he says, "will always be manipulated by people on both sides of the political debate."

Spitzer's study notwithstanding, gay and lesbian activists applaud the mounting scientific evidence regarding the origins of sexual orientation. But even though most results would likely be considered favorable to the gay and lesbian political agenda, activists remain cautious about basing too much political strategy on scientific findings.

"We welcome research that helps us understand who we are," says David Smith, a spokesman for the Human Rights Campaign, a gay lobbying group based in Washington, D.C. "And we've seen a growing body of evidence to indicate there are genetic and biological influences on sexual orientation. But we believe the studies shouldn't have a bearing on public policy. Gay, lesbian, bisexual, and transgendered people should have equal rights regardless of the origins of sexual orientation."

And Shannon Minter, a senior staff attorney at the National Center for Lesbian Rights in San Francisco, is "skeptical that science can ever fully answer the questions to something as humanly complex as sexual orientation. Sure, it's interesting and worth studying, but I'd be careful about jumping to too many conclusions either way."

Mark Stoner shares Minter's ambivalence about finding "the answer" and her wariness that human sexuality can be easily tabulated and measured in the lab.

"It's interesting cocktail chatter, but I don't particularly care what made me gay," says Stoner, who has two older brothers and thus may be a personal example of one theory that links having older brothers with higher levels of prenatal testosterone and thus a greater chance of being gay. "I don't think we'll ever be able to boil it down to a finite set of variables. It's probably genetic and biological and environmental and cultural and social and a whole lot more that we can't squeeze into comfortable definitions. There are always going to be exceptions to whatever rules the scientists discover."

As if to underscore his point, Stoner adds a footnote to his clarinet theory: "Over all the years of doing my survey, I did find one gay trumpet player."

DAHIR, who writes for a number of publications, played the clarinet from age 8 to 17.

The Battle over Gay Teens

What happens when you come out as a kid? How gay youths are challenging the right—and the left

JOHN CLOUD

I n May, David Steward, a former president of *TV Guide,* and his partner Pierre Friedrichs, a caterer, hosted an uncomfortably crowded cocktail party at their Manhattan apartment. It was a typical gay fund raiser—there were lemony vodka drinks with mint sprigs; there were gift bags with Calvin Klein sunglasses; Friedrichs prepared little blackened-tuna-with-mango-chutney hors d'oeuvres that were served by uniformed waiters. Billionaire philanthropist Edgar Bronfman Sr. was there; David Mixner, a gay activist and longtime friend of Bill Clinton's, was holding court with Jason Moore, director of the musical *Avenue Q.*

But the odd thing was that the gay (and gay-friendly) élite had gathered to raise money not for one of its established charities—the Human Rights Campaign, say, or the Democratic National Committee—but for an obscure organization that has quietly become one of the fastest-growing gay groups in the nation, the Point Foundation. Launched in 2001, Point gives lavish (often full-ride) scholarships to gay students. It is one of the few national groups conceived explicitly to help gay kids, and it is a leading example of how the gay movement is responding to the emergence this decade of hundreds of thousands of openly gay youths.

Kids are disclosing their homosexuality with unprecedented regularity—and they are doing so much younger. The average gay person now comes out just before or after graduating high school, according to *The New Gay Teenager,* a book Harvard University Press published this summer. The book quotes a Penn State study of 350 young people from 59 gay groups that found that the mean age at which lesbians first have sexual contact with other girls is 16; it's just 14 for gay boys. In 1997 there were approximately 100 gay-straight alliances (GSAs)—clubs for gay and gay-friendly kids—on U.S. high school campuses. Today there are at least 3,000 GSAs—nearly 1 in 10 high schools has one—according to the Gay Lesbian Straight Education Network (GLSEN, say "glisten"), which registers and advises GSAs. In the 2004–05 academic year, GSAs were established at U.S. schools at the rate of three *per* day.

The appearance of so many gay adolescents has, predictably, worried social conservatives, but it has also surprised gay activists, who for years did little to help the few teenagers who were coming out. Both sides sense high stakes. "Same-sex marriage—that's out there. But something going on in a more fierce and insidious way, under the radar, is what's happening in our schools," says Mathew Staver, president of Liberty Counsel, an influential conservative litigation group that earlier this year won a court order blocking a Montgomery County, Md., teachers' guide that disparaged Evangelicals for their views on gays. "They"—gay activists—"know if they make enough inroads into [schools], the same-sex-marriage battle will be moot."

There are at least 3,000 gay-straight alliances at U.S. schools. Nearly 1 in 10 high schools now has one, as do at least 290 middle schools

Most gay activists would rather swallow glass than say Mat Staver was right about something, but they know that last year's big UCLA survey of college freshmen found that 57% favor same-sex marriage (only about 36% of all adults do). Even as adult activists bicker in court, young Americans—including many young conservatives—are becoming thoroughly, even nonchalantly, gay-positive. From young ages, straight kids are growing up with more openly bisexual, gay and sexually uncertain classmates. In the 1960s, gay men recalled first desiring other males at an average age of 14; it was 17 for lesbians. By the '90s, the average had dropped to 10 for gays and 12 for lesbians, according to more than a dozen studies reviewed by the author of *The New Gay Teenager,* Ritch Savin-Williams, who chairs Cornell's human-development department.

Children who become aware of their homosexual attractions no longer need endure the baleful combination of loneliness and longing that characterized the childhoods of so many gay adults. Gay kids can now watch fictional and real teens who are out on shows like *Desperate Housewives,* the dating show *Next* on MTV and *Degrassi* (a high school drama on the N network whose wild popularity among adolescents is assured by the fact that few adults watch it). Publishers like Arthur A. Levine Books (of

Harry Potter fame) and the children's division at Simon & Schuster have released something like a dozen novels about gay adolescents in the past two years. New, achingly earnest books like *Rainbow Road* (Simon & Schuster), in which three gay teens take a road trip, are coming this month. Gay kids can subscribe to the 10-month-old glossy *YGA Magazine* (YGA stands for "young gay America") and meet thousands of other little gays via *younggayamerica .com* or *outproud.org*. Gay boys can chat, vote for the Lord of the Rings character they would most like to date—Legolas is leading—learn how to have safe oral sex and ogle pictures of young men in their underwear on the ruttish *chadzboyz.com*. Not that you have to search so far into the Web: when University of Pittsburgh freshman Aaron Arnold, 18, decided to reveal his homosexuality at 15, he just Googled "coming out," which led to myriad advice pages.

While the phrase "That's so gay" seems to have permanently entered the (straight) teen vernacular, at many schools it is now profoundly uncool to be seen as anti-gay. Straight kids meet and gossip and find hookups on websites like *facebook.com*, where a routine question is whether they like guys or girls or both. When Savin-Williams surveyed 180 young men ages 14 to 25 for an earlier book, "*... And Then I Became Gay*," he found that nearly all had received positive, sometimes enthusiastic, responses when they first came out. (Many others are received with neutrality, even boredom: University of Washington senior Aaron Schwitters, who was not interviewed by Savin-Williams, says when he came out to his fellow College Republicans at a club meeting last year, "there was five seconds of awkward silence, someone said 'O.K.,' and we moved on.") That doesn't mean young lesbians and gays will never get shoved in the hallway, and multiple studies have shown that gay kids are at higher risk for suicide than their straight peers are. But the preponderance of Savin-Williams' 20 years of research indicates that most gay kids today face an environment that's more uncertain than unwelcoming. In a 2002 study he quotes in the new book, gay adolescents at a Berkeley, Calif., school said just 5% of their classmates had responded negatively to their sexuality.

O.K., that's Berkeley, but the trend is clear: according to Kevin Jennings, who in 1990 founded a gay-teacher group that later morphed into GLSEN, many of the kids who start GSAs identify themselves as straight. Some will later come out, of course, but Jennings believes a majority of GSA members are heterosexuals who find anti-gay rhetoric as offensive as racism. "We're gonna win," says Jennings, speaking expansively of the gay movement, "because of what's happening in high schools right now ... This is the generation that gets it."

Jennings is a spruce, fit, deeply ideological 42-year-old who wants government to spend money to combat anti-gay bias in schools. He often asserts that "4 out of 5" students have been harassed because of their sexual orientation. (He doesn't mention that GLSEN's last big survey, in 2003, found "a significant decline" since 2001 in the use of epithets like *fag*. Or that about the same proportion of kids—three-quarters—hears *fag* as hears sexist remarks.) Regardless, the pro-gay government programs he favors seem highly unlikely in this political environment. That's in part because of the growing influence on the right of another gay force: gays who don't want to be gay, who are

sometimes called, contentiously, "ex-gays." On talk radio, on the Internet and in churches, social conservatives' canniest strategy for combatting the emergence of gay youth is to highlight the existence of people who battle—and, some claim, overcome— their homosexual attractions. Because kids often see their sexuality as riverine and murky—multiple studies have found most teens with same-sex attractions have had sex with both boys and girls—conservatives hope their "ex-gay" message will keep some of those kids from embracing a gay identity. And they aren't aiming the message just at teens. On one of its websites, the Christian group Focus on the Family has warned that boys as young as 5 may show signs of "gender confusion" and require "professional help."

It's important to note that nearly all mental-health professionals agree that trying to reject one's homosexual impulses will usually be fruitless and depressing—and can lead to suicide, according to Dr. Jack Drescher of the American Psychiatric Association, who has studied programs that attempt to alter sexuality. Last month Tennessee officials charged that one of the longest-running evangelical ministries for gays, Love in Action of Memphis, Tenn., was operating unlicensed mental-health facilities. The state said Love in Action must close two residential homes—which include beds for teenagers—or apply for a license. (The ministry's attorney, Nate Kellum, said in an e-mail that the licensure requirement "is intended for facilities that treat mental illness" and not for a "faith-based institution like Love in Action.")

6% of 16-year-olds have same-sex attractions. Gays' mean age of first same-sex contact: 15

Few young gays actually want to change: six surveys in *The New Gay Teenager* found that an average of just 13% of young people with same-sex attractions would prefer to be straight. Nonetheless, gay kids trying to change can find unprecedented resources. As recently as the late '90s, Exodus International, the premier organization for Christians battling same-sex attractions, had no youth program. Today, according to president Alan Chambers, the group spends a quarter of its $1 million budget on Exodus Youth; about 80 of Exodus' 125 North American ministries offer help to adolescents. More than 1,000 youths have visited an Exodus-affiliated website called live hope.org to post messages and read articles like "Homosexual Myths" (No. 2: People are born gay). The website, which started as a modest Texas chat board in the late '90s, now gets referrals from scores of churches in 45 countries. "Twenty years ago, most churches wouldn't even let Exodus in the door," says Scott Davis, director of Exodus Youth. "Now there are open doors all across the country."

Davis and I met in July at Exodus' first ever Youth Day, held at a Baptist convention center outside Asheville, N.C. About

100 people ages 15 to 25 were there to worship, sway their arms to Christian rock, listen to advice about how to stop masturbating ("Replace thoughts that aren't worthy of God with thoughts that are," Davis said) and hear the testimony of adults who say they now live heterosexual lives.

An attractive, married 27-year-old, Davis says he was never drawn sexually to men. Rather, he represents a new group of young, straight Christians who are criticizing older Evangelicals for long denouncing gays without offering them what Davis calls "healing." Davis looks nothing like a stereotypical Fundamentalist; he wears spiky hair, Fauvist T shirts, an easy smile. He first noticed the wave of young people coming out when he was pastor of a student church at Virginia Tech. I asked how his group could succeed when homosexuality has been so depathologized among kids. "GLSEN has 3,000 GSAs, but who knows how many student ministries there are, how many Bible clubs in schools?" he answered. "And my hope is they will be the ones who care for these kids."

In a jarring bit of rhetorical mimicry, many Christians who work with gay kids have adopted the same p.c. tributes to "tolerance" and "diversity" employed by groups like GLSEN. One of the savviest new efforts is called Inqueery (slogan: "Think for yourself"). Founded by a shaggy-haired 26-year-old named Chad Thompson, *inqueery.com* looks at first like a site designed to bolster proudly gay teens. Pink borders surround pictures of stylish kids, and bold text reads, "Addressing LGBT [lesbian, gay, bisexual, transgendered] Issues on High School & College Campuses." Thompson, who realized in fourth grade that he was attracted to boys, remembers hurtful anti-gay jokes, and he is convincing when he denounces such bias. "The Christian church has a sordid history—a history of the televangelists from the '80s who would malign homosexuals and say they're all perverts and pedophiles and going to hell—but didn't actually offer you redemption," he says.

Still, Thompson never accepted a gay identity—"Heterosexuality is God's design," he says—and today he is a leading spokesman for young Christians rejecting homosexuality. Thompson says a new kind of bigotry has emerged—among gays. "Those of us who have chosen not to embrace this orientation are often misunderstood and sometimes even ridiculed," he writes in a pamphlet he distributes at campus speaking engagements. Thompson, who has written a book with the near parodic title *Loving Homosexuals as Jesus Would*, hasn't been completely successful in rejecting his gay desires. He admits he still notices handsome men and says, as though he had an internal Geiger counter, "My attractions are probably about 1% of what they used to be." But the idea that liberals and gay activists are attacking Christian strugglers like Thompson has inspirited and unified social conservatives. The Rev. Jerry Falwell spoke at this year's Exodus conference for the first time, and others have begun to agitate for "equal access" for ex-gays in schools.

Earlier this year, a conservative nonprofit called Parents and Friends of Ex-Gays and Gays (PFOX, whose website says it supports "families touched by homosexuality") approached the PTA about exhibiting at the association's conference. The PTA said no: "From what we saw in the application, it seemed more of an agenda than just a resource for parents," says a PTA official. But the association did allow the liberal group Parents,

Families and Friends of Lesbians and Gays to present an anti-bullying workshop. When I spoke with PFOX executive director Regina Griggs about the PTA'S rebuff, she projected a sense of crepitating resentment: "How can you be more diverse than an organization that says if you're happy being a homosexual … that's your right? But if you have unwanted feelings or are a questioning youth, why can't you make those decisions? I guess diversity stops if you are a former homosexual."

So the Christian right has found its strategy—inclusion, prayer, the promise of change—and the gay movement has found one—GSAs, scholarships, the promise of acceptance. But what of the kids themselves? In July, I met 30 way-out-and-proud LGBT youths at a Michigan retreat arranged by the Point Foundation; these high-achieving Point scholars are getting from $4,000 to $30,000 a year to pay for their educations and are considered by some gays to be the movement's future leaders. A few days later at Exodus' Youth Day in North Carolina, I interviewed 13 of the kids fighting their attractions. Few at either conclave seemed interested in the roles their movements had set for them. Instead they were gay or Christian (or both) in startlingly complex ways.

Take Point scholar Maya Marcel-Keyes of Chicago, for instance. The 20-year-old daughter of conservative activist and former presidential candidate Alan Keyes, Marcel-Keyes has a girlfriend but has dated two boys; identifies herself as queer (not lesbian), pro-life and "anarchist"; and attends Mass whenever she can spare the time from her menagerie. (When Marcel-Keyes and I spoke recently, she and her girlfriend had a rabbit, a ferret, a cockatiel, two rats and two salamanders.) For their part, several of the young Exodus Christians seemed more stereotypically gay— "I love that Prada bag!" a 16-year-old boy at the Youth Day squealed several times—than some of the Point scholars who had been out for years. Others had gone to Exodus with no intention of going straight. Corey Clark, 18, belongs to his GSA at Governor Mifflin Senior High in Shillington, Pa., and says he sees nothing wrong with being gay. He attended Youth Day because he wanted to better understand his evangelical church and friends who say gays should change. "Actually," he says, "I've heard so many good things about gay pride"—in the media and at school—"but I hadn't heard directly about the downside."

It's remarkable that a boy like Clark could grow up in a small town and hear more good than bad about gays. But he still waited until he was 17 to come out. You don't have to be a right-wing ideologue to ask whether it's always a good idea for a child to claim a gay identity at 13 or 14. Cornell's Savin-Williams, who is generally sunny about gay kids' prospects, notes that those who come out early tend to have a harder time at school, at home and with their friends than those who don't.

Perhaps it's not surprising that the straight world isn't always ready to accept a gay kid. But the gay world doesn't seem ready either.

On the first day of the Point Foundation's retreat, which was held in a town on Little Traverse Bay called Harbor Springs, Mich., the 38 students who made the trip were given gift bags that contained, among other items:

- A 9 1/2-oz. jar of American Spoon Sour Cherry Preserves
- A Fujifilm QuickSnap Flash camera

- A small tin of Trendy Mints from Henri Bendel, New York City
- A DVD of the 2001 film *Hedwig and the Angry Inch*, in which a teenage boy is masturbated by an adult
- *The Harbor Springs Visitors Guide*
- The Aug. 16 issue of the gay magazine the *Advocate*, whose cover featured a shirtless man and blared, SUMMER SEX ISSUE.

There was only one Point scholar at the retreat under 18—Zachery Zyskowski, 17, who is in his second year at UCLA. Zyskowski came out at 13, helped start the GSA at his school and graduated valedictorian; he is far too precocious to be scandalized by a magazine or DVD. (He has watched *Hedwig* twice. Point executive director Vance Lancaster says the film, a cult musical about the relationship between a drag queen and a young singer, was already a favorite for many scholars. He also says it "reflects reality": "I don't see the negative repercussions to our students, who are very intelligent, thoughtful and mature.")

But when I opened my gift bag, it occurred to me that gay adults are still figuring out how to deal with gay kids. The gay subculture, after all, had been an almost exclusively adult preserve until the relatively recent phenomena of gay adoption and out teens. Point scholar and Emory College junior Bryan Olsen, who turned 21 in August and has been out since he was 15, told me during the retreat, "It probably sounds anti-gay, but I think there are very few age-appropriate gay activities for a 14-, 15-year-old. There's no roller skating, bowling or any of that kind of thing … It's Internet, gay porn, gay chats."

Olsen believes Point is an exception, and despite the gift bags, he's right. The weekend retreat was packed with anodyne activities such as a boat ride to twee Mackinac Island. Lancaster spends an inordinate amount of energy pairing each scholar with a career-appropriate mentor. The mentors are accomplished and tend to be wealthy—a hedge-fund manager, a university president, movie people—and all undergo background checks.

Point was the brainchild of Bruce Lindstrom, 60, who in 1976 helped Sol Price launch the warehouse retail industry with the first Price Club, in San Diego. Lindstrom had grown up in an evangelical family in Riverside, Calif., and says when his parents and two brothers learned he was gay, they stopped talking to him. His nephew Nathan Lindstrom, 29, says whenever Bruce sent gifts home, the kids were told, "This is from Uncle Bruce, the sodomite."

For years afterward, Lindstrom tried to find a gay organization that was helping kids "not to go through what I went through." He discovered that few gay groups did much for young people. Many gay activists didn't want to fuel the troglodyte notion that they were recruiting boys and girls. GLSEN'S Jennings recalls that when he first started raising money more than a decade ago, "the attitude was either 'Isn't it cute that you're working with kids?' or 'Why are you working with kids? What are you, f——— crazy?'"

By the late '90s, Lindstrom was talking about the idea of a scholarship program with his boyfriend Carl Strickland (who is 29 years younger) and with his old friend John Pence, a San Francisco gallery owner and former social aide to Lyndon

Johnson. One night in 2001 at Lindstrom and Strickland's home—which they call the Point because it sits on a promontory on the Nevada side of Lake Tahoe—the three christened the Point Foundation. Since then, some 5,000 young gays have applied, and 47 Point scholars have been named.

Lindstrom sees the United Negro College Fund and the Rhodes scholarships as his models, and in order to win, Point candidates must prove both academic success and commitment to gay causes. Not surprisingly, many also have biographies resembling Lindstrom's—they come from conservative families that haven't immediately accepted them. Candidates must write an essay on "how you feel you have been marginalized because of your sexual orientation." When scholars were called upon to introduce themselves at the retreat, many offered heartbreaking stories of family repudiation. It was routine to hear sniffling during these presentations, especially from adults.

But when you talk to Point scholars when they aren't performing for donors, you meet kids who are doing a lot better than those plaints suggest. Some remain cut off from their families, but many have repaired relationships with even the most conservative parents. If you read the online Point bio for Matthew Vail, 19, for instance, it says he "sits alone" at family events, "not allowed to have even a gay friend participate in his family life." But in the months since Vail provided the information for that bio, his parents, who live in Gresham, Ore., have softened considerably, and his boyfriend, Jordaan, was actually staying with Vail's father while Vail was at the retreat. Several other scholars also said their online bios dwelled on old wounds and omitted evidence of resilience.

Even those point scholars with the darkest stories of adversity, like Emory's Bryan Olsen, seem more buoyant than Point lets on. I heard Olsen speak to Point donors twice, once in New York City and again in Michigan. Both times he said that after his Mormon family learned he was gay when he was 15, he was sent to a boot camp for wayward teens in Ensenada, Mexico. Olsen says the facility, Casa by the Sea, required residents to wear shoes without backs so they couldn't run. He says that as punishment for a three-meal hunger strike, he was forced to sit in a stress position—cross-legged, with his nose touching a wall—for two hours. Olsen's small face, which is framed by a pop-star haircut that makes him look as though he's still 15, scrunches with tears when he gets to the next part: "I could only come home when I wrote my parents and promised to be straight and Mormon." There were gasps in the room the first time I heard him tell that story.

But much has changed since Olsen returned from Mexico in 2000. He and his parents haven't completely reconciled, and they aren't paying for his education. Olsen says they told him he had to choose between their financial help and "this lifestyle." But Olsen and his partner, Kyle Ogiela—they met in 2002—are welcomed at the family table every Sunday. Ogiela, 26, even works for Randy Olsen, Bryan's father, as the office manager of the family pest-control firm in Woodstock, Ga. As a Mormon, says Randy, 53, "I don't believe that men should be together. I never will. But I love him as my son. And he and his partner are good boys." Randy says his first reaction to Bryan's teen homosexuality was, "I'm going to find him the best hooker I can." But he says he and his wife sent Bryan to Casa not because he was gay but because he was a "totally unruly kid" who was "just so mean ... To go get that scholarship, I understand he had to be the poor little victim. But for three years, my wife and I were the victims." Seconds later, though, Randy yields again: "It's like God put a pair of new glasses on me ... I thought I could talk him out of [being gay]. But it's not something you can talk someone out of."

(As for Casa, Mexican authorities closed it a year ago. The local health minister charged, among other infractions, that Casa was "not equipped with responsible staff to run a pharmacy." James Wall, spokesman for the Utah-based World Wide Association of Specialty Programs and Schools, which ran Casa, says Bryan Olsen once publicly berated the facility's director during school and that he "is probably exaggerating" his stories of abuse. "I wonder if he's ever been [to Casa]," replies Olsen.)

Olsen deeply appreciates what he calls the Point Foundation's "unconditional support." But one night at the retreat, he also said, "I know they sort of want you to focus on the negative when you're telling your story." At the next fund raiser, Olsen resolves, he will tell the donors that he recently went with his mother, one of his sisters and Kyle to Los Angeles to appear on *The Price Is Right*. And Kyle won a new Buick LeSabre.

The point here is not that gay kids don't have to cope with bigotry and bleakness. A Point scholar who asked not to be identified told me he swallowed 17 Tylenols one summer night just before ninth grade—and when that didn't kill him, 30 more the following night. (He merely felt sick the next day; today he is a thriving college student.) He attempted suicide for various reasons—he says his parents ridiculed his desire to pursue acting instead of football—but being gay didn't help. And while Marcel-Keyes says many of her problems have "nothing to do with my sexuality," she has struggled with self-mutilation—at the retreat, her arms bore scars from shoulder to wrist.

Yet, according to Savin-Williams, most gay kids are fairly ordinary. "Perhaps surprising to researchers who emphasize the suicidality, depression, victimization, prostitution, and substance abuse of gay youth, gay teenagers generally feel good about their same-sex sexuality," he writes. A 56-year-old gay man with a slightly elfish mien, Savin-Williams has interviewed some 350 kids with same-sex attractions, and he concludes that they "are more diverse than they are similar and more resilient than suicidal ... They're adapting quite well, thank you."

Such statements have puzzled other researchers. "Ritch has never really acknowledged the fact that the average kid who is gay is facing enormous problems," says Dr. Gary Remafedi, director of the Youth and AIDS Projects at the University of Minnesota. "Most of his subjects have been Cornell students, who are among the highest-functioning students of all." Savin-Williams, who has included many low-income and non-Cornell kids in his work, responds that Remafedi and other clinicians have a warped view because they based early research on gay teens from crisis centers. "Are you only listening to hustlers?" he asks.

Savin-Williams opposes programs designed to change sexuality, but he has won admiration from some ex-gay proponents by writing that "sexuality develops gradually over the course of childhood." Gay identities also develop slowly. Even kids who publicly reveal same-sex attractions can be uncomfortable calling themselves gay; instead they say they are "polysexual" or "just attracted to the right person." Those vague labels sound like adolescent peregrinations that will eventually come around to "Yep, I'm gay." But Savin-Williams says many of the tomboys and flouncy guys we assume to be gay are in reality bisexual, incipiently transsexual or just experimenting.

At many schools around the country it is now profoundly uncool to be seen as anti-gay

Because he routinely sees young gays on MTV or even at school, a 14-year-old may now feel comfortable telling friends that he likes other boys, but that doesn't mean he is ready to enfold himself in a gay identity. "Today so many kids who are gay, they don't like Cher. They aren't part of the whole subculture," says Michael Glatze, 30, editor in chief of *YGA Magazine*. "They feel like they belong in their faith, in their families."

"Increasingly, these kids are like straight kids," says Savin-Williams. "Straight kids don't define themselves by sexuality, even though sexuality is a huge part of who they are. Of course they want to have sex, but they don't say, 'It is what I am.'" He believes young gays are moving toward a "postgay" identity. "Just because they're gay, they don't have to march in a parade. Part of it is political. Part is personal, developmental."

The political part is what worries Glatze. "I don't think the gay movement understands the extent to which the next generation just wants to be normal kids. The people who are getting that are the Christian right," he says. Indeed, several of those I met at the Exodus event had come not because they thought it would make them straight or even because they are particularly fervent Christians. Instead, they were there because they find something empty about gay culture—a feeling that Exodus exploits with frequent declamations about gays' supposed promiscuity and intemperance. "I'm just not attracted to the gay lifestyle, toward gay people—I've never felt a kinship with them," says Manuel Lopez, a lapsed Catholic and University of Chicago grad student who went to the Exodus meeting. "There's a certain superficiality in gay attachments—musicals, fashion ... I do think it's a happier life being straight."

Lopez has only an exiguous notion of what real gay life is like, but such misapprehensions are not uncommon among young people with same-sex attractions. Savin-Williams recalls counseling a kid who, after the third session, referred to his "partner." "And I said, 'Oh, you're gay.' And he said, 'No. I only fall in love with guys, but I'm not "gay." It doesn't have anything to do with me.' He saw being gay as leftist, radical." At Exodus' Youth Day, I met several young gays who spoke of the need to "walk out of" homosexuality because, as a 25-year-old from Boston put it, "I'm not happy going to the clubs anymore," as if being gay were mostly about partying. Frank Carrasco, a 20-year-old from Miami, told me his Exodus counseling had helped cure his porn addiction; Carrasco says that during high school, when he was Bible-club president, he routinely looked at gay Internet porn until sunrise. But he has never had a boyfriend or anything approaching a typical gay life. Carrasco says Exodus has helped him develop some heterosexual attractions, but I met very few at the conference who claimed to be completely straight. (At least two of the young men—one 21, the other 18—hooked up that week and still keep in touch.)

A common refrain from Exodus pulpits is that gays don't form lasting, healthy relationships, but those Exodus youths who seemed most successful in defying homosexual feelings were the ones more interested in exploring themselves than in criticizing gays. "I know gay couples who are in their 40s and 50s who have sex parties and use crystal meth, and I know gay couples who have been in committed, monogamous relationships for 15, 20 years," says Michael Wilson, 22, who lives outside Grand Rapids, Mich. "So people need the facts before they say stuff like that." But while he says he still has gay friends—among them, one of his three ex-boyfriends—Wilson believes God doesn't want him to have relationships with men anymore. He often speaks of his "identity in Christ," and to him that trumps his identity as a gay man. A lot of Exodus youths seemed captives of their Christianity, caught in a hermetic loop of lust and gay sex (or masturbation), followed by confession and grim determination. Wilson is different—calmer, more convincing when he says he communes with God. He doesn't deny that he is still sometimes attracted to men, but he doesn't seem to be struggling. "I don't think God would give you a struggle," he says. "I think he brings freedom."

Until recently, growing up gay meant awaiting a lifetime of secrecy—furtive encounters, darkened bar windows, crushing deracination. That has changed with shocking speed. "Dorothy resonates so much with older gay people—the idea of Oz, someplace you can finally be accepted," says Glatze of *YGA*. "The city of Oz is now everywhere. It's in every high school." That's not quite true, but the emergence of gay kids is already changing the politics of homosexuality. When their kids come out, many conservatives—just ask the Vice President—start to seem uncomfortable with traditionalist, rigid views on gays. But what happens when your child comes out not at 23 but at 13? At least in the short term, it's likely that more gay kids means more backlash.

"It kind of reminds me of the issue of driver's licenses for kids," says the University of Minnesota's Remafedi. "Yeah, it's great they can get around. But there's also a greater chance you can have an accident ... In my own life and generation, we separated ourselves from the straight community. We lived in gay ghettos, and we saw the larger culture as being a culture of repression. Hopefully, some of those walls between cultures have come down. But walking between those worlds takes a lot of skill."

The End of Gay Culture

Andrew Sullivan

For the better part of two decades, I have spent much of every summer in the small resort of Provincetown, at the tip of Cape Cod. It has long attracted artists, writers, the offbeat, and the bohemian; and, for many years now, it has been to gay America what Oak Bluffs in Martha's Vineyard is to black America: a place where a separate identity essentially defines a separate place. No one bats an eye if two men walk down the street holding hands, or if a lesbian couple pecks each other on the cheek, or if a drag queen dressed as Cher careens down the main strip on a motor scooter. It's a place, in that respect, that is sui generis. Except that it isn't anymore. As gay America has changed, so, too, has Provincetown. In a microcosm of what is happening across this country, its culture is changing.

Some of these changes are obvious. A real-estate boom has made Provincetown far more expensive than it ever was, slowly excluding poorer and younger visitors and residents. Where, once, gayness trumped class, now the reverse is true. Beautiful, renovated houses are slowly outnumbering beach shacks, once crammed with twenty-something, hand-to-mouth misfits or artists. The role of lesbians in the town's civic and cultural life has grown dramatically, as it has in the broader gay world. The faces of people dying from or struggling with AIDS have dwindled to an unlucky few. The number of children of gay couples has soared, and, some weeks, strollers clog the sidewalks. Bar life is not nearly as central to socializing as it once was. Men and women gather on the beach, drink coffee on the front porch of a store, or meet at the Film Festival or Spiritus Pizza.

And, of course, week after week this summer, couple after couple got married—well over a thousand in the year and a half since gay marriage has been legal in Massachusetts. Outside my window on a patch of beach that somehow became impromptu hallowed ground, I watched dozens get hitched—under a chuppah or with a priest, in formalwear or beach clothes, some with New Age drums and horns, even one associated with a full-bore Mass. Two friends lit the town monument in purple to celebrate; a tuxedoed male couple slipping onto the beach was suddenly greeted with a huge cheer from the crowd; an elderly lesbian couple attached cans to the back of their Volkswagen and honked their horn as they drove up the high street. The heterosexuals in the crowd knew exactly what to do. They waved and cheered and smiled. Then, suddenly, as if learning the habits of a new era, gay bystanders joined in. In an instant, the difference between gay and straight receded again a little.

But here's the strange thing: These changes did not feel like a revolution. They felt merely like small, if critical, steps in an inexorable evolution toward the end of a distinctive gay culture. For what has happened to Provincetown this past decade, as with gay America as a whole, has been less like a political revolution from above than a social transformation from below. There is no single gay identity anymore, let alone a single look or style or culture. Memorial Day sees the younger generation of lesbians, looking like lost members of a boy band, with their baseball caps, preppy shirts, short hair, and earrings. Independence Day brings the partiers: the "circuit boys," with perfect torsos, a thirst for nightlife, designer drugs, and countless bottles of water. For a week in mid-July, the town is dominated by "bears"—chubby, hairy, unkempt men with an affinity for beer and pizza. Family Week heralds an influx of children and harried gay parents. Film Festival Week brings in the artsy crowd. Women's Week brings the more familiar images of older lesbians: a landlocked flotilla of windbreakers and sensible shoes. East Village bohemians drift in throughout the summer; quiet male couples spend more time browsing gourmet groceries and realtors than cruising nightspots; the predictable population of artists and writers—Michael Cunningham and John Waters are fixtures—mix with openly gay lawyers and cops and teachers and shrinks.

Slowly but unmistakably, gay culture is ending. You see it beyond the poignant transformation of P-town: on the streets of the big cities, on university campuses, in the suburbs where gay couples have settled, and in the entrails of the Internet. In fact, it is beginning to dawn on many that the very concept of gay culture may one day disappear altogether. By that, I do not mean that homosexual men and lesbians will not exist—or that they won't create a community of sorts and a culture that sets them in some ways apart. I mean simply that what encompasses gay culture itself will expand into such a diverse set of subcultures that "gayness" alone will cease to tell you very much about any individual. The distinction between gay and straight culture will become so blurred, so fractured, and so intermingled that it may become more helpful not to examine them separately at all.

For many in the gay world, this is both a triumph and a threat. It is a triumph because it is what we always dreamed of: a world in which being gay is a nonissue among our families, friends, and neighbors. But it is a threat in the way that all loss is a threat.

For many of us who grew up fighting a world of now-inconceivable silence and shame, distinctive gayness became an integral part of who we are. It helped define us not only to the world but also to ourselves. Letting that go is as hard as it is liberating, as saddening as it is invigorating. And, while social advance allows many of us to contemplate this gift of a problem, we are also aware that in other parts of the country and the world, the reverse may be happening. With the growth of fundamentalism across the religious world—from Pope Benedict XVI's Vatican to Islamic fatwas and American evangelicalism—gayness is under attack in many places, even as it wrests free from repression in others. In fact, the two phenomena are related. The new anti-gay fervor is a response to the growing probability that the world will one day treat gay and straight as interchangeable humans and citizens rather than as estranged others. It is the end of gay culture—not its endurance—that threatens the old order. It is the fact that, across the state of Massachusetts, "gay marriage" has just been abolished. The marriage licenses gay couples receive are indistinguishable from those given to straight couples. On paper, the difference is now history. In the real world, the consequences of that are still unfolding.

Quite how this has happened (and why) are questions that historians will fight over someday, but certain influences seem clear even now—chief among them the HIV epidemic. Before AIDS hit, a fragile but nascent gay world had formed in a handful of major U.S. cities. The gay culture that exploded from it in the 1970s had the force of something long suppressed, and it coincided with a more general relaxation of social norms. This was the era of the post-Stonewall New Left, of the Castro and the West Village, an era where sexuality forged a new meaning for gayness: of sexual adventure, political radicalism, and cultural revolution.

The fact that openly gay communities were still relatively small and geographically concentrated in a handful of urban areas created a distinctive gay culture. The central institutions for gay men were baths and bars, places where men met each other in highly sexualized contexts and where sex provided the commonality. Gay resorts had their heyday—from Provincetown to Key West. The gay press grew quickly and was centered around classified personal ads or bar and bath advertising. Popular culture was suffused with stunning displays of homosexual burlesque: the music of Queen, the costumes of the Village People, the flamboyance of Elton John's debut; the advertising of Calvin Klein; and the intoxication of disco itself, a gay creation that became emblematic of an entire heterosexual era. When this cultural explosion was acknowledged, when it explicitly penetrated the mainstream, the results, however, were highly unstable: Harvey Milk was assassinated in San Francisco and Anita Bryant led an anti-gay crusade. But the emergence of an openly gay culture, however vulnerable, was still real.

And then, of course, catastrophe. The history of gay America as an openly gay culture is not only extremely short—a mere 30 years or so—but also engulfed and defined by a plague that struck almost poignantly at the headiest moment of liberation.

The entire structure of emergent gay culture—sexual, radical, subversive—met a virus that killed almost everyone it touched. Virtually the entire generation that pioneered gay culture was wiped out—quickly. Even now, it is hard to find a solid phalanx of gay men in their fifties, sixties, or seventies—men who fought from Stonewall or before for public recognition and cultural change. And those who survived the nightmare of the 1980s to mid-'90s were often overwhelmed merely with coping with plague; or fearing it themselves; or fighting for research or awareness or more effective prevention.

This astonishing story might not be believed in fiction. And, in fiction, it might have led to the collapse of such a new, fragile subculture. AIDS could have been widely perceived as a salutary retribution for the gay revolution; it could have led to quarantining or the collapse of nascent gay institutions. Instead, it had the opposite effect. The tens of thousands of deaths of men from every part of the country established homosexuality as a legitimate topic more swiftly than any political manifesto could possibly have done. The images of gay male lives were recorded on quilts and in countless obituaries; men whose homosexuality might have been euphemized into nonexistence were immediately identifiable and gone. And those gay men and lesbians who witnessed this entire event became altered forever, not only emotionally, but also politically—whether through the theatrical activism of Act-Up or the furious organization of political gays among the Democrats and some Republicans. More crucially, gay men and lesbians built civil institutions to counter the disease; they forged new ties to scientists and politicians; they found themselves forced into more intense relations with their own natural families and the families of loved ones. Where bath houses once brought gay men together, now it was memorial services. The emotional and psychic bonding became the core of a new identity. The plague provided a unifying social and cultural focus.

But it also presaged a new direction. That direction was unmistakably outward and integrative. To borrow a useful distinction deployed by the writer Bruce Bawer, integration did not necessarily mean assimilation. It was not a wholesale rejection of the gay past, as some feared and others hoped. Gay men wanted to be fully part of the world, but not at the expense of their own sexual freedom (and safer sex became a means not to renounce that freedom but to save it). What the epidemic revealed was how gay men—and, by inference, lesbians—could not seal themselves off from the rest of society. They needed scientific research, civic support, and political lobbying to survive, in this case literally. The lesson was not that sexual liberation was mistaken, but rather that it wasn't enough. Unless the gay population was tied into the broader society; unless it had roots in the wider world; unless it brought into its fold the heterosexual families and friends of gay men and women, the gay population would remain at the mercy of others and of misfortune. A ghetto was no longer an option.

So, when the plague receded in the face of far more effective HIV treatments in the mid-'90s and gay men and women were able to catch their breath and reflect, the question of what a more integrated gay culture might actually mean reemerged. For a while, it arrived in a vacuum. Most of the older male generation was dead or exhausted; and so it was only natural, perhaps, that the next generation of leaders tended to be lesbian—running the major gay political groups and magazines. Lesbians also pioneered a new baby boom, with more lesbian couples adopting or having children. HIV-positive gay men developed different strategies for living suddenly posthumous lives. Some retreated into quiet relationships; others quit jobs or changed their careers completely; others chose the escapism of what became known as "the circuit," a series of rave parties around the country and the world where fears could be lost on the drug-enhanced dance floor; others still became lost in a suicidal vortex of crystal meth, Internet hook-ups, and sex addiction. HIV-negative men, many of whom had lost husbands and friends, were not so different. In some ways, the toll was greater. They had survived disaster with their health intact. But, unlike their HIV-positive friends, the threat of contracting the disease still existed while they battled survivors' guilt. The plague was over but not over; and, as they saw men with HIV celebrate survival, some even felt shut out of a new sub-sub-culture, suspended between fear and triumph but unable to experience either fully.

Then something predictable and yet unexpected happened. While the older generation struggled with plague and post-plague adjustment, the next generation was growing up. For the first time, a cohort of gay children and teens grew up in a world where homosexuality was no longer a taboo subject and where gay figures were regularly featured in the press. If the image of gay men for my generation was one gleaned from the movie *Cruising* or, subsequently, *Torch Song Trilogy*, the image for the next one was MTV's "Real World," Bravo's "Queer Eye," and Richard Hatch winning the first "Survivor." The new emphasis was on the interaction between gays and straights and on the diversity of gay life and lives. Movies featured and integrated gayness. Even more dramatically, gays went from having to find hidden meaning in mainstream films—somehow identifying with the aging, campy female lead in a way the rest of the culture missed—to everyone, gay and straight, recognizing and being in on the joke of a character like "Big Gay Al" from "South Park" or Jack from "Will & Grace."

There are now openly gay legislators. Ditto Olympic swimmers and gymnasts and Wimbledon champions. Mainstream entertainment figures—from George Michael, Ellen DeGeneres, and Rosie O'Donnell to edgy musicians, such as the Scissor Sisters, Rufus Wainwright, or Bob Mould—now have their sexual orientation as a central, but not defining, part of their identity. The National Lesbian and Gay Journalists Association didn't exist when I became a journalist. Now it has 1,300 dues-paying members in 24 chapters around the country. Among Fortune 500 companies, 21 provided domestic partner benefits for gay spouses in 1995. Today, 216 do. Of the top Fortune 50 companies, 49 provide nondiscrimination protections for gay employees. Since 2002, the number of corporations providing full protections for openly gay employees has increased sevenfold, according to the Human Rights Campaign (HRC). Among the leaders: the defense giant Raytheon and the energy company Chevron. These are not traditionally gay-friendly work environments. Nor is the Republican Party. But the offspring of such leading Republican lights as Dick Cheney, Alan Keyes, and Phyllis Schlafly are all openly gay. So is the spokesman for the most anti-gay senator in Congress, Rick Santorum.

This new tolerance and integration—combined, of course, with the increased ability to connect with other gay people that the Internet provides—has undoubtedly encouraged more and more gay people to come out. The hard data for this are difficult to come by (since only recently have we had studies that identified large numbers of gays) and should be treated with caution. Nevertheless, the trend is clear. If you compare data from, say, the 1994 National Health and Social Life Survey with the 2002 National Survey of Family Growth, you will find that women are nearly three times more likely to report being gay, lesbian, or bisexual today than they were eight years ago, and men are about 1.5 times more likely. There are no reliable statistics on openly gay teens, but no one doubts that there has been an explosion in visibility in the last decade—around 3,000 high schools have "gay-straight" alliances. The census, for its part, recorded a threefold increase in the number of same-sex unmarried partners from 1990 to 2000. In 2000, there were close to 600,000 households headed by a same-sex couple, and a quarter of them had children. If you want to know where the push for civil marriage rights came from, you need look no further. This was not an agenda invented by activists; it was a movement propelled by ordinary people.

So, as one generation literally disappeared and one generation found itself shocked to still be alive, a far larger and more empowered one emerged on the scene. This new generation knew very little about the gay culture of the '70s, and its members were oblivious to the psychically formative experience of plague that had shaped their elders. Most came from the heart of straight America and were more in tune with its new, mellower attitude toward gayness than the embattled, defensive urban gay culture of the pre-AIDS era. Even in evangelical circles, gay kids willing to acknowledge and struggle publicly with their own homosexuality represented a new form of openness. The speed of the change is still shocking. I'm only 42, and I grew up in a world where I literally never heard the word "homosexual" until I went to college. It is now not uncommon to meet gay men in their early twenties who took a boy as their date to the high school prom. When I figured out I was gay, there were no role models to speak of; and, in the popular culture, homosexuality was either a punch line or an embarrassed silence. Today's cultural climate could not be more different. And the psychological impact on the younger generation cannot be overstated.

After all, what separates homosexuals and lesbians from every other minority group is that they are born and raised within the bosom of the majority. Unlike Latino or Jewish or black communities, where parents and grandparents and siblings pass on cultural norms to children in their most formative stages, each generation of gay men and lesbians grows up being taught the heterosexual norms and culture of their home environments or absorbing what passes for their gay identity from the broader culture as a whole. Each shift in mainstream culture is therefore magnified exponentially in the next generation of gay children.

To give the most powerful example: A gay child born today will grow up knowing that, in many parts of the world and in parts of the United States, gay couples can get married just as their parents did. From the very beginning of their gay lives, in other words, they will have internalized a sense of normality, of human potential, of self-worth—something that my generation never had and that previous generations would have found unimaginable. That shift in consciousness is as profound as it is irreversible.

To give another example: Black children come into society both uplifted and burdened by the weight of their communal past—a weight that is transferred within families or communities or cultural institutions, such as the church, that provide a context for self-understanding, even in rebellion. Gay children have no such support or burden. And so, in their most formative years, their self-consciousness is utterly different than that of their gay elders. That's why it has become increasingly difficult to distinguish between gay and straight teens today—or even young gay and straight adults. Less psychologically wounded, more self-confident, less isolated, young gay kids look and sound increasingly like young straight kids. On the dozens of college campuses I have visited over the past decade, the shift in just a few years has been astounding. At a Catholic institution like Boston College, for example, a generation ago there would have been no discussion of homosexuality. When I visited recently to talk about that very subject, the preppy, conservative student president was openly gay.

When you combine this generational plasticity with swift demographic growth, you have our current explosion of gay civil society, with a disproportionately young age distribution. I use the term "civil society" in its classic Tocquevillean and Burkean sense: the little platoons of social organization that undergird liberal democratic life. The gay organizations that erupted into being as AIDS killed thousands in the '80s—from the Gay Men's Health Crisis to the AIDS Project Los Angeles to the Whitman-Walker Clinic in Washington—struggled to adapt to the swift change in the epidemic in the mid-'90s. But the general principle of communal organization endured. If conservatives had been open-minded enough to see it, they would have witnessed a classic tale of self-help and self-empowerment.

Take, for example, religious life, an area not historically associated with gay culture. One of the largest single gay organizations in the country today is the Metropolitan Community Church, with over 40,000 active members. Go to, yes, Dallas, and you'll find the Cathedral of Hope, one of the largest religious structures in the country, with close to 4,000 congregants—predominantly gay. Almost every faith now has an explicitly gay denomination associated with it—Dignity for Gay Catholics, *Bet Mishpachah* for gay Jews, and so on. But, in many mainstream Protestant churches and among Reform Jews, such groups don't even exist because the integration of gay believers is now mundane. These groups bring gays together in a context where sexuality is less a feature of identity than faith, where the interaction of bodies is less central than the community of souls.

In contrast, look at bar life. For a very long time, the fundamental social institution for gay men was the gay bar. It was often secluded—a refuge, a safe zone, and a clearinghouse for sexual pickups. Most bars still perform some of those functions. But the Internet dealt them a body-blow. If you are merely looking for sex or a date, the Web is now the first stop for most gay men. The result has been striking. Only a decade ago, you could wander up the West Side Highway in New York City and drop by several leather bars. Now, only one is left standing, and it is less a bar dedicated to the ornate codes of '70s leather culture than a place for men who adopt a more masculine self-presentation. My favorite old leather bar, the Spike, is now the "Spike Gallery." The newer gay bars are more social than sexual, often with restaurants, open windows onto the street, and a welcoming attitude toward others, especially the many urban straight women who find gay bars more congenial than heterosexual pickup joints.

Even gay political organizations often function more as social groups than as angry activist groups. HRC, for example, raises funds and lobbies Congress. Around 350,000 members have contributed in the last two years. It organizes itself chiefly through a series of formal fund-raising dinners in cities across the country—from Salt Lake City to Nashville. These dinners are a social venue for the openly gay bourgeoisie: In tuxedos and ballgowns, they contribute large sums and give awards to local businesses and politicians and community leaders. There are silent auctions, hired entertainers, even the occasional bakesale. The closest heterosexual equivalent would be the Rotary Club. These dinners in themselves are evidence of the change: from outsider rebellion to bourgeois organization.

Take a look at the gay press. In its shallower forms—glossy lifestyle magazines—you are as likely to find a straight Hollywood star on the cover as any gay icon. In its more serious manifestations, such as regional papers like the *Washington Blade* or *Southern Voice*, the past emphasis on sex has been replaced with an emphasis on domesticity. A recent issue of the *Blade* had an eight-page insert for escort ads, personals, and the kind of material that, two decades ago, would have been the advertising mainstay of the main paper. But in the paper itself are 23 pages of real-estate ads and four pages of home-improvement classifieds. There are columns on cars, sports, DVDs, and local plays. The core ad base, according to its editor, Chris Crain, now comprises heterosexual-owned and operated companies seeking to reach the gay market. The editorial tone has shifted as well. Whereas the *Blade* was once ideologically rigid—with endless reports on small activist cells and a strident left-wing slant—now it's much more like a community paper that might be published for any well-heeled ethnic group. Genuine ideological differences are now aired, rather than bitterly decried as betrayal or agitprop. Editorials regularly take Democrats to task as well as Republicans. The maturation has been as swift as it now seems inevitable. After all, in 2004, one-quarter of self-identified gay voters backed a president who supported a constitutional ban on gay marriage. If the gay world is that politically diverse under the current polarized circumstances, it has obviously moved well beyond the time it was synonymous with radical left politics.

How gay men and lesbians express their identity has also changed. When openly gay identity first emerged, it tended toward extremes of gender expression. When society tells you that gay men and lesbians are not fully male or female, the response can be to overcompensate with caricatures of each gender or to rebel by blurring gender lines altogether. Effeminate "queens" were balanced by hyper-masculine bikers and muscle men; lipstick lesbians were offset by classically gruff "bull-dykes." All these sub-sub-cultures still exist. Many feel comfortable with them; and, thankfully, we see fewer attempts to marginalize them. But the polarities in the larger gay population are far less pronounced than they once were; the edges have softened. As gay men have become less defensive about their masculinity, their expression of it has become subtler. There is still a pronounced muscle and gym culture, but there are also now openly gay swimmers and artists and slobs and every body type in between. Go watch a gay rugby team compete in a regional tournament with straight teams and you will see how vast but subtle the revolution has been. And, in fact, this is the trend: gay civil associations in various ways are interacting with parallel straight associations in a way that leaves their gay identity more and more behind. They're rugby players first, gay rugby players second.

One of the newest reflections of this is what is known as "bear" culture: heavy, hirsute, unkempt guys who revel in their slovenliness. Their concept of what it means to be gay is very different than that of the obsessive gym-rats with torsos shaved of every stray hair. Among many younger gay men, the grungy look of their straight peers has been adopted and tweaked to individual tastes. Even among bears, there are slimmer "otters" or younger "cubs" or "musclebears," who combine gym culture with a bear sensibility. The varieties keep proliferating; and, at the rate of current change, they will soon dissipate into the range of identities that straight men have to choose from. In fact, these variations of masculinity may even have diversified heterosexual male culture as well. While some gay men have proudly adopted some classically straight signifiers—beer bellies and back hair—many straight men have become "metrosexuals." Trying to define "gay culture" in this mix is an increasingly elusive task.

Among lesbians, Ellen DeGeneres's transition from closeted sitcom star to out-lesbian activist and back to appealingly middle-brow daytime talk-show host is almost a microcosm of diversifying lesbian identity in the past decade. There are still classic butch-femme lesbian partnerships, but more complex forms of self-expression are more common now. With the abatement in many places of prejudice, lesbian identity is formed less by reaction to hostility than by simple self-expression. And this, after all, is and was the point of gay liberation: the freedom not merely to be gay according to some preordained type, but to be yourself, whatever that is.

You see this even in drag, which once defined gayness in some respects but now is only one of many expressions. Old-school drag, the kind that dominated the '50s, '60s, and '70s, often consisted of female impersonators performing torch songs from various divas. The more miserable the life of the diva, the better able the performer was to channel his own anguish and drama into the show. After all, gayness was synonymous with tragedy and showmanship. Judy Garland, Marilyn Monroe, Bette Davis: these were the models. But today's drag looks and feels very different. The drag impresario of Provincetown, a twisted genius called Ryan Landry, hosts a weekly talent show for local drag performers called "Showgirls." Attending it each Monday night is P-town's equivalent of weekly Mass. A few old-school drag queens perform, but Landry sets the tone. He makes no attempt to look like a woman, puts on hideous wigs (including a horse mask and a pair of fake boobs perched on his head), throws on ill-fitting dresses, and performs scatological song parodies. Irony pervades the show. Comedy defines it. Gay drag is inching slowly toward a version of British pantomime, where dada humor and absurd, misogynist parodies of womanhood are central. This is post-drag; straight men could do it as well. This year, the longest-running old school drag show—"Legends"—finally closed down. Its audience had become mainly heterosexual and old.

This new post-gay cultural synthesis has its political counterpart. There was once a ferocious debate among gays between what might be caricatured as "separatists" and "assimilationists." That argument has fizzled. As the gay population has grown, it has become increasingly clear that the choice is not either/or but both/and. The issue of civil marriage reveals this most graphically. When I first argued for equal marriage rights, I found myself assailed by the gay left for social conservatism. I remember one signing for my 1995 book, *Virtually Normal*, the crux of which was an argument for the right to marry. I was picketed by a group called "Lesbian Avengers," who depicted my argument as patriarchal and reactionary. They crafted posters with my face portrayed within the crosshairs of a gun. Ten years later, lesbian couples make up a majority of civil marriages in Massachusetts and civil unions in Vermont; and some of the strongest voices for marriage equality have been lesbians, from the pioneering lawyer Mary Bonauto to writer E.J. Graff. To its credit, the left—gay male and lesbian—recognized that what was at stake was not so much the corralling of all gay individuals into a conformist social institution as a widening of choice for all. It is still possible to be a gay radical or rigid leftist. The difference now is that it is also possible to be a gay conservative, or traditionalist, or anything else in between.

Who can rescue a uniform gay culture? No one, it would seem. The generation most psychologically wedded to the separatist past is either dead from HIV or sidelined. But there are still enclaves of gay distinctiveness out there. Paradoxically, gay culture in its old form may have its most fertile ground in those states where homosexuality is still unmentionable and where openly gay men and women are more beleaguered: the red states. Earlier this year, I spoke at an HRC dinner in Nashville, Tennessee, where state politicians are trying to bar gay couples from marrying or receiving even basic legal protections. The younger gay generation is as psychologically evolved there as any place else. They see the same television and the same Internet as gay kids in New York.

But their social space is smaller. And so I found a vibrant gay world, but one far more cohesive, homogeneous, and defensive than in Massachusetts. The strip of gay bars—crammed into one place rather than diffuse, as in many blue-state cities—was packed on a Saturday night. The mix of old and young, gay and lesbian, black, white, and everything in between reminded me of Boston in the '80s. The tired emblems of the past—the rainbow flags and leather outfits—retained their relevance there.

The same goes for black and Latino culture, where homophobia, propped up by black churches and the Catholic hierarchy respectively, is more intense than in much of white society. It's no surprise that these are the populations also most at risk for HIV. The underground "down-low" culture common in black gay life means less acknowledgment of sexual identity, let alone awareness or disclosure of HIV status. The same repression that facilitated the spread of HIV among gay white men in the '70s now devastates black gay America, where the latest data suggest a 50 percent HIV infection rate. (Compare that with largely white and more integrated San Francisco, where recent HIV infection rates are now half what they were four years ago.) The extremes of gender expression are also more pronounced among minorities, with many gay black or Latino men either adopting completely female personalities or refusing to identify as gay at all. Here the past lives on. The direction toward integration is clear, but the pace is far slower.

And, when you see the internalized defensiveness of gays still living in the shadow of social hostility, any nostalgia one might feel for the loss of gay culture dissipates. Some still echo critic Philip Larkin's jest that he worried about the American civil rights movement because it was ruining jazz. But the flipness of that remark is the point, and the mood today is less genuine regret—let alone a desire to return to those days—than a kind of wistfulness for a past that was probably less glamorous or unified than it now appears. It is indeed hard not to feel some sadness at the end of a rich, distinct culture built by pioneers who braved greater ostracism than today's generation will ever fully understand. But, if there is a real choice between a culture built on oppression and a culture built on freedom, the decision is an easy one. Gay culture was once primarily about pain and tragedy, because that is what heterosexuals imposed on gay people, and that was, in part, what gay people experienced. Gay culture was once primarily about sex, because that was how heterosexuals defined gay lives. But gay life, like straight life, is now and always has been about happiness as well as pain; it is about triumph as well as tragedy; it is about love and family as well as sex. It took generations to find the self-worth to move toward achieving this reality in all its forms—and an epidemiological catastrophe to accelerate it. If the end of gay culture means that we have a new complexity to grapple with and a new, less cramped humanity to embrace, then regret seems almost a rebuke to those countless generations who could only dream of the liberty so many now enjoy.

The tiny, rich space that gay men and women once created for themselves was, after all, the best they could do. In a metaphor coined by the philosopher Michael Walzer, they gilded a cage of exclusion with magnificent ornaments; they spoke to its isolation and pain; they described and maintained it with dignity and considerable beauty. But it was still a cage. And the thing that kept gay people together, that unified them into one homogeneous unit, and that defined the parameters of their culture and the limits of their dreams, were the bars on that cage. Past the ashes of thousands and through the courage of those who came before the plague and those who survived it, those bars are now slowly but inexorably being pried apart. The next generation may well be as free of that cage as any minority ever can be; and they will redefine gayness on its own terms and not on the terms of hostile outsiders. Nothing will stop this, since it is occurring in the psyches and souls of a new generation: a new consciousness that is immune to any law and propelled by the momentum of human freedom itself. While we should treasure the past, there is no recovering it. The futures—and they will be multiple—are just beginning.

First published in *The New Republic*, October 24, 2005, pp. 16-21. Copyright © 2005 by Andrew Sullivan. Reprinted by permission of The Wylie Agency.

UNIT 3

Interpersonal Relationships

Unit Selections

Key Points to Consider

- What makes male-female intimacy difficult to achieve? Have you learned any lessons about yourself and the opposite sex "the hard way?"

- Do we as a society focus too little or too much on sexual mechanics—sexual parts and acts? List at least six adjectives you find synonymous with *great* sex.

- Which do you think is harder—finding a partner or keeping a relationship strong? Why?

- Have you ever felt smothered or too tightly bound in a relationship? Why do you think some people clutch and fear letting go (despite the often quoted advice that with birds or humans letting go is the only way to truly have something)?

- Some people say talking about sex is harder to do with your romantic partner than with a friend or even a stranger. Do you agree or disagree with this statement?

Student Web Site

www.mhcls.com/online

Internet References

Further information regarding these Web sites may be found in this book's preface or online.

American Psychological Association
http://www.apa.org/topics/homepage.html

Bonobos Sex and Society
http://songweaver.com/info/bonobos.html

The Celibate FAQ
http://www.glandscape.com/celibate.html

Go Ask Alice
http://www.goaskalice.columbia.edu

Most people are familiar with the term "sexual relationship." It denotes an important dimension of sexuality—interpersonal sexuality, or sexual interactions occurring between two (and sometimes more) individuals. This unit focuses attention on these types of relationships.

No woman is an island. No man is an island. Interpersonal contact forms the basis for self-esteem and meaningful living. Conversely, isolation results in loneliness and depression for most human beings. People seek and cultivate friendships for the warmth, affection, supportiveness, and sense of trust and loyalty that such relationships can provide.

Long-term friendships may develop into intimate relationships. The qualifying word in the previous sentence is "may." Today many people, single as well as married, yearn for close or emotionally intimate interpersonal relationships but fail to find them. Despite developments in communication and technology that past generations could never fathom, discovering how and where to find potential friends, partners, lovers, and soul mates is reported to be more difficult today than in times past. Fear of rejection causes some to avoid interpersonal relationships, others to present a false front or illusory self that they think is more acceptable or socially desirable. This sets the stage for a game of intimacy that is counterproductive to genuine intimacy. For others a major dilemma may exist—the problem of balancing closeness with the preservation of individual identity in a manner that satisfies the need for both personal and interpersonal growth and integrity. In either case, partners in a relationship should be advised that the development of interpersonal awareness (the mutual recognition and knowledge of others as they

really are) rests upon trust and self-disclosure—letting the other person know who you really are and how you truly feel. In American society this has never been easy, and today some fear it may be more difficult than ever.

These considerations regarding interpersonal relationships apply equally well to achieving meaningful and satisfying sexual relationships. Three basic ingredients lay the foundation for quality sexual interaction: self-awareness, understanding and acceptance of the partner's needs and desires, and mutual efforts to accommodate both partners' needs and desires. Without these, misunderstandings may arise, bringing anxiety, frustration, dissatisfaction, and/or resentment into the relationship. There may also be a heightened risk of contracting AIDS or another STD (sexually transmitted disease), experiencing an unplanned pregnancy, or experiencing sexual dysfunction by one or both partners. On the other hand, experience and research show that ongoing attention to these three ingredients by intimate partners contributes not only to sexual responsibility, but also to true emotional and sexual intimacy and a longer and happier life.

As might already be apparent, there is much more to quality sexual relationships than our popular culture recognizes. Such relationships are not established by means of sexual techniques or beautiful/handsome features. Rather, it is the quality of the interaction that makes sex a celebration of our humanity and sexuality. A person-oriented (as opposed to genitally oriented) sexual awareness, coupled with a whole-body/mind sexuality and an open, relaxed, even playful, attitude toward exploration, makes for joy and pleasure in sexuality.

Great Expectations

Has the quest to find the perfect soul mate done more harm than good? Psychologists provide insight into how the never-ending search for ideal love can keep you from enjoying a marriage or a healthy relationship that you already have.

POLLY SHULMAN

Q: How do you turn a good relationship sour?

A: Pursue your inalienable right to happiness, hot sex, true love and that soul mate who must be out there somewhere.

Marriage is dead! The twin vises of church and law have relaxed their grip on matrimony. We've been liberated from the grim obligation to stay in a poisonous or abusive marriage for the sake of the kids or for appearances. The divorce rate has stayed constant at nearly 50 percent for the last two decades. The ease with which we enter and dissolve unions makes marriage seem like a prime-time spectator sport, whether it's Britney Spears in Vegas or bimbos chasing after the Bachelor.

Long live the new marriage! We once prized the institution for the practical pairing of a cash-producing father and a home-building mother. Now we want it all—a partner who reflects our taste and status, who sees us for who we are, who loves us for all the "right" reasons, who helps us become the person we want to be. We've done away with a rigid social order, adopting instead an even more onerous obligation: the mandate to find a perfect match. Anything short of this ideal prompts us to ask: Is this all there is? Am I as happy as I should be? Could there be somebody out there who's better for me? As often as not, we answer yes to that last question and fall victim to our own great expectations.

Nothing has produced more unhappiness than the concept of the soul mate.

That somebody is, of course, our soul mate, the man or woman who will counter our weaknesses, amplify our strengths and provide the unflagging support and respect that is the essence of a contemporary relationship. The reality is that few marriages or partnerships consistently live up to this ideal. The result is a commitment limbo, in which we care deeply for our partner but keep one stealthy foot out the door of our hearts. In so doing, we subject the relationship to constant review: Would I be happier, smarter, a better person with someone else? It's a painful modern quandary. "Nothing has produced more unhappiness than the concept of the soul mate," says Atlanta psychiatrist Frank Pittman.

Consider Jeremy, a social worker who married a businesswoman in his early twenties. He met another woman, a psychologist, at age 29, and after two agonizing years, left his wife for her. But it didn't work out—after four years of cohabitation, and her escalating pleas to marry, he walked out on her, as well. Jeremy now realizes that the relationship with his wife was solid and workable but thinks he couldn't have seen that 10 years ago, when he left her. "There was always someone better around the corner—and the safety and security of marriage morphed into boredom and stasis. The allure of willing and exciting females was too hard to resist," he admits. Now 42 and still single, Jeremy acknowledges, "I hurt others, and I hurt myself."

Like Jeremy, many of us either dodge the decision to commit or commit without fully relinquishing the right to keep looking—opting for an arrangement psychotherapist Terrence Real terms "stable ambiguity." "You park on the border of the relationship, so you're in it but not of it," he says. There are a million ways to do that: You can be in a relationship but not be sure it's really the right one, have an eye open for a better deal or something on the side, choose someone impossible or far away.

Yet commitment and marriage offer real physical and financial rewards. Touting the benefits of marriage may sound like conservative policy rhetoric, but nonpartisan sociological research backs it up: Committed partners have it all over singles, at least on average. Married people are more financially stable, according to Linda Waite, a sociologist at the University of Chicago and a coauthor of The Case for Marriage: Why Married People are Happier, Healthier and Better Off. Both married men and married women have more assets on average than singles; for women, the differential is huge.

We're in commitment limbo: We care deeply for our partner but keep one stealthy foot out the door of our heart.

The benefits go beyond the piggy bank. Married people, particularly men, tend to live longer than people who aren't married. Couples also live better: When people expect to stay together, says Waite, they pool their resources, increasing their individual standard of living. They also pool their expertise—in cooking, say, or financial management. In general, women improve men's health by putting a stop to stupid bachelor tricks and bugging their husbands to exercise and eat their vegetables. Plus, people who aren't comparing their partners to someone else in bed have less trouble performing and are more emotionally satisfied with sex. The relationship doesn't have to be wonderful for life to get better, says Waite: The statistics hold true for mediocre marriages as well as for passionate ones.

The pragmatic benefits of partnership used to be foremost in our minds. The idea of marriage as a vehicle for self-fulfillment and happiness is relatively new, says Paul Amato, professor of sociology, demography and family studies at Penn State University. Surveys of high school and college students 50 or 60 years ago found that most wanted to get married in order to have children or own a home. Now, most report that they plan to get married for love. This increased emphasis on emotional fulfillment within marriage leaves couples ill-prepared for the realities they will probably face.

Because the early phase of a relationship is marked by excitement and idealization, "many romantic, passionate couples expect to have that excitement forever," says Barry McCarthy, a clinical psychologist and coauthor—with his wife, Emily McCarthy—of Getting It Right the First Time: How to Build a Healthy Marriage. Longing for the charged energy of the early days, people look elsewhere or split up.

Flagging passion is often interpreted as the death knell of a relationship. You begin to wonder whether you're really right for each other after all. You're comfortable together, but you don't really connect the way you used to. Wouldn't it be more honest—and braver—to just admit that it's not working and call it off? "People are made to feel that remaining in a marriage that doesn't make you blissfully happy is an act of existential cowardice," says Joshua Coleman, a San Francisco psychologist.

Coleman says that the constant cultural pressure to have it all—a great sex life, a wonderful family—has made people ashamed of their less-than-perfect relationships and question whether such unions are worth hanging on to. Feelings of dissatisfaction or disappointment are natural, but they can seem intolerable when standards are sky-high. "It's a recent historical event that people expect to get so much from individual partners," says Coleman, author of Imperfect Harmony, in which he advises couples in lackluster marriages to stick it out—especially if they have kids. "There's an enormous amount of pressure on marriages to live up to an unrealistic ideal."

Michaela, 28, was drawn to Bernardo, 30, in part because of their differences: She'd grown up in European boarding schools, he fought his way out of a New York City ghetto. "Our backgrounds made us more interesting to each other," says Michaela. "I was a spoiled brat, and he'd been supporting himself from the age of 14, which I admired." Their first two years of marriage were rewarding, but their fights took a toll. "I felt that because he hadn't grown up in a normal family, he didn't grasp basic issues of courtesy and accountability," says Michaela. They were temperamental opposites: He was a

screamer, and she was a sulker. She recalls, "After we fought, I needed to be drawn out of my corner, but he took that to mean that I was a cold bitch." Michaela reluctantly concluded that the two were incompatible.

In a society hell-bent on individual achievement and autonomy, working on a difficult relationship may get short shrift.

In fact, argue psychologists and marital advocates, there's no such thing as true compatibility.

"Marriage is a disagreement machine," says Diane Sollee, founder of the Coalition for Marriage, Family and Couples Education. "All couples disagree about all the same things. We have a highly romanticized notion that if we were with the right person, we wouldn't fight." Discord springs eternal over money, kids, sex and leisure time, but psychologist John Gottman has shown that long-term, happily married couples disagree about these things just as much as couples who divorce.

"There is a mythology of 'the wrong person,'" agrees Pittman. "All marriages are incompatible. All marriages are between people from different families, people who have a different view of things. The magic is to develop binocular vision, to see life through your partner's eyes as well as through your own."

The realization that we're not going to get everything we want from a partner is not just sobering, it's downright miserable. But it is also a necessary step in building a mature relationship, according to Real, who has written about the subject in How Can I Get Through to You: Closing the Intimacy Gap Between Men and Women. "The paradox of intimacy is that our ability to stay close rests on our ability to tolerate solitude inside a relationship," he says. "A central aspect of grown-up love is grief. All of us long for—and think we deserve—perfection." We can hardly be blamed for striving for bliss and self-fulfillment in our romantic lives—our inalienable right to the pursuit of happiness is guaranteed in the first blueprint of American society.

This same respect for our own needs spurred the divorce-law reforms of the 1960s and 1970s. During that era, "The culture shifted to emphasize individual satisfaction, and marriage was part of that," explains Paul Amato, who has followed more than 2,000 families for 20 years in a long-term study of marriage and divorce. Amato says that this shift did some good by freeing people from abusive and intolerable marriages. But it had an unintended side effect: encouraging people to abandon relationships that may be worth salvaging. In a society hell-bent on individual achievement and autonomy, working on a difficult relationship may get short shrift, says psychiatrist Peter Kramer, author of Should You Leave?

We get the divorce rate that we deserve as a culture, says Peter Kramer.

"So much of what we learn has to do with the self, the ego, rather than giving over the self to things like a relationship," Kramer says. In our competitive world, we're rewarded for our individual achievements rather than for how we help others. We value independence over cooperation, and sacrifices for values like loyalty and continuity seem foolish. "I think we get the divorce rate that we deserve as a culture."

The steadfast focus on our own potential may turn a partner into an accessory in the quest for self-actualization, says Maggie Robbins, a therapist in New York City. "We think that this person should reflect the beauty and perfection that is the inner me—or, more often, that this person should compensate for the yuckiness and mess that is the inner me," says Robbins. "This is what makes you tell your wife, 'Lose some weight—you're making me look bad,' not 'Lose some weight, you're at risk for diabetes.'"

Michaela was consistently embarrassed by Bernardo's behavior when they were among friends. "He'd become sullen and withdrawn—he had a shifty way of looking off to the side when he didn't want to talk. I felt like it reflected badly on me," she admits. Michaela left him and is now dating a wealthy entrepreneur. "I just thought there had to be someone else out there for me."

The urge to find a soul mate is not fueled just by notions of romantic manifest destiny. Trends in the workforce and in the media create a sense of limitless romantic possibility. According to Scott South, a demographer at SUNY-Albany, proximity to potential partners has a powerful effect on relationships. South and his colleagues found higher divorce rates among people living in communities or working in professions where they encounter lots of potential partners—people who match them in age, race and education level. "These results hold true not just for unhappy marriages but also for happy ones," says South.

The temptations aren't always living, breathing people. According to research by psychologists Sara Gutierres and Douglas Kenrick, both of Arizona State University, we find reasonably attractive people less appealing when we've just seen a hunk or a hottie—and we're bombarded daily by images of gorgeous models and actors. When we watch Lord of the Rings, Viggo Mortensen's kingly mien and Liv Tyler's elfin charm can make our husbands and wives look all too schlumpy.

Kramer sees a similar pull in the narratives that surround us. "The number of stories that tell us about other lives we could lead—in magazine articles, television shows, books—has increased enormously. We have an enormous reservoir of possibilities," says Kramer.

And these possibilities can drive us to despair. Too many choices have been shown to stymie consumers, and an array of alternative mates is no exception. In an era when marriages were difficult to dissolve, couples rated their marriages as more satisfying than do today's couples, for whom divorce is a clear option, according to the National Opinion Research Center at the University of Chicago.

While we expect marriage to be "happily ever after," the truth is that for most people, neither marriage nor divorce seem to have a decisive impact on happiness. Although Waite's research shows that married people are happier than their single counterparts, other studies have found that after a couple years of marriage, people are just about as happy (or unhappy) as they were before settling down. And assuming that marriage will automatically provide contentment is itself a surefire recipe for misery.

"Marriage is not supposed to make you happy. It is supposed to make you married," says Pittman. "When you are all the way in your marriage, you are free to do useful things, become a better person." A committed relationship allows you to drop pretenses and seductions, expose your weaknesses, be yourself—and know that you will be loved, warts and all. "A real relationship is the collision of my humanity and yours, in all its joy and limitations," says Real. "How partners handle that collision is what determines the quality of their relationship."

Such a down-to-earth view of marriage is hardly romantic, but that doesn't mean it's not profound: An authentic relationship with another person, says Pittman, is "one of the first steps toward connecting with the human condition—which is necessary if you're going to become fulfilled as a human being." If we accept these humble terms, the quest for a soul mate might just be a noble pursuit after all.

POLLY SHULMAN is a freelance writer in New York City.

In Search of Erotic Intelligence

Reconciling our desire for comfortable domesticity and hot sex

ESTHER PEREL

EVERYBODY'S NOT DOING IT. That's the word from Newsweek, The Atlantic, *and other trend watchers: Couples are having less sex these days than even in the famously uptight '50s. Why? Busy, exhausting lives is the easy answer. But how Americans view eroticism in the wake of recent sexual and social revolutions may be an even bigger factor, according to a growing number of researchers and social observers.*

—The Editors

A few years ago, at a psychology conference, I heard a speaker discuss a couple who had come to therapy in part because of a sharp decline in their sexual activity. Previously, the couple had engaged in light sadomasochism; now, following the birth of their second child, the wife wanted more conventional sex. But the husband was attached to their old style of lovemaking, so they were stuck.

The speaker believed that resolving the couple's sexual difficulty required working through the emotional dynamics of their marriage and new status as parents. But in the discussion afterward, the audience was far less interested in the couple's relationship than in the issue of sadomasochistic sex. Some people speculated that motherhood had restored the woman's sense of dignity, and now she refused to be demeaned by an implicitly abusive, power-driven relationship. Others suggested that the couple's impasse illustrated long-standing gender differences: Men tended to pursue separateness and control, while women yearned for loving connection.

When after two hours of talking about sex no one had mentioned the words *pleasure* or *eroticism*, I finally spoke up. Their form of sex had been entirely consensual, after all. Maybe the woman no longer wanted to be tied up because she now had a baby constantly attached to her breasts—binding her better than ropes ever could. Why assume that there *had* to be something degrading about this couple's sex play?

Perhaps my colleagues were afraid that if women *did* reveal such desires, they'd somehow sanction male dominance everywhere—in business, politics, economics. Maybe the very ideas of sexual dominance and submission, aggression and surrender, couldn't be squared with the ideals of compromise and equality that undergird couples therapy today.

As an outsider to American society—I grew up in Belgium and have lived in many countries—I wondered if these attitudes reflected cultural differences. I later talked with Europeans, Brazilians, and Israelis who had been at the meeting. We all felt somewhat out of step with the sexual attitudes of our American colleagues. Did they believe such sexual preferences—even though they were consensual and completely nonviolent—were too wild and "kinky" for the serious business of maintaining a marriage and raising a family? It was as if sexual pleasure and eroticism that strayed onto slightly outré paths of fantasy and play—particularly games involving aggression and power—must be stricken from the repertoire of responsible adults in committed relationships.

Sexual desire does not play by the rules of good citizenship.

What struck us was that America, in matters of sex as in much else, was a goal-oriented society that prefers explicit meanings and "plain speech" to ambiguity and allusion. Many American therapists encourage clarity and directness, which they tend to associate with honesty and openness: "If you want to make love to your wife/husband, why don't you tell her/him exactly what you want?" These professionals in large part "solve" the conflict between the drabness of the familiar and the excitement of the unknown by advising patients to renounce their fantasies in favor of more reasonable "adult" sexual agendas.

Whereas therapists typically encourage patients to "really get to know" their partners, I often say that "knowing isn't everything." Most couples exchange enough direct talk in the course of daily life. To create more passion, I suggest that they play a bit more with the ambiguity that's inherent to communication. Eroticism can draw its powerful pleasure from fascination with the hidden, the mysterious, and the suggestive.

Ironically, some of America's best features—the belief in equality, consensus-building, fairness, and tolerance—can, in the bedroom, result in very boring sex. Sexual desire and good citizenship don't play by the same rules. Sexual excitement is often politically incorrect; it often thrives on power plays, role reversals, imperious demands, and seductive manipulations.

American therapists, shaped by egalitarian ideals, are often challenged by these contradictions.

In Europe, I see more of an emphasis on complementarity—the appeal of difference—rather than strict gender equality. This, it seems to me, makes European women feel less conflict about being both smart and sexy. They can enjoy their sexual power, even in the workplace, without feeling they're forfeiting their right to be taken seriously. Susanna, for example, is a Spanish woman with a high-level job at an international company in New York. She sees no contradiction between her work and her desire to express her sexual power—even among her colleagues. "If compliments are given graciously, they don't offend. We're still men and women who are attracted to one another, and not robots," she says.

Of course, American feminists accomplished major improvements in women's lives in many ways. Yet without denigrating their achievements, I believe that the emphasis on egalitarian and respectful sex—purged of any expressions of power, aggression, and transgression—is antithetical to erotic desire for men and women alike. (I'm well aware of the widespread sexual coercion and abuse of women and children. Everything I suggest here depends on getting clear consent and respecting the other's humanity.) The writer Daphne Merkin writes, "No bill of sexual rights can hold its own against the lawless, untamable landscape of the erotic imagination." Or as filmmaker Luis Buñel put it more bluntly, "Sex without sin is like an egg without salt."

Many therapists assume that the fantasy life that shapes a new relationship is a form of temporary insanity, destined to fade over a long-term partnership. But can sexual fantasy actually enhance the intimate reality of relationships? Clinicians often interpret the desire for sexual adventure—ranging from simple flirting and contact with previous lovers to threesomes and fetishes—as fear of commitment and infantile fantasy. Sexual fantasies about one's partner, particularly those that involve role-playing, dominance, and submission, are often viewed as signs of neurosis and immaturity, erotically tinged idealizations that blind one to a partner's true identity. Here's an example from a client I worked with (the name changed, of course):

Terry had been in therapy for a year, struggling with the transition from being half of an erotically charged couple to being one-quarter of a family with two children and no eroticism at all. He began one session with what he deemed a "real midlife story" that began when he and his wife hired a young German au pair. "Every morning she and I take care of my daughters together," he said. "She's lovely—so natural, full of vitality and youth—and I've developed this amazing crush on her. You know how I've been talking about this feeling of deadness? Well, her energy has awakened me. I want to sleep with her and I wonder why I don't. I'm scared to do it and scared not to."

I didn't lecture him about his "immature" wishes, or explore the emotional dynamics beneath this presumably "adolescent" desire. Instead, I tried to help him relish the awakening of his dormant senses without letting the momentary exhilaration endanger his marriage. I marveled with him at the allure and beauty of the fantasy, while also calling it just that: a *fantasy*.

"It's great to know you still can come to life like that," I said. "And you know that you can never compare this state of inebriation with life at home, because home is about something else. Home is safe. Here, you're on shaky ground. You like it, but you're also afraid that it can take you too far away from home. And you probably don't let your wife evoke such tremors in you."

A few days later, he was having lunch in a restaurant with his wife and she was telling him of her previous boyfriend. "I'd been thinking hard about what we talked about," he told me, "and at the table I had this switch. Normally, I don't like hearing these stories of hers—they make me jealous and irritated. But this time I just listened and found myself getting very turned on. So did she. In fact, we were so excited we had to look for a bathroom where we could be alone."

I suggested that perhaps the experience of desiring a fresh young woman was what enabled him to listen to his wife differently—as a sexual and desirable woman herself. I invited Terry to permit himself the erotic intensity of the illicit with his wife: "This could be a beginning of bringing lust home," I said. "These small transgressions are acceptable; they offer you the latitude to experience new desire without having to throw everything away."

It amazes me how willing people are to experiment sexually *outside* their relationships, yet how tame and puritanical they are with their partners. Many of my patients describe their domestic sex lives as devoid of excitement and eroticism, yet they are consumed by a richly imaginative sex life beyond domesticity—affairs, pornography, prostitutes, cybersex, or feverish daydreams. Having denied themselves freedom of imagination at home, they go outside to reimagine themselves, often with random strangers. Yet the commodification of sex can actually hinder our capacity for fantasy, contaminating our sexual imagination. Furthermore, pornography and cybersex are ultimately isolating, disconnected from relations with a real, live other *person*.

A fundamental conundrum is that we seek a steady, reliable anchor in our partner, at the same time we seek a transcendent experience that allows us to soar beyond our ordinary lives. The challenge, then, for couples and therapists, is to reconcile the need for what's safe and predictable with the wish to pursue what's exciting, mysterious, and awe-inspiring.

It's often assumed that intimacy and trust must exist before sex can be enjoyed, but for many women and men, intimacy—more precisely, the familiarity inherent in intimacy—actually sabotages sexual desire. When the loved one becomes a source of security and stability, he/she can become desexualized. The dilemma is that erotic passion can leave many people feeling vulnerable and less secure. In this sense there is no "safe sex." Maybe the real paradox is that this fundamental insecurity is a precondition for maintaining interest and desire. As Stephen Mitchell, a New York psychoanalyst, used to say, "It is not that romance fades over time. It becomes riskier."

Susan and Jenny came to see me about their sexual relationship. Susan, a longtime lesbian, set out to seduce Jenny right after they met. Jenny responded, though it was her first lesbian relationship. They moved in together just as Susan was waiting for the arrival of her adopted baby. Once they were a threesome, Jenny thought they were a wonderful family, but completely lost any sexual interest in Susan. Jenny, already in some conflict about her lesbianism, couldn't be a second mom to the new baby, family builder, companion, and passionate lover all at once.

The transition to motherhood can have a desexualizing effect. I reminded them that the mother isn't an erotic image in our culture. Mom is supposed to be caring, nurturing, loving, but, frankly, rather asexual. "Being new parents can be pretty overwhelming," I said. "But can you try to add making love to the list of all the other things you enjoy doing together to unwind and relax? The idea is to make each other feel good, not to solve the fate of your relationship. That's an offer you can't refuse."

At the next session, Jenny reported: "That really loosened us up. We can talk about it, laugh and not be instantly scared."

So many couples imagine that they know everything there is to know about their mate. In large part, I see my job as trying to highlight how little they've seen, urging them to recover their curiosity and catch a glimpse behind the walls that encircle the other. As Mexican essayist Octavio Paz has written, eroticism is "the poetry of the body, the testimony of the senses. Like a poem, it is not linear, it meanders and twists back on itself, shows us what we do not see with our eyes, but in the eyes of our spirit. Eroticism reveals to us another world, inside this world. The senses become servants of the imagination, and let us see the invisible and hear the inaudible."

ESTHER PEREL is on the faculties of the New York Medical Center, Department of Psychiatry, and the International Trauma Studies Program, New York University. She is in private practice in New York.

24 Things Love & Sex Experts Are Dying to Tell You

ELLISE PIERCE

A t REDBOOK, we're dedicated to helping you get the most out of every part of your life—*especially* your love life. That's why we created the REDBOOK Love Network, a brain trust of today's top authorities on relationships, to provide you with the best, most current info on the ins and outs, and ups and downs, of sex and love. Here, our experts share the essential pieces of advice every couple needs.

1 Never underestimate the power of a compliment.

"Every day, tell your partner about one thing they did that you appreciate. Everybody is quick to let their partner know what they didn't do right, and what made you angry. Make sure you balance this with what they do that pleases you. From the small things to the big things, the more you say 'Thank you,' the more of what makes you happy will come your way."

—**Jane Greer, Ph.D., couples therapist and author of *Gridlock: Finding the Courage to Move On in Love, Work, and Life***

2 Sex: Just Do It.

"Have sex—even when you don't want to! Many times, arousal comes before desire. Once you get going, you'll probably find yourself enjoying it. And the more you experience sex, the more your body will condition itself to want it. You'll feel more sensual and energized, and your partner will pick up on this sexy change."

—**Laura Berman, Ph.D., director of the Berman Center in Chicago and author of *The Passion Prescription***

3 Listen more, talk less.

"Communication is 85 percent listening and 15 percent talking. The more you listen, the more you'll enhance communication. Try getting out of the house, taking a long walk without your cell phones, and just looking into your partner's eyes and lis-

tening to him. It's an amazing thing in a relationship when you truly feel listened to!"

—**Neil Clark Warren, Ph.D., founder of eHarmony.com and author of *Falling in Love for All the Right Reasons***

4 Sweep your problems (the little ones) under the rug.

"It really is okay to drop certain subjects and not even come back to them. People think this means you're avoiding key issues. But for everyday little things, successful couples agree to ignore the small problems. It's not worth the aggravation to insist on winning everything."

—**David Wexler, Ph.D., executive director of the Relationship Training Institute in San Diego and author of *When Good Men Behave Badly***

5 Treat your love like a cherished friendship.

"The happiest couples relate to each other with respect, affection, and empathy. They choose their words carefully, avoiding the most poisonous relationship behaviors—criticism, defensiveness, contempt, and stonewalling—and feel emotionally connected."

—**John Gottman, Ph.D., cofounder of the Gottman Institute in Seattle and author of *10 Lessons to Transform Your Marriage***

6 To change your relationship, change yourself.

"In most relationships, we think, I'm right, you're wrong, and I'll try to convince you to change. The truth is, if one person changes, the relationship changes. People say, 'Why do I have to change?' But when I show them how to tip over the first domino, their only question is, "Why did I wait so long?'"

—**Michele Weiner-Davis, couples therapist and author of *The Sex-Starved Marriage***

7 Watch out for harsh comments— they hit harder than you think.

"When you're tired or frustrated, it's easy to slip into being critical of your partner. But remember, negative expressions and comments and behaviors hold much more weight than positive interactions. Make sure that for every one negative interaction, you have five positive interactions to counteract it—a touch, a laugh, a kiss, an act of love, a compliment."

—Scott Haltzman, M.D., Psychiatrist and author of
The Secrets of Happily Married Men

8 Don't knock it till you've tried it… twice.

"Try being adventurous in bed. Even if you don't like something, give it at least two chances before you give up on it—it may grow on you!"

—Laura Berman, Ph. D.

9 Be the first to offer the olive branch.

"Often when there's a problem, each person will wait for the other to take the initiative to work things out. But the longer you wait, the more frustrated you both get and the worse you feel. Try making the first move to break a stalemate. It doesn't mean that you're giving in. You're getting the ball rolling, rather than being stuck."

—Norman Epstein, Ph.D., marriage researcher
and family therapist at the University of Maryland

10 How to be a couple and still be free.

Give the love you want to get. "Put out lots of love and appreciation and doing your share, and you're much more likely to get it back. Put out demands and complaining, and you'll get that back too."

—Tina B. Tessina, Ph.D., couples therapist and author
of *How to Be a Couple and Still Be Free*

11 Fight for your love.

"I've never seen a decent marriage where there wasn't a lot of conflict. Conflict is always the result of uniqueness, the differences between two people rubbing up against each other. Lots of people try to shut themselves down in order to avoid conflict, but any two people living full and vibrant lives are going to clash at some point. If you manage it carefully and thoughtfully, conflict can actually give your marriage a shot of energy. You can have a broader, fuller, more interesting relationship."

—Neil Clark Warren, Ph.D.

12 Sex matters; couple time matters even more.

"Often couples focus on scheduling sex and working very hard on their sex life, and they don't get anywhere. But when they focus instead on spending time together—going to the movies, working on a project together—then often a better sex life will grow out of that."

—Ian Kerner, Ph.D., sex therapist and author
of *She Comes First* and *He Comes Next*

13 Don't get caught up in right or wrong.

"It's easy to fall into a power struggle of who's right and who's wrong, but that prevents you from actually solving the real problem. You're not going to be punished for being wrong, so don't worry about who's right—work together to solve the problem."

—Tina B. Tessina, Ph.D.

14 Feed your relationship.

"People often make their own needs a first priority, and then say they can't get what they want out of the relationship. It's like going to your garden and saying, 'Feed me,' and you haven't put any plants in the ground. Make your relationship your first priority. Maybe your relationship needs more time, more vacation. Maybe you need to put in more positive statements or more moments of connection. Become partners in taking care of this relationship. If you get couples engaged in a mutual project, which is their relationship, no matter what they come up with, it's good. It's the working together that does it."

—Harville Hendrix, Ph.D., founder/director
of Imago Relationship International and author
of *Getting the Love You Want*

15 Words are like food—nurture each other with good ones.

"Say things such as 'I love you,' 'I really appreciate that,' 'I'd love to hear your thoughts about…you name it.' And use more empathetic words, like, 'It seems like you're struggling with this.' You'll communicate genuineness and respect, and make your partner feel loved."

—Alan Hovestadt, Ed.D., president of the American
Association for Marriage and Family Therapy

16 Never mind equality; focus on fairness.

"Everything doesn't have to be 50/50. Having a sense that each person is doing what's fair—even if it's not always equal—is what really makes a happy marriage. That applies not just to housework, but to the relationship itself."

—Barbara Dafoe Whitehead, Ph.D., codirector of the National
Marriage Project at Rutgers University

17 Remember that you were partners before you were parents.

"If you have children, don't forget about your own connection and relationship and put everything into the children. Make relating to each other one-on-one—not just as parents, but as lovers a priority."

—Lou Paget, sex educator and
author of *The Great Lover Playbook*

18 Learn how to communicate without saying a word.

"We are profoundly affected by touch, both physically and emotionally. Happy couples touch each other frequently. A caring touch offers a simple acknowledgment of your partner, saying, 'Way to go' or 'I know that was difficult for you,' without words."

—Alan Hovestadt, Ed.D.

19 Pay back your partner using his or her currency.

"Each of us wants our mate to pay us back for our contributions, to give us positive reinforcement. But this payment needs to be in currency that we recognize. A wife may say, 'The way I show I care is that I make his bed every day,' but if he doesn't even notice that, it's ineffective. Get to know what your partner is looking for and make sure you speak his language."

—Scott Haltzman, M.D.

20 Draw on your successes as a couple.

"One way to bring out the best in a relationship is to focus on what you've done right in the past. For example, if you're trying to break a habit of bickering a lot, think back to a time when you were bickering but ended it differently, with humor or by dropping it or in some other way. Every couple has a big hat of experiences when they handled things well, and it's important to draw on this catalog of successes. Rather than just focusing on the times when things ended negatively."

—David Wexler, Ph.D.

21 Dream a big dream for your relationship.

"When two people dream a great dream for their marriage, they typically see their relationship take a dramatic step in the direction of that dream. Start dreaming big—envision where you want your lives and your relationship to be in 10 years. Then let yourself be inspired by these dreams to make whatever changes are necessary to live these dreams out."

—Neil Clark Warren, Ph.D.

22 See things through each other's eyes.

"A lot of conflict comes from always putting a negative spin on what your partner does. Instead of telling yourself that your partner is being thoughtless or irritating, try to think about it from the other person's point of view—ask yourself, What is going on inside that would make him or her act that way? The behavior might still be a problem, but being aware of your partner's intention can change how you view the problem, and make it easier to communicate about it."

— David Wexler, Ph.D.

23 Cultivate trust to grow intimacy.

"Trust issues are like sparks in a dry forest—you want to deal with them as fast as you can, whether it's something major, like an affair, or something smaller, like a wife sharing intimate things about her marriage with her best friend. You have to remove the masons for lack of trust so that you can both feel safe sharing yourselves deeply."

—Neil Clark Warren, Ph.D.

24 Never lose sight of the romance.

It's important to keep setting aside time for romance. It doesn't always mean that you have to go out for dinner or take a trip. Be imaginative. In fact, I think it's better to have little romantic episodes more often than to have one romantic blowout a year. You want this romantic feeling to be threaded through all your days, so it becomes part of the lifeblood of the marriage."

—Barbara Dafoe Whitehead, Ph.D.

How to Tell Your Potential Lover about Your Chronic STD

Dr. Jeff Gardere

D ating, getting to know someone intimately, or discovering a potential life partner can be exciting and oh so fun! But what most folks forget is that along with reaching out and touching another human being comes an awful lot of responsibility.

So often you hear people talk about protecting themselves when it comes to the dating game. Women will complain that they are afraid of early physical intimacy because they want to "protect" their hearts. Men will brag about how they are double bagging it (two condoms) because they want to "protect" their penises!

But the sad fact of the matter is that while everyone is seeking to "protect" themselves in one way or another, not enough thought is given to being responsible for the well being and protection of those we come in contact with sexually, especially when it comes to physical illness; sexually transmitted diseases (STD's).

The Gifts That Keep on Giving... Bad News

Now I know you're probably thinking, "Oh no Dr. Jeff, please, not another lesson on dating and the dangers of disease!" Besides, a quick visit to the old Doc and some antibiotics will fix the problem lickety-split, right?

Wrong. I'm not talking about the old garden variety STD's like chlamydia, syphilis, and gonorrhea, which are curable through medicine (though some strains of STD's now resist antibiotics). No, I'm discussing the newfangled, modern, chronic STD's that are for the most part incurable, can be dangerous, and depending on the disease, even terminal!

That's right; these are the gifts that keep on giving. I'm talking about genital herpes, genital warts, the variations of hepatitis (A, which is transmitted by fecal matter; B, which is passed through sex; and C, which is transmitted less through sex and more through infected blood). And HIV.

Both hepatitis and of course HIV can cause severe illness and even death. Though these STD's can be managed and placed into remission through medical treatment and healthy living, they always remain and live in their human host.

So that's why we have to go there! That's why we must change our mindset in the dating game from just protecting our own selves from the dangers of STD's, to also being responsible enough to protect our potential lovers from our chronic and transmittable diseases.

The Mental Torment of Unsafe Sex Practices

I cannot tell you how many of my patients have fallen into deep clinical depressions after having been infected with an incurable STD, sometimes on the first sexual contact! On the flip side, I have also worked with patients who are wracked by guilt and depression because they accidentally but carelessly infected a lover (who had no idea that sexual disease was present) through unsafe sex practices.

I am sure that there are sill some disbelievers amongst you who may think that I am exaggerating the potential danger of contracting these STD's. The Center for Disease Control has reported 793,026 cases of AIDS in the US as of June 2001. According to a recent *Newsweek* magazine, over 3 million Americans are infected with Hepatitis C. Results of a recent nationally representative study show 45 million people infected with herpes nationwide. And according to the American Social Health Association, 20 million Americans have human papilloma virus, better know as genital warts.

So there is definitely a more than average profitability that if you are reading this article, you may meet or already be dating someone with one of these chronic diseases, especially herpes or warts, and you might not even know it!

Most STD's Transfer by Accident, Not Intentionally

Now this is not to say that people who have chronic STD's are dangers to society who are looking to infect their lovers. Like Anne Frank, I believe that all people are basically good in nature. I can tell you from my clinical experience that I have never had one patient intentionally pass on an STD. It has always been due to accidental and careless exposure. This is especially true to people who are carriers of herpes or warts.

What STD's Are Like

Unlike HIV and hepatitis, which can be catastrophic to the emotional and physical system, herpes and warts are initially considered to be nothing more than major inconveniences to living. After some time of adjustment they then become very minor to human and sexual functioning. Here's why:

The initial herpes outbreak (the cluster of sores on the genitalia) is usually very painful, and scary as hell. Warts, though not usually painful, can be very unsightly on the genitalia. Both viruses can also cause secondary but treatable problems such as itching and discharge in women.

The psychological effect to anyone with these viruses can be quite upsetting. But after some time, (it varies from individual to individual) the infected person comes to several realizations; it is not a terminal disease, it can be managed, and there can be extremely long periods of time without re-occurrence, especially when a healthy and less stressful lifestyle is adopted.

Add to the mix, effective anti-viral medications that suppress many future herpes outbreaks and the effectiveness of laser surgery to removes warts, and voila, having these STD's becomes part of day-to-day functioning, normally forgotten, especially when in remission.

It's Easy to Get Careless With the Manageable STD's

But therein lies the problem. Because these STD's are so easily managed medically and do not carry the stigma of HIV for example, it is easy to become much more complacent and therefore more careless in transmitting them to others.

Then there are folks who are in remission from herpes or warts and therefore feel no reason to have to reveal their secret until absolutely necessary—or sometimes not at all. Many of them take anti-virals for herpes and are fooled into thinking they are virus free when symptoms are not present.

The truth is that even without obvious symptoms, or even while on medications, you could still be shedding the virus and transmitting the disease. The same thing goes for warts. Just because you do not see warts on your genitalia, it may not mean that you are symptom free. They can be sub-clinical or not easily visible to the naked eye, but still present and infectious. What's more, with females, the herpes lesions or warts can be inside the vagina and not visible unless there is a pelvic examination and or a biopsy.

Even Invisible STD's are Contagious

All of this to say, when it comes to carrying an STD—any STD—and having sex, you can never be totally sure that you are 100 percent safe from passing it on to a lover, no matter how symptom free you think you are. That's why it is essential to be truthful with a partner or potential lover at some point about your condition. Otherwise, you risk unwittingly infecting them, disrupting their lives and you have to live with that guilt for the rest of your life!

So let's get to the heart of the matter as to when and how you should discuss your STD in a relationship with someone you like, love or lust!

Come to Terms with Your Own STD

First and foremost, you must come to terms with your having a chronic STD. Unless you work through it, your self-esteem will be destroyed and you will never be comfortable discussing it with anyone you are attracted to or with whom you are involved. And if you can't deal with it on your own, then get some professional help. Short-term counseling can be very helpful. With my patients who are struggling with this, usually two to three sessions provide enough time and intervention for a healthy adjustment.

The most important realization you must make—whether in therapy, on your own, or even through an informal support group of friends with the same problem—is that *you are not the disease* and *the disease does not define you*. The disease is a small part of you that *can* be managed. Of course for HIV and hepatitis, this psychological and spiritual process takes more time, but can be achieved with hard work.

Timing

The issue of when to tell is strictly a personal choice. But any physician will advise that you should inform your partner of your medical condition before any intimate or sexual contact outside of kissing. The exception is HIV: If there are bleeding gums or sores in the mouth, than you should discuss your status even before any deep kissing.

Also, as a psychologist who has treated many people for issues of living with STD's, it is my opinion that, if you are in the dating game, it is not necessary to share your medical status until there is a conscious decision to take the relationship from an acquaintance or superficial friendship to a more serious track that may lead to emotional and or physical intimacy. I have had patients, however, due to the seriousness of having HIV or hepatitis, for example, who will make their medical status known to friends and potential lovers right away, not just for health reasons, but to establish immediately who is willing to support and walk the long road of survival with them.

How to Talk About It

Again, professional interventions are very helpful in explaining your medical status to a love interest. Many of my patients with chronic STD's have invited their potential partners to a therapy session to discuss the issues and that has worked fabulously. All feelings, anxieties and fears are discussed in a therapeutic manner. Others will arrange for the same forum with a family physician to discuss all the implications, treatment and safe sex options.

If you'd rather keep the shrinks out of it and handle it on your own, I would suggest a quiet place where you can have privacy. The place should be conducive to dialogue, questions, and lots of talking. Maybe a long walk in the park, at the beach, or sitting on a park bench can be the right setting for creating a tranquil environment where thoughtful decisions can be made.

"I know many of you are probably thinking, 'Let my potential lover know about my STD before our first sexual encounter?! Be real, Dr. Jeff, are you trying to destroy my love life?!'"

Provide as much clinical and printed information as you can about the STD. After presenting your information, then just listen as much as possible. Don't try to strong-arm a decision or get resolve in one meeting. Instead, have a series of talks about the matter at different times. Give them time to explore their feelings, concerns and even fears.

Honesty is the Best Policy

I know many of you are probably thinking, "Let my potential lover know about my STD before our first sexual encounter?! Be real, Dr. Jeff, are you trying to destroy my love life?!"

Actually, by taking my advice, I am going to help you make it better! There are many more benefits than drawbacks to being honest about your STD with someone with whom you really want to pursue a relationship. The reality is that anyone who walks away from you after you tell them about your STD would not have worked out anyway. They would not have the emotional strength to support and engage with you in a healthy physical and sexual relationship. But for those souls who are

willing to stay and work it out, you can make decisions together about dealing with the STD and growing the relationship together. That partner will also be very appreciative that they were given full disclosure and the opportunity to participate equally in safeguarding themselves as much as possible from disease.

Again, from the many cases I have worked with in my practice, I can assure you that the difference between getting a chronic STD from a partner who you did not know had it versus the one who explained the possible risks from the beginning is quite different and much more positive.

The Magical Commitment Honesty Can Bring

In a strange but very beautiful and romantic way, sharing this intimate information with your potential lover early in the relationship puts you both on the fast track to communication, honesty, responsibility for one another and even commitment. Think about it; no one should be willing to expose themselves to the possibility of contracting a chronic STD from a partner unless they are committed and willing to make a go at sharing their life with that individual. Then, magically the STD is no longer an issue in the relationship.

The bottom line is living with a chronic STD need not be a physical and emotional burden to any romance. If you handle it honestly and positively at the beginning of a potential romance, it will soon become insignificant. Instead you will have more time and energy for developing a healthy and loving relationship together.

Hey baby, the truth shall set you free!

DR. JEFF GARDERE is a clinical psychologist and author of the book, *Smart Parenting for African Americans*. He appears frequently on TV news and talk shows as well as radio. He can be reached at *myprofessionaladvice.com.*

The Viagra Dialogues

This drug can put the bloom back in sex—but it can also cause relationship problems. Hear what real-life couples have to say about "vitamin V."

DEBORAH PIKE OLSEN

It's 16 years later, but Gary Haub and his wife, Carolyn Acton, still remember how devastating it was when he couldn't make love to her. "I didn't feel like touching her," Gary, now 53, recalls. "I felt like less than a man."

Gary and Carolyn, who live in Irving, Texas, drew apart. "When I hugged Gary, I'd worry that he'd think I wanted more, so I stopped being affectionate," says Carolyn, also 53. Like many women, she blamed herself. "I had put on weight with each of our three children, so I feared Gary no longer found me attractive," adds Carolyn. "Because I wasn't working, I was afraid I was boring." Carolyn became depressed, then angry: "I remember thinking, I'm still the same woman you married."

Finally Gary saw a urologist, who diagnosed erectile dysfunction (ED), a condition caused by aging as well as by certain medical problems. Penile injections helped, but were uncomfortable. Then, in 1998, Viagra appeared. Gary and Carolyn were so pleased with the pill, he has taken it ever since: "I don't know if we'd still be married if Viagra hadn't come along," Gary says bluntly.

Hailed as "vitamin V," Viagra created a stir when it was introduced. Since then, it's helped to repair countless marriages. But many men also use it recreationally—even as an aphrodisiac. "Viagra has evolved into more of a social drug," says Martin Resnick, M.D., chairman of the department of urology at Case Western Reserve University School of Medicine, in Cleveland. "It's being targeted toward men who simply want to perform better." In early TV commercials, the long-married, 70-something former senator Bob Dole extolled the virtues of Viagra. Now virile young athletes do the endorsements. All this makes some wives worry that Viagra will prompt their husbands to cheat—or expect sex on demand. Yet other women are urging the men in their lives to try it.

With two similar drugs (see "Viagra Wannabes") poised to debut this year, Viagra and the hotly debated issues surrounding it are bound to make news again in a major way.

Bring on the Viagra!

At a recent all-girls lunch in Dallas, Viagra was the prime topic of conversation. One woman in her 50s confided that the drug had saved her ten-year marriage. "Sex was a strong part of our relationship," she said. So when her husband could no longer perform, she became concerned: "We needed to connect physically as well as emotionally." And she worried about the impact ED was having on her husband's ego. Finally about a year ago, he tried Viagra, and she declared at the lunch, "I'm very appreciative!"

Women have even started to take the initiative when it comes to Viagra, asking their husband's doctor for a prescription. Domeena Renshaw, M.D., director of the Sexual Dysfunction Clinic at Loyola University in Chicago, recalls a woman in her 60s asking what the drug tasted like—because she wanted to slip a tablet into her husband's hot chocolate!

On Viagra, "he thinks he's Tarzan," says one wife, "but I'm not sure I'm Jane."

Men can be secretive as well. One woman tells of finding a packet of Viagra tucked in her husband's underwear drawer, with one pill missing. When she asked him about it, he confessed he had used it recently but wanted his wife to think his erection had been "natural."

Not Tonight, Dear

Of course, some women are less than thrilled with Viagra. Typically, when a man obtains a prescription, he hasn't been intimate with his wife for at least 18 months. During that time, the dynamics of their relationship may have changed for all sorts of reasons. If a woman is postmenopausal, intercourse may be painful. If her husband hasn't shown affection in years she could have adapted to their more platonic relationship. Or perhaps she craved affection, and when her husband didn't respond, she became resentful or insecure. Suddenly,

In the Works: Viagra Wanna-Bes

Two Viagra-like drugs—Cialis and Levitra—are scheduled to debut this year, pending FDA approval. There is obviously a market: Erectile dysfunction affects an estimated 20 million to 30 million men in the United States. Like Viagra, the new drugs increase blood flow to the penis, triggering an erection in 30 minutes to an hour—or less. But the makers of Cialis and Levitra maintain that their drugs will allow men to have erections over longer periods of time than Viagra does. All three medications can trigger side effects, which may include headaches, facial flush, upset stomach, nasal congestion, or a bluish tinge to the vision. And all are off-limits to men who take a nitrate medicine for heart disease.

Viagra has also been prescribed for women with arousal problems, but it is not approved by the FDA for this purpose—which means no one knows for sure if it's safe and effective. But a new topical medicine for women, called Alista, is in the pipeline. It's designed to increase blood flow to the genital area.

Viagra enters the bedroom—and her middle-aged husband starts acting like a young stud. If he doesn't engage in foreplay, "a woman may feel she's being treated like a receptacle," says Jean Koehler, Ph.D., president of the American Association of Sex Educators, Counselors, and Therapists. And she may fear that if she doesn't respond, her husband will leave her. Dr. Renshaw tells of a woman who called her shortly after Viagra became available. "She said, 'We stopped having sex 20 years ago, and he just came home with Viagra.

I'm 65, and I'm not interested in intercourse. But I have to say yes: If he doesn't do it with me, he'll do if with someone else.'"

Even couples who enjoy lovemaking, Viagra-style, may disagree on how much is enough. When Alfred Pariser, a 63-year-old consultant in Rancho Mirage, California, became impotent after prostate cancer surgery seven years ago, he participated in a study of Viagra and has been taking it ever since. "I felt awful about not being able to have sex with my wife," he says. "Intercourse is one of the great parts of marriage."

His wife, Cheryl, agrees—to a point. "Thank God there's Viagra," she sighs. "Alfred would go nuts if he couldn't have an erection." Still, she says, there are times when "he wants sex more than I do. He thinks he's Tarzan, but I'm not sure I'm Jane."

A Cautionary Tale

Experts insist that Viagra by itself can't solve underlying problems in a relationship. "Sex is about more than erections," says psychologist Eileen Palace, Ph.D., director of the Center for Sexual Health in New Orleans. "Viagra doesn't address the way couples feel about each other." And if a man isn't attracted to his partner, he still may not be able to get an erection with Viagra.

Even if the sparks are flying, Viagra can interfere with spontaneity: The drug must be taken 30 minutes to an hour before intercourse. What's more it doesn't come cheap: Viagra costs about $10 per tablet. "Sometimes I'll take a pill, and Cheryl will change her mind about sex," says Alfred Pariser. "Or we'll fall asleep."

Still, when used properly, Viagra can be liberating. For the Parisers, the drug has been a gift. Says Alfred: "Viagra helped us recapture the intimacy we'd lost."

Save Your Relationship

A breakthrough therapy to find love again

Couples therapy is growing in popularity, but few approaches have proven reliably beneficial. Emotionally Focused Couples Therapy, or EFT, is one that has. This groundbreaking theory of adult love is highly successful, and there is plenty of research to back it up. Here, EFT expert **Susan Johnson,** Ed.D., maps out the nine-step process for rekindling love.

It was Mitchell Irving's affair that finally led him and his wife, Karen, to my office for couples counseling. But the betrayal was merely a symptom of a deeper problem in their 19-year marriage. "He felt like he wasn't getting his emotional needs met at home," says Karen, 45, a mystery-novel writer in Ottawa, Canada. "Maybe that's because he was never here! He was a complete workaholic and didn't come home until midnight every night—for years." When Karen told Mitchell she wanted to spend more time together, he would pull out his calendar and say, "How's lunch next Thursday?" "It would be funny if it weren't so sad," Karen says. "I felt neglected and abandoned, and over time, I withdrew emotionally. Between his not being there in person and my not being there in spirit, we just stopped being able to get close."

The Irvings were perfect candidates for EFT, a short-term approach to marital counseling that seeks to re-create a sense of connection between partners. Unlike the traditional cognitive-behavioral approach, which focuses predominantly on teaching communication skills, EFT hinges on getting partners to recognize that they're both emotionally dependent upon the other for love, comfort, support and protection, much like a child depends on a parent. In my sessions with couples, we get straight to the heart of the matter: the need for emotional security in the relationship. Because without that security, asking troubled couples to trust and confide in each other is like asking people who are standing at the edge of a cliff and staring down a 2,000-foot drop to use their skills of listening and empathy—they can't, because they're too busy feeling afraid.

While a doctoral student at York University in Toronto, I began working with British psychologist Les Greenberg, Ph.D., in designing EFT based on attachment theory, which was developed 50 years ago by psychiatrist John Bowlby. Through his worldwide observations, Bowlby concluded that everyone has an innate yearning for trust and security, or attachment. Children need to feel attached to a parent; adults need to feel attached to another adult, usually a romantic partner. And when those we're attached to can't respond to our needs—maybe one partner is emotionally unavailable—we become anxious and fearful or numb and distant, which sets up dangerous patterns of interaction.

The Irvings' situation is a case in point. Their toxic behavioral pattern, one of the most common, involves a wife who criticizes and becomes contemptuous toward her husband, while he distances himself and stonewalls his wife. "I would tell Mitchell, 'I need you to be around more,' and I meant, 'I miss you,'" Karen explains. "But because of the irritation in my voice, he would hear, 'I am disappointed in you,' and he'd stay away."

(Step 1)
Mary: He doesn't care about anything but work. He has a love affair with his computer. I've had enough.
Harry: You are so difficult. I try to talk to you and all I get is how I can never do anything right.

Patterns like this, which may eventually superimpose themselves onto every element of the relationship, often create a slippery slope to divorce. Recent research by relationship guru John Gottman, Ph.D., author of The Seven Principles for Making Marriage Work, confirms that it's often emotional distance—not conflict—that determines whether a relationship will flourish or begin to disintegrate. After all, every couple fights, but as long as partners can connect emotionally, their relationship should remain healthy. This same notion was also recently supported by Sandra Murray, Ph.D., a psychology professor at the University at Buffalo, State University of New York. Murray's study, just published in the Journal of Personality and Social Psychology, found that partners who feel well-regarded by their mates better handle the occasional hurts that occur in their relationships. So rather than pulling away or lashing out in defense, a confident partner instead draws the offending mate closer to protect the relationship's solidity.

The goal of EFT, therefore, is to help partners feel securely connected by fostering feelings of safety, accessibility and responsiveness. Once in this safe haven, partners are more capable of handling difficult feelings. They more easily process information, deal with ambiguity and see the other's perspective. They also send clearer messages and are better at collaborative problem solving and being assertive. In truth, most distressed couples already have good communication skills—they get along very nicely with other loved ones and co-workers—they just can't apply those skills in their relationship. But if they have a solid emotional connection, if they feel loved and soothed, they'll naturally use the skills they already possess.

Although it's easy for some to dismiss the idea of emotional dependence as antiquated—particularly for women in this post-feminist era—there's no arguing with EFT's success rates. Between 70 and 75 percent of couples report being happy with each other again after undergoing EFT, compared with only 35 percent among those who try cognitive-behavioral counseling. The number of people who experience "significant improvement" is above 90 percent. The dropout rate? Negligible.

(Step 2)
Harry: The more I move away, the madder she gets.
Mary: Right. I feel you've gone off, like, to another land, so yes, I bang on the door louder and louder, trying to get your attention.

So how does EFT go about rebuilding intimacy? It's a nine-step treatment that can take anywhere from 8 to 20 sessions (30, in very complex cases). The first four steps involve helping partners recognize that the problem is not their individual personalities per se, but the negative cycle of communication in which they're stuck. In the next three steps, the therapist works with couples to promote sharing, soothing and bonding, before helping the couple incorporate those acts into everyday life in the last two steps. This final process of showing couples how to keep their connection alive can help prevent relapse.

To better understand how EFT works, it's instructive to see it in action. Take the story of Mary and Harry, married seven years, with one child. Both are managers by profession and very competent, so when they showed up at my office they expressed that they were puzzled by their inability to "manage" their marriage. They said they had lost a sense of intimacy and were no longer making love. In addition, Mary had discovered what she described as "very friendly" e-mails to her husband from a female colleague of his. Although Harry wasn't having an affair—yet—Mary was distraught at the thought of her husband sharing more with this woman than he was with her. Both spouses were thinking about splitting up. But the key snippets of conversations, taken from our sessions together, demonstrate how EFT helped restore their connection.

Step 1. Partners lay their problems out on the table

Describing a recent fight in detail often helps partners begin to identify core problems. Most couples fight about pragmatic issues—doing laundry or paying bills, for instance—but it's the emotional needs underlying these tiffs that need attention. The following conversation between Mary and Harry illustrates their negative pattern of communication as the two argue about Harry's typical reaction to his wife's frequent mood swings: As she complains and criticizes, he gets defensive and withdraws.

Mary: He doesn't care about anything but work. He has a love affair with his computer. I've had enough. I don't even know who he is anymore. [*To Harry*] You never reach for me! Am I supposed to do all the work in this relationship?

Harry: You are so difficult. I try to talk to you, and all I get is how I can never do anything right. It's always the same: You're angry, and you lecture me a thousand times a day, so I guess I do go downstairs to my computer. I get a bit of peace that way.

Step 2. Partners recognize the cycle that's keeping them emotionally distant and try to identify the needs and fears fueling that cycle

As couples more carefully explore the underlying source of their arguments, they begin to realize that the enemy is not the partner but the unhealthy behaviors in their relationship. In this step, I encourage couples to use non-evaluative language to uncover any fears they might have—of rejection, say, or failure—which are driving the relationship dynamic. In the following exchange, note how Harry and Mary are beginning to explore each other's motivations.

Harry [*to me*]: Yes, I do turn away from her, I guess. I try to move away from the message that I'm a big disappointment—that's what I hear—and the more I move away, the madder she gets. Maybe she feels like she is losing me.

Mary: Right. I feel you've gone off, like, to another land. So yes, I bang on the door louder and louder, trying to get your attention, trying to tell you we need to do something.

Step 3. Partners articulate the emotions behind their behavior

At this point, my role is to help both partners understand and clearly explain what's driving their behaviors, while ensuring that the other is also gaining an accurate understanding. Below, Mary realizes that she's not really angry with Harry but frantic to gain his affection. Harry realizes that he withdraws not because he doesn't want to be with Mary but because he doesn't want to be criticized or face his fear that their marriage is in danger.

Mary: I start to feel really desperate. That's what you don't hear. If I can't get you to respond, well...[*she throws up her hands in a show of defeat*].

Harry: I shut down just to get away from the message that I am so disappointing for you. I can't let it in; it's upsetting. In a way, it's terrifying, so I move away and hope you will calm down.

Step 4. Partners realize they're both hurting and that neither is to blame

As the couple begins to see the negative dynamic as the source of their problems, they become more aware of their own needs for attachment, as well as those of their partner. Armed with empathy, partners can now approach their problems with a less combative mind-set. In the following exchange, Mary and Harry begin to see the cycle as a common enemy and discover new hope for the future.

Mary: The more desperate I get, the more I push; and the more scared you get, the more you shut down.

Harry: [*Nods and smiles*] That's it.

Mary: This thing we're doing, it's got us by the throat.

Harry: Maybe it's that we both get scared. I never knew you were so scared of losing me. I never knew you needed me that much.

Mary: Maybe we can step out of this, if we try it together.

(Step 6)
Harry: I never saw how small you felt. I guess you were screaming for me when I saw you screaming at me.
Mary: I didn't think I was getting through to you. I feel awful when you tell me that you were hurting so much that you'd freeze up inside.

Step 5. Partners identify and admit their emotional hurts and fears

At this stage of EFT, my role becomes even more integral in the couple's progress. Their honesty makes them feel increasingly vulnerable, and my job is to encourage and support them and to help them remain responsive to each other. In this exchange, Harry and Mary risk expressing their deepest feelings.

Harry: I don't know how to tell you how deep the pit is that I go into when I hear that I have failed, that I can't make it with you. I freeze. I shut down.

Mary: I never saw that you were hurting. I guess I saw you as calm and in control, almost indifferent, like you didn't need me at all, and that is the loneliest feeling in the world. There is no "us." I am alone, small. I feel like a fool.

Step 6. Partners begin to acknowledge and accept the others feeling and their own new responses to those feelings

After years of believing a partner's behavior indicates one thing, it's difficult to accept that it actually means another. In step six, couples learn to trust these newly revealed motivations and, in turn, experience new reactions to these motivations. Note how Harry and Mary now listen to each other and exhibit mutual compassion.

Harry: I never saw how small you felt. I guess you were screaming *for* me when I saw you screaming *at* me. I don't want you to feel small and alone.

Try Eft At Home

If you and your partner have felt alone, alienated and unable to soothe and support each other for a period of months, you might consider trying Emotionally Focused Couples Therapy on your own. Begin by thinking of a recent argument you've had with your partner and try to detect a pattern of behavior governing it. Don't look to assign blame; just examine the steps in your relationship dance and how those steps cue you and your partner to keep circling around in distress.

Now, allow yourself to be vulnerable for a moment and recognize the fears that might be driving those patterns, such as the fear of being rejected, of being a failure, of being unlovable or abandoned. If you've uncovered any anxieties, try to express them to your partner and ask him or her to reciprocate.

Once you've both shared your fears, rephrase them in terms of what you need from your partner emotionally. If, for instance, you said, "I'm afraid that when you don't return my calls at work it's because you think I'm bugging you, like I'm a nagging wife," you might rephrase that worry and instead say, "I need you to call me back when I leave messages at your office. That shows me that you love me and care about what I have to say." Work together with your partner to incorporate any changes that might help bring you closer in your daily lives.

Trying EFT on your own might be enough to heal your relationship, but you may also find that a professional can help in providing necessary insight. To find an EFT-trained therapist in your area, e-mail the Ottawa Couple & Family Institute at ofci@magma.ca, or contact the American Association of Marriage and Family Therapy by calling (703) 838-9808, or going to www.aamft.org.

CelebrityCounsel

Actors Delta Burke and Gerald "Mac" McRaney were devastated by Delta's depression. Here, they share how couples therapy strengthened their marriage.

Delta Burke

How did depression play into your relationship? When I met Mac we were swept up in our romance, so he didn't know it was anything more than the blues. When I was officially diagnosed, Mac tried to learn along with me what needed to be done. **What happened as you progressed?** Each year I got a little bit better, but Mac was super protective. As I got stronger, it was an adjustment to our relationship. Mac didn't know when he should let me handle things. **How did you confront this problem?** Mac came to therapy with me. The first time, I didn't realize how angry I was. At one point, I started screaming, "I hate you!" He walked out, and I thought. 'There goes my marriage.' But then he came back. **How did couples therapy help?** When we weren't communicating right, Mac's booming voice scared me; I would shut down. The therapist worked with us on recognizing our patterns, it was hard, but it helped us communicate better. **How is your relationship today?** Now we're safe with each other. Everybody goes through scary ups and downs in a relationship. To know that we're really there for each other is wonderful.

Gerald "Mac" McRaney

How did Delta's depression affect you? You know how everybody thinks the entire universe spins around them? At least, I do. Naturally I assumed that I'd done something to disappoint her, that I caused it. **What was your response to her isolation?** I got really protective of her. She was frightened of the press, so I wouldn't let anyone remotely connected to the press near her. **Did this affect you emotionally?** Yes, it got me down because I felt so badly for her, I recall getting frustrated. **Did you ever consider giving up?** No. **You simply loved her too much?** Yup. **Was couples counseling helpful?** Very. I learned that you need a break from time to time; you've got to recharge your batteries. Otherwise you're no good to anybody. **What made you realize this?** The constant reassurance that there was nothing I could do to fix the problem. All I could do was be her husband. **So. you're happy today?** Oh, my God, yes. Just the other night I had to let her know how important she is to me and how glad I am that I'm sharing life with her. **She's a lucky lady.** I'm a terribly lucky man.

Mary: I didn't think I was getting through to you. I feel awful when you tell me that you'd freeze up inside. I guess I was having an impact. I was trying to get you to let me in.

Step 7. Partners are drawn together through the expression of their emotional needs

At this stage, partners are willingly available to each other, so when talking about their vulnerabilities, they're able to assure each other and soothe hurt feelings. This becomes the most emotional part of the therapeutic process as couples like Harry and Mary create a new, bonding cycle that begins to replace the old, destructive one.

Harry: I want you to give me a chance to learn how to be close to you. I can't deal with being labeled a failure. I want to let you in—I want to be close—but I need to feel safe, like you are going to give me the benefit of the doubt.

Mary: It's scary to feel lonely when you turn away. I need reassurance. If I tell you "I need some holding, some 'us' time," I want to know that you'll be there. I want to feel safe again, [In response, Harry holds her tightly.]

Step 8. Partners create new solutions to their problems

In step eight, partners share the new story of their relationship and how hard they worked to rewrite it together. Processing this experience and viewing their history in a different light allows couples to find newer, healthier ways of approaching pragmatic problems. Here we see Harry—who once ran and hid from the relationship—actively create more opportunities to bond with Mary.

Harry: We can have time together in the evening, after the kids are in bed. Let's make coffee and sit together, and if you trust me a little, I'll make us a schedule for nights out. It makes me feel good to know you need time with me.

Step 9. Partners consolidate their new positions and cycles of behavior

After months of work, it's vital that the couple continues to remember what first got them off track and how they found their way back. Without reassessing this process, maintaining this new cycle will lose importance and ultimately lead to a relapse. As Harry and Mary reflect on their therapy experience, both clearly see how they first became distressed and what they did to repair the relationship.

Harry: It was when I got promoted that it all started. I needed to prove myself to everybody. I did get immersed in work, but now when I hear that tone in your voice I remember how much you need me, and I want to reassure you: I am here, Mary. I know we can do this now. We're learning to trust each other again. It's like we are finding the "us" we had when we got married. We still fight sometimes, but these close times make all the difference.

For the right people, EFT can work magic. In fewer than four months, it brought Karen and Mitchell Irving back from the brink of divorce. "We discovered that our marriage was built on these ludicrous underlying assumptions," Karen says now. "Mitchell had this sense of entitlement and believed I should be there for him no matter what. I, coming from a dysfunctional family, believed I wasn't worthy of more consideration than that. When we realized how off our perceptions were, we giggled about it."

More important than the levity these revelations brought were the changes that grew out of them. Mitchell cut back on his office hours and is enjoying spending more time with Karen. And they don't feel childish, as they had before, when asking each other for "close time." "We've learned not to sacrifice intimacy for independence," Karen concludes. "One of the greatest joys of marriage is discovering how much we need each other."

Sadly, for some couples it may be too late. EFT is not designed for people who have tried unsuccessfully to reconnect for so long that they've already mourned the lost relationship and become completely detached. It's also not appropriate for abusive relationships. But if, despite your obstacles, you still desire to make your relationship work, I encourage you to see an EFT-trained therapist.

Learn More About It

The Seven Principles for Making Marriage Work John Gottman, Ph.D. (Three Rivers Press, 2000)

Creating Connection: The Practice of Emotionally Focused Marital Therapy Susan M. Johnson, Ed.D. (Routledge, 1996)

www.emotionfocusedtherapy.org

www.ocfi.ca

SUSAN JOHNSON, Ed.D., is the main proponent of Emotionally Focused Couples Therapy and a licensed clinical psychologist, professor of psychology at the University of Ottawa in Canada, visiting professor at Alliant University in San Diego and director of the Ottawa Couple & Family Institute.

AVIVA PATZ is a freelance writer in Upper Montclair, New Jersey, and a former editor at *Psychology Today*.

Be a Better Couple

There's a new approach to helping you get closer. We give it a try to see how well it works.

DOROTHY FOLTZ-GRAY

Just weeks ago, I considered marriage education a faintly embarrassing process. Why on Earth, when my husband, Dan, and I were perfectly happy, would we sign up for what would surely make us squirm? Yet here we are, about to dive into the murky depths of our relationship in a take home marriage-education course.

Sure, Dan and I like each other. And yes, we've gotten much of the way through raising two boys without jabbing pencils in each other's eyes. But there's this one fight, we've been having, oh, for decades. The gist: I mourn our departure from Chicago, where, as far as I can tell, everything happens. For more than 20 years we've lived in Knoxville, Tennessee, where—as Dan would tell you—the fishing is grand and life is simple.

Our conversations about (someday) moving to a big city quickly get tense. Maybe we could get help with that. Besides, what marriage couldn't use a little shoring up?

Thirty-five years ago, therapists began admitting that marriage counseling (which begins with the premise that something's amiss) wasn't very successful. Back then, only 20 percent of counseled couples rated their marriages happier 2 years after the process. That failure rate spurred a new kind of intervention program: marriage education, where couples learn ways to communicate and resolve differences before a meltdown occurs. Although these courses aren't for couples dealing with severe problems like adultery, violence, gambling, or substance abuse, they do seem to make basically sound unions better. Howard Markman, PhD, and Scott Stanley, PhD, co-developers of the Premarital Relationship Enhancement Program, found that their course raises a couple's odds of staying together by 50 percent up to 5 years after the classes, for example.

The reality, though, is that many couples don't consider marriage education an option, says W. Kim Halford, PhD, director of the Psychological Health Research Center at Griffith University in Brisbane, Australia. That's why he and his colleagues came up with Couple CARE (Commitment and Relationship Enhancement). It's a pioneering, do-it-at-home marital-ed course that uses workbooks, DVDs, and weekly phone sessions with a licensed therapist to guide couples through the process. The six-part series covers self-change, communication, intimacy and caring, managing conflict, sexual intimacy, and looking ahead.

What Can You Find Out?

Doing a course at home sipping sodas, with our feet up and privacy assured (except in this national magazine, but never mind that), definitely makes the idea more appealing. So Dan and I decide to sign up for the program.

Making jokes while huddled in bed one cold Sunday morning, we're feeling a little skittish as we start watching the short DVD. What dust would we kick up?

Concerned, but not deterred, we scribble away in our workbooks, prompted by questions about our families of origin, power and control, gender roles, and conflict. Suddenly, I realize our marriage is more crowded than I thought, my parents astride my shoulders, Dan's parents on his.

Danny talks about how critical his mother had been of his father, and how easy it is to expect the same from me. I share my worries that marriage will simply erase me as it had my mother. It's a relief to find we're not ratting out each other, but our parents. Still, it feels both sad and exciting that, despite many years of marriage, these revelations surprise us.

Two weeks later, we settle into the unit on resolving conflicts. The discussion eventually gets around to our battle about where to live. It doesn't matter that every time the topic comes up, we both recognize that for now we need to stay put.

Usually, I trot out old recriminations and Dan withdraws into angry silence. This time, however, Danny admits that he's bothered by the criticism he anticipates from me on this subject. He recalls a trip we took to Chicago a little more than a year ago. During our visit, as I gushed over the Magnificent Mile, the restaurants, the skyline of the city where we fell in love, he heard, "What a jerk you are for taking me away from here." The trip quickly soured as he lapsed into silence, which in turn made me tense, then angry. Without quite knowing why, we found ourselves fighting.

Fresh Honesty

After working through a few Couple CARE units, our responses are vastly different. Danny explains what bugs him about city life: crime, traffic, the crush. His honesty helps me be more open to his concerns. In fact, the more he shares his feelings, the more relaxed I am about continuing the conversation. Instead of sputtering objections, I find myself agreeing with him. We both want a walking neighborhood, a nearby café, and a spot where traffic isn't synonymous with gridlock. Suddenly, we're envisioning a move we could share.

Indeed, these slight shifts in behavior are the pay dirt of the program. You explore alone and together how your marriage works, then decide what you want to change.

Scott Johnson, PhD, president-elect of the American Association for Marriage and Family Therapy and program director for the Marriage and Family Therapy Doctoral Program at Virginia Tech, thinks that learning how to amend your behavior is the most powerful component of Couple CARE. "The basic message is that you can't change other people," he explains.

Danny wanted to reveal more, I wanted to react less—simple realizations, but ones we both missed until participating in the program. The questions about what works in our relationship and what can use some fine-tuning teased out those insights.

In time, Dan and I began to look forward to each week's phone session with our therapist and the exercises that forced us to think about our marriage in ways we never had before. We knew we'd unravel a few more assumptions, and learn a little more about each other's expectations and sensitivities. In some ways, it was like dating—this person whom I'd already loved for so long had become new to me again.

Dan and I don't take each other for granted. But in a life with kids, fulltime jobs, and a house gathering dust halls, it's easy to adopt a kind of shorthand. In the Couple CARE program, though, we found ourselves talking, sometimes for hours, like two people falling in love.

From *Health Magazine*, January/February 2006, pp. 142, 145-146. Copyright © 2006 by Dorothy Foltz-Gray. Reprinted by permission of the author.

How to Talk About Sex

Whether you have minor problems in bed or a love life dusty with disuse, here's the secret to connecting.

Heidi Raykeil

Ten years ago, before kids and mortgages and All That, my husband and I were experts in the language of love. If sex is a form of communication, well, back then we were on the unlimited calling plan. We may not have always verbally expressed ourselves, but we always conveyed what we meant, physically or emotionally.

Then we had a baby.

Suddenly, I was not only uninterested in sex, I was also strangely confused about how to tell my husband. So while in some ways our daughter's birth brought us closer than ever, in other ways we started to grow apart.

I just didn't know how to explain to J.B. how tired I was, how my body hurt from being pinched and pulled by our baby, and how by the end of the day I couldn't imagine sharing it with anyone else. We both became prickly and defensive: I was sure that when J.B. wrapped his leg over mine at night it meant he was coming on to me (again); when I turned my back and pretended to be asleep, he assumed I no longer found him attractive. Bye-bye, language of love.

Whether it's right after the birth of a baby or a few years down the line, it seems like lots of happily married couples hit the sexual skids when they become parents. And most of them have heard sex therapists on TV and read articles and books, and know they should talk it out.

But there's the rub. Sex is a socially charged and highly personal issue that remains a bit taboo despite our seeming openness. And talking about not having sex? Chances are, the subject comes up when one of you wants it and the other doesn't. Bad time to talk. And who wants to crack open that can of worms later on when it's over? Besides, isn't sex supposed to be fun and spontaneous—like it used to be? Won't talking about it spoil the magic?

"Where's the magic if you're not having sex?" says Valerie Raskin, M.D., author of Great Sex for Moms: Ten Steps to Nurturing Passion While Raising Kids. But how do you start talking? What do you say? And how do you say it so you don't end up bruising egos or booting one of you to the couch? My husband and I started by paying attention to the distinction between how we talked about sex and the details of what we were talking about. To begin:

How to Talk
Just Leap In

Nichole Cook, of Pittsburgh, mom of Eleanor, 8, Odessa, 7, and Izabelle, 6, was embarrassed into silence not long after Eleanor was born: One time during sex she squirted breast milk all over her husband. "I was mortified. I thought it was gross—and totally not normal." Rather than telling him how she felt, though, Cook simply avoided sex altogether for the next couple of weeks.

While talking about sex can be awkward, no one yet has actually died of embarrassment. Dr. Raskin suggests breaking the ice simply by acknowledging how hard it is.

That's what Cook did, a few weeks later. "I was really nervous, but I finally just said, 'That was really embarrassing for me.'" As it turned out, her husband hadn't even noticed and didn't think it was a big deal anyway. "After that, we just made sure we had a towel handy. Now it's something we laugh about."

Rather than letting things build up, talking about it now makes room for more openness later.

Choose the Right Place and Tone

One of the worst fights J.B. and I had about sex was right after a failed attempt at it. I really wanted to be in the mood—even though I wasn't at all—so we got partway into the act before I admitted that things weren't working. We lay in bed trying to "talk" about what had happened. But we were so upset that we ended up blaming, and J.B. stormed angrily out of the room.

Thus, we discovered the importance of environment for having a fruitful discussion of our sex life. Choose a night when nothing else is planned and wait until the kids are asleep. Turn off the TV and the phone. This isn't an inquisition. It's an opportunity to reconnect with each other, to steal an intimate moment in a chaotic life. It's about how you show and share love, about something that should be fun and pleasurable.

J.B. and I have had some of our best talks late at night on our front stoop. We turn off the porch light, pour some wine, and sit side by side. There's something about not looking directly at each other (and the wine, maybe) that lets things flow. It may cut awkwardness to merge your heart-to-heart with an activity—try talking while hiking, or walking, or sorting through your penny jar.

Acknowledge the Problem

This is not the same as agreeing on the cause of the problem. It's just a way to get the conversation rolling. Dr. Raskin calls this "outing the secret—even though it's not really a secret." Begin by stating the obvious: "I know things aren't like they used to be," or "I know we haven't been having sex very much lately." Often, acknowledging this reality, without judgment, can bring a couple closer.

After that big fight, I realized that my husband and I had let things go far too long. While Ramona was napping the next day, I simply said: "I'm having a hard time with sex these days. I hate the way it's come between us, and it must really suck for you, too." The fact that I wasn't trying to deny or make excuses helped J.B. feel comfortable.

After listening to J.B., I realized he wasn't as angry about the situation as I'd thought. It annoyed him that I'd initiated sex when I didn't really want it, but he'd needed to leave the room to cool down because he simply couldn't change gears and talk rationally while he was still aroused. This not only helped me understand why he became so agitated but also made it easier for me to talk about what I was experiencing physically.

Asking and listening without getting defensive is an important part of this process. repeat what your partner's saying and ask if you're understanding correctly. Ask, "is there more you want me to know?"

What Is the Biggest Problem in Your Sex Life Right Now?

- 43% He wants sex more often than I do
- 34% We're both too tired and busy to be in the mood
- 12% Nothing
- 11% A lot about our sex life has changed and we're having trouble adjusting

—*Parenting*'s MomConnection poll

Look Forward, Not Back

Agree to make a fresh start. Don't pull out old fights; avoid generalizing or labeling. Saying things like "You never want sex" or "You're a sex fiend!" is just talking negatively about the past. We all say dumb things; don't waste time fighting about whether they're true.

It's also a bad idea to compare yourself to other couples. What's right for them isn't necessarily what's right for you.

When Holly Wing's husband saw a poll in a magazine that claimed most of its readers had sex a lot more often than they did each month, he kept referring to it—comparing their own not-nearly-so-much stats. Wing, a Berkeley mom of 2-year-old Clio, then started to counter with her own statistics, and before long they were locked in battle. "Instead of solving any problems, we were just getting really good at fighting!"

So stick to what you're feeling ("I feel sad that we're having trouble finding the time to make love") rather than accusations about how you measure up to others.

Stay Positive

"I don't want to talk about sex we haven't had anymore," Wing told her husband after another fight. "If you want to have sex seventeen times a month, well, then, let's go for it!" she said, naming his wildly optimistic ideal. Of course they didn't meet the goal, but the effort did help. Wing felt that her husband realized how hard it is to make time for (and want) frequent sex rather than just complaining about it. And he appreciated her willingness to give it a try.

Shooting for high numbers may not be your solution, but the attitude is admirable. Remind each other that you'll get through this and that you both want to work it out. Instead of saying, "You never woo me anymore," try "Remember that poem you wrote me on our honeymoon? That got me hot!" And if your conversation falls apart and you revert to blaming—stop. Don't try to win. Just end it and try again later when you've both cooled down.

What to Talk About

That There's Love behind Your Lovemaking

If you state explicitly, right up front, that you love and respect each other, and that in talking about this you're only talking about the way you show your love, you're both likely to feel more comfortable expressing your feelings. And keep reminding each other of your love and your mutual desire for each other's happiness—that should be the backdrop to your conversation.

The Meaning of Sex

You can't figure out how to fix your love life if you don't know what you want it to be. So discuss what physical intimacy represents to yourselves and in your relationship.

Women, for instance, often misunderstand the ways in which sex is important for many men. It's not just a matter of stereotypical gotta-have-it male urges but can be a critical form of emotional expression. For whatever combination of reasons, many men feel and express love physically, so they may experience a lack of sex as rejecting not only them but their offering of love as well.

The Definition of Sex

It's a good idea to talk openly about what actually constitutes "sex" to each of you. Is it only intercourse, or does it include other kinds of touching? A husband whose sex drive is at low ebb may be delighted to find that his wife will think him no less a man if he gives her a massage—with or without "extras"—instead of a more "demanding" service.

For Cook and her husband, sharing an understanding that she no longer felt sexual about her breasts was a breakthrough. "I felt like they were just for my kids, not him," she says. With that off the table, they were able to talk about what did still work for both of them.

That It's Not Him. Or You

Many factors mess with parents' love life, only rarely sexual skills or prowess. The list includes exhaustion, a light-sleeping child, hormones, embarrassment about weight gain, lack of time, difficulty shifting gears from parent to lover.

When Heidi Johnecheck, of Petosky, Michigan, mother of Max, 4, and Jaxon, 2, found a magazine article that listed ten reasons it's physically hard for moms to have sex—everything from vaginal dryness to sheer exhaustion—she tore it out and gave it to her husband. "As much as I'd tried to tell him, he just couldn't comprehend what 'I don't feel like it' meant," she says, and he took it personally. "But the article showed that it wasn't just me or just him."

Specific Ways to Make Things Better

Johnecheck and her husband decided to tackle one simple problem head-on: They made a kid-free visit to a local sex shop to buy some lubricants. "We actually made a date together," Johnecheck says, "and decided to just be silly and have fun with it."

Brainstorming about what might help you get back in the swing of things is a great way to move things forward. At the top of the list for most couples? "More private time," says Dr. Raskin. And while scheduling "date night" can help, think about it broadly. If nights out are expensive and infrequent,

what about finding time in the mornings (when women's testosterone levels are highest, resulting in higher libido)? What about Saturday-afternoon naptime (when you'll both be less tired than at night)?

What's the Hardest Thing to Talk About, Sexually?

- 35% Our different levels of interest in sex
- 33% Something specific I'd like him to do differently or improve
- 18% How often we should have sex
- 14% Other

—*Parenting*'s MomConnection poll

Technique

This is not the time to be shy or coy. Be specific about yourself ("I'm finding that it takes me a lot longer to get excited lately"). If you want more mood setting than "Okay, the baby's asleep. Let's do this," ask for it: "First I'd like you to sit through a chick flick with me and hold my hand."

Your body and your life have changed since you had a child. Maybe there's something in particular that you do want that you never did before. Just say it: harder, softer, faster, slower, touch me here. And if you say what you do want your husband to do instead of just what you don't, he'll likely be turned on, too.

For me and J.B., when I finally could say "Not tonight" without worrying it would turn into a fight, a funny thing happened. It became easier for me to say yes. Because once I knew he understood my feelings, we started to address some of the underlying issues: I needed more time for myself, more romance, and more help with our daughter.

Those first years after the birth of Ramona were tough. But four years later I now see talking about sex as just another opportunity for expanding our intimacy—in and out of the bedroom.

HEIDI RAYKEIL's book about her and her husband's romantic life as parents, *Confessions of a Naughty Mommy: How I Found My Lost Libido*, was just published by Seal Press.

UNIT 4
Reproduction

Unit Selections

Key Points to Consider

- In your opinion, what are the most important characteristics of a contraceptive? Why?

- What personal feelings or expectations make you more likely to use contraception regularly?

- Under what circumstances might a person not use contraception and risk an unintentional pregnancy?

- Should contraceptive responsibilities be assigned to one gender or be shared between men and women? Defend your answer.

- In the situation of an unplanned pregnancy, what should be the role of the female and the male with respect to decision making? What if they do not agree?

- If you discovered you or your partner were infertile, what technologies or options would you consider or pursue? Are there any you would not, and if so, why?

- Have you found a fairly comfortable way to talk about contraception and/or pregnancy risk and prevention with your partner? If so, what is it? If not, what do you do?

Student Web Site

www.mhcls.com/online

Internet References

Further information regarding these Web sites may be found in this book's preface or online.

Ask NOAH About Pregnancy: Fertility & Infertility
   http://www.noah-health.org/en/search/health.html
Childbirth.Org
   http://www.childbirth.org
Planned Parenthood
   http://www.plannedparenthood.org

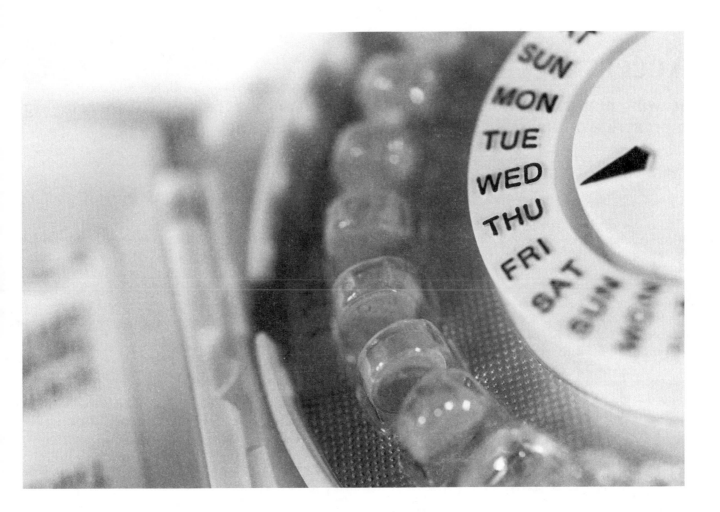

W hile human reproduction is as old as humanity, many aspects of it are changing in today's society. Not only have new technologies of conception and childbirth affected the *how* of reproduction, but personal, social, and cultural forces have also affected the *who*, the *when*, and the *when not*. Abortion remains a fiercely debated topic as well as legislative efforts for and against it abound. Unplanned pregnancies and parenthood in the United States and worldwide continue to present significant, sometimes devastating, problems for parents, children, families, and society.

In light of the change of attitude toward sex for pleasure, birth control has become a matter of prime importance. Even in our age of sexual enlightenment, some individuals, possibly in the height of passion, fail to correlate "having sex" with pregnancy. In addition, even in our age of astounding medical technology, there is no 100 percent effective, safe, or aesthetically acceptable method of birth control. Before sex can become safe as well as enjoyable, people must receive thorough and accurate information regarding conception and contraception, birth, and birth control. However, we have learned that information about, or

even access to, birth control is not enough. We still have some distance to go to make every child one who is planned for and wanted.

Despite the relative simplicity of the above assertion, abortion and birth control remain emotionally charged issues in American society. While opinion surveys indicate that most of the public supports family planning and abortion, at least in some circumstances, there are certain individuals and groups strongly opposed to some forms of birth control and to abortion. Voices for and against birth control and abortion—traditional and newer methods—remain passionate, and face-offs range from academic debates and legislative hearings to work stoppages by pharmacists and protests with or without violence. Supreme Court, legislative, and medical community efforts have been a mixed bag: some seek to restrict the right or access to abortion or the availability of birth control methods, while others seek to mandate freer access to contraceptive and reproductive choice options. Voices on both sides are raised in emotional and political debate between "we must never go back to the old days" (of illegal and unsafe back-alley abortions) and "the baby has no choice."

Access Denied

Growing numbers of doctors and pharmacists across the country are refusing to prescribe or dispense birth control pills. Here's why

CAROLINE BOLLINGER

I n April, Julee Lacey, 33, a Fort Worth, TX, mother of two, went to her local CVS drugstore for a last-minute Pill refill. She had been getting her prescription filled there for a year, so she was astonished when the pharmacist told her, "I personally don't believe in birth control and therefore I'm not going to fill your prescription." Lacey, an elementary school teacher, was shocked. "The pharmacist had no idea why I was even taking the Pill. I might have needed it for a medical condition."

Melissa Kelley,* 35, was just as stunned when her gynecologist told her she would not renew her prescription for birth control pills last fall.

"She told me she couldn't in good faith prescribe the Pill anymore," says Kelley, who lives with her husband and son in Allentown, PA. Then the gynecologist told Kelley she wouldn't be able to get a new prescription from her family doctor, either. "She said my primary care physician was the one who helped her make the decision."

Lacey's pharmacist and Kelley's doctors are among hundreds, perhaps thousands, of physicians and pharmacists who now adhere to a controversial belief that birth control pills and other forms of hormonal contraception-including the skin patch, the vaginal ring, and progesterone injections cause tens of thousands of "silent" abortions every year. Consequently, they are refusing to prescribe or dispense them.

Scenarios like these—virtually unheard-of 10 years ago— are happening with increasing frequency. However, until this spring, the issue received little attention outside the antiabortion community. It wasn't high on the agendas of reproductive rights advocates, who have been preoccupied with defending abortion rights and emergency contraception. But when Lacey's story was picked up by a Texas TV station and later made the national news, Planned Parenthood Federation of America and others took notice.

Limiting access to the Pill, these groups now say, threatens a basic aspect of women's health care. An estimated 12 million American women use hormonal contraceptives, the most popular form of birth control in the United States after sterilization. The Pill is also widely prescribed by gynecologists and family doctors for other uses, such as clearing up acne, shrinking fibroids, reducing ovarian cancer risk, and controlling endometriosis.

"Where will this all stop?" asks Lacey. "And what if these pharmacists decide they suddenly don't believe in a new life-saving medicine? I don't think pharmacists should be in a position to decide these things."

A Matter of Belief

The members of the antiabortion group Pharmacists for Life International say they have every right to make that kind of decision. "Our job is to enhance life," explains the organization's president, pharmacist Karen Brauer, RPh, who first refused to fill prescriptions for some types of birth control pills in 1989. "We shouldn't have to dispense a medication that we think takes lives."

Anti-Pill doctors and pharmacists base their stand on the fact that the Pill isn't perfect: Although it is designed to suppress ovulation and prevent fertilization, both can—and do—occur in rare cases. About 1 woman in every 1,000 who take the Pill exactly as directed becomes pregnant in a given year. But while mainstream experts say ovulation happens only 2 to 3% of the time and fertilization is rare, anti-Pill groups claim both happen frequently. They say most of these fertilized eggs—in their view, nascent human lives—are unable to attach to the hormonally altered uterine lining. Instead of implanting and growing, they slough off. This theoretical action, which scientists can't confirm, is called the post-fertilization effect.

At the heart of the debate between anti-Pill forces and mainstream medicine lies a profound difference of opinion about when pregnancy *and* life begin. The long-standing medical definition of pregnancy, held by the American College of Obstetricians and Gynecologists, is that it starts not when an egg is fertilized, but when the fertilized egg implants in the uterine lining.

This distinction is practical: A pregnancy test won't show a positive result before implantation. "It can't be an abortion before there is a pregnancy," points out David Grimes, MD, a clinical professor in obstetrics and gynecology at the University of

*Not her real name

The Post-Fertilization Effect: Fact or Fiction?

Manufactures of oral contraceptives have long claimed that the Pill provides three lines of defense against pregnancy: It prevents ovulation (most of the time), blocks sperm by thickening cervical mucus, and, should all else fail, theoretically reduces the chances that a fertilized egg will implant in the uterus by hormonally altering the uterine lining.

But does this so-called post-fertilization effect really happen? Truth is, nobody knows. "There is no evidence that the Pill's effect on the uterine lining interferes with implantation or has a post-fertilization effect," says contraception expert Felicia Stewart, MD, codirector of the Center for Reproductive Health Research and Policy in San Francisco. "Documenting it would be a very difficult research task."

David Grimes, MD, a clinical professor in obstetrics and gynecology at the University of North Carolina School of Medicine, says the Pill and other hormonal contraceptives work primarily by preventing ovulation.

Consensus comes from a surprising source. "The post-fertilization effect was purely a speculation that became truth by repetition," says Joe DeCook, MD, a retired OB/GYN and vice president of the American Association of Pro-Life Obstetricians and Gynecologists. "In our group the feelings are split. We say it should be each doctor's own decision, because there is no proof."

Further clouding the issue is the fact that even among women trying to become pregnant—women obviously not taking the Pill—fertilized eggs fail to implant 40 to 60% of the time. They're eliminated when a woman menstruates.

North Carolina School of Medicine and one of the country's leading contraception experts.

But anti-Pill doctors and pharmacists say life begins sooner, at fertilization. Sloughing off a fertilized egg, in their view, is a "chemical abortion."

"Imagine a pharmacist asking a customer whether his Viagra prescription is to enhance sexual performance in his marriage or in an extramarital affair"

"How many women know that if they become pregnant after breakthrough ovulation, these 'contraceptives' will almost always kill any son or daughter they've conceived?" asks the anti-Pill organization Pro-Life America on the group's Web site, ProLife.com.

Surprisingly, there's no science to back the theory that birth control pills really do discourage implantation. This claim, made by contraceptive manufacturers for decades, has never been proven, Grimes says. Even the American Association of Pro-Life Obstetricians and Gynecologists agrees that it's just speculation. {See "The Post-Fertilization Effect: Fact or Fiction?")

Under the Radar

In the past decade or so, the "hormonal birth control equals abortion" view has quietly grown roots in the antiabortion underground. It's spread from doctor to doctor, through local newsletters, in books with titles such as *Does the Birth Control Pill Cause Abortions?* (written by Randy Alcorn, an Oregon based antiabortion pastor and author}, and through lobbying groups that have encouraged lawmakers in Arkansas, South Dakota, and most recently Mississippi to enact "conscience clauses." These legislative provisions protect health care professionals—in this case, pharmacists—who refuse to provide services they oppose on moral, ethical, or legal grounds. At press time, similar legislation had been introduced in 11 more states.

An Internet search turns up thousands of Web sites containing articles with titles such as "The Pill Kills Babies," "Are Contraception and Abortion Siamese Twins?" and "The Dirty Little Secrets about the Birth Control Pill." Hundreds of physicians and pharmacists have pledged not to provide hormonal birth control. Among them: 450 doctors affiliated with the Dayton, OH-based natural family planning group One More Soul; some members of the 2,500 doctors in the Holland, MI-based American Association of Pro-Life Obstetricians and Gynecologists; and a growing number of the 1,500-member Web-based Pharmacists for Life International, says Brauer.

Not even anti-Pill groups know how many doctors and druggists are involved. And while the total is still a small percentage of the nation's 117,500 family physicians and OB/GYNs and 173,000 pharmacists, they are making their presence felt in women's lives and among law and policy makers on both the state and national levels. Their influence is far-reaching and disproportionate to their size—a quiet version of the public shock waves produced by the nation's relatively small number of antiabortion activists.

"Refusing women access to the Pill is a very disturbing trend," says Gloria Feldt, president of Planned Parenthood Federation of America. "The war on choice is not just about abortion anymore. It's about our right to birth control."

There's no science to back the theory that birth control pills really do discourage implantation

Morality versus Public Health

Anti-Pill doctors and pharmacists across the country say the issue isn't about a woman's right to hormonal contraceptives, but about their right to act according to their beliefs. "I feel chemical contraceptives have the potential to harm an embryo," says Mary Martin, MD, an OB/GYN in private practice in Midwest City, OK. "And I decided, based on moral and ethical grounds, that I simply could no longer prescribe them." She stopped writing prescriptions for hormonal birth control in 1999. OB/GYN Arthur Stehly, of Escondido, CA, who hasn't prescribed contraceptives since 1989, says he feels the same way: "I function better and I sleep better at night knowing I'm not giving the Pill."

But at what point does personal belief undermine public health? If more women lose access to hormonal contraceptives, rates of unintended pregnancy and abortions will rise in the United States, predicts Beth Jordan, MD, medical director of the Washington, DC-based Feminist Majority Foundation, an advocacy and research group.

What's more, oral contraceptives aren't only used to prevent pregnancy. The Pill may cut the risk of ovarian cancer by up to 80% and is used by women at high genetic risk for this hard-to-detect and usually fatal cancer. "There are easily more than 20 noncontraceptive uses for the Pill in common practice," says Giovannina Anthony, MD, an attending physician of obstetrics and gynecology at Beth Israel Medical Center in New York City. "This drug saves women from surgery for gynecological conditions like endometriosis, fibroids, and severe bleeding and pain."

Most women's doctors agree that contraceptives are an important tool of good medical care. "I have a hard time with people who market themselves as women's health care physicians but who won't prescribe such a basic part of women's health care," says Anne Drapkin Lyerly, MD, a reproductive rights ethicist and an assistant professor of obstetrics and gynecology at Duke University Medical Center. "We're seeing a growing trend among pharmacists and medical practitioners who consider it acceptable to impose their morality on women's bodies. I don't think moral aspects should be a concern. Imagine a pharmacist asking a customer whether his Viagra prescription is to enhance sexual performance in his marriage or in an extramarital affair. Never!"

Katie Williams's Story

Last winter, 24-year-old Katie Williams encountered a doctor who refused to give her a prescription for the Pill, even though she'd already been taking it for 5 years—originally to relieve extremely painful menstrual cramps. Williams, who had just moved to Milwaukee for a job with an insurance company, realized she was nearly out of Pills. Her roommate recommended the physician who had written a Pill prescription for her a year before: Cynthia Jones-Nosacek, MD, a board certified family doctor with St. Mary's Medical Clinic, a Catholic medical center in Milwaukee. Williams made the appointment, explaining she needed a routine annual exam and a new prescription.

But when she arrived at the office, recalls Williams, "the doctor's assistant told me 'the doctor doesn't write prescriptions for the Pill.' I was totally floored. I just stared at her."

Williams opted to take her chances and see the doctor anyway, thinking the assistant must have been confused. After the doctor finished her exam, Williams asked for her script, explaining she'd been taking the Pill for several years. "The doctor told me she doesn't believe in oral contraceptives and does believe in natural family planning," Williams claims. "I told her 'that's ridiculous.'" Angry, Williams stormed out of the doctor's office.

The Debate over Emergency Contraception

Taken within 72 hours of unprotected intercourse, emergency contraception (EC)—pills containing high doses of estrogen and progestin, the same hormones found in some birth control pills—is 89% effective in preventing pregnancy. Unlike RU-486 (mifepristone) and surgical abortions, EC doesn't work once a woman is pregnant. But many antiabortion groups maintain EC is akin to abortion because it could prevent an egg from implanting. Many pharmacies nationwide, including Wal-Mart, are refusing to dispense it for that reason.

In December 2003, two FDA advisory committees recommended that an emergency contraceptive called Plan B be sold without a prescription, citing scientific evidence that EC is "safer than aspirin." But in May, the FDA declined to give the drug over-the-counter status, saying that teens younger than 16 wouldn't be able to understand the drug's directions. Women's rights groups say the FDA bowed to political pressure from social conservatives.

"We fervently hope that this shameful episode in FDA history will pass and that respect for scientific evidence will prevail once again at the FDA," says Vivian Dickerson, MD, president of the American College of Obstetricians and Gynecologists.

Abortion rights groups claim that EC has the potential to prevent 800,000 abortions each year.

In an interview, Jones-Nosacek, who has been in practice for 21 years, says she stopped prescribing the Pill after discovering a paper written by Salt Lake City family doctor Joseph B. Stanford, MD, an assistant professor of family and preventive medicine at the University of Utah and a recent Bush appointee to the FDA's Reproductive Health Drugs Advisory Committee. "The paper talked about the Pill's post-fertilization effect," says Jones-Nosacek. "After reading it and several other books and papers, I realized I could no longer justify prescribing the Pill."

Although Jones-Nosacek says she may have lost patients over her stand, she thinks most are happy to hear her opinion. "I think most women feel life begins at fertilization," she says. "When they find out the Pill has a potential post-fertilization effect, they're surprised, and some rethink their decision."

As for Williams, she got her prescription that day. Desperate—new to her job, she couldn't afford to take off another day without pay—she asked for help from an employee in Jones-Nosacek's office, who told her there was an OB/GYN in the same building. Williams went there directly and asked one of the doctor's assistants to relay her story to the gynecologist. This new doctor wrote her a prescription, no questions asked. "The doctor's assistant was shocked," says Williams. "She couldn't believe any doctor would refuse to give the Pill to somebody who had already been taking it successfully."

Friends in High Places

Planned Parenthood's Feldt believes anti-Pill groups, like the larger antiabortion movement that spawned them, have been emboldened by the Bush administration's antiabortion policies and appointees. "Pro-life groups know they have friends in high places," she says. In his first budget to Congress, President Bush stripped out a provision that required insurance companies participating in the Federal Employees Health Benefits Program to cover contraceptives. He has also withheld funding for international family planning; signed the Partial-Birth Abortion Ban Act of 2003, which critics say could result in making even second-trimester abortions illegal; and signed the Unborn Victims of Violence Act, which gives a fertilized egg, embryo, or fetus separate legal status if harmed during a violent crime. (Abortion rights groups say that giving a fetus separate legal rights from the pregnant woman opens the door to prosecuting anyone involved in an abortion.)

"The vast majority of people in this country believe access to birth control is a basic right"

Bush also appointed three antiabortion doctors to the FDA Reproductive Health Drugs Advisory Committee: W. David Hager, MD, Susan Crockett, MD, and Stanford. When their committee and the FDA's Nonprescription Drugs Advisory Committee met jointly last December, the group voted 23 to 4 in favor of giving over-the-counter status to emergency contraceptives. Dissenters included Hager, Crockett, and Stanford. In May, the FDA decided not to grant the drug OTC status. (See "The Debate over Emergency Contraception.")

While Hager and Crockett have gone on record saying they do not believe standard birth control pills cause abortions, their colleague Stanford says he has never prescribed them. "I found out in medical school that they may prevent fertilized eggs from implanting, and I decided then that I wasn't ever going to prescribe them," he says. A paper of Stanford's, published in the February 2000 issue of *Archives of Family Medicine*, in which he discusses the post-fertilization effect of the Pill, is often cited by anti-Pill groups.

Federal and state legislators are quietly adopting similar views. US Senator Rick Santorum (R-PA), for example, does not support use of the Pill to prevent pregnancy, his staffers told *Prevention*. In March 2003, during a debate on the Senate floor that touched on emergency contraception, Santorum said, "I will not be supportive of covering medications that would lead to a fertilized egg not [being] implanted in the uterus. I believe life begins at conception. I would not support drugs that would prevent a conceived embryo [from being] implanted."

What's Natural Family Planning?

The natural family planning method (NFP) advocated by Milwaukee physician Cynthia Jones-Nosacek, MD, and other anti-Pill doctors involves avoiding intercourse during the most fertile days of a woman's cycle. Success depends on accurately pinpointing those days by using one or more techniques: tracking changes in cervical mucus, charting the rise and fall in body temperature, using a fertility monitor, and/or relying on the rhythm method, in which a woman and her partner don't have intercourse on certain days in the middle of her cycle. With typical use, the failure rate for NFP can be as high as 25%; for the pill, it's 6 to 8%.

Problems at the Drugstore

Though three states have conscience clauses for pharmacists, there is no such legal provision in Texas, where the CVS druggist refused to fill Julee Lacey's prescription.

The night it happened, Lacey says, she was shocked and responded, "Are you sure? I've had this filled here many times before." But the pharmacist was emphatic. "I just couldn't believe what I was hearing," recalls Lacey. "It was a school night, and I knew I had to put my kids to bed and get organized for work the next morning. I didn't want to run all over town for my Pills." Lacey and her husband complained to the assistant store manager that night and the district manager the next day. Finally, the pharmacy supervisor called and said he would have Lacey's prescription delivered that day. "He apologized and said he was unaware of the pharmacist's moral objections to the Pill. Apparently it was a new belief," says Lacey. (A CVS corporate spokesperson contacted by *Prevention* confirmed Lacey's story. None of the employees has ever been named.)

Pharmacists in other states have refused as well. In 2002, a Kmart pharmacist in Stout, WI, allegedly denied Pills to a student from the local campus of the University of Wisconsin. The state department of regulation and licensing filed a complaint against the pharmacist; at press time a hearing on the matter had not yet taken place.

In 1996, Brauer says, she was fired from a Kmart pharmacy in Delhi, OH, after she refused to sign an agreement to dispense all lawfully prescribed medications regardless of her feelings or beliefs. (She filed suit against Kmart, but since the discount chain is in bankruptcy proceedings, it has never been settled.) "We've known for a long time that birth control pills are abortifacients," she says. "Now it's finally catching on."

Public Opinion

While abortion continues to be a divisive public issue, contraception is not. In fact, 95% of American women use some form of birth control during their childbearing years.

This is no silent majority. When a woman is denied the Pill and the incident becomes public, it triggers a loud response. Case in point: After Lacey's story appeared in the *Dallas Morning News*, there was an enormous outpouring of letters from readers appalled by the pharmacist's actions. "This was a huge issue in our area, and we're a conservative community," says Emily Snooks, director of media relations and communications at Planned Parenthood of North Texas. "People here are still talking about it, simply because the vast majority of people in this country believe access to birth control is a basic right."

But what will you do if, like Kelley, Williams, and Lacey, you encounter a doctor who tells you no or a pharmacist who won't honor your prescription? "If your gynecologist won't prescribe the Pill, find a new doctor—and tell all your friends what has occurred," says Vanessa Cullins, vice president for medical affairs, Planned Parenthood Federation of America in New York City. The same goes for pharmacists who refuse to fill your prescription. The best defense against this grassroots movement, Cullins notes, is another one—in opposition.

CAROLINE BOLLINGER is *Prevention*'s fitness editor.

You Can't Do That on Television

Why abortion doesn't show up on the small screen anymore.

RACHEL FUDGE

On any given evening, you can turn on the TV and surf past images that just a few decades ago were considered too shocking for national broadcast: interracial couples, visibly pregnant women, actual autopsies. You might even catch a comic skit that openly mocks Jesus and God. But there's one thing you're almost guaranteed not to see on television: abortion, despite many of the old you-can't-do-that-on-television taboos have fallen away, abortion, despite being one of the most common medical procedures in the United States, is the one hot-button issue that simply remains too hot for TV.

Robert Thompson, director of the Center for the Study of Popular Culture and Television at Syracuse University, says the portrayal of abortion on TV is "conspicuous by its absence," while in a recent *New York Times* article writer Kate Arthur calls it an "aberration." Although *Roe v. Wade* established a woman's right to choose in 1973, the discourse around abortion and reproductive rights has actually narrowed over the past 30 years, to the point where it has become more difficult to introduce the issue of abortion on a television show than it once was.

The best-known and most widely viewed pop-culture abortion took place in 1972 on *Maude,* a sitcom starring Bea Arthur as a liberal feminist. When 47-year-old Maude, who was married and had a grown daughter, unexpectedly became pregnant, she opted for an abortion, which was legal in New York state at the time. (In a sign of just how different the times were, *Maude's* producers cooked up the abortion storyline in response to a challenge from the group Zero Population Growth—now called Popular Connection—which was sponsoring a $10,000 prize for sitcoms that tackled the issue of population control.)

In the wake of the *Roe* decision, as the basic tenets of second-wave feminism seeped into the American mainstream, serious adult-oriented dramas like *Hill Street Blues* and *St. Elsewhere* featured abortions every season or so, as did the occasional soap opera. (Shortly after *Roe,* Susan Lucci's *All My Children* character had soap opera's first legal abortion, with none of the health or psychosocial aftereffects-sterility, insanity, murder-that would come to, characterize soap abortions in the future.) In the real world, the annual number of abortions steadily increased until 1985, when they leveled off. In the late 1980s and early 1990s, in the face of a growing number of legal challenges to *Roe,* a smattering of storylines revisited the specter of illegal abortions, as if to remind us of what was at stake. On the Vietnam War drama *China Beach,* a young nurse named Holly had an illegal abortion; the show's moral center, leading character Colleen McMurphy, was a staunch Catholic who disapproved of Holly's actions. The popular show *thirtysomething* addressed the issue more obliquely, often using flashbacks to provide distance from the controversial event.

13 percent of unwanted pregnancies end in miscarriage, but on television that number is much, much higher.

With the rise of the prime-time teen soap *(Beverly Hills 90210, Party of Five, Dawson's Creek)* in the mid1990s, it was inevitable that sexually active teen and young adult characters would be confronted with pregnancy, often in the guise of the Very Special Episode. Enter the convenient miscarriage. In the real world, according to the Alan Guttmacher Institute, a nonprofit organization that studies sexual and reproductive health issues, some 13 percent of unwanted pregnancies end in miscarriage, but on television that number is much, much higher. The convenient miscarriage goes something like this: Sympathetic lead character gets knocked up. Agonizing over what to do, SLC sometimes goes so far as to visit an abortion clinic. SLC decides that although she believes in a woman's right to choose, she's going to keep her baby. Moral dilemma resolved, SLC spontaneously miscarries. SLC is sad but realizes that in the end she wasn't really ready to be a mother anyway. Alternatively, the pregnancy turns out to be a false alarm, an even tidier wrap-up to the dilemma. The convenient "miscarriage and the false alarm remain the most popular strategies for dodging abortion since they allow television producers to congratulate themselves for tackling the tough topics without actually having to take a stand.

Recently, however, a handful of shows have approached the issue head-on, even allowing characters to go through with the abortion. HBO's *Six Feet Under* depicted teenage lead Claire matter-of-factly getting an abortion, without endless agonizing or moral anguish. And last year, a two part episode of the made-in-Canada teen soap *Degrassi: The Next Generation* made headlines when 14-

year-old lead character Manny got pregnant, had an abortion (saying, "I'm just trying to do the right thing here. For me. For everyone, I guess"), and didn't express any regret afterward. Alas, U.S. viewers didn't get to see the show: The Viacom-owned cable channel N, which airs *Degrassi* in the United States, refused to show it.

While maude's abortion was truly ground breaking, it inadvertently galvanized the anti-choice movement. When CBS reran the episode six months later, some 40 affiliates refused to air it, and national advertisers shied away from buying ad time, establishing a pattern that remains in effect today. Even more significantly, after the episode first aired, anti-abortion leaders took their case to the Federal Communications Commission, arguing that the fairness doctrine—which mandated equal time for opposing views—ought to cover not just editorials and public affairs but entertainment programming too. Because Maude had an abortion on CBS, they argued, they should have the right to reply on CBS. They lost the case but won the attention of the networks. In 1987 the fairness doctrine itself was struck down, but by that point it didn't matter: The networks had established a pattern of covering their asses by presenting some semblance of balance as a way of diffusing potentially volatile subjects.

In the landmark episode, Maude agonized over the decision, but her daughter reassured her, speaking in the language of the growing feminist movement: "When you were young, *abortion* was a dirty word. It's not anymore." But more than 30 years later, as many of the tenets of the women's liberation movement have become accepted parts of mainstream American culture, *abortion* is a messy, if not exactly dirty, word. Back in 1992, when the sitcom *Murphy Brown* was hailed for its overt feminism and its main character found herself unmarried and unexpectedly pregnant, the *a-word* was never uttered. Diane English, the show's producer, said in a June 1992 *Houston Chronicle* article, "She would have used the word many times, but I wanted a lot of people to watch, and certain words have become inflammatory and get in the way of people hearing what we wanted her to say." In the end, Brown had the baby, igniting the ire of Vice President Dan Quayle (who viewed the character's decision not to wed as an assault on American values) and disappointing many feminists.

During the battle for abortion rights that culminated in the *Roe* ruling, public declarations were an integral tactic of the movement. In an effort to overcome the shame and silence surrounding abortion, women organized public speakouts, at which they talked openly about their illegal abortions. Abortion is a fact of life, they asserted, and it affects women of all colors, classes, and religious and political beliefs. Over the years, as the anti-abortion movement has grown stronger and more organized, the pro-choice movement has struggled to regain this clarity of speech. Young women who were born after *Roe* assert that abortion is a private decision, a private choice that needn't be broadcast—true, but also extremely naive politically.

Veteran TV producer English acknowledged this back in February 2001, when she said to *The New York Times:* "Maybe women. . . only had to think about their Manolo Blahniks for the past eight years under the Clinton administration. If women start to wonder if they will lose the right to have an abortion, perhaps that attitude may change during the next four years."

While poll after poll indicates that a majority of Americans support upholding *Roe v. Wade*, it's also clear that a majority of Americans have deep concerns and moral conflicts about abortion. This ambivalence is reflected in the pro-choice movement, too, as nationally recognized feminist leaders speak of the need to recognize the agony and shame that accompany abortion. Given this roiling mass of conflicting feelings and politics, it's no wonder that a one-hour drama can't get a handle on the issue. As Syracuse University's Thompson points out, "A lot of people strongly feel that there's too much sex on TV, but they will have no trouble watching an episode of *Blind Date* or *Desperate Housewives* in their own home. With abortion, those feelings aren't so easily eliminated in one's TV viewing. No [networks] want to run the risk of powerfully offending people on either side [of the issue]."

As a result, what we see on television isn't likely to satisfy anyone, no matter where they stand. Producers strive for a form of balance by always ensuring that there's a dissenting voice of some sort—friend, relative, or authority figure who ardently asserts the anti-abortion point of view. To pro-choice folks, TV's take on abortion seems unnecessarily harsh, moralizing, and punitive. Rarely, they say, do you see a character undertake an abortion the way many women actually do: with utter confidence that they're doing the right thing in a difficult situation. For now, it's unlikely that TV viewers will ever see one of the desperate housewives unapologetically opting for a second-trimester abortion when she realizes her fetus has profound genetic anomalies, or one of the lissome gals on *The O.C.* sporting one of Planned Parenthood's "I had an abortion" baby tees, proclaiming that ending her pregnancy was the best decision she ever made.

The trashy, ephemeral landscape of pop culture may seem like an unimportant front in the battle for women's rights. But as the 2004 election has shown, the United States is in the midst of an all-out culture war in which public language and pop images are playing a crucial role in shaping the terms of the debate. Thus, the reproductive-rights movement, like the rest of the progressive movement, needs to find new ways to present its case openly and frankly. After all, of the 6 million U.S. pregnancies each year, half are unintended, and some 47 percent of those unintended pregnancies result in abortion. And as history has shown, not talking about it won't make it go away.

From *Utne*, September/October 2005, pp. 43-46. Originally appeared in *Clamor* Magazine, issue 32, May/June 2005. Copyright © 2005 by Rachel Fudge. Reprinted by permission of the author.

Sex, Politics, and Morality at the FDA: Reflections on the Plan B Decision

FRANK DAVIDOFF

On September 3, 2005, I resigned my consultant position with the Food and Drug Administration. I did this to protest the agency's August 26, 2005, decision to delay a final ruling on over-the-counter availability of Plan B, the emergency contraceptive, and I wasn't alone: Susan Wood, the FDA's assistant commissioner for women's health and director of the agency's Office of Women's Health, also resigned at about the same time. What in the world has been going on at the FDA?

Plan B consists of two relatively large doses of a single ingredient, levonorgestrol, a constituent of many birth control pills. Taken twelve hours apart within seventy-two hours after unprotected intercourse, the drug is about 75 percent effective in preventing pregnancy. Importantly for the question of over-the-counter availability, the drug's contraceptive efficacy decreases dramatically during this seventy-two hour window.

Plan B has been available by prescription since 1999. In April 2003, Women's Capital Corporation, which produces Plan B, filed an application with the FDA for approval of over-the-counter marketing of the drug. (Women's Capital Corporation later transferred ownership of the drug to Barr Laboratories.) As it often does in considering such applications, the agency then convened a joint meeting of its Nonprescription Drug and Reproductive Health Drug Advisory Committees (NDAC and RHDAC, respectively) in December 2003 to obtain independent expert opinion on the application. The briefing materials for the meeting were more extensive than usual; they weighed eighteen pounds.

During two days of intensive hearings and discussion, the committees carefully examined the pros and cons of over-the-counter availability; they also heard comments from several dozen members of the public, nearly all in support of approval. In the course of their deliberations, the committees voted twenty-eight to zero that the drug was safe (one member of NDAC commented that the single ingredient of Plan B, levonorgestrol, is the safest drug the committee had yet considered); they voted twenty-seven to one that consumers could properly use Plan B as recommended on the proposed labeling (as judged from the "actual use study" that was part of the sponsor's application); they voted twenty-eight to zero that women

were unlikely to use Plan B as a regular form of contraception; and they voted twenty-seven to one that the actual use study data were generalizable to the overall population of over-the-counter users, including adolescents. At the end of the day, they voted twenty-three to four in favor of approval for over-the-counter availability (I was one of the twenty-three).

In sum, the committees agreed that Plan B met all of the FDA's criteria for over-the-counter availability: 1) an acceptable safety profile based on prescription use and experience; 2) a low potential for abuse; 3) an appropriate safety and therapeutic "index" (the ratio between the toxic and the therapeutic dose); 4) a positive benefit-risk assessment; and 5) demonstrable need for treatment of a condition or illness that is self-recognizable, self-limiting, and requires minimal intervention by a health care practitioner.

While all of that is true, the committees spent most of their time during the hearings considering several complex social, behavioral, and ethical issues—both benefits and side effects or "toxicities"—associated with over-the-counter availability of emergency contraception. FDA advisory committees do occasionally take up issues of that kind; in other meetings, for example, the NDAC struggled at length with the problem that acetaminophen, the active ingredient in Tylenol, is often used for suicidal overdose. But many of the issues raised in connection with the proposed over-the-counter switch of Plan B differed, both quantitatively and qualitatively, from the usual biological and clinical concerns raised by other over-the-counter switches. To start with, the proposed benefits for the switch of Plan B—and the primary explicit rationale for the over-the-counter switch application—were as much social, behavioral, and ethical as they were clinical. They included the likelihood that over-the-counter availability would prevent a large number of unwanted pregnancies and, consequently, a substantial proportion of elective abortions; that it would be of particular importance on weekends, since much unprotected intercourse probably takes place on Friday and Saturday nights, when it is particularly difficult to find a doctor to write a prescription; and that it would cut down on inappropriate, and dauntingly expensive, emergency room visits as a source of prescriptions on short notice for the many women who have no established relationship with a doctor.

But the list of potential social, behavioral, and ethical side effects and toxicities of Plan B's over-the-counter availability was also substantial. First, some members of the RHDAC suggested that requiring a prescription for emergency contraception forces women to see doctors, who can then provide medical evaluations plus education and counseling on contraception. These members argued that over-the-counter availability of Plan B would deprive women of that presumed benefit. Second, because the mechanism by which the drug prevents pregnancy isn't definitely known, some on the committees argued that levonorgestrol could, at least at times, prevent implantation of a fertilized ovum, which some view as a form of abortion, hence unacceptable. Third, easy availability of Plan B could have the social side effect of increased promiscuity, since impulsive sexual encounters might be seen as not having the consequence of an unplanned pregnancy. A related, secondary effect might be an increase in sexually transmitted disease. Fourth, over-the-counter availability might discourage the use of other means of regular contraception. Finally, and importantly, some committee members were concerned about the possibility that the social and behavioral side effects and toxicities associated with over-the-counter availability might be greater in women aged sixteen and younger because women in that age group may be less capable of understanding and following instructions and making appropriate judgments.

During the discussion the committees dealt with each of these issues in considerable depth. As is evident from the votes, the overwhelming majority of committee members appeared to be convinced, largely by the rather extensive published evidence and by the special studies submitted by the sponsor, that the overall benefits of over-the-counter availability of emergency contraception far outweighed its potential risks and harms, whether social, behavioral, or clinical.

The increased control that easier availability would give women over their reproductive lives appeared to most committee members to outweigh concerns about women bypassing doctor visits. After all, women generally consult doctors for contraceptive advice when their sexual activity is to some degree planned. But not all sexual activity is planned, so many women who have had no reason to seek out contraception from a doctor are inevitably exposed to the risk of unplanned and unwanted pregnancy.

As is evident from the twenty-three to four vote, the majority of committee members appeared convinced that the benefits of over-the-counter emergency contraceptive availability far outweighed its potential risks and harms, whether social, behavioral, or clinical.

The available evidence on mechanism of action, limited as it is, strongly indicates that levonorgestrol is a contraceptive, rather than an abortifacient; that is, it appears to prevent fertilization rather than preventing implantation of the fertilized ovum. Among other evidence, the drug is known to be ineffective once pregnancy is established; moreover, as one member of the RHDAC pointed out, this is the same drug that is given to preserve pregnancies in women with spontaneous "threatened abortion."

A variety of clinical studies, some in the United States and others in countries where contraception is available without prescription (there are many), indicate that promiscuity or sexually transmitted diseases do not increase when emergency contraception is available over the counter, nor does use of conventional, preventive contraception decrease. In addition, Plan B frequently produces nausea and vomiting, and repeated use leads to menstrual irregularity, so it is unlikely that women will depend exclusively on it for contraception. Finally, although relatively few women aged sixteen and younger were included in the actual use studies of Plan B, the data that were presented indicated that the youngest women who were studied actually used the drug correctly about as often as older women.

As I thought about the hearings after getting home, I realized that the discussion hadn't considered the issue of spontaneous abortion, a serious omission that in my view prevented the committees from reaching a clear and balanced understanding of the whole abortion issue. Accordingly, several days after the hearings I wrote a letter to the agency, to be included in the public record, which laid out the following concerns. The best studies, using sensitive hormonal assays, have shown that about 30 percent of all pregnancies in women who are using no contraception are spontaneously lost very early after conception, well before the woman knows she is pregnant. Assuming that Plan B prevents pregnancy by preventing fertilization—an entirely reasonable assumption, given current evidence—the over-the-counter availability of Plan B could therefore result in a large decrease in the loss of fertilized ova; in effect, use of Plan B could actually decrease the overall number of "abortions" that would otherwise have occurred (in this case, spontaneously). Moreover, since levonorgestrol is, in fact, a progestational agent that is used to prevent threatened abortion, it is even possible that many, and perhaps most, of the 25 percent of pregnancies that occur despite the use of Plan B (Plan B "failure") could be those that would have otherwise been spontaneously lost early on if the woman had not taken the drug. In this latter case, emergency use of levonorgestrol could, at least in theory, virtually eliminate very early spontaneous "abortion." These considerations suggest that even if Plan B were to prevent as many as 30 percent of pregnancies by preventing implantation of fertilized ova, rather than by preventing fertilization, the overall early loss of fertilized ova in any group of women using Plan B would be no greater than if the drug was not used at all, although drug-induced early loss would replace spontaneous early loss—a tradeoff of uncertain moral significance.

Advisory committee recommendations are not binding on the agency, but the FDA rarely makes decisions that are contrary to those recommendations. Moreover, as a high-level FDA staffer explained to me informally, in the few instances in which the agency's approval decisions went against advisory committee votes, the votes (for reasons that were usually not clear) had been inconsistent with the sense of the committees' own discussions—clearly not the case in the Plan B hearings. It was therefore a considerable surprise, not to mention a serious disappointment, to many of us when the FDA announced its decision in May 2004 that Plan B was "not approvable" for over-the-counter use. The decision seemed to me to be so obviously inconsistent with the evidence that I seriously considered resigning at that time, but I decided not to. I felt an obligation to finish my full term.

It was anyone's guess in May 2004 what drove the FDA to behave in such a seemingly irrational way. True, we had learned during the Plan B committee hearings that some members of Congress had written to the FDA opposing over-the-counter availability, apparently on the grounds that it might foster promiscuity, and some statements in the public hearings had raised concern about the social and behavioral side effects. Moreover, two or three members of the RHDAC had made it clear that they had serious moral concerns because of the possibility, however remote, that in some women Plan B might be acting as an abortifacient. But there was no "smoking gun" to indicate that the agency had actually yielded to direct political pressure from social conservatives. On the other hand, there was no other obvious explanation, either.

In fact, the FDA's May 2004 "not approvable" decision for Plan B did not close the door entirely on the over-the-counter option. The agency offered the sponsor the option of "two tier," age-dependent marketing—that is, making Plan B available over the counter to women over age sixteen, but only by prescription to younger women. As pointed out later, this option is very limited: it would discriminate not only against younger women, but also against those over sixteen who do not have drivers' licenses—usually poor women and those from inner-city neighborhoods.[1] Moreover, being "carded" by a pharmacist in order to buy the drug—a very public process—would be a serious and humiliating invasion of privacy that would intimidate many women and prevent them from obtaining the drug. Despite these disturbing concerns, and despite the fact that such marketing for over-the-counter drugs is virtually unprecedented (nicotine preparations for smoking cessation are not approved for over-the-counter availability to people under age eighteen, but that restriction is consistent with the age restriction for tobacco sales), Barr Laboratories apparently decided it was better to settle for half a loaf and refiled their over-the-counter switch application, which included a plan for dual-level availability.

While this was happening, the FDA's then newly appointed commissioner, Lester Crawford, made a public commitment as a condition of his appointment that the agency would make a definite decision on Plan B's over-the-counter approvability by September 1, 2005. On August 26, 2005, however, the FDA, apparently as the result of a sudden and unexpected *crise de nerfs* over the unprecedented nature of a two-tier marketing system, announced that it would require a ninety-day comment period before it could make a final ruling on over-the-counter availability. Those familiar with the FDA's rulemaking recognized immediately that this nondecision ruling meant the agency could put off a decision on over-the-counter approvability almost indefinitely. There's an old saying that seemed to capture the situation very well: "Fool me once, shame on you; fool me twice, shame on me." At that point, therefore, I decided that the irrationality of the FDA's decision process had crossed the line, and the time had come for me to resign. (Since my term on the NDAC officially ended in May 2005, the position I resigned was actually as a consultant.)

Other information that has surfaced along the way strengthens the inference that the presumed inability of younger women to use Plan B correctly was a smoke screen (or, perhaps more appropriately, a "fig leaf") used to obscure the real pressures for nonapproval. First, it became increasingly clear that many people confuse Plan B with mifepristone, or RU-486—the "French pill"—which is a progesterone antagonist used explicitly to induce abortion.[2] Second, as reported in *Time* magazine, prior to the FDA's August 2005 decision, socially conservative organizations were encouraging their members to flood the White House and Congress with letters and calls opposing over-the-counter approval. Third, W. David Hager, an obstetrician-gynecologist recruited directly by the Bush White House to serve on the RHDAC and one of the four committee members who voted against over-the-counter availability, confirmed that after the committee hearings he had sent the FDA a "minority report" at the behest of "someone at the FDA," whose name he says he is not at liberty to reveal, asking for "more studies" and for "more data on the use of Plan B by young girls."[3] It was also later revealed that in speaking about Plan B to an audience at a Christian college, Hager had said "God has used me to stand in the breach for the cause of the Kingdom."

These suspicions of social conservative pressure received further strong support from the report of the Government Accountability Office released in November 2005.[4] Produced in response to a request by forty-eight members of the U.S. Senate and House of Representatives, the report documents four unusual aspects of the initial "not approvable" Plan B decision process. First, the FDA staff who would normally have been responsible for signing the not-approvable letter disagreed with the decision and refused to sign. Second, high-level FDA management was more involved in the review of Plan B than in the review of any other over-the-counter switch application. Third, the decision not to approve the application may have been made before the scientific reviews were completed. And lastly, the rationale for the decision (the presumed inability of younger women to use the drug appropriately) did not follow the FDA's usual practices—it normally considers extrapolating data from older to younger adolescents to be scientifically appropriate. The exercise of such pressures should not be surprising, however, when we recognize that the FDA is part of the executive branch of government. The FDA commissioner therefore reports to the secretary of the Department of

Health and Human Services who, in turn, reports directly to the president; and the current president makes no secret of his determination to implement a socially conservative agenda by whatever means necessary.

The distressing history of Plan B teaches lessons on at least two points: the special vulnerabilities of the FDA, and the vagaries of resignation as a form of social protest. As a regulatory agency, the FDA is caught in crossfire from several sources. There is pressure from free market advocates, most obviously those in industry, for whom the agency—like all Federal regulators—is anathema; free marketeers truly believe that the economy, medicine, and the public interest would all be better off without the FDA's "paternalistic" control. Accordingly, industry has worked hard, and with considerable success, to reshape the FDA's regulatory role to be more in line with its own interests.[5] Industry has exerted its influence largely through Congress, both because many members of Congress share its free market perspective, and because Congress in turn does possess some control over the shape, size, and function of the FDA. On the other hand, when it perceives that the FDA has allowed the public to be exposed to preventable risks and harms, Congress apparently sees no internal (and political) contradiction in taking the opposite position, coming down hard on the agency and pushing for more stringent regulation. The 1962 Kefauver-Harris amendments mandating that drugs must be shown to be effective as well as safe before they can be marketed came about because of the thalidomide tragedy. The FDA is also subject to direct political pressure from the executive branch, as was apparently the case with the Plan B decision. And finally, the FDA is under constant, detailed, and intensive scrutiny by the media and, consequently, the public. The public's judgments can be swift and harsh, particularly when it perceives that the agency is roiled by conflict of interest, bureaucratic paralysis, and lack of transparency.

It was anyone's guess in May 2004 what drove the FDA to decide Plan B was not approvable for over-the-counter use. While there was no smoking gun to indicate it yielded to direct political pressure, there was no other obvious explanation, either.

Managing these pressures while trying to get its basic scientific and administrative job done is a huge challenge for the agency. Its priority, then, is to manage relationships with the outside world, and for that it requires public trust. Unfortunately, corruption of the decision-making process by political forces, as has happened in the case of Plan B, squanders that trust and tarnishes the agency's image.[6] But the FDA also needs to manage the effects of those pressures internally, particularly their impact on its own employees. Virtually all the FDA staff who worked with the advisory committees struck me as being knowledgeable, professional, competent, and hard working. And although I suspect many FDA staff could have made considerably larger incomes in industry or even academia, several made it clear to me that they chose to stay with the agency because they felt their work was both rewarding and important. I found it particularly distressing, therefore, to be told in September 2005 by a high-level agency official that the staff had become "demoralized and depressed" by the Plan B decision, and to learn that Susan Wood had resigned.

Resigning from an organization is hardly as visible as signing a petition or taking out an ad, nor is it as strident as rioting in the streets; but resigning in protest is certainly a time-honored practice. I had never before resigned in protest, however, and since no one ever taught me in school how to go about it, I was on my own. At first, I wondered whether to do it at all. I would be withholding my expertise, such as it was, from the FDA at a time when it probably needed outside expert help more than ever, and I did feel I had something useful to offer. I knew that, by resigning, I would be letting down my colleagues on the NDAC. And I also knew that my leaving might lead to the appointment of someone worse—someone who believed that social and religious values should trump a rational decision process, based on scientific evidence, which is the agency's mandate.

In the end, I simply decided that the potential value of such a protest outweighed the down side. At the same time, however, just resigning quietly made no sense at all. (As one of my friends put it, "If an FDA committee member falls in the forest and no one hears it, does it make a noise?") In my resignation letter, I therefore told the FDA that I was resigning "publicly," thus declaring my intention to use my resignation actively as leverage for reconsideration of the Plan B decision. (I also told them I would encourage other members of the NDAC to resign, but later reconsidered that decision after a colleague persuaded me that the potential damage to the FDA of multiple simultaneous resignations might be greater than the value of the protest.) Having no clear idea how to turn my resignation into an active protest—how to get the word out, use it for some leverage, "make a fuss"—I fell back on the storied method of social protest: writing a letter to the *New York Times*. Unfortunately, my letter got to the *Times* two days after Hurricane Katrina hit New Orleans, and like so much else, it was washed away in the flood.

It was only when, about two weeks later, I got a call from a *Hartford Courant* reporter asking for an interview that it seemed my protest might gain some traction. The reporter's interest, it turns out, came about only because I had mentioned my resignation to a colleague, and the conversation was passed on through a network of personal connections—the vagaries of chance. The resulting article appeared a few days later as the cover story in *Northeast*, the *Courant*'s Sunday magazine.[7] Since the media seems to find blood in the water irresistible, the *Courant* story was immediately followed by an intense but short-lived media frenzy, which included tapings by National Public Radio, Fox news, and ABC news, not to mention Associated Press and Reuters stories in various newspapers (including the *New York Times*), as well as reports in "The Tan Sheet" and the *British Medical Journal*. But it was only when I began getting e-mail a few days later from friends and colleagues in far-flung places— London, Rome, and Bangkok—that I appreciated fully the reach and power the Internet has given to the media. A number of advocacy groups also approached me, offering to put on press conferences in which I could talk about the Plan B "debacle." That idea seemed attractive at first, but when I considered the possibility of getting tangled up in the agendas of groups I knew nothing about, I decided against it.

In my view, what has brought out the harsh, controlling streak in so many is that emergency contraception has to do with sex, and the resultant co-mingling of sex with politics and morality is highly corrosive.

Has my resignation made any difference at all? It's hard to say. It did lead directly to my being contacted by staffers of two U.S. senators who had questions about "decision-making at the FDA," and this gave me an opportunity to talk at length with them about the Plan B decision. When the GAO report was released, I was invited to discuss it on *The NewsHour with Jim Lehrer* (which I unfortunately couldn't do). I did learn in passing about one or more bills being considered by Congress that would require a definitive decision, up or down, from the FDA on Plan B by "date certain," the default being that over-the-counter availability would be automatically approved if the decision weren't forthcoming by that date. Any relief I felt from the prospect that rationality might be restored to the Plan B decision was quickly extinguished, however, by the realization that such a law would set the terrible precedent of drug approval directly by the unruly politics of Congress, rather than by sober and balanced review of the evidence by the FDA.

How did we get ourselves into such a mess? In my view, what has brought out the harsh, controlling streak in so many people is that emergency contraception has to do with sex, and that the resultant commingling of sex with politics and morality is highly corrosive. Why does sex get people's backs up? Like all powerful forces—terrorism, hurricanes, pandemics— the power of sex can seem appalling, terrifying, something that must therefore be controlled at all costs. And since men exert most organized social control, the control over sexuality is asserted primarily by controlling the sexual and reproductive lives of women. A small number of women apparently also share these views. Furthermore, although several other serious and legitimate concerns—including interests of the state and society, as well as personal, humanistic issues— attach to abortion, one can argue that the abortion issue—particularly not permitting very early abortion—is also in substantial part an expression of the need to control women's sexual lives.

How can we get ourselves out of this mess? It may be both necessary and possible to "fight back" against political attacks on science,[8] but that strategy is likely to be successful only in the short run; deeper structural changes are probably required in the long run to keep from having to fight those battles over and over again. Although a simple solution is unlikely, at least two approaches might help. The first is a greatly increased reliance on transparency. That is, rather than imposing rigid and absolutist control over the availability of a safe and effective drug like Plan B, both doctors and patients would be better off if the public had greater access to the drug, but only on condition that everyone is fully informed about the issues associated with its use. For example, providing everyone with full information about the facts on spontaneous early abortion and possible effects of Plan B on early pregnancy loss would allow those doctors and those women who have serious moral concerns about abortion to make informed choices about using the drug. At the same time, access would not be limited for women for whom these concerns are not a serious barrier to the drug's use. Providing this information through appropriate wording on the package label should be quite possible; I suggested such wording in my December 2005 follow- up letter to the FDA.

The second approach would be to find a way to protect the FDA without diluting its effectiveness. The agency, like all regulators, is currently caught in the crossfire precisely because, by design, it is positioned in the no man's land between the commercial and "guardian" (governmental, academic, legal, religious, and military) worlds. It is therefore subject to the contrasting, often clashing and conflicting "moral syndromes" and pragmatic interests of these two worlds. As the social critic Jane Jacobs has argued, both worlds are necessary for a healthy and well-functioning society.[9] But when one world takes over the functions of the other, the result is a "monstrous hybrid"— think of the Soviet Union's effect on commerce, or, conversely, the effect of commercialism on managed care and HMOs in the United States.[10] However, although each of these worlds needs to keep well within its own domain, they need to interact closely with one another, balancing their interests and working out mutually acceptable solutions if the larger society is to prosper.

That balancing act is a tough one for everyone, and particularly for regulatory agencies, all of which are caught in the middle; moreover, the FDA carries a large added burden because protection of the public health is such a sensitive issue. It has occurred to me, therefore, that it would make sense to convert the FDA into a quasigovernmental agency, like the Federal Reserve and the National Academy of Sciences—supported by public funds and with binding decision-making power over both the standards of scientific evidence and the flow of commerce, but largely out of reach of direct political pressure. I made that suggestion during my discussions with the senate staffers. Unfortunately, they didn't seem impressed.

Notes

1. A.J.J. Wood, J.M. Drazen, and M.F. Greene. "A Sad Day for Science at the FDA," *New England Journal of Medicine* 352 (2005): 1197–99.
2. *60 Minutes*, "The Debate over Plan B," http://www.cbsnews.com/stories/2005/11/22/60minutes/main1068924.shtml.
3. Ibid.

4. United States Government Accountability Office, "Decision Process to Deny Initial Application for Over-the-Counter Marketing of the Emergency Contraceptive Drug Plan B Was Unusual," Report GAO-06-109, http://www.gao.gov/cgi-bin/getrpt?GAO-06-109.

5. M. Angell, *The Truth about the Drug Companies: How They Deceive Us and What to Do about It* (New York: Random House, 2004).

6. Wood, Drazen, and Greene, "A Sad Day for Science at the FDA."

7. R. Buck, "Plan B Casualties," *Northeast Magazine*, October 2, 2005: 3–5.

8. L. Rosenstock and L.J. Lee, "Attacks on Science: The Risks to Evidence-Based Policy," *American Journal of Public Health* 92 (2002): 14–18.

9. J. Jacobs, *Systems of Survival: A Dialogue on the Moral Foundations of Commerce and Politics* (New York: Random House, 1992).

10. F. Davidoff, "Medicine and Commerce. 1: Is Managed Care a 'Monstrous Hybrid'?" [Editorial] *Annals of Internal Medicine* 128 (1998): 496–99; J.G. Coombs, *The Rise and Fall of HMOs: An American Health Care Revolution* (Madison: University of Wisconsin Press, 2005).

FRANK DAVIDOFF, "Sex, Politics, and Morality at the FDA: Reflections on the Plan B Decision," Hastings Center Report 36, no. 2 (2006): 20–25.

From *Hastings Center Report*, March-April 2006, pp. 20-25. Copyright © 2006 by Hastings Center. Reprinted by permission of the publisher and the author, Frank Davidoff.

A Late Decision, a Lasting Anguish

A Kansas doctor is under investigation for performing abortions others won't. His clients say outsiders can't grasp their pain or gratitude.

STEPHANIE SIMON
Times Staff Writer

Wichita, Kan.—The moment is burned forever in her mind: The small exam room, her husband's ashen face, her sobs as the doctor guided a needle into her womb to kill her son.

It's been 4½ years, and still Marie Becker can feel Daniel kicking inside her, kicking and kicking as she choked back hysteria—kicking until the drug stopped his heart and she felt only stillness.

She prayed Daniel would forgive her.

She prayed for forgiveness from God as well. Becker had been taught that abortion was a sin; she wanted so to believe it might also be a blessing. In her seventh month of pregnancy she had learned Daniel had a fatal genetic disorder and his life would be brief and brutal. She wanted to spare him that.

"For the love of God, the last thing I wanted to do was to murder my own child," she said recently. "This was something we did out of love and respect for him."

Becker, who asked to be identified by her middle and maiden names, tells Daniel's story to other pregnant women who find out when they are many months along that their babies are terminally ill or severely disabled. Through an online support group, she listens as they work through their options; if they choose abortion, she tells them what to expect these days she also prays for one of the few doctors in the nation who will take them as patients: Dr. George R. Tiller, who performed her abortion. Specializing in late second- and third-trimester abortions, his clinic here draws women from across the country and around the world.

Tiller's clinic aborted 295 viable fetuses last year and 318 the year before; his website says that he has performed more late-term abortions than anyone else practicing in the Western Hemisphere.

But the clinic is now under criminal investigation for some of those procedures.

Like most states, Kansas does not permit abortions of viable fetuses unless carrying the pregnancy to term would substantially and irreversibly damage the mother's health. Kansas Atty. Gen. Phill Kline is investigating whether Tiller's patients were truly in that much danger. Tiller's lawyers respond that he has "always consistently, carefully and appropriately followed the law in all respects."

Kline, who opposes all abortions, maintains that the mental health concerns some women cite as their main reason for terminating—including depression or anxiety about raising a disabled child—do not justify late-term abortions under Kansas law. He has demanded access to the medical records of dozens of patients. The clinic has appealed to the state Supreme Court; a decision is expected within weeks.

Tiller's patients await the ruling with mounting anger. They say no outsider could ever understand the complex tangle of emotions that brought them to Women's Health Care Services—the psychological and physical strains that made continuing their pregnancies unbearable.

"I don't know what I would have done had [Dr. Tiller] not been available to me," said Katie Plazio, a financial analyst from New Jersey. "That's selfish, I know. I feel selfish. But ... doesn't everyone want the best for themselves and their family?"

Like Becker and most women who spoke for this story, Plazio asked to use her middle and maiden names to protect her privacy. Many of Tiller's patients have not told their co-workers, friends or even close relatives that they had terminated pregnancies. Their abortions were verified by a review of clinic records they supplied.

For Plazio, the heartache began with the unexpected. After a decade of infertility, she was stunned to feel a kick to her ribs as she sat through a meeting in February 2001. She had been dieting for weeks, running five miles a day—and wondering why she still couldn't squeeze into her pants. She was six months pregnant.

Overjoyed, Plazio and her husband scheduled an amniocentesis. The preliminary results were clean; bursting with excitement, Plazio, then 43, bought a baby blanket dotted with pale blue bunnies. Ten days later, her doctor called with devastating news: More complete genetic tests had determined that their son had Down syndrome.

Plazio had studied special education in college; working with adults with Down syndrome, she had seen their lives as lonely, frustrating, full of hurt. She was not sure she could find joy in raising her son to such a future. She didn't think she could cope with what she expected would be a lifetime of sadness and struggle.

Giving her son up for adoption seemed even worse—to wake each morning not knowing where he was, imagining him scared and alone. "I could not live with that fear all my life," Plazio said.

"I don't want anyone to think that I did this all for Matthew," she said. "I was not just sparing him problems. I was sparing my daughter, my husband, me and all those who depend on me I knew the limits of my family and my marriage. Maybe there are families who can handle it all. Maybe they are better people. But I knew I could not do it."

In March 2001, a week into her third trimester, she and her husband flew to Tiller's clinic. They took the bunny blanket and a teddy bear with a big red heart on its chest—a gift to the baby from their daughter, then 11.

Since her abortion, Plazio has suffered such severe panic attacks that she can't drive even as far as the high school to watch her daughter cheerlead. She has gained 60 pounds as she battles depression. The abortion she sought to preserve her mental health has left her deeply shaken; doctors say she suffers from post-traumatic stress syndrome.

Her mental health, she is convinced, would be even worse had she tried to raise a profoundly disabled son—or had she given him up for adoption.

The abortion "released my poor sick baby back to the angels," she said. "The only thing I wish I had done differently was realize I was pregnant months earlier."

Third-trimester terminations like Plazio's are unusual.

About 95% of U.S. abortions are performed within the first 15 weeks of pregnancy, according to the Alan Guttmacher Institute, a nonprofit center for reproductive rights and health research.

About 20,000 women a year seek abortions after the 21st week, which marks roughly the midway point in a pregnancy. Perhaps 1,000 terminate after 24 weeks, when the fetus is generally considered viable. The practice, though rare, makes many Americans uneasy. While 60% say abortion should be legal in the first trimester of pregnancy, 12% say it should be legal in the third trimester, according to a Harris poll conducted in February.

Three clinics in the nation perform abortions in the third trimester. One is in Los Angeles, one in Boulder, Colo. The best-known—recommended by many genetic counselors—is Tiller's bunker-like clinic on a freeway frontage road in Wichita, next to a car dealership. Outside, protesters have erected dozens of white crosses; they maintain a prayer vigil by the gate and try to pull women aside for counseling—especially on Tuesday mornings, when Tiller sees patients seeking late-term abortions.

The women who push past the protesters Tuesdays include young victims of rape or incest who did not realize they were pregnant until just weeks from their due dates. Most are married women with much-wanted pregnancies who got a late diagnosis of fetal anomaly: a malformed heart, a missing brain, an open spinal column, an extra chromosome.

Some of the deformities are lethal. Others are not. A few fall in a gray area: The physical problems might be reparable through surgery, but the operations are risky and grueling.

One patient who had an abortion at 25 weeks in November said she could not bear to imagine surgeons cutting open her daughter's tiny chest to rebuild her heart. The thought of her

Emma spending months of her childhood in the hospital overwhelmed the woman, a 30-year-old technology educator from Virginia who asked to be identified by her middle name, Paige.

"Part of me just wanted to let her die," Paige said. "Is that horrible?"

Marie Becker had the same impulse—and the same question—about her son.

At a four-month ultrasound, the doctor noticed that Daniel's limbs seemed short. She told Becker not to worry, but suggested another ultrasound in a few weeks. At that appointment, Daniel again measured short. Becker was told to come back in another month.

Becker, an accounting clerk, and her husband, a teacher, tried not to dwell on their fears for their first child. They delighted in the ultrasound pictures: Blurry black-and-white images of an arm, a leg, a face. In one, Daniel appeared to be waving; the technician typed a caption: "Hi, mom!"

Becker was 27 weeks pregnant when she went in for her next appointment. By then, it was clear that something was wrong.

A few days later, her doctor confirmed that Daniel had a rare and lethal skeletal disease. His organs were growing normally, but his bones were not; his tiny rib cage was slowly crushing his expanding heart and lungs. "His prognosis was death," Becker said. "Not at 8 years old. Not at 10 years old. Within a few months at most."

In her Florida home, with her husband at her side, Becker wept and prayed for days. Conflicting emotions overwhelmed her. She was scared to carry Daniel to term—scared of how she would react to his deformities. She was afraid to abort, sure she would burn in hell. Her son disgusted her; she wanted him out of her body. She loved him. She wanted to protect him.

Becker, who was then 30, blamed herself for making Daniel sick: Hadn't she taken migraine pills before she knew she was pregnant? Hadn't she sipped a few glasses of wine? Was it that ride at SeaWorld, the one that whirled her around? Had that caused his genes to mutate?

"I was so afraid," she said. "It was bad enough that I had inflicted this on him. I didn't want him to suffer any more."

The week before Christmas, at the start of her third trimester, Becker and her husband flew to Kansas.

Every detail of the trip remains vivid. She remembers staring, transfixed, at the freshly cleaned carpet in the Wichita airport. She remembers driving to the hotel through ice and snow—and turning away from a billboard plastered with gruesome photos of aborted fetuses. On the morning of the appointment, she threw up in the hotel shower, then insisted she needed time to style her hair; her looks seemed the one thing she could control, and she took long minutes applying her lipstick.

When she and her husband turned into the clinic parking lot, a handful of elderly protesters swarmed them, yelling, "Don't go in!" and "You don't have to do this!"

The activists were peaceful that day, but there had been scattered violence: The clinic was bombed in 1986 and blockaded for six weeks in the summer of 1991. In 1993, an antiabortion activist shot Tiller through both arms. He now works in a bulletproof vest. Armed guards pat down patients and walk them through a metal detector at the clinic door. After paying for their abortions—which can cost more than $5,000, depending on the stage of pregnancy—patients wait in a room decorated floor to ceiling with framed letters from grateful women.

"We couldn't stop reading them," Becker said. "When you see how many people wrote letters, when you see how much they love this man, it almost feels like you're being hugged."

Becker still believes that abortion is wrong in most cases. Sitting in her Florida bungalow, her two young daughters playing beside her, she recalled a movie she once saw in Catholic school, of a baby being ripped limb from limb. The image haunts her.

She finds it reprehensible that Tiller aborts healthy fetuses in the first and second trimester (and even, sometimes, in the third trimester when the mother is very young, or a victim of rape). But she cannot censure him too harshly.

For children like Daniel, "the man is a savior," she said. "He's there for women who have nowhere else to go."

With most advanced pregnancies, Tiller performs abortions by injecting the fetus with digoxin to stop its heart. He then gradually dilates the woman's cervix to induce labor. After two or three days of contractions, the women—heavily dosed with pain medication—deliver their babies intact.

Some refuse to look. But many hug their dead children. "It was very important to us to be able to hold her, to give her that kind of respect," said Paige, who aborted her daughter at the end of the second trimester. "This was not just a fetus to me. She was my child."

After Susan Crocker's second-trimester abortion in August, she and her fiance spent three hours cradling their daughter, Isabella, who had Down syndrome. They stroked her scrunched red face and kissed her rounded cheeks. They took pictures of her tiny, almost translucent hands, folded across a green-and-pink striped blanket.

Crocker, a 34-year-old customer service manager, keeps Isabella's ashes in a marble urn decorated with dolphins; she kisses it before she goes to bed each night. Her sons follow her lead. On Halloween, they each gave a Tootsie Roll to Isabella. Jordan, 5, shares his toys with her, propping a little plastic skateboard against the urn.

When a doctor once referred to Crocker as a mother of two, Jamie, the 9-year-old, interrupted indignantly: "No, she has three kids." "Her daughter's in her heart," said Jordan.

Despite her family's support, Crocker, who lives in Texas, has struggled with doubt and depression. "I did the unthinkable," she said. "I ended my baby's life. Sometimes I think, oh God, what if I was wrong?"

Then she thinks about the room where Tiller stopped Isabella's heart. There was a poster on the ceiling of a leaping dolphin. Underneath, it said: "Set them free."

She believes Isabella is free.

"I ended her suffering," she said. "I owe Dr. Tiller greatly. I can never, ever thank him enough."

Crocker sometimes wishes she could talk to the protesters who shouted as she entered the clinic: "Think about your baby!" She would tell them she was thinking of Isabella then, and thinks of her still, every day, with love. She would ask them not to judge.

"You don't know," she'd tell them. "You have no idea. Until it happens to you, you don't know."

Condoms, Contraceptives and Nonoxynol-9: Complex Issues Obscured by Ideology

HEATHER BOONSTRA

During the 1990s, as the AIDS crisis worsened and vaccine research faltered, HIV prevention activists increasingly pinned their hopes on nonoyxnol-9 (N-9). Widely available in the United States for over 50 years as the active ingredient in spermicides, N-9 was shown to kill the AIDS virus in the laboratory. A number of epidemiologic studies further suggested that N-9 conferred some protection against bacterial sexually transmitted infections (STIs) when used alone or in combination with a diaphragm. Researchers and advocates alike anticipated that it would be shown to prevent HIV in human trials as well, clearing the way for a new and relatively inexpensive preventive option to be made available to people around the world living with or at-risk of HIV.

Those expectations were dashed, however, when in 2000 a study of N-9's effectiveness among sex workers in Benin, Cote d'Ivoire, South Africa and Thailand showed that HIV incidence was actually higher among the women using N-9 than among those using a comparison product. But in addition to being a disappointment for HIV prevention efforts, the results also raised questions about the safety of N-9 when used for the purpose for which it was approved, protection against unwanted pregnancy.

Following the results of this study, experts at the World Health Organization (WHO) and the U.S. Centers for Disease Control and Prevention (CDC) conducted a concerted review of the evidence and made a series of recommendations. Based on those recommendations, an ad-hoc coalition of individual experts and women's health and AIDS organizations called on manufacturers to stop adding N-9 to condoms and sexual lubricants. In accordance with the available evidence, however, the coalition stopped short of calling for the withdrawal of noncondom contraceptive products containing N-9 from the market. Meanwhile, anti-family planning activists have been using the N-9 issue to further their ongoing campaign to discredit condoms, and contraceptives in general, as a means of promoting abstinence outside of marriage as the only appropriate answer to STIs and unwanted pregnancy.

Expectations Unfulfilled

N-9 spermicides have been available over-the-counter in the United States since the 1960s and are used by approximately half a million women for pregnancy prevention. N-9 is found in a variety of vaginal contraceptive products, including creams, foams, gels and suppositories—used alone or in combination with the diaphragm or cervical cap. Because N-9 was approved for sale before the Food and Drug Administration (FDA) began to require rigorous efficacy studies, knowledge about N-9's effectiveness against pregnancy in various doses and formulations was limited until recently.

In the late 1980s, when researchers saw that N-9 showed in vitro activity against HIV and other STIs, N-9 was also added to condoms and sexual lubricants. In 1988, Surgeon General C. Everett Koop announced that, based on laboratory tests, condoms with N-9 could provide additional protection against HIV, and public health officials began to advise the use of N-9 for HIV prevention.

Anti-family planning activists have been using the N-9 issue to further their ongoing campaign to discredit condoms, and contraceptives in general, as a means of promoting abstinence outside of marriage.

In 2001, however, after presentation of the preliminary results of a study testing an N-9 gel in a high-risk population of sex workers, WHO convened a technical consultation—experts from developed and developing countries—to review the available evidence from this and numerous other studies and to make recommendations on the use of N-9. WHO released its summary report on N-9 in October 2001 based on this review, and in May 2002,

CDC published its public health guidelines for the use of N-9. The WHO and CDC reports underscore these major conclusions:

- N-9 is not effective against HIV or other STIs and, when used vaginally multiple times a day, can cause genital lesions—a condition that may increase a woman's risk of acquiring HIV.
- Even at low doses, N-9 can cause massive, short-term damage to the rectal epithelium (lining), thereby increasing an individual's risk of contracting HIV and other STIs during anal intercourse.   .
- Although noncondom contraceptive products containing N-9 are moderately effective in preventing pregnancy and safe when used infrequently (no more than once a day), condoms lubricated with a small amount of N-9 are no more effective in preventing pregnancy than are lubricated condoms without N-9.

A Call to Action

In 2002, within months of the CDC report on N-9, HIV and women's health advocates in the United States launched a campaign to caution the public about the appropriate use of N-9 and to encourage responsible behavior by industry. Led by the Global Campaign for Microbicides and endorsed by more than 80 scientists and public health organizations, the open letter makes the following key points:

- Couples engaging in vaginal intercourse should not use products containing N-9 for the prevention of HIV or other STIs, and in no case should these products be used during anal intercourse.
- Manufacturers should remove N-9 from condoms and lubricants, because the small amount of N-9 they contain is dangerous if used rectally and offers no demonstrated contraceptive benefit.
- N-9 contraceptive products designed exclusively for vaginal use remain an important option for pregnancy prevention for women who have sex infrequently and are at low risk of HIV infection; removing these products from the market is unwarranted.

Since the launch of the call to action, nine condom and lubricant manufacturers—including Johnson & Johnson, Mayer Laboratories and the makers of Durex condoms—have discontinued production of N-9 condoms and lubricants. Planned Parenthood Federation of America (PPFA), which joined the call to action, immediately stopped producing N-9 condoms and stopped recommending N-9 as a way to protect against HIV or other STIs. The Office of Population Affairs (OPA) at the U.S. Department of Health and Human Services, which oversees family planning service delivery under the Title X program, sent a copy of CDC's report on N-9 to its regional offices and encouraged them to share the information with grantees. And the New York-based Gay Men's Health Crisis, one of the largest AIDS service organizations in the United States, initiated a public education campaign targeted at men who have sex with men to inform them not to use N-9 condoms and lubricants.

Right-Wing Reactions

To be sure, the controversy over N-9 did not fail to capture the attention of social conservatives in Congress, who have sought to turn the issue to their advantage in their ongoing campaign against the condom (see box). That campaign started in 1999 when, as a member in the U.S. House of Representatives, now-Senator Tom Coburn (R-OK) pushed legislation mandating that condom packages carry a cigarette-type warning that condoms do not protect against human papillomavirus (HPV). Although his directive was never enacted, he was successful in imposing a requirement that FDA reexamine condom labels to determine whether they are medically accurate with respect to condoms' "effectiveness or lack of effectiveness" in preventing STIs, including HPV.

Meanwhile, Coburn and his allies, Reps. Mark Souder (R-IN), Joseph Pitts (R-PA) and David Weldon (R-FL), were quick to respond to the findings of the N-9 sex-worker study upon their release in 2000. Immediately, they called for an investigation by the Government Accountability Office (GAO) into the federal government's actions related to N-9. And before GAO had the chance to respond, Souder's Subcommittee on Criminal Justice, Drug Policy and Human Resources twice called on FDA to pull all N-9 products from the market—the consequences of which would have been serious, especially for those women who, for pregnancy prevention, rely on the diaphragm or cervical cap, which are labeled for use with a spermicide. (Because N-9 is the only spermicide available in the United States, eliminating N-9 products without a substitute would effectively preclude diaphragm and cervical cap use as intended.)

In March 2005, GAO issued its long-awaited report on the federal government's efforts to research and inform the public about N-9 and HIV. By and large, the report recited the succession of research trials that raised concerns about N-9 and the federal government's response. It described how the National Institutes of Health and CDC subsequently stopped conducting and funding research on N-9 and how CDC changed its guidance. In addition, the report gently rebuked FDA for taking so long to inform the public about evidence related to N-9 and HIV transmission. "Since FDA is still in the process of completing warning label changes for N-9 vaginal contraceptive products and condoms, the public may be left in doubt about the appropriate uses of these products until FDA finalizes these warnings," the GAO report concluded. "Further, the public may be at risk if these products are used inappropriately."

HIV and women's health advocates are concerned that the admittedly nuanced and complex messaging that should be taking place around N-9 may not be getting through.

Once again, Coburn and his allies were ready to pounce, and they used the GAO report's release as a spring-board to promote abstinence as the only certain way to protect against

HPV and the Anticondom Crusade

Social conservatives continue to press their campaign to "warn" Americans that condoms do not protect against HPV, some strains of which cause cervical cancer—despite growing recognition within the public health community both that their facts are wrong and that their focus is misplaced.

HPV is an extremely common STI—so common that it is considered a virtual marker for having had sex. But although most women who are sexually active will acquire HPV at some point, very few will develop cervical cancer. In fact, most HPV infections resolve on their own without treatment: As many as 70% of infections clear within one year, and 91% within two.

Because of major advances in detection and prevention, notably the Pap test, cervical cancer has become relatively uncommon in the United States. (The American Cancer Society estimates that 12,200 cases will occur to American women this year, resulting in 4,100 deaths.) According to CDC, regular screening to detect precancerous lesions, which can then be treated, remains the key strategy for preventing cervical cancer. Indeed, the majority of cervical cancer cases in this country occur to women who have not had a Pap test in the last three years ("HPV in the United States and Developing Nations: A Problem of Public Health or Politics?" TGR, August 2003, page 4).

Admittedly, genital HPV cannot be entirely prevented by condom use, because HPV is spread through skin-to-skin contact, not through the exchange of bodily fluids (like HIV). Still, due to the partial protection that can be provided, correct and consistent condom use has been shown to lower the incidence of cervical cancer.

In any event, the debate over condom effectiveness against HPV could be largely made moot by the advent of a vaccine that prevents HPV in the first place. Two such vaccines are in the final stages of testing and could be available within two years. The drug makers, Merck and GlaxoSmithKline, hope the vaccine can be folded into routine medical care for young women. "The best way to prevent infection is to vaccinate the population just before they become sexually active, which is when they're young," Eliav Barr, Merck's senior director of biologics clinical research, told the Newark Star-Ledger. But the anticipated roll-out is already facing opposition from those who fear the vaccine will have a "disinhibiting effect" on young women, giving them a green light to have sex. "The best way to prevent HPV is through abstinence," said Bridget Maher of the Family Research Council to The Star-Ledger. "I see potential harm in giving this vaccine to young women."

pregnancy and STIs. In a joint press release, issued with Weldon, Pitts and Souder in April 2005, Coburn spoke about the "shortcomings" of condoms with regard to both HPV and HIV: "Condoms do not protect against the most common STD—" human papillomavirus (HPV), which causes nearly all cases of cervical cancer—and contraceptives with N-9 increase HIV risk." For his part, Weldon took the opportunity to take a swipe at federally funded family planning programs. Ignoring the actions take by PPFA and OPA following the report from WHO and guidance issued by CDC in 2002, Weldon cited the findings of the GAO report on N-9 as "just another example of how Planned Parenthood, Title X clinics and federal agencies have distorted science to promote a social policy that has the exact opposite impact of the stated goal. We may never know the toll in terms of new HIV cases that have resulted from the promotion and distribution—with taxpayer dollars—of N-9 containing condoms."

Outlook

Looking ahead, FDA is soon expected to propose new labeling for condoms as required by law, and officials have announced that the guidance will include the N-9 issue. And on its own initiative, FDA is looking more broadly at N-9 vaginal contraceptive products. In January 2003, the agency proposed adding a warning to alert consumers that vaginal contraceptives containing N-9 do not prevent the transmission of HIV and other STIs, and that frequent vaginal use (more than once a day) can increase vaginal irritation, which may increase the risk of infection. FDA is expected to finalize the rule for the new warning sometime this fall.

Meanwhile, HIV and women's health advocates are concerned that the admittedly nuanced and complex messaging that should be taking place around N-9 may not be getting through. They remain concerned that N-9 is still being used for lubrication and, mistakenly, for protection against disease, especially during anal intercourse. At the same time, they worry that some women for whom N-9 contraceptives may be appropriate are being scared off.

The work by these advocates to inform the public about N-9 is complicated by the decision of some companies to continue selling N-9 condoms. (Approximately one in five condoms sold in the United States is still lubricated with N-9, accounting for a significant share of the $295 million U.S. market.) Church & Dwight, manufacturer of the top-selling Trojan brand, stands by its decision, arguing that N-9 condoms "remain an important family planning option for couples whose primary concern is pregnancy prevention and who prefer the extra measure of pregnancy prevention that spermicidally lubricated condoms provide"—even though no evidence of extra protection has been demonstrated. (Trojan's label says that "the extent of decreased risk [of pregnancy] has not been established.") Company representatives have also expressed concern that removing N-9 condoms from the market might only further confuse the issue, which they fear would play into the hands of family planning foes and jeopardize the availability of other N-9 contraceptive products. The company notes that it has "proactively revised labeling on all Trojan condoms lubricated with N-9 to help ensure these condoms are used appropriately."

But the Global Campaign's Lori Heise, who initiated the 2002 call to action, says she remains disappointed that companies continue to produce N-9 condoms. "I appreciate the companies' concern about the continued availability of other N-9 contraceptive products, but there is simply no evidence that adding N-9 to condoms provides backup pregnancy protection in case of condom failure. Moreover, in my view, if N-9 condoms were taken off the market, it would do a lot to clarify the issue and take the steam out of the social conservatives' drive to use the issue of N-9 condoms to bash all condoms and promote their morally-based agenda of abstinence outside of marriage."

From *The Guttmacher Report on Public Policy*, Vol. 8, no. 2, May 2005, pp. 4-6, 14. Copyright © 2005 by Alan Guttmacher Institute. Reprinted by permission.

Sex Without Sex? Keeping Passion Alive

MARJORIE OSTERHOUT

Ask a hundred pregnant women if they enjoy sex and you'll hear a hundred different answers. Some have a romp 'em, stomp 'em good time, living it up in their underbelly bikini panties and enjoying the extra endowment nature bestows on their breasts. At the other end of the spectrum you'll find tired, moody, queasy women with a body pillow down the middle of the bed—a hurdle too high for even the most determined lover. And in between are the rest of us: sometimes interested and sometimes not, sometimes feeling sexy and sometimes feeling more like a bloated whale.

It's normal during pregnancy to feel less interested in sex at times. Some pregnant women or their partners may be worried about hurting the baby, even with reassurance from a doctor. For others, intercourse may be uncomfortable, especially in the later stages of pregnancy. Many women feel insecure about their new body shape or just plain old not in the mood. And raging hormones, exhaustion, tender breasts and morning sickness also play a role.

Finding Middle Ground

The key to a satisfying sex life is to communicate about what you each need, want and hope for sexually. This is true throughout life, including during pregnancy. Regardless of how much you do (or don't) want intercourse, sex is not an all-or-nothing deal. Even though there's a watermelon between you and your partner, there's room to be innovative when it comes to physical intimacy. Creative fore-play can be fun and sexy, and it doesn't necessarily need to end in a "touchdown."

Consider the options. Most pregnant women would give almost anything for a good foot rub or back massage. And we're not talking a 1-minute quickie, either: unpack the massage oils, turn down the lights and get horizontal. Don't be shy about telling your partner exactly what aches and what feels good. If you use oil or lotion, stick to stretch-mark creams or specially formulated pregnancy massage oils. Many general massage oils contain essential oils, which can be harmful for pregnant women (especially during the first trimester).

Later in pregnancy, it's safe to use essential oils that are considered soothing as opposed to stimulating (with your healthcare provider's approval). When in doubt, use oils that are derived from flowers rather than herbs. Safe bets include lavender, bitter orange, or ylang ylang. When massaging essential oils into your skin, dilute them first in a "carrier oil" (such as almond oil), not-too-hot bath water or lotion. To scent the air, put four to six drops in a bowl of hot water or a diffuser. You can also put a couple of drops on a cotton ball and place it under your pillow.

Oral sex can be a fun and safe alternative to intercourse, but tell your partner not to blow air forcefully into your vagina. Blowing hard could cause an air embolism, where air enters your blood-stream and is potentially dangerous for both mother and baby. Normal breathing shouldn't interfere, though, so enjoy!

Showering together is another way to enjoy physical intimacy without the pressure to have sex. Offer to wash if he'll dry, break out the expensive body wash and take your time. Warm water is powerfully relaxing, and showering together is a great way to be intimate and prepare for a good night's sleep.

Even something as simple as sleeping naked (or almost naked) with your partner can promote togetherness. Skin-on-skin contact is comforting and intimate, and the best part is that it lasts all night long. If you can't sleep comfortably without wearing a bra or support belt, that's okay. Naked legs tangled together can be just as nice. Kissing, caressing and holding each other can be very satisfying, too, especially if you are feeling anxious or stressed.

Sometimes sex drives are lopsided and one person wants sex more than the other—a lot more. In general, partners should respect each other's sexual desire (or lack thereof). But if your partner is about to implode from sexual frustration and you have the energy to stay awake for a few more minutes, go for it. Your hands and mouth are powerful ways to satisfy your partner, and it's okay to have an occasional one-sided romp.

When No Means No

Dr. Valerie Davis Raskin is a clinical associate professor of psychiatry at the University of Chicago Pritzker School of Medicine and author of *Great Sex for Moms: Ten Steps to Nurturing Passion While Raising Kids*. According to Dr. Raskin, it's not necessarily important for pregnant couples to maintain their physical connection. But, she says, it is important to maintain a "loving, intimate connection. Sex is one way couples do that, but temporary breaks in physical intimacy do not necessarily cause a problem in the long run. The key is that both partners feel respected and 'heard' when it comes to negotiating sexuality around childbearing (or any other time)."

If your partner is about to implode from sexual frustration and you have the energy to stay awake for a few more minutes, go for it.

If you and your partner are concerned about having sex for health reasons, ask your medical caregiver whether or not it's safe. Since orgasm and semen can cause mild contractions, many caregivers advise against intercourse if you have any of the following conditions:

- A higher-than-average risk for miscarriage
- A history of premature labor or birth
- Unexplained vaginal bleeding or discharge
- Abdominal cramping
- Leaking amniotic fluid
- An incompetent cervix
- A dilated cervix
- Placenta previa
- A multiple pregnancy
- Your water has broken
- Any sexually transmitted disease, including unhealed herpes lesions in you or your partner

If physical intimacy of any kind is too uncomfortable for you, remember to practice small kindnesses that can keep you and your partner connected emotionally. Cooking dinner and arranging for a fantastic date may not seem like grand gestures, but small things make a difference. Send your partner a sweet email, browse baby-name books together or go shopping together for baby items. And don't forget to express your love and thanks for kindnesses received.

About the author: **MARJORIE OSTERHOUT** is a freelance writer in Seattle.

From *ePregnancy*, July 2004, pp. 28–29. Copyright © 2004 by ePregnancy. Courtesy of ePregnancy Magazine, www.epregnancy.com.

A Tale of Two Mothers

Two mothers. Three babies. One thoroughly modern tie: Samantha Wood was hired to be Pam Guagenti's surrogate— and the pair have been great friends ever since

CYNTHIA HANSON

I t was 10:30 in the morning, and life hectic as usual for Pam Guagenti, of Torrance, California; with a phone between her ear and a shoulder, she was carrying a wailing Kyle, one of her 3-month-old twins, while chasing son Chase, a rambunctious toddler who had just managed to remove half his clothes. When Pam's friend Samantha Wood, 34, and her sons Aidan, 7, and Kail, 4, walked in on the chaos, Pam was relieved. "So glad you're here," she said. "Could you give the baby his bottle?"

Later, the two moms found some calmer moments to chat. "They keep sending you this stuff when you have a baby," Samantha said at one point, fishing baby-formula coupons out of her purse and handing them to Pam. Pam happily accepted—she hadn't been receiving any coupons herself. In fact, Pam had never even been pregnant: Samantha had given birth to all three of Pam's children.

Samantha was hired to be a surrogate—an "oven," as Samantha herself likes to say—to carry embryos created by Pam and her husband, Gary. Such parenthood partnerships, known as "gestational" surrogacies (as opposed to ones in which the surrogate contributes her egg *and* carries the baby), are booming, and not just for well-to-do celebrities like Joan Lunden: In the U.S. over the past two decades, an estimated 20,000 babies have come into the world through surrogacy. In 2000 alone, 1,210 babies were born of gestational surrogacies, double the number in 1997.

But while technology has made pregnancy by proxy a rather routine miracle, the process still has the potential to be an emotional and psychological nightmare—making Pam and Samantha's relationship the most astonishing part of it all. "I went into this figuring the couple would send me pictures of the child once a year," says Samantha, holding baby Kyle in her arms. Adds Pam, laughing, "I wanted a baby, not a friendship! But when I met Sam, I knew she'd be more than just a surrogate." Indeed, their experience spawned a special bond neither woman could have ever imagined, and has made the whole experience more meaningful for both of them.

The Baby Bill

How the costs of having a surrogate child add up for prospective parents*:

Agency fee:	$12,000
IVF procedures:	$13,000
Insurance policy:	$200
Medical screenings:	$5,000
Pregnancy care:	$5,000
Freezing/storing eggs:	$920
Lawyer's fee:	$6,000
Surrogate's fee:	$17,000
Total:	**$59,120**

*All costs are approximate.

From Heartbreak to Hope

Pam Guagenti's journey began in 1989, when she was 16 and living in Phoenix. Her mother, concerned that her youngest daughter had not started to menstruate, took Pam to a gynecologist. A pelvic exam revealed that Pam had been born without a uterus, a rare condition called Rokitansky syndrome. It meant she'd never be able to bear children.

"I was upset, but I didn't want to discuss it with anyone—not my doctor, my mother, my three older sisters or the counselor my mother wanted me to see," Pam recalls. "Everybody kept saying, 'You can adopt.' There's nothing wrong with adoption, but I didn't want to hear about it then." An ultrasound revealed that Pam had two ovaries—which gave her hope that she might someday have kids. "I knew about surrogacy from a TV movie," she says, "so even though it was controversial, I knew it was an option."

In 1994, while at Arizona State University, Pam met Gary Guagenti, a business major. She fell fast for his easygoing charm, and after only two weeks of dating, she felt close enough to him to bring up her condition. He was sympathetic, supportive and undeterred. He told her, "I'm not falling in love with you for what you can give me, but for who you are."

The couple wed in April 1998, then put their family plans on hold to concentrate on their jobs, hers as a kindergarten teacher and his as the owner of a Snap-on Tools franchise. In August 1999, they consulted Bill Yee, M.D., a fertility specialist. "I was very determined to have a baby of my own, somehow," says Pam. If her ovaries produced eggs, Dr. Yee explained, an embryo could be created with Gary's sperm. An ultrasound confirmed that Pam did indeed ovulate. "It's possible for you to have children," Dr. Yee told an elated Pam. "The next step is to find a surrogate."

Searching for a Soul Mom

Of the 10 surrogacy agencies they contacted, the Guagentis were most impressed with Building Families Through Surrogacy, in Lake Forest, California, and its director, Carol Weathers. A former accountant, Weathers, 39, started the agency in 1991 after watching a co-worker struggle with infertility, which affects an estimated 6 million couples nationwide. Since then, 105 surrogates in her program have delivered a total of 152 babies.

Most of her clientele are middle-class couples who are willing to pay a hefty price for a chance at biological parenthood—about $60,000, of which the surrogate receives $17,000. Each contract signed is for one pregnancy; should a surrogate fail to get pregnant, she does not receive any funds. Many clients foot the bill by taking out loans, as the Guagentis did.

Most surrogates in Weathers' program are about 30 years old, married and working; all are natural mothers of their own children, so they are known to have carried a pregnancy successfully. Everyone must pass a rigorous screening process that includes a home visit, a criminal background check and filling out a 587-point questionnaire to gauge emotional health. The Guagentis had to undergo similar psychological testing.

The prospective parents seal the partnership by signing an agency contract and a separate agreement with the surrogate; the specifics on these agreements can vary, but all need to be ironclad, since there aren't many laws governing surrogacy. And the surrogate must agree to relinquish all rights to the baby at birth.

The Guagentis were told they might have to wait up to six months to be paired with a surrogate. But three months after signing the contract, Samantha Wood, a part-time nurse in Poway, California, spotted an ad for Building Families Through Surrogacy in a parenting magazine and contacted Weathers. For years, she had toyed with the idea of becoming a surrogate, having watched a friend struggle with infertility. "I couldn't imagine being told that I was unable to have children," says Samantha. "I knew I'd be a good candidate: I have a 'fixer' personality. And I enjoy being pregnant—even giving birth." After many lengthy discussions, she persuaded her husband, Tristan, a Navy medical dive technician, to let her proceed. In December, Samantha passed the psychological screening and Weath-

ers matched her with Pam, who lived two hours away. The pair seemed to be a good fit: They shared similar middle-class upbringings and family values and both had gregarious personalities.

Soon after, the Guagentis and Woods met for the first time for dinner at a steakhouse. The couples talked for five hours about everything from their families to their careers. Finally, Gary turned to Tristan and asked, "I assume you're supportive, but how do you really feel about Samantha's becoming a surrogate mother?"

Tristan put down his fork. "When she told me she wanted to do this, I was so touched I almost cried," he said. Samantha was stunned. "You never told me that," she said, touching his arm.

Then Pam spoke up. "Why do *you* want to become a surrogate?" she asked Samantha.

"I want to help someone who can't have a baby the traditional way," Samantha responded.

Pam ventured her next question tentatively: "If you deliver a baby girl, would you want to keep her?"

"I wouldn't want your daughter," Samantha replied, smiling. "If I want a baby girl, I'll try for one with my husband."

Pam's eyes filled with tears. "I don't know why I'm crying," she said.

"Because you're going to have a baby," said Samantha. And with that, their adventure in baby-making began.

The Conception Connection

The odds for a successful journey through the technical part of the process were in the women's favor: Pam, then 27, was young enough to produce healthy eggs, and Samantha had a history of normal pregnancies and deliveries. In February 2000, the women went to Gabriel Garza, M.D., and Arthur L. Wisot, M.D., of a fertility practice called Reproductive Partners, which has performed more than 40 successful procedures with surrogates in the last five years. Pam received hormone injections to stimulate her ovaries and Samantha got doses of estrogen to prepare her uterus to accept an embryo. Of the 11 eggs retrieved from Pam, eight were fertilized with Gary's sperm. Dr. Wisot transferred two embryos to Samantha, in the hope that one would implant (each embryo has about a 20 percent chance of becoming a fetus). The remaining eggs were frozen. A blood test in April revealed the best possible news: Samantha was pregnant. "We were both at the doctor's office when we found out, and we were screaming and crying and hugging each other," says Pam. The Guagentis decided to keep the sex of the child a surprise. "We'd used enough technology already," says Pam.

Throughout the pregnancy, the women kept in touch by phone, and each month Pam accompanied Samantha to her prenatal checkups and to visit with the midwife they chose to deliver the baby at the hospital. "I didn't want to miss anything," says Pam, who resigned from teaching at the end of the school year. "Since I always wondered how it would feel to have a baby moving inside of me, Samantha called when the baby kicked for the first time and described the sensation." Pam kept

The Virtual Womb

Will the miracles of medicine make surrogacy obsolete?

Women like Pam Guagenti may soon have more options in their quest to become mothers. Medical science has already introduced uterus transplants: In April 2000 a Saudi Arabian woman received another woman's uterus. Even though the transplant ultimately failed, scientists say that it was a milestone in the treatment of infertility.

Now even more remarkable developments are under way. According to news reports, scientists in Japan have created an artificial womb capable of incubating a goat fetus for up to three weeks. Similar work is happening in the U.S. as well. Hung-Ching Liu of the Center for Reproductive Medicine and Infertility at New York's Cornell Medical Center has already gotten mouse embryos to survive for up to two weeks in an artificial environment. Liu and fellow researchers are also working on techniques to grow human endometrial tissue, with the hope that they will someday be able to use it to repair damaged uteruses.

While researchers like Liu believe their work creating artificial wombs will offer women who can't have a baby new hope, others are concerned. "This might seem like a feminist career woman's dream," satirized columnist Tony Blankley in the conservative *Washington Times*. "Not only can she avoid the messy part of conception, but she needn't miss a day of work due to pregnancy." Adds Jeremy Rifkin, writing in the liberal *Guardian*, "What kind of child will we produce from a liquid medium inside a plastic box?" Given the recent advances in reproductive technology, it may not be long until we find out.

—*Leslie Laurence*

But Wait—Is Surrogacy *Ethical?*

We asked prominent ethicists: Is it morally okay for one woman to carry the baby of another?
—*Anne Cassidy*

"Helping infertile couples have babies is a highly ethical thing to do—and surrogacy is a piece of that. As long as everyone understands going in what his and her rights and obligations are, it can be a good way to help people have a family who couldn't otherwise."
—*Arthur Caplan, Ph.D., professor and director of the Center for Bioethics at the University of Pennsylvania, in Philadelphia*

"When a woman hires another woman to carry her baby for her, it reduces pregnancy to a 'job' and women to vessels. It also makes us forget about the relationship between a mother and her fetus. The fetus is connected to her—it is the flesh of her flesh—no matter what the genetic tie."
—*Barbara Katz Rothman, Ph.D., professor of sociology at City University of New York*

And pregnancy is hard on your body. There are easier ways to make money."

Pam faced her own struggles. She occasionally grieved because she wasn't the one carrying her child. "Once in the supermarket," she recalls, "there was a very pregnant lady people were gushing over and I felt like saying, 'Well, I'm eight-and-a-half months pregnant, too.' But they wouldn't have understood."

On December 26, 2000, the Guagentis' phone rang at 3:15 A.M. "I think I'm in labor," Samantha blurted. Everyone raced to the hospital, and the Guagentis, Tristan and Carol Weathers joined Samantha in the birthing room. Gary stood by Samantha's head, feeling somewhat awkward, as Pam held one of Samantha's legs and Tristan the other. Calmly and without pain medication, Samantha delivered Chase Maxwell, 9 pounds, 21 inches. As they'd planned, the midwife placed Chase on Samantha's stomach, Gary cut the umbilical cord and Samantha passed him to Pam's open arms.

"Look at your baby," Samantha said, beaming at the Guagentis. Weathers snapped a picture of that moment—a moment, the women agree, that perfectly captures their surrogacy experience. "Most women who've just pushed out a 9-pounder will look at the baby, but my bond was with Pam, and so in the picture I'm looking at her," says Samantha. "Short of the birth of my own two children, it was the most special moment of my life." The image also captured Tristan rubbing his wife's back, looking fairly pleased himself.

As Pam cuddled Chase, marveling at how his almond-shaped eyes looked just like Gary's, she felt overcome with affection and respect for Samantha. "I didn't feel jealous," recalls

a scrapbook with pictures of a pregnant Samantha so, she says, "I could show my child this wacko thing his parents did!"

Samantha says she found Pam supportive, but not suffocating. "She never called to see if I was eating my vegetables. She was very protective, though, to the point where she almost hired a housekeeper for me." And the baby turned out not to be their only bond. Over lunches and trips to the mall, Pam and Samantha discussed their vacation plans, even their marriages. "If I'd met Pam under different circumstances," says Samantha, "I definitely would have chosen her as a friend."

Unlike other close friends, though, the women sometimes found themselves defending their relationship. "I'd be out to dinner and strangers would ask, 'When is your baby due?' And I'd say, 'It's not mine, I'm a surrogate' and they'd say 'Oh, you make a lot of money doing that,'" says Samantha. "I'd just laugh it off. I wasn't about to get into an argument." Seventeen thousand dollars is definitely a tidy sum, Samantha concedes, "but surrogacy is a huge commitment—on my part, my husband's part, my children's part.

Pam. "I was in awe of her selflessness and willingness to give us the greatest gift that anyone ever could."

Overcome with joy at being parents after so long, the Guagentis also had the happy knowledge that they wouldn't have to stop now that they were a little family of three. Earlier, after having discussed it with her husband, Samantha made them an offer they couldn't refuse: "I'll do it again whenever you're ready."

More Great Expectations

Over the next months, Pam and Samantha kept in touch, swapping photos and tales of motherhood. "Pam called all the time for baby advice," recalls Samantha. "I'd originally assumed I'd be paired with someone who'd been trying to get pregnant for years; I never thought I'd be the older woman in the relationship." Occasionally, their families got together for barbecues.

In the summer of 2001, when Chase was 7 months old, the Guagentis decided to accept Samantha's offer. In January 2002, their remaining three embryos (frozen from the first round of treatments) were transferred into Samantha's uterus. She didn't become pregnant. The women were disappointed, but determined. On an increased dosage of ovarian stimulation medication, Pam produced 29 eggs, and 25 developed into embryos. Dr. Wisot placed two in Samantha's uterus. Two weeks later, Samantha was pregnant and this time, the ultrasound detected two heartbeats. Pam and Gary were ecstatic.

The second pregnancy progressed smoothly and on November 12, 2002, Samantha gave birth with the Guagentis and Tristan again by her side. First to arrive was Ella, weighing 6 pounds, 6 ounces and 19 inches. Kyle followed at 6 pounds, 1 ounce, also 19 inches. Pam started bawling. As for Samantha, "I was relieved that the babies were healthy, and I was very tired!" A month later, they got together at Pam's house for a baby shower; Samantha made a cross-stitched sampler for the twins and gave Pam a charm bracelet with three booties and a heart.

The women still talk on the phone once a month and see each other as much as their jam-packed family lives will allow. Samantha says she always gets choked up seeing Pam's kids. "When I look at them, I know they're not mine. But I do have a connection, in the way I imagine foster mothers must feel. After

Would You Do It?

Here are your candid responses to a recent LHJ.com poll:

Is it ethical for a woman to carry another couple's biological child?

55%	Yes, even if the parties aren't related
24%	Yes, if it's being done for a family member
21%	No

Would you ever become a surrogate mother?

41%	No
17%	Yes, for my sister
17%	Yes, for a stranger
13%	Yes, for a friend
12%	Yes, for another close relative

Typically, a surrogate mother is paid $10,000 to $20,000. For you to be a surrogate mother, how much money would you have to be offered?

40%	No amount of money would be enough
20%	$10,000 to $20,000
5%	at least $50,000
5%	at least $100,000

I had Chase, Pam's mother told me, 'You're family now.' I'm not just the surrogate."

During the women's last visit, Samantha's 4-year-old fell in love with baby Ella. "Kail was calling her 'My girlfriend.' He said he wanted to marry her," says Samantha, laughing. "I looked at Gary and said, 'That would be weird me giving birth to my own daughter-in-law!'"

Pam plans to have her kids call Samantha by her first name; as soon as they are old enough to understand, she'll explain Samantha's relationship to them. But she knows she'll never be able to put into words the gratitude she feels in her heart. "My sister has three kids, and every time she got pregnant, I'd look at her and think, When is it going to be my turn?" says Pam. "Thanks to Samantha, I got my turn."

The Birds and the Bees and Curious Kids

Questions about sex come up when you least expect them—and sooner than you think. Here, the answers you need.

MARGARET RENKL

I once believed the birds and the bees weren't my problem. My husband would expertly field all the tough questions about sex our three sons threw our way: All I'd have to do is stand beside him and nod.

No such luck. When the topic finally came up, Dad was out for the evening. I was loading the dishwasher, and the boys were in the family room watching a nature show. From my post in the kitchen, I heard this serious PBS voice say, "Sex between sharks can get quite rough." A second later our oldest, 8-year-old Sam, appeared in the doorway with a funny look on his face.

I considered distracting him— "Ready for dessert, sweetie?"— long enough for his father to get home. But we'd always tried to be open about body parts and functions in our house, and I didn't want to freeze up just when straight talk was needed most.

I told him we'd talk at bedtime, and kept my promise. After our usual songs and stories, I took a deep breath and plunged into those shark-infested waters. "So, that show made you have some questions," I said. "Want me to answer them?" I told him the whole story—about how males and females make babies together, with the male depositing his sperm in the female. My son was appalled and disgusted—but also intrigued.

Variations on "the talk" don't always come up at convenient times or in predictable ways. So be prepared: below, the best strategies for handling the kinds of scenarios that catch parents most off guard.

Your 3-year-old is fascinated by her baby brother's diaper changes. "What's that?" she asks, pointing at his penis. How to respond: You may be tempted to change the subject quickly, and fasten that diaper even faster, but it's best to be matter-of-fact. "Some parents teach their children the names of every body part except the genitals, skipping them as if they don't exist," says Mark Schuster, M.D., a pediatrician and coauthor of *Everything You Never Wanted Your Kids to Know About Sex (But Were Afraid They'd Ask)*. That can give kids the idea that talking about your private parts is taboo. So instead say, "That's how you can tell the difference between a girl and a boy. It's called a penis. You have a vagina."

Of course, just because you use the correct term doesn't mean she'll get it right on the first try. Nashville mom Laura Hileman once heard her 3-year-old son explaining to his brother, "Boys have penises, and girls have china." And don't be surprised if the question comes up again and again while your little one sorts it all out.

Hoping to demystify the potty for your toddler, you let her watch you pee. Soon she asks, "Why do you have hair down there?" How to respond: "Young children ask simple questions and don't need more than simple, partial answers," says Virginia Shiller, Ph.D., a licensed clinical psychologist in private practice in New Haven, Connecticut, and author of *Rewards for Kids!* Just say that it's natural for grown-ups to have hair in places that children don't, especially under their arms, between their legs, and, for men, on their faces. Birmingham, Alabama, mom Joan Watkins explained to her daughter Lora, 4, that when Lora gets to be a big girl like her mother and her aunts, she'll have hair covering her private parts, too.

Toddlers are big on imitation, and they're fascinated by the potty, so it's natural for them to wonder what you're up to in there. Letting your child join you in the bathroom from time to time is a good way to teach her there's nothing wrong or dirty about the human body.

Your child tells you her classmate has two mommies. "How can that be?" she asks. How to respond: Homosexuality may seem like a confusing subject—especially for kids who haven't even gotten the concept of heterosexuality down yet. But your explanation doesn't have to be complicated: "In Ginny's family, her two mommies love each other the way that Daddy and I do. So they live together, and both take care of Ginny."

The topic may also come up after your child hears a homosexual slur. Christi Cole's daughter Caitlyn, 6, said a boy at school had been telling kids in her class, "You're gay"—so of course she wanted to know what that meant. The Augusta, Georgia, mom explained that sometimes boys fall in love with boys and girls fall in love with girls, but that the boy at Caitlyn's school probably didn't really understand what he was talking about. Then she reminded her daughter that calling people names isn't nice and might hurt someone's feelings.

You're in line at the grocery store when your pre-schooler looks up and asks, "Why is my penis getting hard?" **How to respond:** If a question arises at an inopportune moment, it's okay to give an incomplete answer, along with a promise to fill in the rest later on. In this case, you can say quietly, "Oh, that happens sometimes. It will get soft again soon."

Joan Watkins says that when her two kids ask questions in an inappropriate place, she replies, "That's a really great question. We can talk more about it in the car, if you want." But it's important to come back to the question once you do get in the car: "Remember what you asked when we were at the store? Do you still want to talk about it?"

You've explained that when a mommy's egg and a daddy's sperm combine, a baby begins to grow. Now your 6-year-old asks, "How does the sperm get to the egg anyway?" **How to respond:** Explaining intercourse doesn't have to be a big deal. You might start by saying, "Daddies have to be close enough to mommies so the sperm can come out of their body and get into the mommy. The sperm comes out of the daddy's penis and goes right into the vagina, a special place in mommy's body made for keeping the sperm safe and helping it get to the egg." If your child asks additional questions, offer a slightly more detailed explanation: "A penis is made to fit into a vagina sort of like an arm fits into a sleeve."

Some parents use this talk as an opportunity to introduce a moral framework for sexuality. When her older child first asked the question, Watkins said, "God had a great plan for mommies and daddies to make babies. He designed them differently so they fit together like a puzzle. The sperm comes out of a daddy's penis and swims inside the mommy's body till it reaches the egg."

Your preschooler has been content so far with vague sex information like "Babies grow inside mommies." But now she wants to know what happens next: "How does the baby get out of there?" **How to respond:** Again, accurate but uncomplicated answers are best. Try, "Most babies come out through the mommy's vagina." If your child asks a follow-up question, you can add, "The vagina is like a tube inside the mommy. It stretches really wide so the baby can get outside."

If that doesn't satisfy your child, there may be another question behind the first, one she's too shy to ask. At 4, Loree Bowen's daughter, Kendall, repeatedly asked how her new baby brother or sister would get out, even after learning about the vagina. Finally, the Yorba Linda, California, mom realized her child was wondering whether her new little brother or sister would emerge covered with poop or pee. "So I told her there was a special opening just for babies, and we were done," she says.

Your grade-schooler's friend tells him how to get to an x-rated website. You walk into the family room later and find him staring at a naked woman on the screen. **How to respond:** First, try not to get angry. Your son's interest is only natural. Still, you need to make it clear that such material isn't appropriate for kids. Find a way to condemn the pornography nonjudgmentally without condemning him for his curiosity. Tell him calmly, "That's a website for adults; you need to stick to sites for kids." Then bookmark the sites you've approved—and be sure to download some parental controls for the family computer.

Contributing editor **MARGARET RENKL** lives in Nashville with her husband and three kids.

UNIT 5

Sexuality Through the Life Cycle

Unit Selections

Key Points to Consider

• Do you remember trying to get answers about your body, sex, or similar topics as a young child? How did your parents respond? How did you feel? Do you hope your children will ask you questions about sex? Why or why not? Which topics or questions do you expect will be hardest for you to handle and answer?

• How do you view sex and sexuality at your age? In what ways is it different from when you were younger? How do you perceive the changes—positively, negatively, not sure—and to what do you attribute them? Are there things you feel you have missed? What are they?

• Close your eyes and imagine a couple having a pleasurable sexual interlude. When you are finished, open your eyes. How old were they? If they were younger than middle age, can you replay your vision with middle-aged or older people? Why or why not? How does this relate to your expectations regarding your own romantic and/or sexual life a few decades from now?

• Do you ever think about your parents as sexual people? Your grandparents? Was considering these two questions upsetting for you? Embarrassing? Explain your answers as best you can.

Student Web Site

www.mhcls.com/online

Internet References

Further information regarding these Web sites may be found in this book's preface or online.

American Association of Retired Persons (AARP)
http://www.aarp.org
National Institute on Aging (NIA)
http://www.nih.gov/nia/
Teacher Talk
http://education.indiana.edu/cas/tt/tthmpg.html
World Association for Sexology
http://www.tc.umn.edu/nlhome/m201/colem001/was/wasindex.htm

Individual sexual development is a lifelong process that begins prior to birth and continues until death. Contrary to once popular notions of this process, there are no latent periods in childhood or old age during which the individual is nonsexual or noncognizant of sexuality. The growing process of a sexual being does, however, reveal qualitative differences through various life stages. This section devotes attention to these stages of the life cycle and their relation to sexuality.

As children gain self-awareness, they naturally explore their own bodies, masturbate, display curiosity about the bodies of the opposite sex, and show interest in the bodies of mature individuals such as their parents. Exploration and curiosity are important and healthy aspects of human development. Yet it is often difficult for adults (who live in a society that is not comfortable with sexuality in general) to avoid making their children feel ashamed of being sexual or showing interest in sexuality. When adults impose their ambivalence upon a child's innocuous explorations into sexuality, fail to communicate with children about this real and important aspect of human life, or behave toward children in sexually inappropriate ways, distortion of an indispensable and formative stage of development occurs. This often leaves profound emotional scars that hinder full acceptance of self and sexuality later in the child's life.

Adolescence, the social stage accompanying puberty and the transition to adulthood, proves to be a very stressful period of life for many individuals as they attempt to develop an adult identity and forge relationships with others. Because of the physiological capacity of adolescents for reproduction, sexuality tends to be heavily censured by parents and society at this stage of life. However, prevailing societal messages are powerful, conflicting, and confusing: "Just Say No" … "Just Do It"; billboards and magazine ads using adolescent bodies provocatively and partially undressed; "romance" novels, television shows, MTV, movies with torrid sex scenes; seductive teenage "boy" and "girl" singers and bands, as well as, more open exposure of same-sex or multisex couplings; and Internet chat rooms and My Space or Face Book pages. In addition, individual and societal attitudes place tremendous emphasis on sexual attractiveness (especially for females) and sexual competency (especially for males). These physical, emotional, and cultural pressures combine to create confusion and anxiety in adolescents and young adults about whether they are okay and normal. Information and assurances from adults can alleviate these stresses and facilitate positive and responsible sexual maturity if there is mutual trust and willingness in both generations.

Sexuality finally becomes socially acceptable in adulthood, at least within marriage. Yet routine, boredom, stress, pressures, the pace of life, work, or parenting responsibilities, and/or lack of communication can exact heavy tolls on the quantity and quality of sexual interaction. Sexual misinformation, myths, and unanswered questions, especially about emotional and/or physiological changes in sexual arousal/response or functioning, can also undermine or hinder intimacy and sexual interaction in the middle years.

Sexuality in the later years of life has also been socially and culturally stigmatized because of the prevailing misconception that only young, attractive, or married people are sexual. Such an attitude has contributed significantly to the apparent decline in sexual interest and activity as one grows older. However, as population demographics have shifted and the baby boomer generation has aged, these beliefs and attitudes have begun to change. Physiological changes in the aging process are not, in and of themselves, detrimental to sexual expression. A life history of experiences, good health, and growth can make sexual expression in the later years a most rewarding and fulfilling experience, and today's aging population is becoming more vocal in letting their children and grandchildren know that as we age we don't grow out of sex, but that, in fact, like fine wine, it can get better with age.

The Sexual Revolution Hits Junior High

The kids are doing more than baring bellies: They're shocking adults with their anything-goes behavior

KIM PAINTER
Special for USA TODAY

Picture the mating rites of middle-schoolers. Perhaps you imagine hand-holding and first kisses, girls trying out eye shadow, boys sneaking a peek at vulgar men's magazines.

Now look again, through the eyes of increasingly concerned educators and experts:

• Researchers in Washington, D.C., recently started a program to prevent early sexual activity. They planned to offer it to seventh-graders, but after a pilot study decided to target fifth-graders—because too many seventh-graders already were having sex.

• Jo Mecham, a nurse at a Bettendorf, Iowa, middle school, says she overhears "pretty explicit sexual talk" from boys and girls in her "conservative" community. And despite a dress code, girls come to classes looking like bare-bellied rock stars: "They'll leave the house totally OK, and when they get to school, they start disrobing."

• Joey Zbylut-Birky, a middle-school teacher in Omaha, recently asked students to think about "where they feel most comfortable" as part of an assignment to write song titles about themselves. A group of giggling boys piped up with comments about receiving oral sex.

The list goes on. Middle schools that used to do without dress codes now must send home exhaustive inventories of forbidden garments, from tube tops to too-low hip-huggers. Schools that used to handle crude language on a case-by-case basis now must have "no-profanity" policies. And sexual-harassment training is a normal part of middle-school curriculum.

The world "is rougher, it is sexier and it has reached down to touch boys and girls at younger ages," says Margaret Sagarese, who, with Charlene C. Giannetti, has written several books on parenting, including the new *The Patience of a Saint: How Faith Can Sustain You During the Tough Times of Parenting*.

Baby-boomer parents who thought that nothing would ever shock them are shocked by the way their young teens talk, dress and perhaps even behave, Sagarese says.

"Things have changed," says Jude Swift, 52, a mother of five whose youngest is an eighth-grade boy. "I think a great deal of it is due to the media and what kids see on TV, in magazine ads, in videos…. It's all about being sexy."

The world 'is rougher, it is sexier' and it's harder for teens to avoid it

Swift, of Camillus, N.Y., says she picked up a *Teen People* magazine the other day and "I was amazed. It was page after page of young teens dressed in very provocative ways and in very provocative poses."

Young girls "do not see anything wrong in looking that way," says Zbylut-Birky, the Omaha teacher. And, she says, "they don't see the difference between how they should look for a party and how they should look in an educational setting."

Boys Want to Look Sexy, Too

Even boys face increasing pressure to look sexy, says Sagarese: "There are 12-year-old boys going to GNC and taking all kinds of supplements because they want abs the same way girls want breasts."

Of course, many girls who dress like Britney Spears and many boys who talk like Eminem don't go beyond nervous note-passing in their actual romantic lives.

Zbylut-Birky, who overheard the oral-sex banter, says, "A lot of times they use that kind of language to impress their peers, but there's really nothing going on there."

But for some substantial minority of middle schoolers, something very risky—including intercourse and oral sex—is going on, some experts say. In 1995, government researchers asked teens over age 15 whether they'd had sexual intercourse by age 14; 19% of girls and 21% of boys said yes. In 1988, the numbers were 11% for girls and the same 21% for boys, says the Washington, D.C.-based research group Child Trends. Data for 2002 are just being collected.

Another study, using different methods, followed 12- to 14-year-olds between 1997 and 1999 and found 16% of girls and 20% of boys reported sex at 14 or younger, says Child Trends researcher Jennifer Manlove.

Sex by age 14

Kids (15 and older) who say they had had intercourse by age 14:

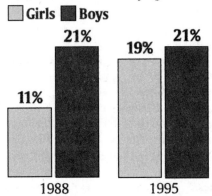

As for oral sex, a 2000 study from the Alan Guttmacher Institute in New York caused a firestorm by suggesting that more young teens were engaging in that activity—possibly as a way of remaining technical virgins in the age of abstinence education. That study was based on scattered, anecdotal reports of increased oral herpes and gonorrhea of the throat.

No nationwide, scientific study has actually asked young teens, or older teens for that matter, whether they have oral sex.

"A lot of alarm parents feel on this issue is based on anecdotal information," says Bill Albert, spokesman for the Washington, D.C.-based National Campaign to Prevent Teen Pregnancy, a private, non-profit group working to reduce teen pregnancy.

But some of the anecdotes are hair-raising.

"The other day at school, a girl got caught in a bathroom with a boy performing oral sex on him," says Maurisha Stenson, a 14-year-old eighth-grader at a Syracuse, N.Y., middle school.

When the Lights Went On

Denyia Sullivan, 14, attends a different Syracuse middle school but says she's seen and heard about similar things. One time, a girl performed oral sex on a boy in the gym bleachers during a movie. "The teacher turned on the light and there they were," Sullivan says. "Everybody was looking and laughing."

The two girls also say there's more than oral sex going on. Sullivan can think of five pregnant girls at her school, which includes sixth-, seventh- and eighth-graders. Stenson guesses that "almost 50%" of kids at her school, for seventh- and eighth-graders, are engaging in some kind of sex.

"This is happening; they are telling the truth," says Courtney Ramirez, who directs the Syracuse Way to Go after-school program, designed to help kids succeed in school and avoid risks. Both girls are peer educators in the program.

"Youths are really getting involved in things a whole lot sooner than we thought," Ramirez says.

But other experts say that without good, current numbers on nationwide trends, they can't even say with any confidence that early sex is increasing. "It could be getting worse, it could be getting better, we just don't know," Albert says.

One problem is that the best government studies are done infrequently. Another is that researchers—and the public—are squeamish about asking detailed sex questions of young teens. And when they do ask, they aren't sure youngsters always understand the questions or answer truthfully. Albert's organization will try to fill in the gap later this year with a report based on data from around the country.

But many educators and parents have heard the alarms and are acting now. Krystal McKinney directs a program that offers sex education and life-skills training to middle-school girls in the Washington, D.C., area. Since the 2000 Guttmacher oral sex report, she and her staff have redoubled efforts to make sure that girls understand the risks.

"We have kids who think you can't get diseases from oral sex," she says. "Kids think they know everything, but we challenge that."

With the youngest teens, clear information is crucial, says Xenia Becher, a mental health educator at the Syracuse after-school program.

Recently, she says, she asked some 13- to 15-year-olds to define sex. "They had trouble coming up with an answer," she says. "Some said it had to be between a male and female and a penis and vagina had to be involved.

"So I asked, 'What about if two men were involved?' 'Well,' they said, 'I don't know what that is, but it's not sex.'"

Becher also trains parents to discuss sex with their kids. She tells them that their voices matter, even in a sex-soaked culture.

"When you get down to what's right or wrong, popular culture is going to have an influence, but the stronger internal voice comes from you," she says.

Becher admits that setting limits and encouraging independence can be a real balancing act. When her own 13-year-old daughter dressed for a dance in a pair of "those nasty hip-huggers" and a short top, Becher says, she asked her to think how she'd look when "she was waving her arms around on the dance floor." But she didn't make her daughter change.

"You've got to pick your battles," she says.

Parents Shouldn't Back Off

"Kids really do care what their parents think," says Kristin Moore, president of Child Trends. "They don't really want their parents to back away. But a lot of parents do back away at this age."

Some parents, she says, are so intimidated by a child's hostile behavior and demands for privacy that they give far too much ground. "Sometimes parents are home during a party but have no idea what is going on at the party."

Mark Gibbons, an Augusta, Ga., father of two girls ages 8 and 12, says that he and his wife are doing everything they can to stay involved. They try to talk to their daughters about everything. "We've told them that it may sometimes be embarrassing, but that we'd rather they get their information from us," he says.

"I talk to them all the time," says Lauryn, a seventh-grader who takes classes for gifted and talented kids. She does say that she prefers to discuss boyfriends with her mom.

Nevertheless, when Lauryn has friends over, Gibbons says he keeps his ears open. When she's instant messaging on the computer, he says, "Every once in a while, I'll just wander over there and ask who she's talking to. And I do look at her little directory and make sure all those user names are people that I know. We try not to show that we're being nosy, but we are."

Gibbons also chaperones middle-school dances. It's a window into his daughter's larger world—one that, even in a community of "pretty well-behaved kids," can be shocking, he says. "Some of the dancing they do is kind of risque, to say the least."

Lauryn says she appreciates her parents' involvement: "I believe it does makes a difference.... I have never gotten into trouble." And she says she does know kids who are getting into sexual trouble. "At some of the parties I go to, people playing 'Truth or Dare' will say that they've already 'done it,'" she says.

Meanwhile, Gibbons says he recently got a reminder that it is never too early to discuss sexual values. Third-grader Tayler "came home and said one little girl took a boy behind a tree and they were French kissing.... I said, 'Well, do you think that is wrong?' She said, 'Yes.'"

But while parents are right to watch and worry, some may be worrying too much and enjoying too little about their children's pubescent years, says Sagarese, the parenting author. "I can't tell you how many parents have come up to me at speeches and they are apoplectic that their daughter is kissing. They feel like the first kiss is a runaway train that will lead to AIDS or pregnancy."

Her co-author, Giannetti, says, "Parents need to take a deep breath and a step back and remember what it was like to be a young adolescent."

Sometimes, Sagarese says, a first kiss is just a first kiss—and the same lovely rite of passage it was in a more innocent time.

From *USA Today Newspaper*, March 17, 2002, pp. 1-2. © 2002 by Kim Painter. Reprinted by permission of the author.

The Cuddle Puddle of Stuyvesant High School

Researchers find it shocking that 11 percent of American girls between 15 and 19 claim to have same-sex encounters. Clearly they've never observed the social rituals of the pansexual, bi-queer, metroflexible New York teen.

ALEX MORRIS

Alair is wearing a tight white tank top cut off above the hem to show her midriff. Her black cargo pants graze the top of her combat boots, and her black leather belt is studded with metal chains that drape down at intervals across her hips. She has long blonde curls that at various times have been dyed green, blue, red, purple, and orange. ("A mistake," she says. "Even if you mean to dye your hair orange, it's still a mistake.") Despite the fact that she's fully clothed, she seems somehow exposed, her baby fat lingering in all the right places. Walking down the sterile, white halls of Stuyvesant High School, she creates a wave of attention. She's not the most popular girl in school, but she is well known. "People like me," she wrote in an instant message. "Well, most of them."

Alair is headed for the section of the second-floor hallway where her friends gather every day during their free tenth period for the "cuddle puddle," as she calls it. There are girls petting girls and girls petting guys and guys petting guys. She dives into the undulating heap of backpacks and blue jeans and emerges between her two best friends, Jane and Elle, whose names have been changed at their request. They are all 16, juniors at Stuyvesant. Alair slips into Jane's lap, and Elle reclines next to them, watching, cat-eyed. All three have hooked up with each other. All three have hooked up with boys—sometimes the same boys. But it's not that they're gay or bisexual, not exactly. Not always.

Their friend Nathan, a senior with John Lennon hair and glasses, is there with his guitar, strumming softly under the conversation. "So many of the girls here are lesbian or have experimented or are confused," he says.

Ilia, another senior boy, frowns at Nathan's use of labels. "It's not lesbian or bisexual. It's just, whatever . . . "

Since the school day is winding down, things in the hallway are starting to get rowdy. Jane disappears for a while and comes back carrying a pint-size girl over her shoulder. "Now I take her off and we have gay sex!" she says gleefully, as she parades back and forth in front of the cuddle puddle. "And it's awesome!" The hijacked girl hangs limply, a smile creeping to her lips. Ilia has stuffed papers up the front of his shirt and prances around on tiptoe, batting his eyes and sticking out his chest. Elle is watching, enthralled, as two boys lock lips across the hall. "Oh, my," she murmurs. "Homoerotica. There's nothing more exciting than watching two men make out." And everyone is talking to another girl in the puddle who just "came out," meaning she announced that she's now open to sexual overtures from both boys and girls, which makes her a minor celebrity, for a little while.

When asked how many of her female friends have had same-sex experiences, Alair answers, "All of them." Then she stops to think about it. "All right, maybe 80 percent. At least 80 percent of them have experimented. And they still are. It's either to please a man, or to try it out, or just to be fun, or 'cause you're bored, or just 'cause you like it . . . whatever."

With teenagers there is always a fair amount of posturing when it comes to sex, a tendency to exaggerate or trivialize, innocence mixed with swagger. It's also true that the "puddle" is just one clique at Stuyvesant, and that Stuyvesant can hardly be considered a typical high school. It attracts the brightest public-school students in New York, and that may be an environment conducive to fewer sexual inhibitions. "In our school," Elle says, "people are getting a better education, so they're more open-minded."

That said, the Stuyvesant cuddle puddle is emblematic of the changing landscape of high-school sexuality across the country. This past September, when the National Center for Health Statistics released its first survey in which teens were questioned about their sexual behavior, 11 percent of American girls polled in the 15-to-19 demographic claimed to have had same-sex encounters—the *same* percentage of all women ages 15 to 44 who reported same-sex experiences, even though the teenagers have much shorter sexual histories. It doesn't take a Stuyvesant education to see what this means: More girls are experimenting with each other, and they're starting younger. And this is a conservative estimate, according to Ritch Savin-Williams, a professor of human development at Cornell who has been conducting research on same-sex-attracted adolescents for over twenty years. Depending on how you phrase the questions and how you define sex between women, he believes that "it's possible to get up to 20 percent of teenage girls."

Of course, what can't be expressed in statistical terms is how teenagers think about their same-sex interactions. Go to the schools, talk to the kids, and you'll see that somewhere along the line this generation has started to conceive of sexuality differently. Ten years ago in the halls of Stuyvesant you might have found a few goth girls kissing goth girls, kids on the fringes defiantly bucking the system. Now you find a group of vaguely progressive but generally mainstream kids for whom same-sex intimacy is standard operating procedure. "It's not like, *Oh, I'm going to hit on her now*. It's just kind of like, you come up to a friend, you grab their ass," Alair explains. "It's just, like, our way of saying hello." These teenagers don't feel as though their sexuality has to define them, or that they have to define it, which has led some psychologists and child-development specialists to label them the "post-gay" generation. But kids like Alair and her friends are in the process of working up their own language to describe their behavior. Along with gay, straight, and bisexual, they'll drop in new words, some of which they've coined themselves: polysexual, ambisexual, pansexual, pansensual, polyfide, bi-curious, bi-queer, fluid, metroflexible, heteroflexible, heterosexual with lesbian tendencies—or, as Alair puts it, "just sexual." The terms are designed less to achieve specificity than to leave all options open.

To some it may sound like a sexual Utopia, where labels have been banned and traditional gender roles surpassed, but it's a complicated place to be. Anyone who has ever been a girl in high school knows the vicissitudes of female friendships. Add to that a sexual component and, well, things get interesting. Take Alair and her friend Jane, for example. "We've been dancing around each other for, like, three years now," says Alair. "I'd hop into bed with her in a second." Jane is tall and curvy with green eyes and faint dimples. She thinks Alair is "amazing," but she's already had a female friendship ruined when it turned into a romantic relationship, so she's reluctant to let it happen again. Still, they pet each other in the hall, flirt, kiss, but that's it, so far. "Alair," Jane explains, "is literally in love with everyone and in love with no one."

Relationships are a bitch, dude."

Alair is having lunch with Jane, Elle, and their friend Nathan at a little Indian place near Jane's Upper West Side apartment. Jane has been telling the story of her first lesbian relationship: She fell for a girl who got arrested while protesting the Republican National Convention (very cool), but the girl stopped calling after they spent the night together (very uncool).

"We should all be single for the rest of our lives," Alair continues. "And we should all have sugar daddies." As the only child of divorced parents, Alair learned early that love doesn't always end in happily ever after and that sex doesn't always end in love.

Nathan looks across the table at her and nods knowingly. He recently broke up with a girl he still can't get off his mind, even though he wasn't entirely faithful when they were together. "I agree. I wholeheartedly agree," he says.

"I *disagree*," says Elle, alarmed. She's the romantic of the group, a bit naïve, if you ask the others.

"Well," says Nathan. "You're, like, the only one in a happy relationship right now, so . . ."

Alair cracks up. "Happy? Her man is gayer than I am!" (Jane, the sarcastic one, has a joke about this boy: "He's got one finger left in the closet, and it's in Elle, depending on what time it is.")

"But at least she's happy," argues Nathan.

"When I'm single, I say I'm happy I'm single, and when I'm in a relationship I seem happy in the relationship. Really, I'm filled with angst!" says Elle.

Nathan rolls his eyes. "Anyone who says they're filled with angst is definitely *not* filled with angst."

He's got a point. In her brand-new sneakers and her sparkly barrettes, Elle is hardly a poster child for teenage anxiety. She makes A's at Stuyvesant, babysits her cousins, and is engaging in a way that will go over well in college interviews.

Then again, none of them are bad kids. Sure, they drink and smoke and party, but in a couple of years, they'll be drinking and smoking and partying at Princeton or MIT. They had to be pretty serious students to even get into Stuyvesant, which accepts only about 3 percent of its applicants. And when they're not studying, they're going to music lessons, SAT prep, debate practice, Japanese class, theater rehearsal, or some other résumé-building extracurricular activity.

Their sexual behavior is by no means the norm at their school; Stuyvesant has some 3,000 students, and Alair's group numbers a couple dozen. But they're also not the only kids at school who experiment with members of the same sex. "Other people do it, too," said a junior who's part of a more popular crowd. "They get drunk and want to be a sex object. But that's different. Those people aren't bisexual." Alair and her friends, on the other hand, are known as the "bi clique." In the social strata, they're closer to the cool kids than to the nerds. The boys have shaggy hair and T-shirts emblazoned with the names of sixties rockers. The girls are pretty and clever and extroverted. Some kids think they're too promiscuous. One student-union leader told me, "It's weird. It's just sort of incestuous." But others admire them. Alair in particular is seen as a kind of punk-rock queen bee. "She's good-looking, and she does what she wants," said a senior boy. "That's an attractive quality."

"The interesting kids kind of gravitate towards each other," Elle had explained earlier. "A lot of them are heteroflexible or bisexual or gay. And what happens is, like, we're all just really comfortable around each other."

Still, among her friends, Elle's ideas are the most traditional. Her first kiss with a girl was at Hebrew school. Since then, she's made out with girls frequently but dated only guys.

"I've always been the marrying type," she says to the table. "Not just 'cause it's been forced on me, but 'cause it's a good idea. I really want to have kids when I grow up."

"Have mine," offers Alair.

"I will," Elle coos in her best sultry voice. "Anything for you, Alair."

Jane blinks quickly, something she has a habit of doing when she's gathering her thoughts. "They will probably have the technology by the time we grow up that you two could have a baby together."

"But, like, if Alair doesn't want to birth her own child, I could."

"I'll birth it," Alair says, sighing. "I just want you to raise it and pay for it and take care of it and never tell it that I'm its parent. 'Cause, I mean, that would scar a child for life. Like, the child would start convulsing." Everyone laughs.

"You'd be an awesome mom, I think," says Elle. Her own mom puts a lot of pressure on her to date a nice Jewish boy. Once, Elle asked her, " 'Mom, what if I have these feelings for girls?' and she said, 'Do you have feelings for boys too?' I'm like, 'Yeah.' And she's like, 'Then you have to ignore the ones you have for girls. If you can be straight, you have to be straight.' " Elle asked to go by a nickname because she hasn't told her mother that she's not ignoring those feelings.

Even as cultural acceptance of gay and bisexual teenagers grows, these kids are coming up against an uncomfortable generational divide. In many of their families, the 'It's fine, as long as it's not my kid' attitude prevails. Some of the parents take comfort in the belief that this is just a phase their daughters will grow out of. Others take more drastic measures. Earlier this year at Horace Mann, when one girl's parents found out that she was having a relationship with another girl, they searched her room, confiscated her love letters, and even had the phone company send them transcripts of all her text messages. Then they informed her girlfriend's parents. In the end, the girls were forbidden to see each other outside school.

Even Jane, whose parents know about her bisexuality and are particularly well suited to understanding it (her mother teaches a college course in human sexuality), has run up against the limits of their liberal attitudes. They requested that she go by her middle name in this story. "My mom thinks I'm going to grow up and be ashamed of my sexuality," she says. "But I *won't*."

To these kids, homophobia is as socially shunned as racism was to the generation before them. They say it's practically the one thing that's not tolerated at their school. One boy who made disparaging remarks about gay people has been ridiculed and taunted, his belongings hidden around the school. "We're a creative bunch when we hate someone," says Nathan. Once the tormenters, now the tormented.

Alair is one of the lucky ones whose parents don't mind her bisexual tendencies. Her dad is the president of a company that manages performance artists and her mom is a professional organizer. "My parents are awesome," she says. "I think they've tried to raise me slightly quirky, like in a very hippie little way, and it totally backfired on them."

" 'Cause you ended up like a hippie?" Nathan asks.

"No, 'cause I went further than I think they wanted me to go." Despite the bravado, there's a sweetness to Alair. She sings in the Trinity Children's Choir. She does the dishes without being asked. She's a daddy's girl and her mother's confidante, though she hasn't always managed to skirt trouble away from home. She got kicked out of her middle school, Columbia Prep, after getting into an altercation with a girl who had been making her life miserable. ("I threw a bagel at her head, all right? I attacked her with a bagel.")

"My mom's like, 'Alair, I don't understand you. I want to be a parent to you but I have no control at all . . . As a person you're awesome. You're hilarious, you entertain me, you're so cool. I would totally be your friend. But as your mother, I'm worried.' "

"I can't say I was pleased," her mother tells me about first learning of Alair's bisexual experimentation. "But I can't say I was upset either. I like that she's forthright about what she wants, that she values her freedom, that she takes care of herself. But I have all the trepidations a parent has when they learn their child is becoming sexually active."

Of course, none of these kids will have to deal with their parents quite this directly in another year or so—a fact of which they are all acutely aware. College is already becoming a pressing issue. Everyone thinks Elle is going to get into Harvard. "If I fail physics, my average drops like a stone," she frets. Alair and Nathan want to go to the same college, wherever that may be.

"You do realize," Alair tells him, "that, like, we're two of the most awesome people in the school."

"We would room," Nathan says. "We would totally room."

"Fuck yeah. But I'm gonna need a lock on my door for like, 'I'm bringing these five girls home, Nathan. What are you doing tonight?' " She mimics his voice, " 'I'm reading my book.' "

"Ouch!" Nathan scowls at her.

"It's the Kama Sutra!"

"Oh, right, right."

"I've actually read the Kama Sutra," Alair informs the table. "Some of that shit just isn't gonna work."

"I know!" says Jane. "We have three editions at my house."

"Like, I've tried it. You need a man that's like 'Argh!' " Alair pumps her arms up above her head. "I've got one of those guys, actually." She's talking about Jason, the boy she was hanging out with last night, another frequenter of the cuddle puddle. "He's so built."

"He's in love with you," Jane says drily.

"No, he's not!"

"Yes he is!"

"How could he *not* be in love with Alair?" Nathan reasons.

Jane nods in Alair's direction. "He bought you gum."

"He bought you gum." This cinches it for Nathan. "Yeah, he loves you. He wants you so in his underwear."

Alair looks at him blankly. "But he already has that. We're friends." There's no need to bring love into it.

But later, back at Jane's apartment, as the afternoon is turning to night, Alair has the look of, if not love, at least infatuation, as she waits in the hallway for the elevator to take her back down. Only it's not Jason she's saying good-night to—it's Jane. "You make my knees weak," she says. And then to cut the tension: "I showered for you and everything." She leans in and gives Jane a kiss.

It practically takes a diagram to plot all the various hookups and connections within the cuddle puddle. Elle's kissed Jane and Jane's kissed Alair and Alair's kissed Elle. And then from time to time Elle hooks up with Nathan, but really only at parties, and only when Bethany isn't around, because Nathan really likes Bethany, who doesn't have a thing for girls but doesn't have a problem with girls who do, either. Alair's hooking up with Jason (who "kind of" went out with Jane once), even though she sort of also has a thing for Hector, who Jane likes, too—though Jane thinks it's totally boring when people date people of the same gender. Ilia has a serious girlfriend, but girls were hooking up at his last party, which was awesome. Molly has kissed Alair, and Jane's ex-girlfriend first decided she was bi while staying at Molly's beach house on Fire Island. Sarah sometimes kisses Elle, although she has a boyfriend—he doesn't care if she hooks up with other girls, since she's straight anyway. And so on.

Some of the boys hook up with each other, too, although in far fewer numbers than the girls. One of Alair's male friends explained that this is because for guys, anything beyond same-sex kissing requires "more of a physical commitment." If a guy does hook up with other guys it certainly doesn't make the girls less likely to hook up with him; and the converse is obviously true.

Of course, the definition of "hooking up" is as nebulous as the definition of "heteroflexible." A catchall phrase for anything from "like, exchanging of saliva" to intercourse, it's often a euphemism for oral sex. But rules are hazy when you're talking about physical encounters between two girls. As Alair puts it, "How do you define female sex? It's difficult. I don't know what the bases are. Everyone keeps trying to explain the bases to me, but there's so many things that just don't fit into the base system. I usually leave it up to the other girl."

Elle elaborates by using herself as an example. At a recent party, she says, she "kissed five people and, like, hooked up with two going beyond kissing. One of them was a boy and one of them was a girl. The reason I started hooking up with the guy is because he was making out with this other guy and he came back and was like, 'I have to prove that I'm straight.' And I was standing right there. That's how it all began." The guy in question became her boyfriend that night; even though the relationship is all of a week old, she calls it her second "serious" relationship. "At least I'm intending for it to be serious." (It lasted eleven days.)

The cuddle puddle may be where a flirtation begins, but parties, not surprisingly, are where most of the real action takes place. In parentless apartments, the kids are free to "make the rounds," as they call it, and move their more-than-kissing hook-ups with both genders behind locked bathroom doors or onto coat-laden beds. Even for bisexual girls there is, admittedly, a *Girls Gone Wild* aspect to these evenings. Some girls do hook up with other girls solely to please the guys who watch, and it can be difficult to distinguish between the behavior of someone who is legitimately sexually interested and someone who wants to impress the boy across the room. Alair is quick to disparage this behavior—"It kinda grosses me out. It can't be like, this could be fun . . . is anyone watching my chest heave?"—but Jane sees it as empowering. "I take advantage of it because manipulating boys is fun as hell. Boys make out with boys for our benefit as well. So it's not just one way. It's very fair."

She's not just making excuses. These girls have obliterated the "damned if you do, damned if you don't" stranglehold that has traditionally plagued high-school females. They set the sexual agenda for their group. And they expect reciprocation. "I've made it my own personal policy that if I'm going to give oral sex, I'm going to receive oral sex," says Jane. "Jane wears the pants in any relationship," Ilia says with a grin. "She wears the pants in *my* relationship, even though she's not part of it."

When the girls talk about other girls they sound like football players in a locker room ("The Boobie Goddesses of our grade are Natalie and Annette," or "Have you seen the Asian girl who wears that tiny red dress and those high red sneakers?," or "Carol is so hot! Why is she straight? I don't get it"), but there's little gossip about same-sex hookups—partly because the novelty has by now worn off, and partly because, as Alair puts it, "it's not assumed that a relationship will stem from it." It seems that even with all the same-sex activity going on, it's still hard for the girls to find other girls to actually date. Jane says this is because the girls who like girls generally like boys more, at least for dating. "A lot of girls are scared about trying to make a lesbian relationship work," she says. "There's this fear that there has to be the presence of a man or it won't work."

But dating gay girls isn't really an option either, because the cuddle-puddle kids are not considered part of the gay community. "One of the great things about bisexuality is that mainstream gay culture doesn't affect us as much," says Jane, "so it's not like bi boys feel that they have to talk with a lisp and walk around all fairylike, and it's not like girls feel like they have to dress like boys." The downside, she says, is that "gays feel that bis will cheat on them in a straight manner." In fact, there's a general impression of promiscuity that bisexual girls can't seem to shake. "The image of people who are bi is that they are sluts," says Jane. "One of the reasons straight boys have this bi-girls fantasy is that they are under the impression that bisexual girls will sleep with anything that moves and that's why they like both genders, because they are so sex-obsessed. Which isn't true."

If you ask the girls why they think there's more teenage bisexual experimentation happening today, Alair is quick with an explanation. "I blame television," she says. "I blame the media." She's partly joking, giving the stock answer. But there's obviously some truth to it. She's too young to remember a time when she couldn't turn on Showtime or even MTV and regularly see girls kissing girls. It's not simply that they're imitating what they've seen, it's that the stigma has been erased, maybe even transformed into cachet. "It's in the realm of possibilities now," as Ritch Savin-Williams puts it. "When you don't think of it as being a possibility, you don't do it. But now that it's out there, it's like, 'Oh, yeah, that could be fun.'" Of course, sexy TV shows would have no impact at all if they weren't tapping into something more innate. Perhaps, as research suggests, sexuality is more fluid for women than it is for men. Perhaps natural female intimacy opens the door to sexual experimentation at an age when male partners can be particularly unsatisfying. As one mother of a cuddle-puddle kid puts it, "Emotionally it's safer—it's difficult in this age group to hold onto your body. You're changing. There's a safety factor in a girl being with a girl." Then, laughing, she asked that her name be withheld. "*My* mother might read this."

It's true that girls have always experimented, but it's typically been furtive, kept quiet. The difference now is how these girls are flaunting it. It's become a form of exhibitionism, a way to get noticed at an age when getting noticed is what it's all about. And as rebellions go, it's pretty safe. Hooking up with girls won't get them pregnant. It won't hurt their GPA. It won't keep them out of honor societies, social groups, the Ivy League.

In the end, the Stuyvesant cuddle puddle might just be a trickle-down version of the collegiate "gay until graduation." On the other hand, these girls are experimenting at an earlier age, when their identities and their ideas about what they want in a partner are still being formed. Will it affect the way they choose to live their adult lives? Elle is determined to marry a man, but Alair and Jane are not so sure. Maybe they won't get married at all, they say, keep their options open. "I have no idea," says Alair. "I'm just 16."

A few weeks later, the guys are hanging out in Nathan's room. Jason is stretched out on the bed and Ilia is leaning back in a chair by the desk, and it's pretty clear that nothing much is happening this afternoon. Just some guitar playing, some laying about. Then the girls show up and things get more interesting. Alair and Jane have brought a couple of friends, Molly and Nikki. Molly doesn't know for sure if she's bisexual, but "I have my suspicions," she says; she's hooked up with Alair before. Nikki is with her friend Jared, who she's sort of but not really dating. He makes out with boys but considers Nikki his "soul mate"; she's totally straight but kisses girls. "I kiss anything pretty, anything beautiful, anything worthwhile," she says.

Nikki runs her hands through Jane's hair. "You look awesome! I love this shirt. I love your hair." Jane crosses the room to sit in Alair's lap, and Alair wraps her arms around her. That reminds Nikki of something.

"Wait! Let me show you guys the next painting I'm doing," she says, pulling from her backpack a photograph of Alair asleep on the beach in a striped bikini. It's a sexy picture, and Nikki knows it.

Chinese food is ordered, guitars strummed, an ice cube is passed around and for no apparent reason everyone is required to put it down their pants. It's just another afternoon of casual flirtation. The boys showing off for the girls, the girls showing off for everyone. No strings attached. In theory, anyway. Most of the kids say they hate relationships, that they don't want to be tied down, that they want to be open to different possibilities and different genders from minute to minute, but there is a natural tendency—as natural perhaps as the tendency to experiment—to try to find connection. Like it or not, emotions get involved. If you look closer, you can see the hint of longing, the momentary pouting,

the tiny jealousies. Jared can't take his eyes off Nikki, but Nikki seems interested mainly in Alair. Jason, too, is angling for Alair's attention, but Alair is once again focused on Jane. And Jane, well, Jane might actually be in love.

She is in a particularly good mood today, quick to smile, and even more quick to drop into conversation the name of the boy she recently started dating, a tall, good-looking senior and one of the most popular kids at Stuyvesant. Later, while rummaging for silverware, she casually mentions that they may start dating exclusively.

"Ugh!" Alair exclaims, grabbing her by the hips and pulling her away from the drawer. "What about me?"

"Let's put it this way," Jane counters, grinning and snatching up a fork. "I'm not interested in any other *guys*."

Still, it's clear that Jane really likes this guy. And Alair seems a little rattled. Her fortune cookie reads, "You are the master of every situation." Except perhaps this one.

Later, after the lamps have been switched on and the takeout eaten, both girls are on a love seat in the living room, leaning into each other, boys and dirty dishes strewn about. Jane starts showing off what she can do with her tongue, touching her nose with it, twisting it around, doing rolls. Everyone is impressed.

"My tongue gets a lot of practice," she says.

"Why don't you practice on me?" Alair demands. "I'll hook up with you." It's clear that she means more than kissing.

Jane blinks a few times. "I'm scared I'm going to be bad at it," she finally says. She's being coy, just putting her off, but there's a bit of sincerity to her nervousness.

"You won't be bad at it," Alair reassures her. She pulls Jane between her legs and starts giving her a massage, running her hands up and down her back, pushing her hair aside to rub her neck. When the massage is over, Jason comes over to Alair, grabs her hand, kisses it. For the rest of the evening, he stays close to her side, but she stays close to Jane.

The next day when I meet up with Alair on her way to choir practice, she tells me that nothing ever happened with Jane that night. She's decided to give up on her. Jane's with someone else, it's official, and there's no room in the relationship for her. "But you know what," she says, mustering a smile. "They're, like, monogamous together, and I'm really happy for them. And being their friend and seeing them so happy together totally beats a fling." She pauses. "It really does."

Your Turn: Give Students the Knowledge to Make Wise Choices About Sex

Three out of four respondents to November's Your Turn believe schools should teach a comprehensive sex education curriculum. Abstinence-only education, they say, is unrealistic for media-savvy teens who may already be having sex.

As a Minnesota reader put it, "If public schools don't teach a comprehensive sex education curriculum, Madonna will."

This Your Turn marks the debut of the ASBJ Reader Panel, a group of readers who are joining an e-mail conversation with us to supplement the printed Your Turn question. (Interested? Sign on at **www.asbj.com/readerpanel**.)

At this early stage, the Reader Panel is a resounding success. We've received hundreds of responses and many thoughtful comments. We can't print them all, but we can offer a representative sample of your views.

In addition to the 75 percent who supported a comprehensive sex-ed curriculum, 16 percent favored abstinence-only education, 8 percent offered various other responses, and 1 percent said, "Don't teach sex education at all."

Like the reader who cautioned against ceding sex education to Madonna, many of you said it was unrealistic, dangerous, and even dishonest to teach abstinence only when many teens are having sex and will continue to do so regardless of what their teachers tell them.

"The program should stress the importance of abstinence but must be comprehensive," said Lee Doebler, a board member from Alabama. "We cannot ignore the fact that many teens are sexually active and that sexual activity is beginning earlier and earlier as children reach puberty at an earlier age."

"Teaching abstinence-only sex education is like teaching nutrition without covering sugars and fats," added another reader. "Abstinence should certainly be emphasized in the curriculum; however, students should be given all the information so they could make that determination for themselves."

William Higgins, a board member from Washington state, said he favors a strong abstinence message along with other information. "It is urgent that we get a handle on the number-one addictive drug of choice among our youth—sex," he said. "I advocate a comprehensive program of graduated information,

based on age and grade level, that has a strong emphasis on abstinence. The idea is to keep kids smart—and safe!"

While we want students to abstain, there are other things we need to teach them along with abstaining that will strengthen their resolve, said Kim S. Rogers, a board member from North Carolina. "We cannot force our children to abstain. And if we don't educate them on the emotional and physical stress of teen sex, that has the effect of diluting the importance of abstaining—which, in my opinion, is the ultimate goal of sex education. Not talking about it doesn't make it go away."

Many of those favoring the abstinence-only approach said sex education should be handled by parents, not schools.

"Parents have the right and duty to decide how to present this information to their children," said an Indiana board member.

Added Texas Superintendent Paul Vranish: "It seems that 'how-to' instruction should best be left to parents."

Such "how to" instruction can give teens a false sense of confidence, several readers said. As one Missouri board member put it, "There is too much false information being taught about the safety of the use of condoms as it relates to 'safe sex.'"

Ann Johnson, a registered nurse and Indiana board member, said she favors abstinence-only education as the best way to deter students from making choices that could harm them physically and psychologically.

"I believe students need to understand the anatomy and physiology of human reproduction," Johnson said. "It is also important to have some discussion on the emotional and hormonal changes that occur in developing from preteen to adolescent to young adult and on the financial, emotional, and physical demands that result from unplanned and too early pregnancies."

Among those favoring no sex education in school was Perry Shumway, a board member in Idaho. "If sex education weren't taught at all in public schools, private institutions, such as families, churches, and youth groups, would step up to the plate and fill in the void," Shumway said.

However, most respondents agreed with Linda Smith Kortemeyer, an Iowa board secretary/treasurer who said abstinence only isn't enough.

"If we adopt a curriculum limiting what children are allowed to learn because of our restrictive beliefs, we basically are telling children we don't believe in their ability to work through life's difficult problems," Kortemeyer said. "When we encourage them to learn all they can, we tell them we have faith in their abilities to make the right choices. ... Children may not make the same choices as we did, but they will have the opportunity to make decisions based on the knowledge we provided them. Hopefully, these choices are made with wisdom and courage."

Sex & Love: The New World

More middle-aged people than ever are single, and they're finding the rules have changed. STDs and Internet dates. Aging bodies and kids at home. Who knew?

BARBARA KANTROWITZ

He expected to end up alone, so did she. Joe Germana, 49, had been married to Jane, "the love of my life," for 17 years. Diane Barna, 51, had been in a committed relationship with the same man for nearly a quarter of a century. Then, three years ago, Germana and his two young daughters returned to their Parma, Ohio, home after a brief shopping trip and found Jane dead from a medication reaction. "It was an absolute kick in the gut, a nightmare," he says. "Dating was the last thing on my mind." When Barna's longtime partner died last year, she, too, thought her romantic life was over. "I knew what love was, and not everyone gets that lucky," says Barna, a legal secretary who lives in Olmsted Falls, Ohio. "I had a great job, a good circle of friends, a lot of interests, and I thought I just wasn't going to settle for something in pants."

But love at midlife is full of surprises. You'll see.

The 77,702,865 Americans born between 1946 and 1964 came of age in the era of sex, drugs, and rock and roll. And while the last two may have lost some appeal over the years, sex and relationships remain front and center as the oldest boomers turn 60 this year. That's largely because more boomers are single than any previous cohort of forty to sixtysomethings. According to the Census Bureau, 28.6 percent of adults age 45 to 59 were unattached in 2003, compared with only 18.8 percent in 1980. (Of those, 16.6 percent were divorced, 2.9 percent were widowed and 9.1 percent had never been married.) And many of these singles are on the prowl. In a recent AARP survey, up to 70 percent of single boomers said they dated regularly. Of those between 40 and 59 years old, 45 percent of men and 38 percent of women have intercourse at least once a week.

29% of adults age 45 to 59 were unattached in 2003, up from 19% in 1980, says the U.S. Census Bureau.

In the 1970s and '80s, gay men and women who didn't have the option of marriage pioneered this pattern of evolving social connections. But for boomers in 2006, the issues have shifted. Gay or straight, they worry about the effect on their kids, especially if they became parents late in life. It's one thing to get an all-clear from a 23-year-old son or daughter but quite another to date around when you've got a preschooler in the house.

Images of middle-aged sex are beginning to permeate popular culture, from Jack Nicholson and a nude Diane Keaton in "Something's Gotta Give" to Charles and Camilla (together at last). Romance novelist Susan Elizabeth Phillips, who has nine New York Times best sellers to her credit, often includes passionate older couples in her books. "In the one I'm working on now, the secondary love story is between this geezer rocker and a woman who was once his groupie," she says. "They're both in their early 50s." In real life, there's Mick Jagger, still seeking satisfaction at 62. Author Gail Sheehy, who defined life journeys with "Passages" in the 1970s and "The Silent Passage" (on menopause) in 1991, has a new offering: "Sex and the Seasoned Woman," which promises to prove that women over 50 are "spicy... marinated in life experience."

20% of older singles have sex once a week or more, according to AARP. An additional 2% have sex daily.

That's a sea change from a generation ago, when older singles were out of the game. "You were supposed to stay home and be a grandparent at 50," says University of Washington sociologist Pepper Schwartz, 59, a twice-divorced single boomer herself and the author of "Finding Your Perfect Match." But boomers, Schwartz says, are "very clear about what they want, and they're willing to go looking for it." A whole new industry is gearing up to help with everything from drugs for erectile dysfunction to sex toys designed to appeal to boomers' more elevated sense of style (higher-quality silicone, according to Rebecca Suzanne, marketing manager of Babeland). Gyms across the country are introducing low-impact classes to attract boomers who want to firm up flabby thighs and jelly bellies in order to attract an equally fit partner. Boomers are flaunting their sexuality. "It's a situation of enjoying what's there," says Helen Gurley Brown, whose 1962 book "Sex and the Single Girl" ushered in a new era of openness about women and desire. "Sex is such an enjoyable activity at any age," says Brown, 83. "Why delegate it only to the young?"

Among older singles, 22% of men are looking for someone to marry or live with, compared with just 14% of women.

Why indeed? Although boomers usually still meet the old-fashioned way—through friends, neighbors or relatives—a growing number are searching online. Jim Safka, CEO of Match.com, says that people over 50 make up his site's fastest-growing segment, with a 300 percent increase since 2000. Some sites, like PrimeSingles.net, cater specifically to the over-50 crowd. Others attract boomers with more-specialized requirements like religion (BigChurch.com for Christians and Jdate.com for Jews) or sexual orientation (OurPersonals.com for gays). "Even 25 years ago, most people were reliant on their friends to fix them up," says family historian Stephanie Coontz, of the Evergreen State College in Washington. "People in their 40s and 50s don't want to be hanging out at bars. Now they have access to this incredible pool of single people their age."

61% of sexually active older singles report they're having unprotected sex.

The web helped Joe Germana start dating again. Two and a half years after Jane's death, he began to think about "reconnecting." He missed "the sweetness, the intimacy of a woman." But he was uncomfortable going to bars or clubs. "I'm in my 40s, not my 20s, and I was never a player," he says. "The thought of hitting on people just wasn't what I'm about." His thoughts wandered to his college girlfriend, and, amazingly, he found her on Classmates.com. They exchanged emails and discovered that both had lost spouses and had other experiences in common. After two months, they reunited. "There were huge sparks, a lot of mutual attraction, and a weekend that was very passionate," he says. "It felt so natural. In the back of my mind I thought, could we pick this up where we left off?"

The answer turned out to be no. Like many men his age, Germana was looking for a new life companion. But many boomers aren't eager to settle down. American women in their 40s and 50s are better educated and more affluent than any previous generation of women at midlife, and that has transformed the way they view dating. They don't necessarily want or need to center their lives on a man. In the AARP survey, only 14 percent of women said their most important reason for dating was to find someone to live with or marry, compared with 22 percent

of men. College professor Katherine Chaddock, 58, coauthor of "Flings, Frolics and Forever Afters: A Single Woman's Guide to Romance After Fifty," has a full schedule with work, her writers' group, her book club, her kids' visits home from college, her mixed-doubles tennis matches and her trips to the gym. For now, Chaddock says, her ideal relationship would be a "flex time" romance. "I could really enjoy on a fairly long-term basis somebody who lives and works about 100 to 200 miles away, somebody I saw every weekend, Friday through Sunday," she says. "Then we'd take a break and I could go back and talk to my cats and do silly stuff and wear my teeth-whitener strips around the house."

41% of older singles meet through friends, neighbors or relatives.

Although even the most fit 50-year-old can't compete with her 25-year-old body, women are learning to accept some of the sags that come with aging—and using a little cosmetic surgery to cope with the rest. Peggy Northrop, editor in chief of More magazine, which aims at women over 40, says midlife women "are not so uptight about their bodies as they were when they were younger. Their feeling is: if I'm naked and smiling, what's your problem?"

For boomer women, this freedom at midlife may turn out to be an unexpected benefit of the feminist movement of the 1970s. "People used to say to me that because of all these changes in our society, a lot of women were going to end up lonely in their old age," says Coontz. "Well, you couldn't prove it by the ones I know." Single women in their 40s and 50s often have vast friendship networks that they've developed from college through years in the workplace and community activities. "They take vacations to meet up with friends and they have very rewarding lives without a partner," says Coontz. "It's a stunningly new ball game."

Victoria Lautman, a single mother in Chicago, thinks of herself as a poster girl for the fortysomething divorced woman. "That's not because I've got men coming up the wazoo," she says. "It's mainly because I'm very social. I give a lot of parties." Lautman, a broadcast journalist, says she is far happier than she was when she was married. "The traditional view of the divorced woman is that they're just in purgatory, waiting until the next heavenly messenger shows up," she says. "I would so much rather be alone for the rest of my life than be mired in a bad relationship." At the moment, her 11-year-old son is the main man in her life. But she's definitely looking ahead. "At some point, when my son's a teenager, he's not going to need me," she says. "And when I'm 52, hopefully I'll still pass for 42, and I won't have to go for the 80-year-olds."

The longer they're single, the harder it is for boomer women to settle down. Cecilia Mowatt, 45, a lawyer turned consultant, always thought she would be married, but time passed quickly. "I was busy leading my life, doing my corporate career, all the Junior League stuff and philanthropic stuff to give back, and I kind of forgot about what I wanted to do for me in terms of a personal life," she says. But she admits she has become accustomed to her freedom and has come to cherish it. "Marriage is no easy thing," she says. "That partnership requires work every single day, and a commitment that's incredible."

For boomer men, the new rules can be bewildering at first but ultimately liberating. Lawyer Alan Kopit, 53, re-entered the dating scene in 2003 after a marriage that lasted nearly 18 years. "It used to be that a guy called the girl and set up the date," says Kopit, who lives in a Cleveland suburb. "Now a woman can just as easily call me and ask if I want to get together." This shift makes dating a lot more balanced, he says. A generation ago, it was the women who sacrificed a post-divorce social life to care for the children. But Kopit, like many divorced dads, is always thinking about the effect dating has on his daughters, ages 16 and 12, who live with him four nights a week. "I have to fit dating around my parental responsibilities," he says.

Even though he knew things weren't going well, Joe Germana tried to revive the relationship with his former classmate. He calls this effort "simpleton thinking with the brain between my legs." But they both had full lives and lived hundreds of miles apart. The situation was impossible. Eventually, they stopped communicating. "It was horrible," he says. Heartbreak in your 40s is a much slower-healing wound. But he still wanted love in his life, so a few months later he signed up on eHarmony.com, figuring that having to pay a fee might "weed out" women who weren't serious. After weeks of e-mails, he finally found a woman with potential. She liked classical music, bike rides and walks in the park, and had two kids close in age to his own. She worked in an office, as he did, and was recently divorced.

Only one hitch. She was 10 years younger.

"Their feeling is: if I'm naked and smiling, what's your problem?" —Peggy Northrop

In past generations, the age game always worked in favor of men. The assumption was that they could readily date down the calendar while women couldn't. But as Germana was about to find out, those rules have changed. Germana and the younger woman hit it off on their first date, and things moved "slowly, very slowly" until her 40th birthday. He bought her 40 long-stemmed roses and says he was "rewarded" for his patience. And so it began—lots of passion and lots of late nights. Paradise? Not exactly. "The lifestyle was killing me," Germana says. "I'm not used to all those late nights." He began to long for his quieter and more sedentary lifestyle. The younger woman took off on her annual camping trip with her kids. By the time she came back, the relationship had fizzled. "She needed someone younger and more exciting," he says, "and I needed a break since I was half dead."

Women in their 40s and 50s fantasize about younger men for the same reasons older men have always chased hot young babes—pure and simple lust. But reversing the sexes adds some interesting quirks. Think of the groundbreaking affair between Samantha Jones, the aggressive publicist on "Sex and the City," and her gentle boy toy, Smith Jerrod. She guided his career, gave him the benefit of her experience and expertise, and he gave her compassion and loyalty when she battled cancer. And he was one amazing lover.

"In real life, Kim Cattrall, the 49-year-old actress who played Samantha, is in a relationship with 27-year-old Alan Wyse, a private chef whom she describes as an old soul. "He's not a very young 27-year-old," Cattrall says. And, she adds, "he's in the culinary world, and making food is a very nurturing thing." After playing a sexually adventurous character, Cattrall found it hard to have a relationship with a man her own age because she thought they were trying to compete with Samantha. A younger man, she says, doesn't feel that need to outdo her. "The thing I really enjoy," she says, "is that I can show him my world and what I think about something. He's not closed down." She recently introduced him to the movie "Harold and Maude," the story of a special relationship between a 20-year-old man and a woman in her 70s. He loved it, of course.

But men who date younger women say that's their only option if they want to have a family. Even though Jim Bixby, a 46-year-old chemical engineer in Chicago, lives in a big city, he's finding it tough to meet women and started looking online about a year ago. In the first part of 2005, he had about 18 dates with six different women. "I was so jazzed," he says. "Then reality sank in. At some point, I realized I was drawing from the DNA cesspool." A number of the women had what he calls "extreme behavior" and a lot of "issues." One constantly swore even in ordinary conversation, and another e-mail correspondent turned out to be from Poland and was looking for a way to come to the United States. When he looks into his future, he's hoping he'll be a father instead of a 60-year-old dating 24-year-old women. "That's just gross," he says.

54% of older singles say the best thing about their lives is their independence and personal freedom.

But not impossible. Thanks to the pharmaceutical industry, physical limitations to sex as men get older are vanishing. The percentage of men suffering from erectile dysfunction increases dramatically with age. Viagra and its cousins are helping men stay sexually active, although that can pose unexpected challenges for women, says Dr. Lee Shulman, a professor of obstetrics and gynecology at Northwestern University and a board member of the Association of Reproductive Health Professionals. If a man has "36 hours of an erect penis, that's a lot of pressure, especially for those women for whom intercourse has become painful," he says. "She may try more oral sex to keep him at bay, but eventually, he's going to want to do the horizontal mambo." The solution: vaginal lubricants and moisturizers and possibly local estrogen therapy for women who want to stay in shape for sex.

As Joe Germana continued his search, Diane Barna was also tentatively starting to date. She tried online dating and "absolutely loathed" her experiences. After being in a couple for so long, she found the new rules daunting. Who makes the first call? Who pays for dinner? Does the three-date rule still apply? Who brings the condom? And (a really delicate issue) how do you ask if that someone has been tested for HIV? On all except the last, there are no real guidelines, says syndicated columnist Amy Dickinson, but she advises her readers to have a very specific discussion of their sexual histories. "Getting an HIV test together is the modern equivalent of exchanging class rings," says Dickinson, a 46-year-old single mother herself.

But Barna couldn't do it. "Oh, God," she groans. "That's kind of intimidating."

Though single boomers are having sex regularly, only 39 percent invariably use protection, according to the AARP study. "To me those are pretty alarming figures," says Linda Fisher, AARP's research director. From 1990 to 2004, the cumulative number of AIDS cases in adults 50 and older grew sevenfold, from 16,288 to 114,981. The increase reflects people who were infected early on and have survived because of antiviral medication, but experts who study aging and AIDS are concerned that the problem of new infections in older adults may be more serious than the statistics reflect.

Many boomers just don't have a sense of danger about sex. They came of age before the HIV epidemic and never learned how to negotiate condom use or testing with their partners. In fact, women over 50 are at risk for developing HIV from heterosexual sex because their thinner vaginal walls are more susceptible to cuts and tears. Women of all ages represent the fastest-growing segment of new HIV cases, and the number of new infections among older women is rising rapidly: between 1988 and 2000, women's share of AIDS cases among those 50 and older nearly doubled, from 8.9 percent to 15 percent.

One day, Germana's younger girlfriend shared her tale with Barna, a frequent lunch companion. Despite the failure of her friend's relationship with Germana, Barna was intrigued. "There I was, alone, hearing about this really nice guy who takes care of his kids, works hard, who is close to my age, who somebody else thought was kind of boring. I thought, give me some of that boring. He sounds absolutely perfect." Because there were no hard feelings, the younger woman agreed to act as a facilitator, e-mailing pictures and asking Germana if he wanted to meet Barna. The answer was yes.

"I have to fit dating around my responsibilities as a parent." —Alan Kopit

Six months later, Germana and Barna think of themselves as a serious couple. "This is a good person, a good man, and I'm very comfortable," says Barna. And the three-date rule? Not a problem. "At our age," says Barna, "if sex presents itself, if you're comfortable with your partner, why wait for three dates? Just go for it." Germana agrees that age shouldn't be a barrier, but having a full life in your 40s and 50s puts different strains on dating. "There are more pressures just from life itself," he says. "You are generally established at work, working hard, long hours, you have kids and family obligations—and just obligations in general." His daughters were troubled at first by his dating, and he thinks they were worried that he wouldn't spend enough time with them. But now he says things are OK. Barna says her adult son had no problem with her dating again. In fact, she believes he's happy for her. "He's probably thinking, 'I'm not going to have to take care of Mom'," she says, laughing. "Besides, I know he wants me to be happy." And for now, she is.

With Joan Raymond, Karen Springen, Pat Wingert, Anna Kuchment and Raina Kelley

Staying Up Late with Sue

ANNE MATTHEWS

S ue Johanson, sex guru, has three grown kids, two grand-children, three books, a nursing degree and not one but two hit TV programs. Thirty weeks a year, live from Toronto's SkyDome, she broadcasts *The Sunday Night Sex Show,* a favorite in Canada since 1996.

In 2002 she added a second hour especially for the U.S. audience. *Talk Sex With Sue* airs late nights on the Oxygen cable network, and some 4.2 million Americans now stay up to catch her tips and quips, from the latest in lubricants to the odds of a male over 35 having a heart attack during intercourse.

Johanson, a leading sex educator in Canada for more than three decades, will discuss absolutely anything except the year she was born. "Sometime in the 20th century" is about as specific as she gets. Gray hair gives her credibility, and she knows it. "Nothing reduces inhibitions like a grandmother sitting on TV talking about whips, willies and warts," she says.

She's the Julia Child of sex, unflappable and candid. Fans know she likes to knit and sew, bake sourdough biscuits, putter at her Ontario lake cottage and go to yard sales—"I'm cheap!"

On camera, she is a born ham, especially when sharing condom advice: "If you wanna be mine, cover your vine!"; "Shroud the moose before you let loose!" Every week she delves into her Pleasure Chest—actually an old sewing basket, thriftily relined with red velvet—and offers tabletop demos of sex toys. On a live broadcast, this can be risky. Audiences have seen her battle a smoldering vibrator and a badly out-of-control vacuum pump. Sex toys that are dishwasher-safe get a special nod of approval.

The heart of her shows is the call-in segment. Erectile dysfunction, pregnancy and yeast infections are the most common worries; always, Johanson's answers reassure and teach as well as amuse. This is an international public education project that only looks like standup comedy. Her approach is slangy but never vulgar. She has never been bleeped. And you can't beat her command of statistics: What percentage of American teens have their first sexual experience in automobiles? "Twelve percent. You never see that in car commercials." What percentage of women over 80 continue to have sex? "Thirty percent. Finding a man that age with working parts is another story."

Johanson works in the tradition of the wisecracking advice columnist who uses reader queries to explain human behavior. Like Dear Abby and Ann Landers, she tackles sensitive topics head-on, and like Dr. Ruth Westheimer, she displays a frankness that can be jaw-dropping. Sex aids for quadriplegics?

Bondage play after a bypass? Sue covers it all. Canadians seem to love it, stopping her on the street or at the grocery store for detailed sex advice. Americans politely murmur that they really, really like the show.

Credentials and Credibility

Born in Ontario to an English-Irish family, married young to a Swedish-Canadian electrician employed by a public utility, Johanson is a registered nurse with postgraduate training in family planning, human sexuality and counseling and communications. These credentials underpin her credibility. Her ability to talk easily with teenagers about sexual issues led her to create, in 1970, the first birth control clinic in any North American high school. She still does 60 shows live and 30 lectures a year; for her countless courses, talks and media presentations on smart sex, she received in 2001 the prestigious Order of Canada award, that nation's version of knighthood.

Good sex after midlife interests Johanson—and her audience. "Who says you shouldn't have exciting sex at 70?" she asks. "If fitness and flexibility allow, do it, try it, don't limit yourself by age. 'Oh dear, I'm 50, I can't, I shouldn't.'" The key, she believes, is the quality of the relationship with one's partner. Enjoyable sex calls for drive, enthusiasm, imagination.

And understanding. "As we get older the body changes—no more firm, young, bodacious tatas. Your waistline is gone, you've got turkey neck and wrinkled skin. ... You're not sure what a partner will think? Well, your partner has the same worries. That manly chest has slipped south. ... Talk about it ahead of time. Say, 'I'm going to find this a little difficult—my body works, but it isn't so beautiful.' And they'll likely reply, 'Thank goodness! Me too!'"

Not Just for the Young

Arousal in both sexes takes longer with age, Johanson explains, and the need for orgasm diminishes dramatically. But the need for a sex life is evergreen, even if grown children try to interfere, or shame ("Mother! At your age!"). Sex in nursing homes and assisted-living communities is growing more common, she adds; in Canada, facilities often include a "love nest" on the premises, with double bed, flowers, candles and a good radio/CD player. Improvised intimacy works, too. "Privacy can be as

Getting More Out of Your Love Life

Tips from Sue Johanson:

1. Skip burgers and fries. Good nutrition makes you feel much better, and makes for better sex. "Eat junk food," she says, "and all you want to do is fight over the remote control."

2. Games are good. Try phone sex—he on one extension, she on another. Try hide-and-seek, on the floor, in the dark, in the nude. "Find each other, then have fun under the coffee table."

3. Toys work, too. "Go to a sex store together, buy small, low-cost items to start, check them out, then invest more once you know what you like."

4. Choose a time when both feel ready for lovemaking. Wake up your partner at midnight with caresses and a sultry "Hi, big guy!" Someone with arthritis may do best in the morning, after a good night's sleep. "When we were young," Johanson points out, "we could never have sex during the day—the kids would hear."

5. If you have a physical restriction, or just the aches and pains of aging:
- Take an anti-inflammatory 20 minutes ahead of time.
- Together, take a romantic hot bath, with lights low, and candles and incense by the tub.
- Keep extra pillows nearby in case of leg or foot cramps.
- Have cream or gel handy.
- Warm the bed with an electric blanket.

6. Pleasurable positions? Spoon-fashion. Side-by-side. The X position. Or female-on-top. Try chair sex: It's easy on the joints.

7. And try the following books:
- Her latest, *Sex, Sex and More Sex*, coming out this month.
- *The Ultimate Guide to Sex and Disability*, by Cory Silverburg, Miriam Kaufman and Fran Odette.
- *The New Love and Sex After 60*, by Robert Butler and Myrna Lewis. "Get the book and stand well back!"

simple as a Do Not Disturb sign on a room door, which means 'Meals and meds can wait. We are having fun in here.'"

Johanson's weekly call-ins still demonstrate the widespread belief that sex is the property of the young. That's changing. Aging boomers, she says, will permanently redefine post-50 sex. Women in their 70s and 80s have begun asserting their ongoing interest in a sex life. Sue calls such people "cougars"—older women who enjoy sex, always did and have no intention of giving it up. Recently she spoke to an 85-year-old woman whose male partner is 35. No complaints from either side; quite the contrary.

"So why accept arbitrary age parameters?" Johanson asks. The basic rules of sex apply at every life stage. "Use your head, plan ahead, know what you're doing, never let sex just happen." At 18 or 80, she advises, "Don't always expect multi-orgasmic bliss. Pleasure, sure. Affection, definitely. Sex should be energizing. Enjoyable. And a bit of a giggle."

ANNE MATTHEWS *is a nonfiction writer in Princeton, N.J.*

UNIT 6

Old/New Sexual Concerns

Unit Selections

Key Points to Consider

- What does your college or university do about date or acquaintance rape? Are there education or prevention programs? How is a report of an assault handled? How do you think these issues should be handled on campuses?

- How do you feel about laws restricting sexual behaviors (for example, age limits, marital requirements for engaging in sex, or laws making specific sexual behaviors illegal)? Which laws would you add or change related to sexual issues or behaviors?

- What are your criteria for consent when two (or more) people engage in a sexual behavior? What do you recommend as safeguards against misunderstanding, confusion, and assault?

- How would you react to finding out that your partner is logging onto "adult" Internet sites? Asking you to watch explicit "adult" videos together? Being unfaithful? Asking you to participate in an open relationship or swinging? Would any be grounds for ending the relationship?

- How important to you is sexual intimacy, including the frequency of sexual intimacy within your partner relations? What would you be willing to do to remedy interest level differences, and would a continuing need discrepancy be grounds for ending the relationship?

Student Web Site

www.mhcls.com/online

Internet References

Further information regarding these Web sites may be found in this book's preface or online.

The Child Rights Information Network (CRIN)
http://www.crin.org

Infertility Resources
http://www.ihr.com/infertility/index.html

Third Age: Love and Sex
http://www.thirdage.com/romance/

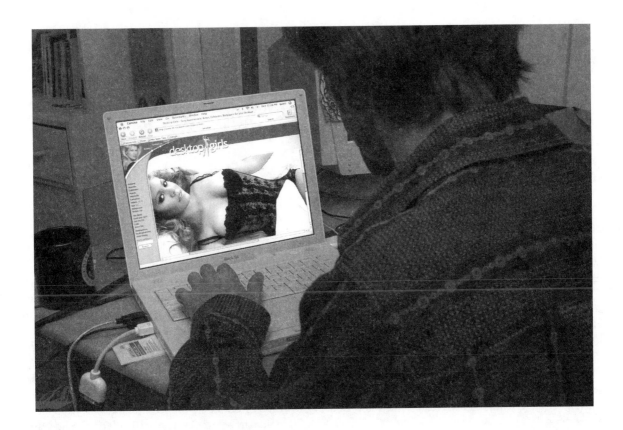

This final unit deals with several topics that are of interest or concern for different reasons. Also, as the title suggests, it combines "old" or ongoing topics and concerns with "new" or emerging ones. In one respect, however, these topics have a common denominator—they have all taken positions of prominence in the public's awareness as social issues.

Tragically, sexual abuse and violence are long-standing occurrences in society and in some relationships. For centuries, a strong code of silence surrounded these occurrences and, many now agree, increased not only the likelihood of sexual abuse and violence, but the harm to victims of these acts. Beginning in the middle of the twentieth century, two societal movements helped to begin eroding this code of silence. The child welfare/child rights movement exposed child abuse and mistreatment and sought to improve the lives of children and families. Soon after, and to a large extent fueled by the emerging women's movement, primarily "grass-roots" organizations that became known as "rape crisis" groups or centers became catalysts for altering the way we looked at (or avoided looking at) rape and sexual abuse.

Research today suggests that these movements have accomplished many of their initial goals and brought about significant social change. The existence and prevalence of rape and other sexual abuse is much more accurately known. Many of the myths previously believed (rapists are strangers that jump out of bushes, sexual abuse only occurs in poor families, all rapists are male and all victims are female, and so on) have been replaced with more accurate information. The code of silence has been recognized for the harm it can cause, and millions of friends, parents, teachers, counselors, and others have learned how to be approachable, supportive listeners to victims disclosing their abuse experiences. Finally, we have come to recognize the role that power, especially unequal power, plays in rape, sexual abuse, sexual violence, and, a term coined more recently, sexual harassment. However, as current events have shown us, the battle is far from over and sexual abuse continues to have consequences for victims, those connected to them, as well as, society as a whole.

As we, as a society, have sought to expose and reduce abusive sex, it has become increasingly clear that all of society and each of us as individuals/potential partners must grapple with the broader issue of what constitutes consent: What is non-abusive sexual interaction? How can people communicate interest, arousal, desire, and/or propose sexual interaction, when remnants of unequal power, ignorance, misinformation, fear, adversarial sex roles, and inadequate communication skills still exist? Finally, another layer of perplexing questions that confront the proactive/reactive dilemma: What is, or should be, the role of employers, school personnel, or simply any of us who may be seen as contributing on some level due to awareness or complicity to an environment that allows uncomfortable, abusive, or inappropriate sexual interaction? Conversely, is it possible that we could become so "sensitive" to the potential for abuse that combined with our discomfort, anger, and fear we could become hysterical vigilantes pushing an eager legal system to indict "offenders" who have not committed abuse or harassment?

The Sex Offender Next Door

Megan's Law was supposed to protect us from neighborhood predators. But in too many places, kids are still in danger.

AMY ENGELER

The sounds of children and splashing water caught Francine Johnson's attention on a weekday afternoon last May. Wondering if school had let out early, she looked out her window at her neighbor's above-ground pool and saw a half dozen young boys, each around eight years old, playing in the water. With them was Robert Forzano, the strapping blond automobile mechanic who lived next door to Johnson in suburban Rancho Cordova, California. She was puzzled, thinking it odd that Forzano, 42, who didn't socialize with other adults in their neighborhood, would be playing with children in the middle of a school day. "Whenever I saw him, he was standoffish with me. Kind of gruff, really," says Johnson. "So this was strange."

Johnson mentioned the pool party to her husband that night; and she kept up her vigil, watching boys come and go on several other afternoons. Both her backyard and Forzano's opened onto the busy White Rock Community Park, and the local elementary school was just across the street. In fact, the school's principal, Fay Kerekes, could nearly see Forzano's house from where she stood as kids poured into her school each morning. But there was one shocking fact that neither of these women knew: Forzano and his roommate, tow truck operator Brian McDaniel, 42, were both convicted child molesters.

Forzano had served four years in prison for molesting boys under age ten in Ventura County, California; after his parole, he moved in with McDaniel, who had a similar record of lewd acts with a child under age 14 (the men are thought to have met in prison). The two melted into this community outside Sacramento just as easily as they might have a decade earlier, before the passage of Megan's Law.

That landmark piece of legislation was named after seven-year-old Megan Kanka, murdered in 1994 by a convicted sex offender who lived across the street from the Kankas' New Jersey home. After Megan's death, her grief-stricken mother, Maureen, campaigned tirelessly for a law that would prevent other parents from having to endure a similar tragedy. In May 1996, President Clinton signed a law requiring all states to make information about pedophiles and rapists available to the public. But Congress gave the states a lot of leeway in how they accomplished this goal. "Putting a law in place is one thing," Maureen

Kanka says today. "Having law enforcement and the state work together to see that the registries are as up-to-date as possible and that they're being used effectively is another."

Had Forzano lived in Texas, Florida, or another state that is aggressive about implementing Megan's Law, the police might have been sent to the White Rock Elementary School to warn the principal that a convicted pedophile had moved in little more than a block away. Or flyers with his photo might have been handed out to neighbors by law-enforcement officials. But at the time, California's version of Megan's Law was among the most permissive in the country. Plus, California was doing a poor job of enforcing the requirements they did have: In 2003, 30 to 40 percent of the state's 100,000 convicted sex offenders were missing from the registry.

Luring the Children into a Trap

Forzano, at least, kept his appointments with the sheriff's office, spoke politely to detectives, and provided a correct address. But with the California state registry not yet online, his neighbors could have learned about Forzano's criminal history only by going to the police station, signing an application, and looking him up on a CD-ROM. Or, for $10, they could have called a 900 number to get information. Not surprisingly; says Laura Ahearn, executive director of the New York-based advocacy group Parents for Megan's Law, no neighbors made the call. "When Megan's Law was passed, there was so much hope that these laws would be strong," she says. "But some states have deluded the public into thinking they are being protected when they aren't."

Forzano and McDaniel kept their lawn trim and their driveway full of cars. Many mornings, Forzano would stand outside working under the hood of his old Mustang, greeting children who passed by on their way to school. Forzano's appearance caused no alarm—his tanned face and thick neck looked youthful and macho. To the eight-year-olds in the neighborhood, he was simply "Bob," or "my friend Bob." Forzano's young "friends"—almost a dozen boys between seven and 12 years old, mostly from low-income families newly arrived from Ukraine, according to the police—kept quiet as Forzano "groomed" them, as the long seduction of young victims is called. The friendly greetings over the hood of Forzano's Mustang turned into conversations in the park. Once Forzano was no longer a stranger, or someone to be feared, the boys came through the chain-link fence in his backyard and into the pool, police say, and then up the steps into his house. Forzano plied them with sodas and snacks and movies that weren't available at home and gave the older boys a refuge from school. "The parents didn't realize that their kids were skipping school," says Sgt. Micki Links, who is in charge of the sex offender registry for the Sacramento County Sheriff's Office. "The kids didn't want anyone to know, to stop a good thing. And when they said, 'We were at Bob's house,' the parents thought it was a little friend, not an adult."

Forzano kept his pool parties going for several weeks, police say, until Deputy Steve Wright, a resource officer with the Folsom-Rancho Cordova Unified School District, looked into curious absences by two boys from the nearby Mills Middle School. The boys wouldn't say where they had been, so the school asked for Wright to be put on the case. He got the boys to admit they'd been hanging out with an adult named Bob. Wright drove them past the house for confirmation, ran a check on the license plate of a car in the driveway, and learned of Forzano's status as a registered sex offender. Wright listened with concern as the boys talked about playing in Forzano's pool and in his house, sometimes with their seven- and eight-year-old brothers, students at White Rock Elementary School. One of those younger brothers, police learned, appeared to be Forzano's intended victim. Forzano showed the boy some child pornography, which is often the first step toward coercing sexual acts.

What the Search Warrant Revealed

At dawn on May 25, 2004, Principal Kerekes was awakened by a call from the sheriff's office. Now that someone was obviously in danger, California state law allowed police to warn the school about a sex offender. Principal Kerekes signed for the Megan's Law disclosure and received a rap sheet on Forzano. At the same time, the police, with a warrant, entered the men's neat, wood-shingled house and found a stash of child pornography on McDaniel's computer, a hidden video camera set up to capture children undressing and urinating, and a wealth of toys and games. "It was pretty scary," says Sergeant Links, "to see that these two grown men had more Walt Disney videos than most parents."

The next day, the police announced the arrest of Forzano on two felony charges of molesting or annoying a child under 14 (for improper touching in the pool) and on a misdemeanor—using a camcorder to film someone unknowingly for sexual gratification. They also arrested McDaniel for possessing child pornography.

By summer's end, only a brown spot on the ground hinted at the place where Forzano's pool had once stood. McDaniel tore it down after he bailed himself out of jail, while his housemate remained in custody awaiting prosecution. Later, McDaniel was

convicted and sentenced to a 180-day work furlough program and three years' probation. In September, Governor Arnold Schwarzenegger signed a bill giving Californians Internet access to more of the state's sex offender registry. Meanwhile, a federal grand jury indicted Forzano for possessing, receiving, and distributing pornography of minors. (State charges are still pending.) The offense carries a maximum 60-year prison term. As of press time, he had not yet entered a plea. But if convicted, Forzano won't be around children for a very long time to come.

What Parents Need to Know About Megan's Law

Below, Karen Terry, Ph.D., editor of a Megan's Law sourcebook and an associate professor at John Jay College of Criminal Justice in New York City, answers questions on how to make Megan's Law better.

Q: What are the basic requirements of the law?

Anyone who commits any type of sexual offense (against a child or an adult) must register with the police as soon as he's released from prison. The offender has up to 30 days, depending on the state, to appear at the police station and give his address, a photo, and sometimes a DNA sample.

But states have a lot of leeway with public notification, the second part of the law. Most states rank sex offenders into three tiers: Level I is low risk (of reoffending), Level II is moderate risk, and Level III is high risk (known in some states as sexual predators). In almost every state, only information about Level III offenders is available to the public.

And each community can handle the notification differently. Some counties release names and photos only on the Web. Some have a book of names at the police station. In other areas, police will go door-to-door or hold a town meeting. Others will put up a poster at the post office. In some jurisdictions in Louisiana, the offender has to personally go door-to-door and tell neighbors that he is a sex offender.

Q: The law has been in place for almost ten years. How well is it working?

The law has been very helpful in investigations. When a crime occurs, the police look at the registries, match up the modus operandi, and they have a list of people to talk to. As for prevention of future crimes, supervision of convicted sex offenders—when the police can drop by an offender's house at any time to look for evidence of kids or any sign of relapse—may be effective. It's important for sex offenders to know that someone is watching them. Plus, these laws are popular because the public feels protected. But that may be a false sense of security; Megan's Law hasn't really been studied, and we can't prove that it deters future sexual assaults.

Q: What parts of the law need fixing?

The biggest issue is keeping the registries up-to-date. Some states, such as Florida, have been very good at this; others are having a hard time keeping up. Offenders move around quite a bit. They may register with a false address, or they don't reregister when they move. Or they just take off immediately and never register. Most places don't have the resources to follow up. For instance, New York City has a monitoring unit with wonderful, hard-working, diligent officers. But seven officers are in charge of about 4,000 sex offenders.

Q: When the law was passed, some groups worried about vigilantism against sex offenders and privacy infringement. How has this played out?

The courts have pretty much decided that an offender's right to privacy is less important than public safety. The offender may be stigmatized or verbally abused, but that's not unconstitutional. But it does bring up another issue with Megan's Law: Generally, child molesters have poor self-esteem and don't relate well to adults, so their treatment involves learning to improve their social skills and form relationships with adults. But if they live in Texas, where one judge has made them put a sign in their yard that says "I am a sex offender" or a bumper sticker on their car, they are likely to be ostracized.

They can't make friends or have appropriate sexual relationships, so it can start the cycle of offending again. Plus, if the notification process is too stigmatizing, offenders may not register, which is the part of the law that has been shown to be most helpful to law enforcement.

Q: What should parents do?

Look at the Internet registries. If a child molester lives down the street, show his picture to your child and say, "Take a good look at this person. This person has harmed children before. Stay away from him." But even if you don't find anyone on the registry in your area, it would be a mistake to say, "Phew! No sex offenders on my block. We're OK." Sex crimes are highly underreported. Sex offenders who are actually quite dangerous don't appear on those registries. Consider this: Nine times out of ten, the offender will be someone the child knows and not the stranger at the end of the block. So say to your child, "If anyone, including Uncle Joe or Aunt Sue, touches you in a way that's improper, you need to tell me."

Silent No More

Survivors of sexual abuse can begin to heal the pain of the past by speaking out

ROBIN D. STONE

My journey from victim to survivor began when I was about 9 years old. My younger sister and I were sleeping over at an uncle's house in the country. I adored my uncle, and I curled up on his lap to watch the late-night movie. Everyone else was asleep when, sometime later, he led me by the hand to a dark corner of his house. There he fondled my growing breasts and rubbed my crotch. When he was finished, he sent me to bed, warning me never to tell anyone what he had done. "The incident," as I now refer to it, was five minutes of confusion, horror and profound embarrassment. Its impact has lasted a lifetime.

Like many children who've been violated and warned to keep quiet, I did as I was told. Through years of family gatherings and church functions, I kept my distance from my uncle as I built a wall of silence around myself. Inside it, my secret began to take root in my life, and as a tree's roots slowly conform to their surroundings, so was I shaped by my inability to give voice to what had happened to me. Deep down, I believed that I had done something to deserve what happened, and even as I wrestled with that, there were periods when I managed to convince myself that it was really no big deal. Still, I decided that I shouldn't get too close to men, or anybody else for that matter. Even God was not exempt. I remember thinking that if God really existed, he wouldn't have let my uncle touch me.

Though some may find it difficult to understand how five minutes can forever affect the course of a life, those who have been sexually violated know all too well the residue of humiliation and helplessness that the experience leaves behind. Not telling about the abuse only compounds its effects. Indeed, some find that secrecy can become a way of life. Kristen (name has been changed), whose older cousin repeatedly forced her to have intercourse with him from ages 9 to 12, says, "There was a real connection between my not telling about the abuse and withholding other things about my life as well. You become good at hiding because you fear that if you don't, others will be able to see the shameful truth of what happened to you."

Sooner or later, though, the secret must be reckoned with, because the silence that helps us cope in the beginning can lead to anxiety, depression, addiction, memory loss, cancer, promiscuity and sexual and reproductive problems. "There's a mind-body-soul connection," explains Maelinda N. Turner, a Van-

couver, British Columbia, social worker with a degree in divinity who has worked mostly with Black and Latino clients. "It may sound New-Agey, but if emotions aren't released, they hide in the body as disease."

A Quiet Epidemic

Because sexual violence—being forced or coerced to perform sexual acts—is fueled by the abuser's need for power and control, those who have less power, such as children, are often more vulnerable. Indeed, children under 12 make up about half of all victims of sexual assault. And not surprisingly, the rates of rape and other forms of sexual assault are higher in poor and urban areas, where so many feel powerless. As a result, experts say, Black women have a disproportionately higher risk of assault.

In recent years, even as overall crime rates have fallen, the incidence of rape and sexual abuse has risen. At least one in four women, and one in six men, will experience some form of sexual abuse in their lifetime. And according to some estimates, as many as one in four young women on college campuses will become a victim of rape or attempted rape, although half of those violated won't think of it as such. That's partly because almost 70 percent of rape and sexual-assault victims know their offender as an acquaintance, friend, relative or intimate partner, and we're loath to see people close to us as rapists. Think about it: If a mugger beats a woman as he steals her purse, she'd report that to the police. But if an associate rapes a woman after she has invited him up for a drink, she thinks about the line of questioning ("You did invite him up, didn't you?") and decides to keep it to herself. The bottom line: Fear often keeps us quiet and can even keep us from admitting to ourselves that we have been criminally violated. There's the fear of what people will think and what they'll say. There's the fear of retaliation. The fear that you won't be believed. Fear that you'll jeopardize existing relationships. Fear that somebody will go to jail. Fear that you'll be alone. And fear that you actually invited it. The fear can be so overwhelming that many victims of abuse actually repress the memory as a way of coping.

So why are we so reluctant to talk about sexual violence? Well, first we'd have to be willing to talk about sex, which many of us find uncomfortable. "We're certainly not the only

Healing the Hurt

Iyanla Vanzant

1. Talk to someone. Find someone you trust and let them know what happened. Tell them exactly how you feel. Do not participate in the conspiracy by remaining silent.

2. Keep a journal of thoughts and prayers. Even after talking, the thoughts continue to circle in your mind. Write down what you think and feel, then write a prayer to have those thoughts and feelings healed.

3. Avoid asking yourself why. Asking why deepens the wound and feeds the feelings of shame and guilt. An unanswered why shifts the responsibility onto your shoulders.

4. Keep your body moving. The trauma of sexual abuse gets locked in the muscles and tissues of the body. You must exercise to free yourself of the effects of the emotional and mental trauma. Dancing, swimming or yoga can help you rebuild and regain a healthy relationship with your body.

5. Talk to yourself. Learn to love yourself by creating powerful, loving affirmations that support and encourage you. Affirmations let you know that you are still okay.

6. Rehearse the confrontation. Write out what you would say to your abuser, and write the response you believe the abuser would have. Keep writing both sides of the story until you experience peace. Repeat this exercise as many times as necessary.

7. Realize it was not your fault. Whether you were abused as a child or an adult, avoid blaming your appearance, behavior, inability to escape, lack of retaliation or fear for the violation.

8. Don't run from the memories. You only delay your healing when you avoid, deny or resist the memory of the experience. Instead, draw a picture that represents what you feel. When you are done, burn it!

9. Create a safe place. Choose a place in your home that you can decorate with comforting objects, or go to a park or some other easily accessible location. Claim it as a safe haven. When you go to your safe place, sit quietly, pray, meditate or just hold loving thoughts about yourself.

10. Get professional help or support. Do not deny yourself healing support and encouragement. Find a counselor, therapist or support group with whom you can continue to explore and share your thoughts and feelings.

---

group that's silent regarding abuse," says Gail E. Wyatt, Ph.D., author of *Stolen Women: Reclaiming Our Sexuality, Taking Back Our Lives* (John Wiley & Sons). "But we're the only group whose experience is compounded by our history of slavery and stereotypes about Black sexuality, and that makes discussion more difficult."

Because so few of us tell, nobody knows how big the problem of sexual violence really is. All statistics are based only on *reported* assaults, and, according to the 1999 National Crime Victimization Survey from the U.S. Department of Justice, sexual assault is reported only about 28 percent of the time, making it the least reported violent crime in the United States. Untold numbers continue to suffer in silence, sleepwalking through their days, alive but not truly living, compressing their feelings so they won't feel pain.

For survivors of sexual abuse, there is no one formula for recovery, but every path to healing ultimately requires that we speak out about the ways in which we have been violated. On the following pages, three women (names and identifying details have been changed) give voice to their stories of abuse and silence—and they discover, in the telling, a way to finally move beyond the secrets that have haunted them for so long.

Dangerous Games

Stephanie, a 31-year-old artist, rarely makes her way from her East Coast home to the rural midwestern town where she grew up. Home reminds her of the "games" she and her two sisters used to play with their father. "When Mama was away, Daddy would put us on his lap and feel us up," says Stephanie, the middle sister. "He'd call us into his room one at a time. He'd start with a hug or a tickle, and then he'd touch my breast. We knew what was happening. My sisters and I had a code. We'd say, 'Okay, in five minutes, you've got to come and get me.'" Throughout the girls' childhood, their father would call the eldest sister the most often. Today that sister escapes the pain of those memories through the use of illegal drugs and alcohol. Stephanie's youngest sister struggles with overeating. On the surface, Stephanie, who is single, seems highly functional compared with her sisters. She is full of energy and has a host of friends and a calendar packed with theater dates, parties and book-club meetings.

When I ask Stephanie how she feels about what her father did to her and her sisters, she seems surprised. She has never thought much about it, she says, adding, "What's done is done." But she quickly contradicts herself. "Things have built up over the last few years," she admits. "I'm at the point where I hate

Safeguarding Our Children

Few of us actually teach our children how to protect themselves from sexual abuse, despite the fact that 67 percent of all reported victims of sexual assault are under 18, according to a recent Department of Justice survey. How do we empower our kids to defend themselves, and to create an environment in which they'll feel free to tell us anything?
Here are ways to start:

Give children the appropriate vocabulary so that words like *vagina, breast* and *penis* aren't foreign to them. Naming intimate body parts helps your child claim them in a healthy way.

Respect their boundaries. If Aunt Sally wants a kiss and your little one resists, don't force the issue. Children pushed to submit to affection may begin to feel that grown-ups' demands are more important than their own physical limits.

Teach them about inappropriate touching. "Say to your child, 'Nobody should touch you there,' or 'Nobody kisses you on the mouth,'" says New York clinical psychologist Dorothy Cuningham, Ph.D. Introduce concepts gradually, starting around age 3 and depending on your child's ability to understand. But don't put off talking about inappropriate touching, Cunningham warns. Toddlers can be the most vulnerable.

Encourage children to express their feelings. "You can't have closed communication and then expect it to be open if there's sexual misconduct," Cunningham points out. "Invite your children to talk to you. Don't just ask 'How's school?' Ask 'How's your teacher?' and 'What did you do today?' Get a sense of their relationships and friendships." Give feedback so your child knows you're listening and responsive. And don't be afraid to ask direct questions. For example, you might periodically ask your child "Has anyone ever tried to touch you in a way you did not like, or asked you to touch them in a way that made you uncomfortable?" One woman, abused by an older relative for years during her childhood, says that if her mother had asked her a direct question, her painful secret would have come out.

Teach children that it's okay to question authority— especially those in authority who make them feel uncomfortable. This can be a challenge for those of us raised to "do as you're told" by grown-ups. But children should never feel that they have no choice.

Know your child. "If you're tuned in, you know when she's upset," Cunningham says. If a once-carefree child becomes moody, withdrawn and unresponsive, don't dismiss it as phase. If your child suddenly doesn't want to go to Uncle Fred's house, pay attention. If your youngster becomes preoccupied with mature sexual concepts, don't assume it's just something picked up at school. Question your child gently, and above all, let her know you love her unconditionally.

—R.S.

---

when my father even answers the phone. Yet when I do go home, I don't want him to know that I feel uncomfortable. He's this old man and he does love me. It's all bizarre."

Stephanie believes her abuse is to blame for her struggle to become truly intimate with men. "For a long time, I didn't like to be touched," she says. "It made me feel kind of helpless." Her sisters, too, have had trouble sustaining relationships. Neither has ever married, but each has a child.

"The great wound of sexual abuse," explains social worker Maelinda Turner, "is that it leads you to believe you're not worthy to celebrate the gifts of the power of your sexuality without fear, question or judgment." I ask Stephanie if she and her sisters have ever considered talking with a professional. She shrugs: "I feel like you're supposed to just go on with your life."

Turner sees patterns typical of sexual-abuse victims in Stephanie and her sisters. "You can find ways to escape from the pain," she explains. "Work, drugs, food. You can be successful, smart and busy, but eventually it sneaks up on you. At

some point you need to slow down and deal with what happened and how it has affected your life."

She stresses that unless their father gets counseling, the sisters have to contend with the fact that when their children are around him, they, too, will be in danger. That concern became quite real a few years ago, when one sister suspected their father had begun to abuse her 6-year-old son. Her fear for her son led her to finally confront her father about the abuse she and her sisters had suffered. As the secret tumbled out, her mother reacted with disbelief. "You all must have done something," she said lamely, apparently not knowing how else to respond. Stephanie's father insisted nothing had happened with his daughters or his grandson, and her mother let the issue drop. Stephanie's sister, dismayed by her parents' denial and needing to protect her son, now avoids her parents' home.

That episode was the first and last time the sisters ever openly discussed the abuse with their parents. Turner believes that the entire family will need to go into therapy if real healing is to occur, but she acknowledges that it is unlikely that

Stephanie's parents will ever move past their denial. Mothers who can't acknowledge their daughters' abuse have often been abused themselves, she reflects. Until they can deal with their own demons, they can't help their daughters. "It's like a cancer," Turner says. "If your grandmother had it and your mother had it, you're susceptible."

As for her father, Stephanie is resigned. "People are who they are," she says. "Rather than have him live out his last days being miserable, I've made a conscious decision to make him feel comfortable." A soft sigh escapes her as she adds: "That just leaves me waiting until he dies."

Sex, Money, Drugs

Evelyn's eyes say she's 50. In fact, she is only 35. She grew up in a comfortable home in New York City with her parents, sister and two brothers. When she was 10, her brother's teenage friend began to creep up to her bedroom to fondle her. He'd give her candy to keep silent. Evelyn finally threatened to tell when he pressured her to "let him put his thing in me." Then he left her alone. In junior high, she fell into a clique of girls who regularly visited the principal's office. "We let him feel us up, and he gave us money and good grades," she says. The principal was fired when one of the girls became pregnant and told. No one else in the clique breathed a word.

At 16 Evelyn befriended a man who owned a neighborhood store. He invited her into the basement for drugs and sex. Not long after, she got pregnant and dropped out of school to have his child. She was in the ninth grade and could barely read. "I was always used to a man taking care of me," she says. At 18 she met Benny, who fed her crack habit and then beat her. Desperate to escape him, Evelyn left her baby with her mother and took off on her own. Soon she was prostituting to buy crack. "It didn't matter what they did to me," she says of the countless tricks she turned. "I just wanted my money."

Author Gail Wyatt, a professor of psychiatry at UCLA, observes that by the time Evelyn was a teenager, she had been conditioned to see herself as a sexual object and sex as a means to an end. Evelyn's case is extreme, Wyatt notes, but in all sexual relationships it's important to ask, "Is my body just being used to get me something?"

Evelyn quickly sank into a miserable routine of sex, violence and drugs that consumed two decades of her life and drained her self-worth. In crack houses she would often emerge from her haze naked and bruised, knowing she had been raped. "I was too afraid to go to the cops," she says. "Why would they believe me? I wanted to die. I asked God why I wasn't dying." She was too ashamed to tell her family she needed help: "I didn't want them to see me; I didn't want to disgrace them."

Indeed, her unwillingness to reveal to her family her earliest incidents of abuse—first by her brother's friend, then by the principal and later the store owner—may have led to Evelyn's pattern of abusive sexual encounters. As Wyatt observes, family dynamics are frequently at the root of our silence around issues of sex and sexuality. "An abuse victim's decision not to tell says a lot about whom they trust, their loneliness and isolation," she explains. "Sometimes there's an emotional distance in the

family. It's difficult to talk about sex if you're not talking in general. And abusers will tell you they can sense vulnerable, needy kids."

Evelyn, still vulnerable and needy as an adult, eventually entered an upstate treatment program, where her pattern of abusive sexual encounters continued: She had sex for money with men on staff. She got caught and kicked out and headed back to the streets. Eventually she landed in Project Greenhope, a Manhattan rehabilitation and drug-treatment residence for women who've had trouble with the law. More than a year later, she's clean and fortunately AIDS-free, and through counseling she's coming to understand the roles sexual abuse and silence have played in her life. Soon she will be on her own, and with only $117 a month in welfare, she will need to find a job and a home. "I'm learning to love myself, but I'm scared to death," she admits. "I've never paid a bill in my life."

While Wyatt applauds Evelyn's efforts so far in turning her life around, she cautions that Evelyn will need long-term psychotherapy to help her reclaim her own power over her body: "This young woman was conditioned to give her power away," Wyatt says, adding that Evelyn needs to develop positive relationships with women, perhaps other graduates of her treatment center, and steer clear of the temptations of old friends and habits. She encourages Evelyn to avoid sexual relationships altogether until she gets in touch with her own sexuality. "This is not just about sex," Wyatt says. "This is her whole life."

Longing for Nurturing

Behind Kim's fiery spirit and quick wit is a wounded, still grieving young woman. She's overweight, but she has "too many other things to work on" besides dropping pounds. She's single and often lonely, though she has a boyfriend of seven years. Before him, by her own account, she had a string of mostly empty sexual relationships, 40 in all. "I used to confuse sex with love," she says. Now 34, she still finds it hard to believe that a man could want more than sex from her, saying, "I'm afraid people will leave if they see the real me."

Kim can identify exactly when these feelings of worthlessness began. Her stepfather started fondling her during bath time when she was about 7, and by the time she was 11 he had graduated to intercourse. "I went from crying to just giving in to fighting to get him away from me," she says. She felt she had no choice but to remain silent: Her stepfather had warned that if she told her mother, a prominent southern political activist, he'd kill them both. To prove his point, he'd sharpen his knives and clean his gun in front of Kim.

And so she endured routine rapes by the man who was supposed to be taking care of her while Mommy was out saving the world, beatings when she threatened to tell, and a pregnancy and horrifying miscarriage that she suffered through alone at age 16. "I knew my stepfather was the father," she wrote in a journal, "and just like everything else he had done to me, I could not tell anyone about it."

When Kim was 19, her stepfather pressed one time too many for sex. She resisted and he slapped her, and in her anger she found the courage to tell her mother. Kim was stunned when her mother responded by accusing her of seducing her stepfather and ordered her out of the house. Forced to live with friends and family for a while, Kim eventually moved out on her own. Many years later, she would learn that her mother herself had been sexually abused by a relative. Through therapy she would come to understand that her mother had no inkling of how to protect or support her daughter. At the time, though, Kim was devastated.

"Sometimes I think I shouldn't have said anything," Kim says through tears. "I paid a price: I had to change my life. I had no degree, no job, no skills, nobody but me. What I've lived through is incomprehensible. I lost a good part of my life." She tries to describe the physical and psychological impact of her past: "I constantly have indigestion. When I'm afraid, I want to throw up. I'm always waiting for the other shoe to drop, for something to rock my semblance of being normal."

Dorothy Cunningham, Ph.D., a clinical psychologist with a private practice in New York, explains that Kim's situation was made worse by her mother's denial: "When a parent refuses to accept what's going on, they're often thinking about what it could do to their career and to their family," Cunningham says. "It took a lot of courage for Kim to say this happened, and the mother left her child to heal herself."

Kim has been trying to do just that. Now working toward her college degree, she has been in therapy for years, though she admits she doesn't go as often as she should. "Sometimes it's too hard," she says. Yet therapy is crucial to Kim's healing process, Cunningham says. "There's a loss of innocence, a loss of childhood and family," she explains, and Kim needs to mourn that loss. Therapy can be a safe place to grieve.

Cunningham also sees in Kim a woman who needs to get angry. "People who stay in victim mode blame themselves," she says. "They see themselves as bad and dirty. In some ways that's safer than unleashing the anger that's inside. You need to give yourself permission to be angry. Say 'I deserved to be listened to; I deserved protection.' When you're a victim, you don't feel like you deserve anything. When you're angry, you're moved to action; you're empowered."

One of the most difficult memories for an abuse victim to deal with is the sensation of physical pleasure that she may have experienced. Even now, Kim struggles to understand how she could have felt pleasure while being raped. "It was like looking forward to a lover," she says, her voice almost a whisper. "And as much as I looked forward to it, it repulsed me too."

As disturbing as Kim finds this aspect of her abuse, her experience is not uncommon. "It's very difficult for many to accept," Cunningham confirms. "You can be terrified and confused but still have an orgasm. Kim should know that her body did what bodies are supposed to do—it responded to touch. That's how bodies are made. She needs to know she's not a perverted soul."

Seven years ago, after Kim's stepfather died, she began to reach out to her mother. But their conversations often spiral into accusations and tears. Though she still longs for the nurturing that she feels she missed while growing up, Kim recognizes that she is more likely to get it from supportive friends and family members than from her mother. "She is what she is," Kim sums up, "but I still love her. And I know I'm going to be okay."

Common Ground

While every experience of sexual abuse is different, some common therapeutic themes emerge: We need to understand the role of power in our relationships, and hold our abusers accountable for their actions. And we must learn to treat ourselves kindly as we work to come to terms with what happened. "You can't mark progress or breakthroughs," Maelinda Turner says of the healing process, "but you can look back six months or a year and know that you're in a different place."

My own healing took years. I was 21 when my mother and stepfather finally sensed my discomfort around my uncle and gently encouraged me to tell them about it. My parents were surprisingly calm, and I felt enormous relief that I could finally let go of my secret. But when my mother called my uncle to confront him, he denied everything, which left my parents to decide whom they should believe. Fortunately for me, they believed their daughter. Some heated family discussions followed, and it was eventually agreed that a few relatives should be informed so they'd know not to leave their kids vulnerable. My uncle steered clear of me, and life went on.

But even after I shared my experience with my parents, I didn't really deal with the *effects* of it for another 12 years. During that time, the 9-year-old girl in me was still feeling a 9-year-old's feelings. And so, about four years ago, with the help of a psychotherapist, I began the hard work of untangling the secret from my life, pulling up its deeply rooted feelings of shame and fear and self-doubt.

When I look back on my experience, I see that the most difficult aspect of my abuse was not the telling, of what happened to me—it was carrying the burden of silence for all those years. In my own journey toward healing, I'm learning to counter the 9-year-old's thoughts that even now sometimes play in my mind. I'm learning not to be afraid of inviting attention by speaking up or standing out or even by writing. I'm learning that I didn't deserve what happened to me, and that I have a right to be angry at my uncle. I'm also learning that I can have warm, close relationships.

I married a man whose love was strong enough to breach the wall I'd built around myself, and who understood why I needed to take this healing journey. We have a young son who is my heart and joy, and I'm doing work that fulfills me. I used to wonder where I might be if not for what happened in that dark corner so many years ago. But I now see that in spite of what happened, I'm embracing life, moving out of the long shadow of silence and doing what I can to help myself, and others, heal. And like so many survivors, I carry on.

Getting Help

If your child tells you she has been abused, assure her that she did the right thing in telling and that she's not to blame for what happened. Offer her protection, and promise that you will promptly take steps to see that the abuse stops. Report any suspicion of child abuse to your local child-protection agency or to the police or district attorney's office. Consult with your child's physician, who may refer you to a specialist with expertise in

163

trauma. A caring response is the first step toward getting help for your young one.

If you know a sister who has been sexually assaulted, encourage her to seek out a group or individual therapist who is trained to counsel her. These resources can help:

Books

Surviving the Silence: Black Women's Stories of Rape by Charlotte Pierce-Baker (W.W. Norton & Co., $23.95).

I Never Called It Rape: The Ms. Report on Recognizing, Fighting and Surviving Date and Acquaintance Rape by Robin Warshaw (HarperPerennial, $13).

I Never Told Anyone: Writings by Women Survivors of Child Sexual Abuse edited by Ellen Bass and Louise Thornton (HarperCollins, $13).

I Can't Get Over It: A Handbook for Trauma Survivors by Aphrodite Matsakis, Ph.D. (New Harbinger, $16.95).

Organizations

Rape, Abuse and Incest National Network (RAINN), 635-B Pennsylvania Ave., S.E., Washington DC 20003; (202) 544–1034; (800) 656-HOPE (hot line directs you to a crisis counselor). Or contact the group on-line at rainn.org or rainnmail@aol.com.

Association of Black Psychologists, P.O. Box 55999, Washington DC 20040; (202) 722–0808.

National Association of Black Social Workers, 8436 W. McNichols St., Detroit MI 48221; (313) 862–6700.

National Black Women's Health Project, 600 Pennsylvania Ave., S.E., Suite 310, Washington DC 20003; (202) 543–9311.

Survivors of Incest Anonymous, P.O. Box 190, Benson MD 21018; (410) 893–3322.

Men Can Stop Rape, P.O. Box 57144, Washington DC 20037; (202) 265–6530 or mencanstoprape.org.

ROBIN D. STONE, editor-in-chief of essence.com, is writing a book about Black women survivors of sexual abuse. She is reachable by E-mail at womenwise@aol.com.

Where Girls Marry Rapists for Honor

Turkey is working with agencies to combat widespread abuse of women. Education and tougher laws are part of the reform effort.

AMBERIN ZAMAN
Special to The Times

Diyarbakir, Turkey—Rojda was 13 when she was raped two years ago by a neighbor in this hardscrabble Kurdish province. In order to "cleanse" her honor, she was forced to marry her attacker in an unofficial Islamic-style ceremony. He later was convicted of raping a 7 year-old boy and has been imprisoned.

But Rojda's troubles were far from over, according to an account of her ordeal provided by her family and attorneys. She allegedly was raped again in March by her father-in-law, who she said demanded she prostitute herself to earn her keep. When Rojda refused, the relatives and attorneys charge, a group of men held her down and sliced off her nose.

Police raided their home after being tipped off by neighbors, who heard her cries. The men were briefly detained, then set free—though they have since been rearrested.

Rojda's story is not unusual: Human rights groups and Turkish officials say violence against women is widespread in Turkey, though statistics are hard to come by because so many attacks go unreported. They blame the violence on poverty, a lack of education and the patriarchal structure prevalent in much of Turkish society.

As this nation seeks to become the European Union's first predominantly Muslim member, its Islam-rooted government has teamed up with the EU and other international groups to combat abuses through a series of nationwide projects and campaigns.

Their efforts are evident here in Diyarbakir, where the bar association is training local administrators to understand and implement new laws that, among other things, broaden women's rights and stiffen penalties for their abusers. The $500,000 project is being funded by the EU.

"We have trained 700 officials over the past year; awareness is growing," association President Sezgin Tanrikulu said last week. One such trainee learned of Rojda's plight soon after her alleged attackers were initially freed. He took her to Tanrikulu, complaining that justice had not been served.

Rojda, a childlike figure with enormous dark eyes set above her disfigured nose, looked terrified, recalled Tanrikulu. "We pressed fresh charges on her behalf, and the men were rearrested," he said.

Her mother, Serife, who lives in a muddy tent on the outskirts of the nearby town of Cinar, said that Rojda "was my prettiest girl" before the attack. Serife, who carried a sickly child—her 10th—from a pouch strapped to her back, said she would "not find peace" until her daughter was avenged.

Their attorneys requested that Serife and her daughter be identified only by their first names.

If found guilty on separate counts of rape and assault, the men could face up to 22 years in prison, said Meral Bestas, an attorney at the bar association's women's advisory center, which is handling Rojda's case.

Staffed by six female lawyers, the center offers free legal advice to women. Bestas said her clients are often illiterate and in polygamous and abusive marriages. Many are afraid to seek help.

"Their men view us as a subversive, corrupting influence and order them to stay away," Bestas said.

Across from the center, in the Hasirli slum area, social worker Handan Coskun goes about empowering women in subtler ways. She supervises a free laundry service, which attracts hundreds of women and their children every week.

The laundry doubles as a school where women are taught to read, write and use birth control. They are also informed of their legal rights.

"I felt stronger, safer after the courses," said Naile Gungor, a 49-year-old mother of seven, as she stuffed her wash into a machine.

Like many here, she is a refugee from one of thousands of villages that were razed by Turkish security forces during a 15-year separatist insurgency led by rebels of the Kurdistan Workers Party, or PKK. Government plans to repatriate the villagers have been marred by a resurgence in violence after the PKK—which has renamed itself the Kurdistan Freedom and Democracy Congress, or KADEK—ended a five-year cease-fire last year.

With dozens of refugees crammed into tiny concrete shacks in shantytowns that have sprung up across the southeast, "abuse and incest have permeated people's genes," said Coskun, the social worker.

Another big part of tackling violence against women involves educating men, said Meltem Agduk, a consultant with the United Nations Population Fund.

The U.N. agency recently devised a program to discourage conscripts from engaging in domestic violence.

With all Turkish men older than 18 required to perform 15 months of military service. the campaign should have far-reaching effects. Agduk predicted during an interview in Ankara, the Turkish capital.

In a similar vein, the government last year instructed thousands of state-employed Muslim clerics to preach against "honor killings." slayings committed by male relatives of women and girls accused of staining their family's reputation.

Under Turkey's new penal code that will come into effect June 1, sentences for such crimes will be significantly increased. In the past, those convicted could get sentences reduced to as few as three years in prison because protecting the family's honor was seen as a mitigating circumstance. Now they will serve as much time as any other convicted murderer.

Despite such efforts. the killings continue.

This year in the province of Batman, east of Diyarbakir, an 18-year-old girl was shot to death by her brother for wearing blue jeans.

A Cruel Edge

The painful truth about today's pornography—
and what men can do about it.

Robert Jensen, Ph.D.

After an intense three hours, the workshop on pornography is winding down. The 40 women all work at a center that serves battered women and rape survivors. These are the women on the front lines, the ones who answer the 24-hour hotline and work one-on-one with victims. They counsel women who have just been raped, help women who have been beaten, and nurture children who have been abused. These women have heard and seen it all. No matter how brutal a story might be, they have experienced or heard one even more brutal; there is no way to one-up them on stories of male violence. But after three hours of information, analysis, and discussion of the commercial heterosexual pornography industry, many of these women are drained. Sadness hangs over the room.

One women who has held back throughout the workshop, her arms wrapped tightly around herself. Now, finally, she speaks. "This hurts. It just hurts so much."

Everyone is quiet as the words sink in. Slowly the conversation restarts but her words hang in the air:

It hurts.

It hurts to know that no matter who you are as a woman you can be reduced to a thing to be penetrated, and that men will buy movies about that, and that in many of those movies your humiliation will be the central theme. It hurts to know that so much of the pornography that men are buying fuses sexual desire with cruelty.

Even these women, who have found ways to cope with the injuries from male violence in other places, struggle with that. It is one thing to deal with acts, even extremely violent acts. It is another to know the thoughts, ideas, and fantasies lie behind those acts.

People routinely assume that pornography is such a difficult and divisive issue because it's about sex. I think that's wrong. This culture struggles unsuccessfully with pornography because it is about men's cruelty to women, and the pleasure men sometimes take in that cruelty. And that is much more difficult for everyone to face.

"At least our society still brands rape a crime."

There are different pornographic genres, but my studies of pornographic videos over the past seven years have focused on the stories told in mainstream heterosexual pornography. By that I mean the videos and DVDs that are widely available in the United States, marketed as sexually explicit (what is commonly called "hard-core"), rented and purchased primarily by men, and depict sex primarily between men and women. The sexual activity is not simulated: What happens on the screen happened in the world. This mainstream pornography does not include overt bondage and sadomasochism, explicit violence, urination or defecation, although such material is widely available in shops, through the mail, or on the Internet. (There's also, of course, an underground market for child pornography—the only porn clearly illegal everywhere in the United States.)

To obtain mainstream pornographic videos for study, I visited stores that sold "adult product" (the industry's preferred term) and asked clerks and managers to help me select the most commonly rented and purchased tapes. I wanted to avoid the accusation that feminists analyzing pornography only pick out the worst examples, the most violent material, to critique.

While many may find what is described here to be disturbing, these are not aberrations. These rapes are broadly representative of the 11,303 new hardcore titles that were released in 2002, according to *Adult Video News*, the industry's trade magazine. They are standard fare from a pornography industry with an estimated $10 billion in annual sales. They are what brothers and fathers and uncles are watching, what boyfriends and husbands and, in many cases, male children are watching.

What kind of stories does this mainstream pornography tell the all-American boy—and what does that mean for the girl next door? Here are three examples:

- The 2003 film "Sopornos 4" was produced by VCA Pictures, one of the "high-end" companies that create films for the "couples market." These films, sometimes called "features," typically attempt some plot and character development. The industry claims these films appeal to women as well as men.

The plot of "Sopornos" is a takeoff on the popular HBO series about New Jersey mobsters. In the last of six sex scenes, the mob boss's wife has sex with two of his men. Moving through the standard porn progression—oral sex and then vaginal sex—one of the men prepares to penetrate her anally. She tells him: "That fucking cock is so fucking huge. … Spread [my] fucking ass. … Spread it open." He penetrates her. Then, she says, in a slightly lower tone, "Don't go any deeper." She seems to be in pain. At the end of the scene, she requests the men's semen ("Two cocks jacking off in my face. I want it.") and opens her mouth. The men ejaculate onto her at the same time.

- "Two in the Seat #3," a 2003 "gonzo" release (meaning, there is no attempt to create characters or story lines) from Red Light District, contains six scenes in which two men have sex with one woman, culminating in a double-penetration (the woman is penetrated vaginally and anally at the same time). In one scene, 20-year-old Claire, her hair in pigtails, says she has been in the industry for three months. Asked by the off-camera interviewer what will happen in the scene, she replies, "I'm here to get pounded." The two men then enter the scene and begin a steady stream of insults, calling her "a dirty, nasty girl," "a little fucking cunt," "a little slut." After oral and vaginal sex, she asks one to "Please put your cock in my ass." During double-penetration on the floor, her vocalizations sound pained. She's braced against the couch, moving very little. The men spank her, and her buttock is visibly red. One man asks, "Are you crying?"

Claire: "No, I'm enjoying it."
Man: "Damn, I thought you were crying. It was turning me on when I thought you were crying."
Claire: "Would you like me to?"
Man: "Yeah, give me a fucking tear. Oh, there's a fucking tear."

- Finally, there's "Gag Factor 10," a 2002 release from JM Productions also in the "gonzo" category. One of the 10 sex scenes involves a woman and man having a picnic in a park. While she sits on the blanket, he stands and thrusts his penis into her mouth. Two other men who walk by join in. One man grabs her hair and pulls her head into his penis in what his friend calls "the jackhammer."

At this point the woman is grimacing and seems in pain. She then lies on the ground, and the men approach her from behind. "Eat that whole fucking dick. … You little whore, you like getting hurt," one says. After they all ejaculate into her mouth, the semen flows out onto her body. She reaches quickly for the wine glass, takes a large drink, looks up at her boyfriend, and says, "God, I love you, baby." Her smile fades to a pained look of shame and despair.

I can't know exactly what the women in these films were feeling, physically or emotionally. But here is what BellaDonna, one of the women who appeared in "Two in the Seat #3," told a television interviewer about such sex scenes: "You have to really prepare physically and mentally for it. I mean, I go through a process from the night before. I stop eating at 5 p.m. I do, you know, like two enemas, and then the next morning I don't eat anything. It's so draining on your body."

Even if the pain shown in the above scenes is acted and not real, why don't directors edit *out* pained expressions? I see only two possible answers: either they view such pain as being of no consequence to the viewers' interest—and hence to the goal of maximizing film sales—or they believe viewers enjoy seeing the women's pain. So why, then, do some men find the infliction of pain on women during sex either not an obstacle to their ability to achieve sexual pleasure or a factor that can *enhance* their pleasure?

I believe it's all about the edge.

There are only so many ways that human beings can, in mechanical terms, have sex. There are a limited number of body parts and openings, a limited number of ways to create the friction that produces the stimulation and sensations. That's why stories about sexuality generally tap into something beyond the mechanical. When most nonpornographic films deal with sex, they draw, at least in part, on the emotions most commonly connected with sex: love and affection. But pornography doesn't have that option, since my research has shown that men typically consume it to *avoid* love and affection and go straight to sexual release.

And that means pornography, without emotional variation, will become repetitive and uninteresting, even to men watching primarily to facilitate masturbation. So pornography needs an edge.

When the legal restrictions on pornography gradually loosened in the 1970s and '80s, anal sex captured that edge, because it was seen as something most women don't want. Then, as anal sex became routine in pornography, the gonzo genre started routinely adding double-penetrations and gag inducing oral sex—again, acts that men believe women generally do not want. These days, pornography has become so normalized and so mainstream in our culture that the edge keeps receding. As Jerome Tanner put it during a pornography directors' roundtable discussion featured in *Adult Video News*, "People just want it harder, harder, and harder, because… what are you gonna do next?"

It's not surprising that the new edge more and more involves overt cruelty—an easy choice given that the dynamic of male domination and female submission is already in place in patriarchy. All people are capable of being cruel, of course. But contemporary mainstream heterosexual pornography forces the question: Why has cruelty become so sexualized for some men?

Feminist research long ago established that rape involves the sexualization of power, the equation in men's imaginations of sexual pleasure with domination and control. The common phrase "rape is about power, not sex" misleads, though; rape is about the fusion of sex and domination, about the eroticization of control. And in this culture, rape is normal. That is, in a culture where the dominant definition of sex is the taking of pleasure from women by men, rape is an expression of the sexual norms of the culture, not violations of those norms. Sex is a sphere in which men are trained to see themselves as naturally dominant and women as naturally passive. Rape is both nominally illegal and completely normal at the same time.

"Pornography, however, is sold to us as liberation."

By extension, there should be nothing surprising about the fact that some pornography includes explicit images of women in pain. But my question is: Wouldn't a healthy society want to deal with that? Why aren't more people, men or women, concerned?

Right-wing opponents of pornography offer a moralistic critique that cannot help us find solutions, because typically those folks endorse male dominance (albeit not these particular manifestations of it). Conversely, some feminists want us to believe that the growing acceptance of pornography is a benign sign of expanding sexual equality and freedom. Meanwhile, feminist critics of pornography have been marginalized in political and intellectual arenas. And all the while, the pornographers are trudging off to the bank with bags of money.

"Why has cruelty become so sexualized for some men?"

I think this helps explain why even the toughest women at rape crisis centers find the reality of pornography so difficult to cope with. No matter how hard it may be to face rape, at least our society still brands it as a crime. Pornography, however, is not only widely accepted, but sold to us as liberation.

I don't pretend to speak for women; my focus is on men. And I believe that the task for men of conscience is to define ourselves and our sexuality outside of the domination/submission dynamic. It is not easy: Like everyone, we are products of our culture and have to struggle against it. But as a man, I at least have considerable control over the conditions in which I live and the situations in which I function. Women sometimes do not have that control. They're at far more risk of sexual violence, and they have to deal with men who disproportionately hold positions of power over them. Mainstream pornography tips that power balance even further.

For example, when a female student has a meeting about a research project with a male college professor who the night before was watching "Gag Factor 10," who will she be to him? Or when a woman walks into a bank to apply for a loan from a male loan officer who the night before was watching "Two in the Seat #3," what will he be thinking? And when a woman goes in front of a male judge who the night before was watching "Sopornos 4," will she be judged fairly?

But some will argue: How can you assume that just because men watch such things they will act in a callous and cruel man-

ner, sexually or otherwise? It is true that the connection between mass-media exposure and human behavior is complex, and social scientists argue both sides. But taken together, the laboratory evidence, the research on men who abuse, and the voluminous testimony of women clearly indicate that in some cases pornography influences men's sexual behavior. Pornography may not *cause* abuse, but it can be implicated as an accessory to the crime.

If we could pretend that these images are consumed by some small subset of deviant men, then we could identify and isolate those aberrant men, maybe repair them. But men who consume these images are everywhere: men who can't get a date and men who have all the dates they want. Men who live alone and men who are married. Men who grew up in liberal homes where pornography was never a big deal and men who grew up in strict religious homes where no talk of sex was allowed. Rich men and poor men, men of all colors and creeds.

When I critique pornography, I am often told to lighten up. Sex is just sex, people say, and I should stop trying to politicize pornography. But pornography offers men a politics of sex and gender—and that politics is patriarchal and reactionary. In pornography, women are not really people; they are three holes and two hands. Women in pornography have no hopes, no dreams, and no value apart from the friction those holes and hands can produce on a man's penis.

As with any political issue, successful strategies of resistance, I would suggest, must be collective and public rather than solely personal and private. Pornographers know that to be true—which is why they try to cut off the discussion. When we critique pornography, we typically are accused of being people who hate freedom, sexually dysfunctional prudes who are scared of sex, or both.

Pornographers also want to derail any talk of sexual ethics. They, of course, have a sexual ethic: Anything—and they mean anything—goes, and consenting adults should be free to choose. I agree that choice is crucial. But in a society in which power is not equally distributed, "anything goes" translates into "anything goes for men, while some women and children will suffer for it."

There are many controversial issues in the pornography debate, but there should be nothing controversial about this: To critique pornography is not repressive. We should be free to talk about our desire for an egalitarian intimacy and for sexuality that rejects pain and humiliation. That is not prudishness or censorship. It is at attempt to claim the best parts of our common humanity: love, caring, empathy. To do that is not to limit anyone. It is to say, simply, that women count as much as men.

ROBERT JENSEN, PH.D., journalism professor at the University of Texas at Austin, is the co-author of *Pornography: The Production and Consumption of Inequality* and author of *Citizens of the Empire: The Struggle to Claim Our Humanity*.

Sexual Heroin

Variant arousal patterns are an obstacle to intimacy

BARRY MCCARTHY AND JENNIFER CINTRON

When a bewildered woman finally confides to friends that her husband or partner has been avoiding sex for months, or that the couple's rare liaisons are filled with awkwardness and self-doubt, the questions on many lips often are: Is he having an affair? Could he be gay? In our clinical experience, more often than not, the answer is no—homosexuality and extramarital affairs aren't, by a long shot, the only explanations for the male sexual avoidance that brings couples into marital or sex therapy. Far more frequently than most people imagine, we discover the man has another sexual secret: he's involved in a *compulsive variant arousal pattern* as absorbing, erotic, and hard to kick as sexual heroin.

There's a reason why pornography is the most financially successful business on the Web, with thousands of websites catering to every conceivable fetish. According to experts in the field of male sexual behavior, including Gene Abel and Michael Metz, some two to five million men have either a variant or deviant arousal pattern. Variant patterns, like fetishistic preoccupation with high-heeled shoes, or toes, or rubber, or cross-dressing, may be secret and shame filled, but they harm nobody physically. Deviant patterns, like pedophilia, exhibitionism, and frotteurism (when a person rubs against another to high arousal or orgasm, usually on public transportation), by contrast, are either illegal, or cause harm to others, or both.

Therapists working with couples in which variant arousal patterns are a problem must move on two fronts simultaneously; the intense, secret compulsion must be confronted and the couple's damaged sexual relationship must also be restored. This is urgent work; good therapy for sexual secrets and dysfunction can determine whether the marriage survives or fails. The adage in marital therapy is that good sex alone can't make a marriage, but bad sex can sink it.

A Romance Gone Sour

Take, for instance, Paula and Keith. They were in their early thirties and had been together for four years and married for nearly two when they came for their first therapy session with Barry McCarthy. They were filled with self-doubt and blame, each secretly fearing that their marriage wouldn't survive. Their relationship, they said, had begun in a bloom of romantic love and almost daily lovemaking. But after six months, Keith's passion had dimmed markedly. Despite their deep, genuine affection for each other, their bedroom had become an awkward place. Spontaneity, playfulness, and erotic charge had given way to fumbling self-consciousness. Nothing seemed to flow. Paula worried secretly that her husband didn't find her attractive because he avoided sex altogether and wouldn't say why. The last time they'd made love had been on their honeymoon 20 months earlier. The more Paula asked what was wrong and looked for reassurance, the more Keith avoided not only sex, but any discussion of sex. The decline in their mutual happiness, Keith implied during that mutually blaming first session, was at least partly Paula's fault: she'd gone from being optimistic and self-confident to pessimistic, dependent, and constantly nagging and seeking reassurance.

Case Studies

After our joint initial meeting, I saw Keith and Paula separately. (I find this the most efficient way of getting a client to quickly disclose sexual secrets, and to find out what meaning their mutual sexual distress holds in the narrative of their past and present lives.) Paula told me that when Keith avoided sex, she went into a spiral of self-doubt about her own attractiveness and the viability of the marriage itself. Was it her? (She had a long scar on her thigh; perhaps it turned Keith off.) Was it him? (Perhaps he was, as her friends suggested, gay.) Or was it them? (Perhaps the marriage just wasn't viable.) And Keith's failure to even acknowledge a problem was making her feel crazy in addition to self-doubting.

Paula very much wanted children and genuinely loved Keith, but she didn't want to bring a child into a non-sexual marriage that she feared wouldn't survive. She worried that she might be following in the footsteps of her mother, who'd been divorced twice from men with hidden duplicities and fragilities: one had turned out to be a compulsive gambler; the other had bragged about fantasized financial successes that never materialized.

Neither of those, it turned out, were Keith's secrets. But he had plenty of them. When I met with him alone, he told me haltingly that, for decades, he'd been secretly arousing himself during masturbation with fantasies—and later, pornography—of being spanked. He'd never breathed, a word of this to Paula, out of shame and fear of humiliation.

As an adult, his sexual relationships with women had followed a familiar pattern: first, in the novelty of a new relationship, he'd be carried along on a river of intense sexual excitement. He'd allow himself to hope that, this time, things would be different, and that this new love would allow him to leave behind his solitary sexual fetish forever. But after six months to a year, the newness would wear off, and he'd become afraid of being impotent during standard-issue "vanilla sex." So he'd simply stop having it. Meanwhile, he'd return to his favorite cyberporn websites, which specialized in domination and spanking. Once or twice a day, he'd go online, enter his credit card number, and follow the orders of a distant dominatrix beamed onto his flatscreen by webcam, while he masturbated to orgasm.

Such variant arousal patterns typically begin in childhood or adolescence, and are reinforced by thousands of highly ritualized, erotically charged experiences of solitary masturbation. The combination of shame, secrecy, repetition, and orgasm makes it almost impossible to stop these activities, which is why we use the metaphor of sexual heroin.

Keith, for instance, was hooked. He told me that his spanking fetish had gotten started with childhood feelings of guilt and a need for acceptance and forgiveness. He remembered trying to spank himself at the age of 10 after he'd done something wrong. He first masturbated to orgasm at age 12, while fantasizing about being spanked and then being told he was loved and a good boy. Instead of experimenting with a wide variety of sexual fantasies, as most adolescents do, he'd repeated versions of this one scenario over and over, grooving a deep, narrow channel in his neurophysiology and sexual psyche. (This is at the core of a fetish: narrow in scope, highly erotic, ritually-repeated, and kept as a shameful secret.) Keith told me that he felt great love for Paula and also wanted to preserve the marriage and start a family. But he felt hopeless about changing a sexual pattern that dominated him as completely as his paid cyber-dominatrices did.

A Secret Revealed

The fourth session was a feedback session. I noted that both Keith and Paula had congruent goals, including having a satisfying and stable marriage, a sexually rewarding relationship, and a family. All were hopeful signs. Then I turned to Keith and described his secret variant arousal pattern as an "intimacy disorder." Rather than developing an intimate and interactive sexual style with Paula, he'd retreated into his secret fetish. That gave him a predictable sexual arousal and payoff, at the cost of blocking out Paula, her sexuality, and any sense of giving himself to the unknown. Giving yourself to the unknown is the hallmark of sex with another human being—interactive sex is, by its nature, unpredictable.

Paula's first reaction to this information, contrary to Keith's fear, was shock, surprise, relief, and uncertainty. She could stop worrying that it was something about her. But what was expected of her now? If she spanked him, would that make everything okay?

Keith felt vulnerable, exposed, and relieved. "It's as if a 500-pound weight is off my shoulders," he said. "But now it's in the middle of the room, and I don't know what we'll do with it." To which Paula replied, "Now that it's 'we,' we'll figure it out."

The couple was on the same page, and we could work together to develop a two-pronged therapeutic plan. On the one hand, they needed to rebuild the sexual relationship between the two of them and restore Paula's sexual confidence. On the other, they needed to address the fetish and explore whether it could serve any purpose in their sex life.

Opening up the secret at first made both of them vulnerable: Paula now had a new reason for worrying that Keith could never really find her attractive, and Keith worried that Paula couldn't really love him now that he'd revealed his fetish. So I gave them homework designed to help them rekindle their sexual confidence and intimacy. On one Saturday morning, Paula was to tell Keith all the things she found attractive about him—from his physical traits to his sexuality to his personality to his work style. Then she was to make one to three requests that would make Keith more attractive to her. These were to be requests, not demands: Keith had a choice of accepting, modifying, or rejecting them without fear of negative consequences.

When they reported back to me at the next session, Paula had told Keith that she saw him as a hardworking, caring, physically attractive guy; she particularly liked his eyes and his long fingers, with their gentle caresses. She asked that he look at and kiss her when they began a sexual encounter, and to hold her and talk afterward. Her other major request was that he be sexually honest with her Keith agreed.

A couple of days later, it was Keith's turn. He told Paula he found her warmth and optimism, as well as her sparkling eyes and athletic body, attractive. He also asked her to wear sexy outfits—a request she modified by suggesting they go to Victoria's Secret and shop together, which they did. The exercise proved to be highly motivating, especially for Paula. She felt affirmed that Keith did find her both loveable and desirable, and that his commitment to the marriage and a family was high. This gave her a safe base from which she could take more personal and sexual risks—being freer in initiating sexual encounters, and allowing herself to be both sensual and erotic.

Paula began the next therapy session by saying she felt closer to Keith than at any time since their wedding, and was glad that he'd shared his spanking fetish. She was committed to the marriage, but she needed to hear from Keith what he wanted.

Keith was equally resolute about his love for Paula and desire for a successful marriage, but unsure of what to do about his fetishistic arousal pattern. He understood that it was a major roadblock in their intimate relationship. Could the fetish be integrated into their sexual style? Could spanking be a part of their foreplay-pleasuring scenario—a bridge to greater shared pleasure? '

As I often do when dealing with a variant arousal pattern, I suggested that Keith first bring Paula into his secret sexual world, showing her the sex websites, and playing out the spanking fetish. This would help them determine whether the fetish could play a role in their shared sexuality. Keith was hesitant, embarrassed, and anxious—this had always been his secret domain. Paula, by contrast, was eager. Parts of the next two sessions were spent on clarifying guidelines for this experimental exercise. They agreed on the following: Keith was to show Paula what was erotic to him about the cybersex websites, and she was to be open and nonjudgmental. They'd discuss their feelings about the experience at their next therapy session.

Entering Keith's World

That Saturday, they sat down in Keith's home office and linked up to one of the websites he frequently accessed. Paula watched as Keith played out the cybersex spanking ritual with the dominatrix, including masturbating to orgasm. This proved to be a very powerful experience for both of them. Despite her best efforts to be nonjudgmental, Paula found the ritual mechanical and antierotic, utterly lacking in either intimacy or playfulness. She simply couldn't imagine incorporating it into their sex life. Keith's reaction was even more dramatic. Enacting the ritual in front of Paula made it much less sexy: the excitement was so inextricably bound up with its illicitness and secrecy.

In their next session, Paula told Keith: "This is really not about me or us. It's your secret childhood world. I want to really be with you sexually. The fetish is a wall, not a bridge, for us sexually." It was clear to her that maintaining this secret world of forbidden pleasure would destroy any chance they had of marital intimacy. At this point, Keith began to get that his spanking ritual wasn't a harmless sexual outlet. Rather it was a compulsively destructive sexual heroin, which could defeat any chance he had to maintain his marriage. This session was Keith's moment of truth. He announced he was willing to give up his fetish.

But how? Many therapists mistakenly believe that improving the relationship dynamics within the couple alone will magically resolve the problem. It doesn't work that way, any more than better communication alone solves one partner's addictive involvement with alcohol, gambling, or cocaine. Without getting into the controversy over exactly what constitutes an "addiction," it's safe to say that compulsive habits are devilishly difficult to break, especially when they're secret, satisfiable 24/7, and erotically charged. I didn't want to put either Keith or Paula in the position I've seen couples in before, in which a man agrees to give up the fetish, but secretly returns to it until it again dominates his sexual desire, thoughts, and arousal. When this happens, the wife feels doubly betrayed: not only has her sexual self-confidence been undermined for a second time, but her partner has lied to her. The fetish alone doesn't produce a fatally flawed marriage. But when a fetish is combined with dishonesty and a lack of effective support for change, the marriage dies. That's why I had them make a commitment to not keeping any sexual secrets from each other.

To support change, I worked in individual sessions and in joint sessions. First, Keith and I worked together on the meaning he gave to fetishistic sex. He had to learn that "comparisons are odious" and to stop comparing the erotic charge of his fetish, in a decontextualized way, with that of couples sex. If he did, the fetish would always win out, just as a shot of heroin will always beat a stroll in the park for pure bodily pleasure. For him, the erotic intensity of the fetish was 100 on a scale of 100. Intimate, interactive sex might never become more intense than an 85.

New Scenarios

Then I worked with the couple together, creating erotic scenarios that would be inviting and pleasurable. The challenge to Paula was to stay sexually self-confident and in touch with her own desires—to find and keep her own positive sexual voice—rather than worry about Keith's arousal. The challenge for him was to stay involved in intimate, interactive sex, and not retreat behind his fetish fantasy.

To address Keith's fear of being insufficiently aroused, I got the couple to focus on multiple erotic stimulation, both before and during intercourse. He also started exploring a wider range of sexual fantasies, ones that had been cut off in his adolescence by his focus on his spanking fetish. Keith's two favorite erotic scenarios in the pleasuring—foreplay period turned out to be standing while he gave his wife oral breast stimulation and Paula gave him manual stimulation. The second scenario involved kneeling, rubbing his penis between Paula's breasts, and doing manual clitoral stimulation. During intercourse, Keith was highly responsive to testicular stimulation, enjoyed changing intercourse positions two or three times, and liked to intermix circular thrusting with in-out thrusting. Soon they were involved in an upward erotic interactional spiral: Paula got turned on when Keith stimulated her, and when she verbalized this, it turned Keith on all the more.

Changing a ritual as firmly entrenched as Keith's spanking fetish is a challenging process. The sources of support for the change must come from a number of directions. Here these included not only Paula's clear message about the unacceptability of Keith's continuing the fetish and the need for ongoing couples therapy, but also the 12-step Sex Addicts Anonymous (SAA) group I referred Keith to and his sponsor from that group who supported him in abstaining completely from his fetish. The role of the sponsor, a member of SAA who had a personal experience with the power of fetishistic behavior and all the ways people who live in the grip of such rituals can try to "play the system" without really changing their sexual behavior, was especially important. Another member of the group, who was very sophisticated with computer software, installed a system to block fetish material from Keith's computer. It also tracked his computer activity, allowing Paula to know if her husband had visited any porn sites.

More important, Keith agreed to a "24-hour rule," wherein he'd disclose to Paula any internet, pictorial, or written use of spanking-fetish material within a day. Paula had no desire to be the "sexual police," nor did Keith want her to play that role; he saw her as his intimate friend who was committed to helping him break the fetish pattern. Together, they worked out a system in which, once a week, Paula would conduct a five-minute check-in and ask if Keith had been in any high-risk situations. Within three months, their sexual comfort and confidence had improved so markedly that they decided to try to become pregnant, a decision that provided a special charge to their new sexual style.

I'm struck repeatedly by how, in healthy couples, sex is only a small, positive part of a good marriage, while sexual dysfunction, conflicts, secrets, and avoidance are so fatally destabilizing and draining. Problems like the one Paula and Keith faced can destroy marriages when one spouse is either unwilling or unable to face the issue, or feels so wounded or demoralized that he or she can't maintain the motivation necessary to resolve the problem. What made treatment with Keith and Paula successful where many other men regress to their secret world or continually relapse? In this case, it became impossible for Keith not to recognize the negative consequences of not changing. He got a strong, coherent message from multiple sources—his therapist, spouse, SAA group members, and sponsor—that his fetish was an addictive "poison" that could only be dealt with through total abstinence. Beyond that, Keith had the incalculable advantage of being invested enough in making his marriage to Paula work that he was willing to undergo the soul-searching struggle needed to bring a truly intimate, interactive sexuality into his life.

Case Commentary

DAVID TREADWAY

The question Barry McCarthy and Jennifer Cintron pose in their case study is how best to treat shame-based, erotically turbo-charged, secret behavior. Can the opening up of such a secret and exposing the ritual behavior become a bridge to intimacy, or will it remain a wall blocking a couple from developing a sexual bond? It would appear that McCarthy and Cintron's answer is that, while the couple can become more intimate by sharing their secrets and their vulnerability, sexual behavior such as Keith's spanking fetish must be pathologized if treatment is to succeed.

But was this the only possible successful outcome for this case? Must all sexually variant behavior be treated using the addictions model McCarthy and Cintron employ here? I understood Keith's preoccupation with spanking as a pattern growing out of childhood in which he tried to comfort himself by administering his own spanking as a prelude to reassuring himself that he was lovable. Given Paula's initially empathic and compassionate response, I was left wondering whether, in this case, they could have found a way of incorporating Keith's vulnerabilities and needs into their sexuality as a couple, while doing away with the secrets or shame.

Case Studies

McCarthy and Cintron appear to have done a good job helping this couple share their deepest vulnerabilities. But if he wanted to give this couple a chance to explore together Keith's need for spanking and redemption with composure and empathy, then the assignment to have Paula watch him go through his ritual with a long-distance dominatrix on the internet seems almost guaranteed to insure that she'd be repelled and Keith would be shamed. I'd have preferred that McCarthy and Cintron invite them to consider trying some sexual role-play in the intimacy and privacy of their marital bed, to see whether they could have successfully helped Keith to stop using the internet and strangers for comfort.

I once treated a man who, after his mother's death, developed secret erotic behavior using women's lingerie for self-comfort and soothing. Before coming to see me, he'd secretly dressed in his wife's underwear for years. However, once the shame and secret were exposed, his wife was able to let him wear her panties in their love making sometimes. She was able to indulge him, in part, because of her empathy for the yearning and grief that was expressed in his seeking solace in his mother's lingerie drawer. Eventually, he was able to bring his sexual and emotional energy to her, rather than to get caught up in rigid rituals involving intimate clothing and other variant behavior. This achievement could never have happened if he'd been asked to show her the world of cross-dressing pornography that he regularly visited on the internet.

My case example doesn't contradict McCarthy and Cintron's. Their article describes a thought—provoking case with a positive outcome. However, the challenge for us therapists is always to keep in mind the different-strokes-for-different-folks rule, especially in the area of sexuality, where there's so much idiosyncratic yearning and vulnerability. I'd have preferred it if McCarthy and Cintron had helped this couple expand their sexual repertoire to include some of Keith's yearnings, while, of course, keeping the addiction model in reserve in case he couldn't redirect his compulsion and continued to retreat to cybersex and/or if Paula, despite her best efforts, found role-playing her husband's scenario too repellent for her. For me, the key to the case was giving them the choice.

Authors' Response

We appreciate David Treadways's commentary and couldn't agree more with the guidelines he presents for working with variant sexual behavior: increasing empathy and compassion, not reinforcing shame, and bearing in mind that in sexual matters, as elsewhere, there are always "different strokes for different folks."

Nevertheless, in this case, and with many men and couples, the compulsive sexual behavior/sexual heroin model is actually more liberating (and truthful) than pathologizing. Keith's ritualistic sexual pattern needed to be understood without shaming him, but both Keith and Paula realized it wasn't a sexual scenario that could be successfully integrated into their couple sexual style. Helping the couple make a "wise" sexual choice is the crucial clinical issue.

BARRY MCCARTHY is a professor of psychology at American University in Washington, D. C., a clinician at Washington Psychological Center, and author of *Rekindling Desire* and *Coping with Erectile Dysfunction*. **JENNIFER CINTRON** is a graduate student in the psychology Ph.D. program at American University. Contact: mccarthy 160@ comcast.net.

DAVID TREADWAY, PH.D., is the director of the Treadway Training Institute in Weston, Massachusetts. He's the author of *Dead Reckoning: A Therapist Confronts His Own Grief* and *Intimacy, Change and Other Therapeutic Mysteries*. His website is drdavidtreadway.com. Contact: dctcrow@aol.com.

Letters to the Editor about this department may be e-mailed to letters@psychnetworker.org.

The Secret Lives of Wives

Why they stray: With the work place and the Internet, overscheduled lives and inattentive husbands—it's no wonder more American women are looking for comfort in the arms of another man

LORRAINE ALI AND LISA MILLER

When groups of women get together, especially if they're mothers and have been married for more than six or seven years, and especially if there's alcohol involved, the conversation is usually the same. They talk about the kids and work—how stressed they are, how busy and bone tired. They gripe about their husbands and, if they're being perfectly honest and the wine kicks in, they talk about the disappointments in their marriages. Not long ago, over lunch in Los Angeles, this conversation took a surprising turn, when Erin, who is in her early 40s and has been married for more than a decade, spilled it. She was seeing someone else. Actually, more than one person. It started with an old friend, whom she began meeting every several months for long dinners and some heavy petting. Then she began giving herself permission to flirt with, kiss—well, actually, make out with—men she met on business trips. She understands it's a "Clintonian" distinction, but she won't have sex with anyone except her husband, whom she loves. But she also loves the unexpected thrill of meeting someone new. "Do you remember?" She pauses. "I don't know how long you've been married, but do you remember the kiss that would just launch a thousand kisses?"

I DO, I DO
Not every bride is willing to forsake all others

Erin started seeing other men when she went back to work after her youngest child entered preschool. All of a sudden she was *out there*. Wearing great clothes, meeting new people, alive for the first time in years to the idea that she was interesting beyond her contributions at PTA meetings. Veronica, on the other hand, fell in love with a man who was not her husband while she was safely at home in the Dallas suburbs looking after her two children. Hers is the more familiar story: isolated and lonely, married to an airline pilot, Veronica, now 35, took up with a wealthy businessman she met at a Dallas nightclub. Her lover gave her everything her husband didn't: compliments, Tiffany jewelry, flowers and love notes. It was, in fact, the flowers that did her in. Veronica's lover sent a bouquet to her home one afternoon, her husband answered the door and, in one made-for-Hollywood moment, the marriage was over. Now remarried (to a new man), Veronica says she and her friends half-jokingly talk about starting a Web site for married women who want to date. "I think there might be a market in it," she says. There is. Wives who want extramarital sex—or are just dreaming about it—can find what they seek on Yahoo!, MSN or AOL.

BLIND EYE
Few husbands suspect their wives cheat

Much has changed since Emma Bovary chose suicide with arsenic over living her life branded an adulteress—humiliated, impoverished and stripped of her romantic ideals. In the past, U.S. laws used to punish women who cheated; in a divorce, an unfaithful wife could lose everything, even the property she owned before marriage. Newer laws have been designed to protect these women. The reality is this: American women today have more opportunity to fool around than ever; when they do fool around, they're more likely to tell their friends about it, and those friends are more likely to lend them a sympathetic ear. They probably use technology to facilitate their affairs, and if they get caught, they're almost as likely to wind up in a wing chair in a marriage counselor's office as in divorce court. Finally, if they do separate from their husbands, women, especially if they're college educated, are better able to make a go of it—pay the bills, keep at least partial custody of the children, remarry if they want to—than their philandering foremothers. "It was just so ruinous for a woman to be caught in adultery in past times, you had to be really driven or motivated to do it," says Peter D. Kramer, clinical professor of psychiatry at Brown University and author of "Should You Leave?" "Now you can get away with it, there's a social role that fits you."

Just how many married women have had sex with people who are not their husbands? It's hard to say for sure, because people lie to pollsters when they talk about sex, and studies vary wildly. (Men, not surprisingly, amplify their sexual experience, while women diminish it.) Couples therapists estimate that among their clientele, the number is close to 30 to 40 percent, compared with 50 percent of men, and the gap is almost certainly closing. In 1991, the National Opinion Research Center at the University of Chicago asked married women if they'd ever had sex outside their marriage, and 10 percent said yes. When the same pollsters asked the same question in 2002, the "yes" responses rose to 15 percent, while the number of men stayed flat at about 22 percent. The best interpretation of the data: the cheating rate for women is approaching that of men, says Tom Smith, author of the NORC's reports on sexual behavior. When Michele Weiner-Davis, a marriage counselor and founder of the Divorce Busting Center in Woodstock, Ill., started practicing 20 years ago, just 10 percent of the infidelity she knew of was committed by women. Now, she believes, it's closer to 50 percent. "Women have suddenly begun to give themselves the same permission to step over the boundary the way that men have."

A rise in female infidelity, though titillating, does not do much to clarify the paradoxes in American culture surrounding sex. Taboos about female sexuality are falling away; together, Dr. Phil and "Sex and the City" have made every imaginable sex act fodder for cocktail-party conversation. At the same time, Americans developed a lower tolerance for infidelity: 80 percent of Americans say infidelity is "always wrong," according to the NORC, up from 70 percent in 1970. Popular opinion is on to something: infidelity can be devastating. If discovered, it can upend a marriage and create chaos in a family. Nevertheless, in America, as in other parts of the world, a double standard continues to thrive: boys will be boys, but girls are supposed to be good. Even though women are narrowing the gap, men still do the bulk of the domestic damage. "Bill Clinton, who we're all loving on TV—he's a charmer. The poor, weak, wandering guy is kind of a cultural norm," says Elizabeth Berger, a psychiatrist in Elkins Park, Pa., and author of "Raising Children With Character." A weak or wandering mother is a scarier image, she adds.

What would she do without her cell phone or computer? 'I can't even imagine,' Amanda says.

Popular culture has always been full of unfaithful wives, but even today's fictional cheaters share something that sets them apart from the tragic Anna Karenina or the calculating Mrs. Robinson. Their actions may cause their lives to unravel, but the new philanderers aren't victims. When, on the HBO series "The Sopranos," Carmela finally took a lover after putting up with her mob-boss husband's extracurricular antics for years, audiences cheered. (Her lover was a cad in the end, but the dalliance gave Carmela a secret source of strength.) Sarah, the heroine of

this year's best-selling novel "Little Children," falls in love with a handsome stay-at-home dad she meets at the playground; the affair doesn't last, but it gives her the impetus she needs to leave her husband, a weaselly man with a fetish for the underpants of a swinger he met online. And with her role in the 2002 movie "Unfaithful," Diane Lane created an iconic new image of a sexually adventurous wife. Beautiful and well dressed, Connie Sumner has what looks like a perfect life, and she fools around not because she's miserable but simply because she can (a decision that soon makes her life a lot less perfect).

"Women always say 'thank you' for that role, and at first I wasn't sure how to take that," says Lane, who adds that the character was capable of far more denial than she could ever be. "I mean, she was cheating and lying. Then I realized it was because she wasn't a victim. She made a choice to have an affair. It's not something you often see."

Where do married women find their boyfriends? At work, mostly. Nearly 60 percent of American women work outside the home, up from about 40 percent in 1964. Quite simply, women intersect with more people during the day than they used to. They go to more meetings, take more business trips and, presumably, participate more in flirtatious water-cooler chatter. If infidelity is an odds game, then the odds are better now than they used to be that a woman will accidentally bump into someone during the workday who, at least momentarily, interests her more than her husband does. There's a more subtle point embedded in here as well: women and men bring their best selves to work, leaving their bad behavior and marital resentments at home with their dirty sweatpants. At work, "we dress nicely. We think before we speak. We're poised," says Elana Katz, a therapist in private practice and a divorce mediator at the Ackerman Institute for the Family in New York City. "And many people spend more time out in the world than with their families. I think sometimes people have the idea that [an affair] will protect the marriage." They get a self-esteem boost during work hours and don't rock the boat at home. "In some paradoxical sense this may be a respite, a little break from the marriage."

"I wasn't out there looking for someone else," says Jodie, 34, a marketing professional in Texas and mother of two. (NEWSWEEK talked at length to more than a dozen women who cheated, and none of them wanted her real name used.) Her continuing affair with a co-worker started innocently enough. She liked his company. "We would go to lunch together and gradually it started feeling like we were dating." At Christmas, Jodie asked her husband of 10 years to join her at the office party, and when he declined, the co-worker stepped in. "We just had so much fun together and we laughed together and it just grew and grew and grew until . . . he kissed me. And I loved it."

'He tells me my skin is soft,' says Marisol. 'I know it sounds stupid, but it makes me feel sexy again.'

It's not just opportunity that fuels the impulse to be unfaithful; it's money and power as well. American women are better educated than they've ever been. A quarter of them earn more money than their husbands. A paycheck and a 401(k) don't guarantee that a woman will stray, but if she does, they minimize the fallout both for her and for her children. The feminist Gloria Steinem once said, "Most women are one man away from welfare," but she recently amplified her views to NEWSWEEK: "Being able to support oneself allows one to choose a marriage out of love and not just economic dependence. It also allows one to risk that marriage." In other words, as women grow more powerful, they're more likely to feel, as men traditionally have, that they deserve a little bit of nooky at the end (or in the middle) of a long, busy day.

And like their fathers before them, these powerful women are learning to savor the attentions of a companion who is physically attractive but not as rich, successful—or as old—as they are. In his practice in Palo Alto, Calif., family therapist Marty Klein sees a rise in sexual activity between middle-aged women and younger men. "Forty-year-old women have more of a sense of entitlement to their sexuality than they did before the 'Hite Report,' the feminist movement and 'Sex and the City'," he says. A story currently circulating in Manhattan underscores his point. It seems that a group of 6-year-old girls from an elite private school were at a birthday party, and the conversation turned to their mommies' trainers. As the proud mothers listened nearby, one youngster piped up: "My mommy has a trainer, and every time he comes over, they take a nap." The wicked laughter this story elicits illustrates at least what is dreamed of, if not actually consummated.

The road to infidelity is paved with unmet expectations about sex, love and marriage. A woman who is 40 today grew up during the permissive 1970s and went to college when the dangers of AIDS were just beginning to dawn. She was sexually experienced before she was married and waited five years longer than her mother to settle down. She lives in a culture that constantly flaunts the possibility of great sex and fitness well after menopause. "Great Lovers Are Made, Not Born!" read the ads for sex videos in her favorite magazines; "What if the only night sweats you had came from a good workout?" ask the ads for estrogen therapy.

COVER-UP
Working women say hiding flings is a cinch

At the same time, she's so busy she feels constantly out of breath. If she's a professional, she's working more hours than her counterpart of 20 years ago—and trying to rush home in time to give the baby a bath. If she's a stay-at-home mom, she's driving the kids to more classes, more games, more playdates than her mother did, not to mention trying to live up to society's demands of perfect-momhood: Buy organic! Be supportive, not permissive! Lose five pounds! Her husband isn't a bad guy, but he's busier than ever, too, working harder just to stay afloat. And (this is practically unmentionable) therapists say they're seeing more cases of depressed male libido. It turns out he's too tired and stressed to have sex. An affair is a logical outcome of this scenario, therapists say: women think they should be having great sex and romantic dates decades into their marriage, and at the same time, they're pragmatic enough to see how impossible that is. Couples begin to live parallel lives, instead of intersecting ones, and that's when the loneliness and resentment set in.

Marisol can't remember the last time her husband paid her a compliment. That's why the 39-year-old grandmother, who was pregnant and married at 15, looks forward to meeting with her boyfriend of five years during lunch breaks and after work. "There is so much passion between us," she says. "He tells me my skin is soft and that my hair smells good. I know it sounds stupid, but that stuff matters. It makes me feel sexy again."

Ironically, the realities of the overprogrammed life make it easier, not harder, to fool around. When days are planned to the minute, it's a cinch to pencil in a midday tryst—and remember to wear the lace-edged underwear—at least compared with trying to stay awake and in the mood through "Law & Order." And as any guileless teenager knows, nothing obscures your whereabouts better than an Internet connection and a reliable cell phone. Amanda's husband has no idea she has six e-mail addresses, in addition to an account specifically for messages from her boyfriend Ron. Amanda, a customer-service rep in L.A., uses e-mail to flirt with Ron, then turns to her instant messenger or cell phone when it comes to setting up a rendezvous. "Text messaging is safer than e-mailing," says Amanda, 36, who's been married for eight years. What would she do without her mobile or computer? "No cell phone? I can't even imagine."

Along with its 4 million porn sites, the Internet has exploded with sites specifically for people who want to cheat on their spouses—sites like "Married and Flirting" at Yahoo, "a chat room dedicated to those who are married but curious, bored or both!!" These sites contain all the predictable pornographic overtures, but also such poignant notes as this: "Ok, I know it is late almost 11:30 my time and I am still up on this pitiful Friday night. Hubby STILL at work."

Online romances have a special appeal for married women. For one thing, you don't have to leave the house. "You can come home from work, be exhausted, take a shower, have wet, dripping hair, have something fast to eat and then, if you're feeling lonely, you can go on the Internet," says Rona Subotnik, a marriage and family therapist in Palm Desert, Calif. On the Web, women can browse and flirt without being explicit about their intentions—if they even know what their intentions are. Clicking past porn, women prefer to visit sites that dovetail with their interests, such as chess, bridge or knitting, explains Peggy Vaughan, author of "The Monogamy Myth" and host of dearpeggy.com, a Web site for people with unfaithful spouses. "They find somebody else who seems to think like they do, and then they gradually move from that to an instant message, and then they wake up one day and they cannot believe it happened to them," says Vaughan. Last year Vaughan did a survey of a thousand people who visited her Web site, and 70 percent of the respondents were women. Her results, though not scientific, are remarkable: 79 percent said they were not looking for love online. More than half said they met their online lover in person, and about half said the relationship culminated in sex. Sixty percent said their spouses had no idea.

Wayward Wives 101

Throughout history, women, both real and imagined, have shown that when it comes to infidelity, it's not solely a man's world. Here's a crash course.

Bathsheba
CIRCA 100 B.C.
Spotted bathing by a voyeuristic King David, the married Bathsheba obliges his demands for a royal romp. Pregnant with David's child, Bathsheba stands by as he murders her husband; the child conceived with the king dies.

Guinevere
FIFTH OR SIXTH CENTURY
Though accounts of the myth vary, one fact is almost indisputable: Guinevere, betrothed to King Arthur, fell for Sir Lancelot. In some versions, their first kiss ignited their undying love. In others, they united during a rescue.

Catherine the Great
EIGHTEENTH CENTURY
She needed to produce an heir to the Russian throne but her husband (and cousin), Peter III, was impotent, sterile and mad. Somehow, though, she conceived five children.

Hester Prynne
'THE SCARLET LETTER' (1850)
Assuming her husband is lost at sea, Hester takes up with the town's Puritanical preacher. After giving birth to his child Pearl, Hester is forced to sew her guilt onto her garment.

Emma Bovary
'MADAM BOVARY' (1857)
The 19th century's material girl, Emma is more interested in couture and cash than in her husband. But the debts and suspicions mount, and rather than swallow her pride, she swallows arsenic.

Anna Karenina
'ANNA KARENINA' (1878)
Vronsky loves Anna. Anna loves Vronsky. Anna is married. What to do? She begins seeing Vronsky, and seeks divorce from her husband to no avail. Trapped, she throws herself under a train.

Ingrid Bergman
1949
The cold war started, but this Swedish star's affair with director Roberto Rossellini had Americans steaming mad. After leaving her family, she retreated into a seven-year acting hiatus.

Elizabeth Taylor
1963
Talk about a serial spouse. While filming the 1963 movie "Cleopatra," Taylor—then with hubby number four, Eddie Fisher—fell for her costar Richard Burton. She ran off with Burton soon after.

Mrs. Robinson
'THE GRADUATE' (1967)
A restless housewife, Mrs. Robinson (Anne Bancroft) seduces Ben (Dustin Hoffman) shortly after his college graduation. When he begins dating her daughter, the middle-aged ice queen exacts revenge by sabotaging their relationship.

Francesca Johnson
'THE BRIDGES OF MADISON COUNTY' (1995)
A lonely Iowa farm wife (Meryl Streep) plays tour guide to a rugged National Geographic photographer (Clint Eastwood). They begin looking at bridges but have eyes only for each other.

Camilla Parker Bowles
1994
Rumors of an illicit affair began to circulate as Prince Charles's highly publicized marriage to Diana became strained. Two weeks ago he added Camilla to his financial accounts.

Connie Sumner
'UNFAITHFUL' (2002)
Connie (Diane Lane) is a well-to-do Weschester mother and wife until she literally collides with a sensual, 28-year-old French bookseller on the street. The steamy affair leads to a murder of passion.

Carmela Soprano
'THE SOPRANOS' (2004)
Ever-faithful while husband Tony slept around, Carmela finally had sex with her son's guidance counselor this past season. A.J. wound up with a passing grade in English, and Carmela reunited with Tony.

John LaSage was shocked to come home one day and find his wife of 24 years had disappeared. No note, no phone call, nothing. He'd bought her a computer four months previously, he says, and he knew something was wrong: she'd stay up until 3 or 4 a.m., browsing online. She told him she was doing research for a romance novel she was writing, he says, and after her disappearance, he hacked into the computer to investigate. "She had set up a chat room that was called . . . gosh . . . 'Smooth Legs.' And so guys would come in there and flirt with her. I have transcripts. I can't tell you how excruciating it was to read the e-mails from people supposedly speaking with my wife, but she wasn't talking like my wife. That was just weird." Two weeks later he discovered she had left the country, he says. "I wasn't the perfect husband. I would have done a lot of things differently, but I never got the chance," says LaSage, who has

since founded an online support group (chatcheaters.com) for people with spouses who stray.

In 1643 Mary Latham, who was 18 years old and married, was hanged in Massachusetts with her lover James Britton. Since then, adultery has been a crime in many states. A woman accused of adultery could, in divorce court, lose her home, her income and her children. All that changed in the 1970s, when most states adopted "no fault" and "equitable distribution" divorce laws, in which nearly all the assets accrued to either partner during the marriage belong to the marriage and, in a divorce settlement, are split evenly. And unless a woman (or man) has been flagrantly or inappropriately sexual in front of the children, or has, in the frenzy of an affair, neglected them, infidelity does not legally affect settlements or custody. In researching her book "The Price of Motherhood," journalist Ann Crittenden found, however, that an implicit bias against female adultery still prevails in the country's predominantly male courtrooms—and that when it came to settlements, that bias was costly to women. "There may be no fault as grounds, but fault has not left the system," she says.

Unearthing infidelity is shattering to any spouse. Men can be as traumatized as women by such a revelation; they can also be more surprised. David, 39, a government worker in Washington, D.C., discovered his wife was cheating the day she told him she wanted a divorce. "Never in a million years did I think it was possible." He found out later that his wife had started seeing someone at work, someone David knew fairly well because the two couples often met socially. Once the reality set in, he couldn't get images of his wife and the other man out of his head. Beset by nightmares, he started taking antidepressants. "I felt shame for what had happened, like I couldn't keep a person happy enough to stay with me." Now, eight months later, David is beginning to date again. His divorce should be final this month.

Just over half of all cases of female infidelity end in divorce, says Susan Shapiro Barash, a professor of gender studies at Marymount Manhattan College and author of "A Passion for More: Wives Reveal the Affairs That Make or Break Their Marriages." But that number may be shrinking. The conservative-marriage movement, as well as recent books like Judith Wallerstein's "The Unexpected Legacy of Divorce," have created a backlash against separation and raised consciousness about the seriousness of its effects on children. Therapists who see the overworked professional set say they've noticed an interesting trend: people who have children and marry late in life tend to be less interested in cheating than their contemporaries who married earlier—and more willing to work it out when a woman (or man) does stray. These women have spent a lot of time alone, and they're wise to the benefits of companionship. They've also waited a long time to have families and have a realistic sense of what's at stake. "I think people try to stay together," says Alvin Mesnikoff, a psychiatrist with a private practice in New York. In spite of the temptations, "women want a relationship, and they're willing to work hard at it."

Divorce or no, how do responsible parents protect the hearts of their children when they're in the midst of heartbreak themselves? Therapists say kids don't care whether it's Mom or Dad who fools around—all they care about is knowing they're safe and that their lives will remain stable. It's difficult, but parents who are dealing with a revelation of infidelity need to protect young kids from the facts of the case, as well as from their own anger. "There are very few things I will be absolute about, and this is one of them," says Katz. "Everything [children] ask for is not something they want. And if they ask, you should say, 'Yes, you're right. Things are tense around here, but this is between Mom and me'."

Explaining infidelity to older children is somewhat more complicated. If a 15-year-old turns to his mom and asks, "How long has this been going on?" a truthful answer may be in order, says Berger, the Elkins Park psychiatrist. And if he asks, "How could this happen?" "It may be reasonable for Mom to say, 'You don't understand, dear, that Dad has been cheating on me'," Berger says. Sometimes correcting the record is all right. "There's noth-

ing gained by one parent being a martyr to the other parent's mistreatment." What parents need to avoid at all costs is to wrap the children into the drama by treating them as confidants.

Nadine grew up in a small, Midwestern town, and when she was 13 years old, her mother cheated on her father, moved to a town two hours away and married the other man. "There weren't any fights, nothing crazy," says Nadine, who at 28 lives in a big city and works in finance. "We sat down at Christmas. We discussed that Mother was leaving; it was nothing we had done." She and her siblings continued to live with her father; her mother went to school conferences and games as she had always done. Her parents remained, as she puts it, "best friends." But Nadine's teenage years were difficult. She never warmed up to the new man. She felt abandoned.

'Do you remember that kiss?' Erin asks. 'The kiss that would just launch a thousand kisses?'

In retrospect, Nadine understands what pushed her mother to be unfaithful. Beautiful and intelligent, her mother was stifled by her life's low horizons, and her father, a stand-up guy, was probably a little bit boring. The new man promised travel, wealth and adventure; her father was the kind of guy who'd say, "Why go around the world? You'll get plane-sick." And although she and her mother have made a kind of peace—"I got tired of making her cry," she says—she thinks the affair eroded any kind of trust she has in marriage or love. She can't stay in long relationships. "Ever since I could date, all I could think was, 'I will never, ever, ever do what my mom did.' I will never have a man take care of me. I have been called an ice princess in the past. I feel in some way my mom sold out and kind of fell for something."

Who said being married and raising kids was easy? The good news is that the wounds inflicted on a family by a woman's infidelity are not always critical. Therapists say couples often can—and do—get past it. Sometimes the husband sees it as a wake-up call and renews his efforts to be attentive. Sometimes, especially if neither party is too angry, too defensive or too far out the door, the couple can use it as an opportunity to air grievances and soothe old hurts. Sometimes the woman sees the dalliance for what it is, a fling, and takes it with her to the grave. In her study of good marriages, Wallerstein found that an affair did not necessarily damage family life—especially if it fell into the category of a "one-night stand." "In good marriages this doesn't dominate the landscape, and the kids don't know," she says. She remembers interviewing a 30-year-old man, who said that when he was 9, his mother had an affair, but his father assured him that they would stay together. The man said: "I learned from my father that anything worth having is worth fighting for." When lunch is over and the wine wears off, most women will admit that if they were the prize in a fantasy duel between an imperfect but loving husband and a handsome stranger, they'd root for the husband every time.

With Vanessa Juarez, Holly Peterson, Karen Springen, Claire Sulmers, William Lee Adams, and Raina Kelley.

My Cheatin' Heart

When love comes knocking, do you answer the door?

DAPHNE GOTTLIEB

L et's just get this out in the open.
I was 14 and madly in love for the first time. He was 21. He made me suddenly, unaccustomedly beautiful with his kisses and mix tapes. During the year of elation and longing, he never mentioned that he had a girlfriend who lived across the street. A serious girl. A girl his age. A girl he loved. Unlike inappropriate, high school, secret me.

The next time, I was 15 and visiting a friend at college. It was a friend's friend's boyfriend who looked like Jim Morrison and wore leather pants and burned candles and incense. She was at work and I wanted him to touch me. She found out. I don't know what happened after that.

I was 19 and he was my boyfriend's archrival. I was 20 and it was my lover's girlfriend and we had to lie because otherwise he always wanted to watch. I was 24 and her girlfriend knew about it but then changed her mind about the open relationship. We saw each other anyway. I was 30 when we met—we wanted each other but were committed to other people; the way we look at each other still scorches the walls. I turned thirtysomething and pointedly wasn't invited to a funeral/a wedding/a baby shower because of a rumor.

I am a few years older now and I know this: That there are tastes of mouths I could not have lived without; that there are times I've pretended it was just about the sex because I couldn't stand the way my heart was about to burst with happiness and awe and I couldn't be that vulnerable, not again, not with this one. Waiting to have someone's stolen seconds can burn you alive, and there is nothing more frightening than being willing to take this free fall. It is not as simple as we were always promised. Love—at least the pair-bonded, prescribed love—does not conquer all. It does not conquer desire.

Arrow, meet heart. Apple, meet Eve.

Call me Saint Sebastian.

Out there in self-help books, on daytime television shows, I see people told that they're wrong to lust outside their relationships. That they must heal what's wrong at home and then they won't feel desire "inappropriately." I've got news. There's nothing wrong. Desire is not an illness. 'We who are its witnesses are not infected. We're not at fault. Not all of us are running away from our relationships at home, or just looking for some side action. The plain fact about desire is that sometimes it's love.

If it were anything else, maybe it would be easier. But things are not as simple as we were always promised: Let's say you're a normal, upstanding, ethical man (or woman) who has decided to share your life with someone beloved to you. This goes well for a number of years. You have a lot of sex and love each other very much and have a seriously deep, strong bond. Behind door number two, the tiger: a true love. Another one. (Let's assume for the moment that the culture and Hollywood are wrong—we have more than one true love after all.)

The shittiest thing you can do is lie to someone you love, yet there are certain times you can choose either to do so or to lie to yourself. Not honoring this fascination, this car crash of desire, is also a lie. So what do you do? Pursue it? Deny it? It doesn't matter: The consequences began when you opened the door and saw the tiger, called it by its—name: love. Pursue it or don't, you're already stuck between two truths, two opportunities to lie.

The question is not, as we've always been asked, the lady—beautiful, virtuous, and almost everything we want—or the tiger-passionate, wild, and almost everything we want. The question is, what do we do with our feelings for the lady *and* the tiger? The lady is fair, is home, is delight. The tiger is not bloodthirsty, as we always believed, but, say, romantic. Impetuous. Sharing almost nothing in common with the lady. They even have a different number of feet. But the lady would not see it this way. You already know that.

You can tell the second love that you can't do this—banish the tiger from your life. You can go home to the first, confess your desire, sob on her shoulder, tell her how awful you feel, and she (or he) will soothe you. Until later, when she wonders if you look at all the other zoo animals that way, and every day for a while, if not longer, she will sniff at you to see if you've been near the large cat cages. Things will not be the same for a long time. And you've lost the tiger. Every time the housecat sits on your lap, you tear up thinking of what might have been, the love that has been lost. Your first love asks you what's wrong and you say "nothing." You say nothing a lot, because there's nothing left, nothing inside.

So instead, let's say you go home and tell your first love, *This new love is a love I can't live without. What can we do?* She will say, *All right, I want to meet her right away. I get all holidays and weekends with you, and there will be no sleepovers with the new love, and I expect the same for myself, and you are never to call her any of the nicknames you have ever used for me,* and the whole thing starts to remind you of a high school necking session—under the sweater; over the bra, but not under it.

You feel like an inmate all the time, and, moreover, where is your first love tonight? She's out with someone you've never met while you're out with your second love, who once had been amenable to an affair. She looks at you sadly and says, "So you think I'm only a half-time tiger?" Her fangs are yellowed and sharp and she finds herself unable to stop staring at the clock, which shows when you will have to leave her to return to the lady.

Maybe there is no "happily ever after" here, but I think there's an "after." I have been the first love; I have been the second; and I have tried to decide between my own firsts and sec-

onds. I have walked through each ring of fire, and I've found no easy answers. It could be that hearts are dumb creatures, especially mine. It could be that there are no good answers. Whether we're admitting desire, lying about it, denying it, or fulfilling it, the consequences are staggering, sometimes ruinous.

So, heart firmly sewn onto sleeve, assured that there is an "after," what can we do but stride forth? It seems clear that no system—polyamory, monogamy, or stand-on-your-head-for-me-will sanitize the astonishing highs and the bereft lows of desire and betrayal. And even if they did, who wants a sanitized heart? So it's up to us: to work together, to love what's so human about us, to understand that the risk of love is loss, and to try to grant desire without eviscerating ourselves. I'm not sure how to do this, but I'm still trying. Because above all, I know this: It's grace to try, and fail, and try again.

A version of this essay appeared as the introduction to *Homewrecker: An Adultery Reader* (Soft Skull Press, 2005), edited by Daphne Gottlieb.

The New "Mixed" Marriage

Working with a couple when one partner is gay

JOE KORT

When we think of a "mixed marriage," we typically imagine two individuals of different races or religions. But the mixed-orientation marriage—with one straight spouse and one who's gay or lesbian—is just as real, though far more likely to operate underground. This long-shrouded partnership burst into public view in August 2004, when New Jersey Governor James McGreevey went on national TV to come out as a "gay American," while his wife, Dina, stood stock-still by his side, her mouth arranged in a frozen smile. More recently, best-selling author Terry McMillan (*How Stella Got Her Groove Back*) publicly denounced her husband, Jonathan Plummer, for carrying on clandestine affairs with male lovers. Suddenly, America was buzzing about the "horror" and "tragedy" of straight and gay individuals united by marriage.

Let me be clear at the outset: I'm not against mixed-orientation marriages per se. They can, and do, work well for some couples. What I don't support are mixed-marriages that are steeped in secrecy, which is how these relationships too commonly operate.

Living a Lie

During my first appointment with Eric, he told me that he'd had some homosexual experiences and wasn't sure whether he was gay, bisexual, or a sex addict. The manager of a major export company, 48-year-old Eric had been married to his wife, Ann, for 25 years, and the couple had a teenage son and daughter. But even before he'd gotten married, Eric admitted, he'd had frequent and elaborate sexual fantasies about men.

When he was 21 years old, a college therapist told him what he badly wanted to hear: that his urges were simply sexual perversions that would pass. The therapist further advised him not to act on these "perversions," but to go forth and lead a healthy heterosexual life. Deeply relieved, Eric decided to marry Ann, whom he'd dated during his senior year of college, and to keep his homoerotism to himself.

At first, Eric felt he pulled it off pretty well. He loved his wife and enjoyed sex with her, though he often used images of men to stay aroused and reach orgasm. For a number of years, he didn't act on his homosexual urges, so he didn't feel bad about them. Occasionally, he'd masturbate to porn, but he was careful to throw the magazines out afterward. Overall, Eric's lack of romantic feelings for other men convinced him that his urges were "simply" sexual, not part of full-fledged gay identity. He told himself he was "heterosexual with a bit of kink."

Then, several years into the marriage, the couple bought a home computer, and Eric's delusions quickly began to unravel. Secretly, he began surfing gay-porn sites and entering chat rooms. Before long, he found himself meeting men for anonymous sexual encounters. "But all this time, I loved Ann and believed in monogamy, so I felt horribly guilty for cheating," he told me.

One night, as he surfed the web, he stumbled upon an internet club expressly for married gay men who wanted monogamy with another man without leaving their wives. He immediately joined the group, and soon afterward met Harris, who lived in a nearby city and was also married. They "clicked" online, met soon afterward, and agreed that they'd found the perfect arrangement. They told their wives they'd met at a business conference and discovered that they both enjoyed fly fishing, which gave them the excuse to spend whole weekends alone together, for enthusiastic sex and—for Eric, at least—deepening intimacy.

But their idyll was short-lived, for Harris soon announced that he wanted to have sex with other men. Eric was devastated. He plunged into a depression so black that Ann couldn't help but notice. Finally, sleepless and distraught, he called me.

After listening to his story, I pulled no punches. "You're not living with integrity," I told him.

He exploded. "This from a gay therapist? For a response like that, I could have called Dr. Laura!"

I assured him that I didn't necessarily disapprove of his having an intimate relationship with a man, even though he was married. "The issue is that you're keeping secrets, deceiving your wife, and aren't being congruent with yourself." I said. "If you both had an open relationship, with informed consent on her side, that would be different."

"You have no idea what my life is like!" Eric shouted. "You've never had a wife and kids you loved, and because of it, faced giving up someone you're mad about." He started crying. "Maybe you're not the right therapist for me," he said between sobs. "I need someone to support me and help me make this work."

"Make what work?" I inquired.

"Having a relationship with both my wife *and* my boyfriend. I don't want to lose either of them."

I gently told Eric that if he wanted someone to approve his living a lie with his wife and himself, he was correct—I wasn't the right therapist for him. "Until you get honest with yourself and your wife," I said, "I can't support your belief that having sex with someone outside of marriage is okay." Even more important, I told him, "Until you act from a place of integrity, I don't think you'll feel any happier or more whole than you are right now."

If Eric wasn't prepared to tell his wife, I said, there was another viable option—to stay married and make a commitment to never again act on his homosexual urges. I made very clear that my perspective on this was different from practitioners of Reparative Therapy (RT), who tell gay people that sexual reorientation is possible and, indeed, highly advisable. I believe that's nonsense. However, I do believe that people who self-identify as homosexual, but don't wish to come out as gay, can choose to create a heterosexual lifestyle.

But Eric wasn't open to this option, either. At the end of the session he left quickly, mumbling over his shoulder that he'd call if he wanted to reschedule. I figured there was a good chance I'd never hear from him again. But a month later, he called, sounding desperate. His depression and anxiety had worsened. "I gotta tell her," he said.

Coming Out

When a gay person comes out to his or her straight spouse, the couple is likely to embark on a roller-coaster ride of emotional stages that often encompass humiliation, revenge, renewed hope, rage, and, finally, resolution. While each couple is unique, these stages can serve as a rough road map for therapists trying to help mixed-orientation couples make sense of their feelings, communicate honestly, and, ultimately, make informed, healthy decisions about their future.

When Eric told Ann that he was homosexual, she was stunned and horrified. "Did you marry me just to have kids?" she railed. "Were you just using me all along?" When he then admitted that he'd been having an affair with Harris, her hurt and horror turned to cold fury. Blaming him for ruining her life, she ordered him out of the house and threatened to tell their two teenage children and their families of origin. She also planned to see a divorce lawyer to get full custody of the kids. "You do realize," she hissed, "that no judge would let a homosexual even have visitation rights!"

Beneath Ann's rage was a deep sense of humiliation. "What kind of a person was she to choose a homosexual husband?" she wondered. Eric, in turn, felt humiliated by Ann's accusatory response, which only reinforced a lifetime of shame about his essential "wrongness." I explained to Eric that Ann was trying to shame him because of the humiliation she felt, but that he needed to take her threats of reprisal seriously. At my suggestion, he asked her to join him for a therapy session, and she reluctantly agreed.

Before they came in, Ann sent me a long e-mail detailing everything she knew about Eric's dysfunctional childhood, neurotic personality traits, inadequate fathering, problematic work and sleep habits, and more. This wasn't unusual. Typically, when spouses learn that their partner is gay; their first response is to focus on their partner's failings.

As the joint session got underway, Ann was quick to let me know that she didn't trust me. "Why would a gay therapist be interested in helping us decide whether to stay together?" she demanded. She wasn't sure she wanted to stay with Eric, she said, but she wanted to keep the possibility open. Her concerns made sense to me, and I explained my perspective on mixed-orientation marriages. "If you both want it to work, then so do I," I assured her.

For most of that first session, I listened to, and validated, Ann's flood of thoughts and feelings. Both Ann and Eric wept, insisting that they wanted to stay together but weren't sure it was possible.

I then appealed to Ann's sense of integrity. If she wanted to remain married, it needed be a conscious choice free of shame and darkness. But Ann was unwilling to look at her contribution to the issues in the marriage. Spouses in all marriages—gay or straight—choose partners, in part, to meet certain unconscious needs. I tried to explain to Ann that straight individuals rarely marry gay people accidentally. Either they have sexual issues themselves or they need emotional distance from their partners. Ann didn't want to hear any of this. Instead, she projected all of their problems as a couple onto Eric I spent our next several meetings trying to facilitate clear, open communication between them. What did each of them want? Ann made it clear that she couldn't tolerate Eric's having a relationship with both her and Harris. "You'll have to choose," she told him. But soon afterward, Harris made the choice for Eric by breaking off with him. Eric was crushed, although his boyfriend's decision also clarified for Eric what he wanted—or at least what he thought he wanted. Now that he'd lost Harris, he couldn't face the possibility of losing Ann, too. He apologized for hurting her, and told her he wanted to stay married. "I love you, and I promise to stay faithful," he said.

The Honeymoon

This new pledge of fidelity initiated the next stage of the coming-out process for Eric and Ann as a couple: a kind of honeymoon period of renewed hope and mutual appreciation. Because Eric truly loved Ann, and because he'd empathized with her pain, she began to feel she'd been reunited with the man she married. Eric, for his part, was profoundly grateful that Ann was willing to take him back. "She's a saint!" he told me, his voice edged with awe.

Shortly after they reunited, Ann stopped coming to see me. She also refused to see another therapist or attend a support group for straight partners married to gay partners. But Eric continued on in therapy. Before long, he acknowledged that he'd begun to feel restless and dissatisfied. He loved Ann and his kids; there was no question about that. But with no homosexual outlet, his life felt flat and empty.

Eric's growing dissatisfaction initiated the next stage of the couple's process, when they become aware of the limits of the possible. While still hurt, Ann was genuinely happy to have Eric back. But, the absence of a man's emotional and sexual companionship weighed increasingly heavily on him. Increasingly depressed, he found himself surfing internet porn sites once again, and drifting into chat rooms. Before long, he was telephoning men and meeting them for sex—and, he hoped, for love.

Late one night, Ann caught Eric making arrangements on line to hook up with a new man. After an explosive fight, they returned to my office together. "I love you," he told her in that session, "but I have to be who I am. I want to stay married to you and have affairs with men." I still remember my sense of foreboding when Ann, looking strained and pale, agreed to his terms. This type of arrangement can sometimes work out, but only when the straight spouse is willing to take a long, close look at herself. So far, I hadn't seen any willingness on Ann's part to do that. I strongly recommended she get some individual therapy, but she assured me, "I can handle this on my own."

Eric continued to meet men, but now told Ann the truth about his plans. Between dates, he'd often sit in their driveway for hours talking on his cell phone with guys he'd met online. From Eric's vantage point, Ann seemed to be adjusting pretty well to their "new marriage." Then one night Eric returned home from a date to discover that Ann had told their son and daughter that their father was gay. He was stunned and furious. "How dare you tell them without my permission," he raged, "and without letting me be part of the process!"

"What was I supposed to do?" Ann countered bitterly. "You're out all hours meeting guys, and I'm left here worrying sick you'll be killed!"

Back into therapy they came.

Ann stubbornly held to her position that she'd told the kids only because she was worried out of her mind, not because she was furious at Eric. Firmly, I told them that I believed that neither one of them was behaving either with respect to themselves or their relationship. As far as I could tell, I said, Ann wanted a full-time, monogamous husband—sexually and emotionally. Eric wanted a boyfriend as well as a wife who was reasonably happy with the arrangement. Their aims were incompatible.

For the next few sessions, I worked on encouraging both of them to examine and identify their authentic relationship needs. Within a few weeks, Eric decided to come out as a gay man—in his words, to live "as the person I've been all along." Ann, for her part, realized that it was impossible to make the marriage work. They decided to divorce

Getting Real

When I work with people in mixed-orientation marriages like Eric and Ann's, my goal is neither to help them to stay married or to get divorced. Instead, it's to help partners come back into integrity with themselves and each other. It's truly up to the couple, not to me, to discover what's right for them.

That said, I tend to start from a place of hope for the relationship. Unless one partner definitely wants out of the marriage, I start by asking a couple how their marriage can continue. I work with each partner on what he or she really wants.

I realize that many therapists disapprove of a gay husband and straight wife staying together under any circumstances. Sign of an intimacy disorder. Some might urge the couple to consider divorce to allow both parties to move on with their lives. Other clinicians might advise the gay husband to remain the sexually faithful partner he promised to be on his wedding day. I once held this belief myself—that anything less than monogamy betrayed the relationship. Now I'm open to the various arrangements that couples adopt.

The principal reason I've changed my mind it that I've now sat with many couples who've struggled long and hard over a divorce or separation when, in the end, that wasn't at all what they wanted. So I've come to accept that there are a number of instances in which responsible nonmonogamy between partners is a viable option. One such instance is when the couple is older, has invested emotionally, financially, and psychologically in each other, and want to be together in their later years. Another is when the couple has become best friends, and the marriage is sacred to them. A third is when the man is emotionally heterosexual and physically homosexual.

The idea here isn't to change the orientation of the gay spouse. That's impossible. Rather, it's to accept the couple as they are and honor what they want.

In doing this kind of work, taking a thorough history on both partners is essential. While Ann refused to participate, I was able to do some effective family-of-origin work with Eric. He grew up in a family that demanded obedience, and therefore Eric learned early on to get his needs met underground. I helped him see that his depression stemmed, in part, from his inability to openly make decisions for himself and allow himself to experience the consequences of those decisions. Gradually, I helped him feel safe enough to do this.

Ann still hasn't gotten help. She remains angry at Eric for "ruining her life." This outcome isn't the norm: many gay and straight spouses who divorce ultimately become friends. While Eric wants friendship, particularly for his children's sake, Ann has made it clear she's not interested. Meanwhile, Eric has done his best to talk with his teenage kids about who he is, why he's made the decisions he has, and how much he loves them. At this point, they're more aligned with their mother.

In the meantime, Eric has met a man with whom he wants to spend the rest of his life. He continues to regularly visit his children, but doesn't talk about his gay life or bring his partner around, at their request. I hope that, eventually, the children will develop a separate relationship with Eric and accept his life as a gay man with a new partner, just as they would if their parents had divorced and Eric had married another woman.

It's often hard for me to sit with mixed-orientation couples, since I get in touch with my anger at living in a society that shames gays and lesbians into role-playing heterosexuality. If gays were treated with respect and empathy to begin with, much personal suffering and chaos could be spared. As comedian Jason Stuart says, "I wish you straight people would let us gay people get married. If you did, we'd stop marrying you!"

Case Commentary

Michele Weiner-Davis

Couples decide their marriages are doomed for a litany of reasons. Some say that, though they love their spouses, they're no longer *in love*. Others find the spark has gone out of their sexual relationships. Still others feel that the endless arguments about children, in-laws, and money are so divisive that the marriage has been drained of mutual respect and caring. To me, a psychotic optimist about the possibility of personal and relationship change, these are nothing more than garden-variety problems that, with a heavy dose of problem-solving, can easily be resolved.

But because sex is such a fundamentally important part of marriage, what happens when one spouse finds him- or herself yearning to be with a same-sex partner, despite many years of marriage? No amount of "I-messages," active listening, or willingness to compromise alters sexual orientation.

This is the problem Joe Kort faces on a regular basis, and I have great respect for his interest in helping these couples find their way. Nonetheless, there were times in reading about Eric and Ann that I found myself wondering, "How might I have handled this case differently?" As I reflected on this, several major issues emerged.

One of the most important lessons I've learned in my work with 11th-hour couples is that, regardless of my personal opinions, unless I join equally with *both* spouses, change becomes unlikely and resistance almost inevitable. I've become convinced that the art of doing good marital work lies in our ability to have both spouses leave our offices feeling that we're on his or her side. After all, we often ask people to stretch outside their comfort zones. But, unless they see us as genuine allies, why should they?

With that in mind, I wondered whether Kort really connected with Ann. Let's face it, she was inappropriate and irritating. Her anger and blaming would easily push the buttons of even the most accepting of therapists. But I put myself in her shoes for a moment and tried to imagine what it would be like to discover in an instant that the man I married and thought I knew more intimately than anyone in the world wasn't who I thought he was. Talk about having the rug pulled out from under you!

So, while I'd draw a line in the sand about Ann's anger and threats, I'd try to help both Ann and Eric see how her cruel behavior was really a symptom of the shock, grief, and fear she was undoubtedly feeling. Normalizing in this way might have softened the blow of her actions for Eric, while, at the same time, painting a more humane picture of Ann. This might have allowed them to join in their shared pain, rather than become opponents.

Also, I suspect that marital work may have been doomed from the start because of a theoretical belief held by Kort—that mixed marriages can only work if straight spouses are willing to examine the underlying dysfunctional reasons they marry gays. I know many, many people who simply don't have "gaydar"; they don't pick up on their spouses' homosexual tendencies. And I don't think this means they have an unconscious need for emotional/sexual distance in their relationships.

If owning up to her own reasons for marrying a gay man was the sort of personal growth Kort was expecting of Ann, I can completely understand why she resisted it, along with his other suggestions for individual therapy and support groups. From my perspective, since both Ann and Eric were interested in saving their marriage if at all possible, what they needed was help in defining the parameters of their newly emerging relationship, which was headed toward uncharted territory. I couldn't help

but wonder whether Ann's meltdown resulted, not from her inability to cope with her anger about having to develop a mixed marriage, but from poor communication regarding their mutual expectations around his dating behavior.

Kort's work shines a light on one other issue that's become increasingly clear to me over the years—a marriage is about more than the person to whom you're wedded. I recently worked with a man who loved his wife, but was not in love with her, and was wildly passionate about the woman with whom he'd been having an affair. He admitted he didn't understand why he felt so confused and stuck, because he knew he'd rather be with his affair partner. I explained that, in life, our choices are never simply about one issue versus another: every choice in life is about package deals. I asked him to weigh the attributes not of the women in his life, but of the packages they encompassed. When he did so, his marital package won hands down, despite the sizzle of his affair.

How does this relate to Kort's work with Ann and Eric? Marriage isn't always about achieving personal satisfaction. While I'd certainly encourage Eric to honor and explore his need for same-sex relationships, I'd work overtime to help preserve the family unit, and not simply for the reasons Kort proposes—a shared history, friendship, companionship in old age, etc.—all personally driven goals. What about the kids? Conspicuously missing from Kort's list of acceptable reasons to stay in the marriage is a relationship with your children.

Am I suggesting Eric stay for the sake of the kids? That would be okay with me, but that's not what I'm proposing here. Nevertheless I can't help but wonder how Eric feels now, months or even years later, having sated his homosexual yearnings and become a "regular visitor" of his not-yet-accepting children? Is that the package he wanted?

Author's Response

Weiner-Davis' commentary is comparing apples to oranges: she juxtaposes her heterosexual male client's affair with a woman to the affair of a gay husband with another man. But for the gay spouse, cheating isn't just an indication of a relationship issue; it's his attempt to resolve a personal identity crisis about his fundamental sexual and romantic orientation. Eric had to decide not just whether he could make some changes in his marriage, but whether his marital partner was the wrong gender.

My work with couples assumes that each partner has an equal investment in creating and maintaining the type of closeness or distance—including emotional and sexual—that exists between them. Straight spouses often look back at themselves and admit they unconsciously needed a partner who couldn't be fully available to them. In mixed marriages, these spouses happen to be gay. Nevertheless Ann was unwilling to examine anything other than Eric's "bad" behaviors. Try as I did to join with her, she was unwilling to accept any insights about herself from support groups or individual therapy with myself or another therapist. Had she been willing to do so, she could have come to understand her own personal and relational dynamics.

With all couples, my work is about *shared* responsibility. When one partner in a relationship has an addiction, they're an addicted couple. When the woman is pregnant, they're pregnant. When one has an affair, they both share the burden of how it evolved and how to resolve it.

I would never advise anyone, gay or straight, to stay in a marriage only for the sake of the kids. This burdens the children and would have denied Eric's fundamental identity as a gay man, keeping him invisible.

Weiner-Davis supports my concern about a therapist's countertransference with these couples when she writes, "I put myself in [Ann's] shoes . . . and tried to imagine what it would be like to discover in an instant that the man I married and thought I knew more intimately than anyone in the world wasn't who I thought he was." As therapists, our job is to put on our clients' shoes and take off our own. Doing this is no easy task, but it's mandatory if we're to do good work. Weiner-Davis winds up by doing what too many do to gay

spouses: giving them all the blame for their situation, rather than having empathy for both partners within the context of the culture as a whole.

JOE KORT, M.S.W., is an openly gay psychotherapist in Royal Oak, Michigan. His forthcoming book, *10 Smart Things Gay Men Can Do To Find Real Love*, includes a chapter on heterosexually married gay men. For more information, go to www.gayaffirmativepsychotherapy.com. Contact: joekort@joekort.com.

MICHELE WEINER-DAVIS, M.S.W., is a marriage and family therapist in Woodstock, Illinois, and author of *The Sex-Starved Marriage; The Divorce Remedy*; and the bestsellers *Divorce Busting; Change Your Life and Everyone In It*; and *Getting Through to the Man You Love*. Contact: dbusting@aol.com.

Good Sex: Why We Need More of It and a Lot Less of the Bad Stuff

JENNIFER ROBACK MORSE

Lots of Americans today—young and old—are coping with deep problems related directly or indirectly to sex. Many have been burned by current sexual practices—such as hook-ups that create emptiness, or cohabiting relationships that go nowhere—and are looking for new ways to build a loving physical relationship with a member of the opposite sex. Many would welcome, more generally, a fresh way to strengthen their relationships with loved ones. They need some help balancing not just "love and career," or "work and family," but some even bigger things. Their desire for independence and autonomy must be balanced with their equally important longings for interdependence, closeness, and even neediness at times. Men and women alike would love to find an alternative to the sterile "struggle for equality" in relationships. They have an intuition that freedom is something more profound than just the right to do as you please, but they aren't quite sure what that deeper secret might be.

Finding true love, good sex, and spousal happiness is not easy in modern America because we are working with a batch of concepts that are actively in our way. Today's favorite ideals of equality and freedom, however attractive and appropriate in the political or economic realm, are not adequate bases on which to build happy home lives. Love relations and family life are distinct social spheres that need concepts and ideas of their own, not just hand-me-downs from politics and economics.

And there is much more at stake in the successes and failures of our love lives than just personal happiness and private feelings. It matters to the rest of the world whether we succeed at sex, love, and family life because bad sex, bad love, and bad family life often produce bad children.

A free society needs people with consciences who can control themselves and use freedom without bothering other people too much. Research shows that the groundwork for the conscience is laid during the first 18 months of our lives, in our relationship with our parents. Without that foundation, a child is much more likely to grow up without an ability to govern himself. Thus, your ability to succeed at sex, love, and marriage has the potential to strengthen a free society, or significantly weaken it.

You might object that not every couple has children. Maybe you yourself don't. But there is a second reason your marriage

matters to the rest of the world, a reason that is independent of children. *Human sexuality is the great engine of sociability.* Sexuality builds up the relationship between the couple, and this relationship then becomes the basis of higher society.

The widespread disappointments in family life since the 1960s are predictable consequences of some very dumb ideas. In the last half of the twentieth century, we distilled from the Western tradition of freedom a peculiar elixir of pure sexual and personal freedom. We came up with the idea that *freedom means being completely unencumbered by human relationships.* A person is free only it he or she avoids relationships that generate financial, sexual, or parental dependency. A person, it is claimed, is not free if he or she must be responsible for an unexpected child. A person is not free if he or she feels pressed to remain married.

A society that defines freedom in this way—as the absence of totally committed human relationships—will not remain free. Only by meeting obligations to each other do we produce a new generation deserving of liberty, and able to exercise it responsibly. Moreover, individuals who define freedom in this commitment free way are abandoning the very thing that has the best chance of making them happy.

Yet people continue to acquiesce in many of the assumptions of the sexual revolution, mostly because no appealing substitute seems to be on the horizon. Many Americans think the only alternative to anything-goes sex is something between *The Stepford Wives* and the Taliban. They imagine that if it weren't for free love, women would all beat home in dresses and high heels, in their spotless kitchens with cookies in the oven, robotically waiting for the Beaver to come home from school. If it weren't for the sexual revolution, citizens would be facing prosecution left and right for deviant sexual acts. Without modern sexual mores, America would be one step away from the *burkha* and public stoning for adultery.

How different the truth is.

Sexual intimacy is a social good; it instantly creates small societies.

Sex Makes Us Concerned for Others

The interplay between our self-centeredness and our need for other people is at the heart of sexual activity. Our desire for sexual satisfaction draws us out of ourselves, and into relationships with other people. The sexual urge provides a motive force for sociability. In this way, good sex is the foundation of community.

Our self-centeredness easily comes to the surface in daily life. That's a part of our human nature. So what human impulses are universal enough and powerful enough to lure people out of themselves, and into productive interdependence? The most reliable instinct is the sexual urge. Sexual desire has a powerful ability to make selfish adults aware of other people, and has the potential to make them truly concerned about the welfare of another person.

Potential lovers must *win* each other's love. That means they have to pay attention to one another. They must develop a genuine concern for the other, what he or she likes, wants, feels. Part of the courtship process is to discover who the other person really is, what makes them tick, what pleases them. The lovers must come to know the unique quirks of the other person. It is the sexual impulse that makes that other person interesting, and initiates the relationship.

We don't automatically become genuinely interested in the person to whom we are sexually attracted. It is certainly possible to view another person as simply a means to satisfy our sexual desire. We can think of sexual activity as just another recreational pastime, something fun to do on a Saturday night. We can reduce the other person to an object, interchangeable with other potential sex partners. But in a relationship between two adults of approximately equal strength, neither side will long stand for being used in this way.

The sexual urge thus has the potential to make us more sociable than our natural self-centeredness might first suggest. We have to become aware of the other person as a person—in order to win their affection and their willingness to be sexual with us.

Sex Builds Connection

Sexual activity has two natural purposes; procreation and spousal unity. The procreation part is pretty obvious; the idea of "spousal unity," though, may require some explanation. Spousal unity means that sex builds attachments between the husband and wife It is the feature of human sexuality that makes it distinct from purely animal sexuality.

Casual sex, instead of being a source of bond-building, is just a consumer activity.

The two organic purposes for sex have something in common: they both build community. Procreation literally builds the community by adding new members. Spousal unity builds community by stabilizing marriage and family relationships.

Through the sexual act, men and women connect to each other in a powerful way that carries over into the rest of life.

Most of us have mixed feelings about this connectedness created by sex. We are sometimes vexed by our dependency upon someone else. At the same time, this interdependence can charm and thrill. We love the connection; our bodies cry out for it. Together with a spouse, we can do what neither of us could do alone: bring a new person into existence. Not to mention that we really enjoy one another in the sexual act.

Because reproductive technology has made it possible to separate sexual activity from procreation, we have lost sight of the community-building features of sex. Since we can now do a technological end-run around the procreative function of sex, we seem to think we can also bypass the spousal unity function. But building bonds between sexual partners is every bit as "natural" a consequence of sex as procreation is. The connection between spousal unity and sexual activity is imprinted on the body just as the procreative function is. Neither our bodies nor our souls will allow us to completely undo the connections between sexual activity, devoted love for another adult, and babies. So our ability to build worthy societies depends upon these connections more than we are sometimes willing to admit.

Modern physiology is discovering that the attachments we feel toward our sexual partners are more than mere feelings, and more than cultural conditionings. A relationship is a physiological event. And there are slightly different aspects to the physiology for men and for women, which I'll discuss next.

The Importance of Human Touch

Women need help in raising their offspring through a long period of dependency. We need help in protecting our young, and in obtaining resources for their survival. This is easy to see among primates. Males help provide food, territory, and safety for the mother and her young. The elements of primate physiology that support the social structure contribute to the survival of the group.

We sometimes imagine that we are exempt from the biological rules of survival. After all, in a modern economy a woman and her offspring can physically survive without the help of a man. A woman can even get herself artificially inseminated and have a child without performing a sexual act. The biochemistry of the body, however, works against our attempts to be completely independent of a mate.

Women connect to their sex partners, and to their children, partly via a hormone called oxytocin. This hormone spikes during orgasm, and is heavily involved in the birth process and breast feeding. Oxytocin rises in response to touch, and it in turn promotes touching. It also promotes other forms of affectionate behavior and parenting instincts.

A woman's oxytocin level surges at sexual climax, during labor, and while suckling a child. Her body is literally changed by these community-building acts. The flood of oxytocin increases her desire for further touch with both her mate and her child. The hormone itself connects her to her child and her child's father. This chemical connection builds cooperation between parents for the benefit of their child.

This physiological reality helps explain a couple of otherwise puzzling bits of social science data. First, couples who think they can avoid the commitment of marriage while still having many of its benefits by cohabiting find that the reality is much trickier. They don't realize that their hormones may create an "involuntary chemical commitment" even if their minds have set boundaries. The very process of spending time together, touching each other, having sex, and sleeping next to each other night after night creates a powerful bond, partly biochemical, between the partners.

Bonding hormones also help explain the remarkable propensity of battered women to return to the very men who abused them. Our hormonal response to touch, to sex, and to proximity is so powerful it can trump our better judgment about what is truly in our interests. This may explain why domestic violence is so much more prevalent among cohabiting couples than among couples who decided to marry without cohabiting.

The oxytocin factor may also explain why arranged marriages, so strange to educated Westerners, actually work out well in many cases. We assume that married couples in arranged marriages stay together either because they had no culturally acceptable alternatives or because they started with low expectations for emotional fulfillment within marriage. But arranged marriage is the norm in many successful cultures, and immigrants to the U.S. who come here with parentally arranged marriages will commonly tell you that they grew to share as much love with their partners as any married couple. This may be partly due to the biochemical impact of being in a close, physical, and intimate relationship. The relationship itself creates its own hormonal glue.

By uncoupling sexual activity from spousal unity, we have capsized the whole natural order of sexuality.

Sex Sews Men to Women

While oxytocin helps to bind women to their sexual partners and their babies, something slightly different is at work in male physiology. Vasopressin, primarily a male hormone, has sometimes been called the "monogamy molecule." Less is known about vasopressin than about oxytocin, but the preliminary facts suggest that vasopressin helps to counteract the male tendency to "play the field."

Men also have their own well-documented reactions to sex that tend to tie them to a single mate. On the dark side, there is jealousy. Jealousy appears to be such a common reaction among men that we may safely call it "natural," and some psychologists believe jealousy helps men to connect with their sexual partners.

After all, a man doesn't feel jealous or possessive toward every woman he sees. He feels jealous about a woman he is in a serious relationship with, particularly one he has had sex with. And his jealousy makes it hard for him to just walk away from her and her offspring. A woman doesn't want to be abandoned

by the father of her child; she wants a man who will stick around and contribute. She is thus less likely to choose a man who philanders. So any man who wants to be attractive enough to a woman that she will attach herself to him must fight his tendency to play the field. Jealousy helps him do this.

There is much more at stake in our love lives than just personal happiness. It matters to other Americans whether we succeed—because bad sex and bad family life usually produce damaged children.

The man's body tells him that having sex with a woman puts that particular woman into a new and different category. This is not merely an attractive woman: this is *his* woman who may give birth to his child. She is, therefore, different from other females. The sex act has put her in a more important category.

This hints at the brighter side of male attachment; loyalty. Men are capable of heroic loyalty to women and children. Men will work for a lifetime at jobs they don't like in order to support their families. Despite the common image of divorced men as "deadbeat dads," most meet their child-support obligations, sometimes at tremendous cost to themselves. Part of the fathering instinct is a drive to protect, provide, and take responsibility for others. This male impulse seems to be triggered when a man is needed or trusted by someone beloved. Usually it's a mate or child who triggers this loyalty response. Sometimes it's a beloved country. The spark in both cases is the man's love, and the love he gets in return.

The view that most men, most of the time, have no attachment to their sex partners is a caricature of reality. While it may be true that men attach to their sex partners less than women do, men are not simply looking for sexual release. Men merely attach in a somewhat different way.

To illustrate this, I'll ask my male readers to perform a thought experiment. Imagine you've gone to bed with an attractive woman. She invites you to do whatever you wish sexually. However, she just lays there. She does not respond at all. She doesn't resist, but she doesn't encourage you either. In fact, she gives no sign of feeling anything one way or another. You successfully ejaculate. She quietly asks if you are finished.

Why isn't this satisfying? What is missing? You got your orgasm. You got sexual release. You had the experience of bedding an attractive woman. But there is something wrong. It is obvious what is missing: her caring. The woman's response matters to the man.

Take a different example: The woman is very responsive, very passionate. But when it is all over she tells you, matter-of-factly, that she was fantasizing about her high school sweetheart the whole time. Why does this also feel all wrong?

In the first case, you are using her. In the second case, she is using you. And both make you feel lousy.

So even for men—who are allegedly indifferent to emotions—the relationship matters. A man might not have any particular need to talk about his feelings of connection, neediness, and attachment. But most men would be disturbed by a completely unresponsive or totally manipulative woman. In short, men have feelings about sex beyond mere lust. They have feelings about the quality of the relationship. Those feelings are just somewhat different from women's.

Sex and Sociability

All of this means that sexual activity is necessarily related to our sociability. Sex is especially important in creating and maintaining the most basic of social groups: the family. Our bodies ensure that we enjoy sex so that we will do it and keep the species going. Our bodies help us to connect to our mates so we will stick together to raise our young to maturity and independence. We respond to our emotions as well as to our reason.

The ability to create community is biologically based. Reptiles don't bother: They lay their eggs, maybe help incubate them, and then walk (or slither) away. It is the part of the brain that is uniquely mammalian that actually cares about offspring, and about specific mates.

The human tendency to attach to our sexual partners is thus more than simply cultural conditioning; it is built into us. Societies differ in how they structure spousal attachments, but the basic desire to connect to one's sexual partner has deep physiological roots. We can construct, deconstruct, and reconstruct our cultures all we want, but we are more likely to be satisfied with the outcome if we work with our biology rather than against it.

Our bodies cry out for connection with our sex partners. By having sex, we attach ourselves to each other, and the natural result is a little community, often with a baby at its center. The gift of sex to the world, therefore, is something quite wonderful: human commitment.

But perhaps I should say commitment to each other is the gift of *rightly ordered* sex, because for many people in modern America, sex now has relatively little to do with building community of any kind. Sex is treated as a purely private matter, in the narrowest sense of private.

The sexual revolution has been profoundly anti-social. By uncoupling sexual activity from both procreation and spousal unity, we have—"capsized the whole natural order of sexuality. Instead of being an engine of sociability and bond-building, sex has become a recreational activity, a consumer good. Instead of being something that draws us out of ourselves and into responsibilities toward others, our sexual activity focuses us inward, on ourselves and our own desires. A sexual partner is not a person to whom I am irrevocably connected, but rather an object that satisfies me more or less. And we all know what we do with objects that no longer satisfy us: we discard them.

I believe this shift in worldview is at the heart of today's culture wars. One side believes that the meaning of human sexuality is primarily individual and private—to obtain personal pleasure and satisfaction. The alternative view is that sex is essentially a social activity—whose purpose is to build communal loyalty, starting with the spousal relationship and adding on from there.

Why Recreational Sex Is Anti-Social

The terms "private" and "public" are often treated today as if they are mutually exclusive. But these terms come from economics and politics, and are not entirely applicable to sexuality and the family. When we describe something as "private" we usually mean that it concerns only one or two individuals, and has no effects on other people. When we describe something as "public" we often mean that it is under the jurisdiction of governmental authorities, something we are understandably reluctant to cede for sexual activity. So if the only analytical categories are "public" and "private," that pretty much means sex is "private."

Many Americans think the only alternative to anything-goes sex is something between *The Stepford Wives* and the Taliban.

But sex doesn't meet the technical definition of private. One's sexual activity potentially has very significant consequences for other people, some of them quite negative. There are "victims" involved in some forms of sex, even when adults have consented.

No one, anywhere on the political spectrum, really wants to give other people jurisdiction over sex. Just the same, it doesn't make sense to ignore the legitimate interests that other people have in your sexual activity. This suggests that simply contrasting the "private" from the "public" does not do justice to the inner workings of the family and sex life.

There is another possible category: the "social." This can help us understand a sphere of activity that is properly outside the scope of government, yet still concerns others beyond merely the individuals involved. Sexual activity is social in exactly this sense.

Let me illustrate the social aspect of sex by making a confession. During my student days, I more or less did the whole sexual revolution. I tried most of the hare-brained things I'm now writing about: adultery, fornication, cohabitation, group sex, same-sex sex. I had an abortion. I was married and divorced.

I got to be an expert on what doesn't work. And it was not a jolly time. I hurt myself and other people.

I can't credibly blame anybody else. It was my fault. I was wrong. I am now sorry for the harm I caused myself and others, harm that I can never fully repair.

But I will not give a full confession, precisely because of the social aspect of sex. The reason I won't tell of every sexual encounter I've ever had is because *the other people involved have feelings and interests.* They may not appreciate me telling "my" story as though it was a private possession.

When I was young, I had the idea that my sex life was my private property. I needed that idea. It gave me permission to do what I did. But I was wrong. My sex life is not really my private property.

Every sexual act I have ever participated in has been fully consensual. I never raped anybody; nobody ever raped me. The persons I had sex with never consented to me telling my version of our story any time I choose, however.

Yet this is exactly where the logic of a solely personal approach to sexuality leads us. This sexual encounter is mine, for me to do with as I please. The only thing that prevents people from running off at the mouth is a sense of common decency. But why do we consider sexual reticence to be "decent?" I think it is because we instinctively know that the sexual act creates a "we" out of two "I"s. The sexual story becomes a shared story. The private space between sexual partners belongs to them both; one person cannot take full possession of it, or divide it in half.

Sexual intimacy is necessarily a social good. It instantly creates a small society. We have the potential to create either functioning little platoons that contribute to the wider community, or dysfunctional non-societies that tear it down.

The Costs of Anti-Social Sex

Suppose a young couple decides to get married. Their families have reason to celebrate. The marriage draws one new member into each of the existing families. Everybody is excited about the children the marriage might produce, sometimes years in advance. They will be somebody's nieces, nephews, grandchildren, and cousins; they will be born into a pre-existing social network, with ready-made relationships.

The sex life of the married couple is not public. They don't report on it to other family members. They don't need a government permit for it. But at the same time, it is not exactly private either. Their sex life has social ramifications across generations.

Now imagine another couple about the same age, who choose to have sex without getting married. No one in either of their families necessarily knows or approves of the relationship; it is understood that their sexual relationship is a private matter between two individuals only. No one, no matter how close to them, has the right to express an opinion about it.

Perhaps a baby results from this sexual activity. Maybe the relatives are excited. More likely, they are secretly worried about the demands the new baby will place upon the unmarried parents—and upon members of the extended family. Will the father stick around and support the baby and mother? Will the mother accept his involvement? Will she make demands on the rest of the family for financial and emotional support, and perpetual babysitting? With no long-term commitment between the parents, the baby is a potential drain on everyone.

For the father, the appeal of not getting married is that he can have sex, father a child, and then do what he wants about it after. He does not have to be accountable to the mother or her child, unless she jumps through all the legal hoops necessary to make him accountable.

Likewise, the unmarried mother may believe that she can have her baby without being tied down to the father. She may seriously underestimate the amount of interaction she'll end up having with him. She may misjudge the complications of having to deal with a man she didn't like well enough to marry. She

probably didn't really think about having children and grandchildren in common with this man for the rest of their lives.

Both the woman and the man may enter the situation thinking they are freer than if they were married. They are mistaken, because the marriage commitment creates a series of obligations, benefits, and understandings for both of them. Marriage provides a context of stability in which those needs can be met, help provided, and conflicts worked out. Sex outside of marriage deprives them of the opportunity to integrate these parts of their lives.

Adultery is another example of anti-social sex. When two people who are married have sex with others, this activity tears down an existing community of love, instead of building up a new one. Nobody is excited for this couple and the offspring they might produce. Their relationship is a source of pain and deprivation for their spouses and children. Their relationship may disrupt two households, permanently, with effects that reverberate for generations.

It is a simple truth: adultery and divorce can impose massive and pervasive costs on other people, even those unrelated. The family court system is burdened with trying to resolve the problems generated by the disrupted marriage. The school system is taxed by having to deal with stressed-out children of parents preoccupied with new lovers or contentious splits. The police and criminal justice system are taxed by continual "Amber Alerts" for missing children, who all too often turn out to be kidnapped by their own parents.

> **When I was young, I had the idea that my sex life was my private property. I needed that idea. It gave me permission.**

There are other costs of irresponsible sex. Some women repeatedly get pregnant and have abortions. Sometimes people produce children they have no means of supporting. Nobody thinks freedom means being allowed to impose costs on other people. But in our "no-fault" sexual environment, we are barely able to acknowledge that anti-social sex does this regularly.

Recreational Sex That Isn't Fun

I dispute the widespread idea that mutual consent is the only criterion for judging the morality or appropriateness of sexual activity. We can give our consent to acts that are harmful to ourselves and others. To make consent the only standard of morality comes close to saying we can never make moral mistakes. But some decisions, on reflection, clearly work out better than others. And the variety of negative sexual experiences a person might have is much broader than simply coerced sex.

For instance, "date rape" is said to be reaching epidemic proportions on college campuses. What exactly is date rape, and why is it a problem?

Date rape is unwanted sexual activity that can be distinguished from ordinary rape by the absence of violence. If a woman's date attacks her and forces her to have sex that is rape without adjectives. But date rape often involves alcohol consumption, or cloudiness on who did what, said what, and meant what. She didn't say "no" firmly enough. She wasn't clear in her own mind what she wanted. She allowed herself to be talked into something and then regretted it later.

Perhaps the date rape crisis is mostly a political creation. Some argue that feminists invented the concept of date rape to keep men on edge and on the sexual defensive. But even if there is such a political agitation, why is the claim of unwanted sexual activity a plausible vehicle for a power grab? There must be something about the idea of date rape that resonates with people's experiences.

I tried most of the things I'm now writing about. I got to be an expert on what doesn't work. And it was not a jolly time.

I once had a college student describe to me something he and his fraternity brothers called "The Walk of Shame." This is when a guy slinks back into his frat house or dorm room early in the morning after a sexual encounter, not wanting anybody to see him. He can't quite put his finger on the source of his embarrassment; more often than not, it has nothing to do with this particular woman. The problem is that he had sex with someone he isn't connected with, respectful of, or even well acquainted with. And he doesn't want to have to explain himself.

What is this all about? Certainly not the moral disapproval of roommates—college campuses are now about the least judgmental places on earth. Presumably the sexual encounter was consensual, so he didn't violate anybody's rights. Presumably he and the female in question used contraception, so there isn't concern about pregnancy. Presumably he was able to achieve orgasm. He satisfied today's Big Three criteria for moral acceptability in a sexual encounter. Yet this young man doesn't want to be accountable for that sexual act. The reality is, it was disappointing. It is a source of embarrassment.

The whole premise of the sexual revolution is that sex is just another recreational activity. But no one really believes this. If sex was really no big deal, just another activity, then being talked into unwanted sexual activity should be no more consequential than being talked into going to a ball game when you would have preferred a movie, and the whole idea of date rape would be absurd.

An advocate of consumer sex might reply that the distress college co-eds feel about this casual sexual interaction simply reflects vestigial moral codes that unreasonably condemn sexual activity. But is this believable? Contemporary campuses transmit almost no disapproval of sexual activity of any sort. Students have nearly unregulated opportunities for sexual encounters in their co-ed dorms. Some college courses are thinly veiled pornography classes. It seems unlikely that students are showing up in date rape crisis centers out of some sort of lingering prudery.

And if the encounters that end up being described as date rapes are only about misused power, not about sex, as many feminists insist, this wouldn't be a subject anyone would agonize over. If an acquaintance stole my purse or walked off with my stereo, I'd have no problem calling the cops and smearing the guy to everyone on campus. I wouldn't be plagued by any self-doubt, sense of betrayal, or shame. I'd just be angry.

It is the sex that makes everything feel different. The offense is more intense, because it is an assault on the interior of the person. The fact that a sexual assault by a presumed friend can be worse in some respects than a similar assault by a stranger demonstrates that sexual activity cannot be evaluated without considering the relationship in which it is embedded.

Either sex is a big deal, or it isn't. If it is really no big deal, then unwanted sexual activity shouldn't be particularly traumatic. Colleges could save money and trouble by shutting down their date-rape crisis centers and telling co-eds to grow up and get over it. But what it sex really is a big deal? Then we can't very well categorize it as just another recreational activity. And every serious person knows which of these things is true.

The Guilty Hook-Up

Still, recreational sex has become the norm on many college campuses, where the "hook-up" is now a recognized pattern. A hook-up is when a girl and a guy get together for a physical encounter without expecting anything further. While only a minority of female students admit that they themselves hook up "frequently," students report that hook-ups are not uncommon.

The biochemistry of the body works against our attempts to be completely independent of a mate.

Some say it is easier to have sex than to talk intimately. "People just get really weirded out...neither...are willing at all to talk about their feelings.... It is easier to hook up with someone as opposed to talking." Others report they hook up as a way of avoiding a commitment and a painful breakup. Many women feel awkward and empty after these encounters, researchers report. Some feign indifference, but still hope the guy will call.

The hook-up is often associated with drinking. Students will go to a party, get very drunk, and find themselves in a sexual situation. Sometimes they place themselves in these situations specifically because they want sex but want to avoid romantic entanglements. The binge drinking problem on campuses is thus more closely related to the sexual environment than people are prepared to admit.

But if it is really perfectly normal to have morally indifferent sex—sex without any commitment or connection to the other person—why bother to get drunk? Why not stay sober to enjoy the full pleasure of sex? If the heart, soul, and body really believe the intellectual argument that sex is no big deal, the need to get intoxicated doesn't make sense. It seems students are anesthetizing themselves with alcohol to diminish bad feelings flowing from this noncommittal, indiscriminate sexual activity.

Co-ed dorms facilitate these destructive patterns. Students could certainly find ways to have casual sex without the co-ed dorm, but is there any doubt that this living arrangement makes it easier? Supporters claim co-ed living arrangements prepare students for real life. There actually aren't many real life situations, though, in which a large number of unrelated men and women live in such close and intimate proximity with each other. As two professors who have studied this syndrome observe, "if co-ed dorms offer 'real life' training, it appears to he an early training in booking up and cohabitation, but little else."

So is there something wrong with encouraging cohabitation? Unfortunately, voluminous research shows that the practice increases the likelihood of unhappiness, instability, and domestic violence. Even if a cohabiting couple ultimately marries, they tend to report lower levels of marital satisfaction and a higher propensity to divorce.

Many people imagine that living together before marriage is like taking a car for a test drive. The "trial period" gives couples a chance to discover whether they are compatible. "You wouldn't buy a car without taking it for a test drive, would you?"

Here's the problem with the car analogy: The car doesn't have hurt feelings if the driver dumps it back at the used car lot and decides not to buy. The comparison works fine if you picture yourself as the driver. It stinks if you picture yourself as the car.

The "test drive" metaphor implies I am going to drive you around the block a few times, withholding judgment and commitment until I have satisfied myself about you. You are not permitted to have any feelings about this trial run. Just behave normally. Pay no attention to my indecision, or my periodic withdrawals to evaluate your performance. Try to act as you would if we were married, so I can get a clear picture of what sort of spouse you might be. You just pretend to be wed; I'll just pretend to be shopping.

Cohabiting couples, social scientists find, are likely to have one foot out the door throughout their relationship. They rehearse not trusting. They tend to hold back. I am sorry to say that I learned this from experience. My husband and I lived together before we were married, and it took us a long time to unlearn the habits of the heart that we built up during those cohabiting years.

Living together is not just a glorified roommate situation. The body knows the difference between sexual activity and other forms of camaraderie. We have a deep longing to be cherished by the person we have sex with, a longing that is not fooled by our pretense of indifference.

"We're living together" is a way of avoiding a decision. Once a couple begins asking "should we get married?" they bring the intellect more fully into the decision making process. People can't slide into marriage in quite the same way they slide into cohabitation. People decide to get married. They offer an account of themselves. They tell others what they are doing and why. They invite witnesses to come and celebrate. A person doesn't quite do any of that when moving in with a partner, a few possessions at a time.

Good, Bad, Wrong, and Right

Since "wrong" and "right," "good" and "bad" are no longer useable terms in our judgment-free world, we don't have many adjectives available for describing a negative sexual encounter. Yet, as any experienced person knows, some rendezvous feel all wrong. Even if the sex was voluntary, and appropriately contracepted, it just felt all icky. (There's no other word.)

Having sex makes a person uniquely vulnerable, both physically and emotionally. We don't just give our bodies to the other person during sex. Our whole spiritual, emotional, and psychological being is bound up in the act.

Look at the variety of non-physical harms we might experience during a voluntary sexual encounter. We might feel used or manipulated. We might feel ignored while the other person attends to their own orgasm. We might feel like a chump because the whole experience mattered more to us than to the other person. If we allow sex to mean a lot, we leave ourselves more open to being hurt. A person might resist letting sex mean very much—by holding back, protecting herself from the potential bad feelings that flow from vulnerability. But in the process, we've "protected" ourselves from many potential good feelings as well. And we have ourselves become people who use others.

Our ability to describe unsatisfactory sex is now extremely cramped by the premise that all voluntary sex is acceptable. We've collapsed all the possible delineations or categories into rape (bad) and consensual sex (good). If these are the only permissible categories, then every voluntary sexual act is essentially indistinguishable from any others.

> **A society that defines freedom as the absence of committed human relationships will not remain free.**

It is now difficult to say "I feel cheap." Or "I feel used." Or "This was all wrong." The words are inexplicable to someone with the stunted moral vocabulary of the modern, anything-goes mind. So in order to make sense of the powerful feeling that something dreadfully wrong happened, some contemporary women reinterpret the deeply icky act as an assault. That's the sort of place you end up once you define sex as nothing more than a recreational activity, or an interaction of plumbing parts. Properly speaking, sexuality should be primarily about building up the relationship between a man and a woman. Take the relatedness out, and suddenly sex is a lot less enjoyable, wholesome, and productive.

To Persuade Is Not to Impose

I am not now, nor have I ever been, a member of any governmental body. I have never lobbied for legislative change, or brought a lawsuit as a means of altering society. I have neither wish nor authority to "impose my morality" on anybody. The only kind of power I seek is the power to persuade.

And why should I go to the trouble of trying to persuade complete strangers? I have found through my own experience that it's extremely difficult to figure out the meaning of human sexuality on your own. By the time you have conducted enough trials and errors to learn that your initial premises were false, you've lost a lot of time. You may have wasted your prime years of sexual enthusiasm trying to decide what sex means, what type of partner to look for, how to treat him or her, and what you can reasonably expect in return. You may be menopausal by the time you figure it all out!

This is part of what older people ought to offer younger people: the benefit of experience and hindsight. That way you don't have to make it all up as you go along. More generally, moral codes exist to give us helpful signals of what prior men and women over many generations have found to be most true and valuable.

I am willing to share my experience that the moral premises of the sexual revolution will not usually sustain lifelong love; that, instead, they will usually bring unnecessary trouble. An ethical code that puts the sex act on approximately the same moral plane as eating a meal will do that.

To those who hold that sex is best when it has no limits, I also want to suggest that you don't know what you are missing. Keeping sex within reasonable, time tested boundaries is not only more wholesome, it is also more enjoyable.

JENNIFER ROBACK MORSE is a research fellow at Stanford's Hoover Institution, and author of *Smart Sex: Finding Life-Long Love in a Hook-Up World* (Spence), from which this essay is adapted.

Pillow Talk

A conversation with Stephen and Ondrea Levine about lust, the meaning of marriage, and true intimacy

NINA UTNE

What is a good long-term relationship? *When we asked the question around the office and among our friends, we heard a lot of fear and even more relief. Fear because asking questions inevitably rocks the boat of marriage and family. Relief because after we admit that there are few long-term relationships to emulate, we can begin an honest exploration of how to do it differently. Stephen and Ondrea Levine, with three marriages behind them, have made their marriage work for 26 years and have raised three children. They work as counselors and writers, with a focus on death and dying as well as relationship issues. Good relationships are entirely idiosyncratic, they say, but self-respect, clarity of intent, and commitment to growth are the key elements. Ondrea says each of us has to start by answering the question "What do you want out of this very short life?" But ultimately, Stephen says, it's about "when you get to just loving the ass off that person and you still don't know what love means."*

Nina: We hear a lot about how relationships begin, and plenty about how they end. But there's not a lot of honest talk about how to make them last—or, for that matter, why they should.

Ondrea: Once the lust of the first couple of years wears off, once the other person is off the pedestal, and you're off the pedestal, and you're facing each other and you see each other's craziness, frailties, vulnerabilities—that's when the work really starts. The initial intensity of the passion cools, and love comes to a middle way, a balance. You have to have something more than the fact that you're in love to keep it going and keep it growing.

Nina: And what is that something?

Stephen: I think relationships persevere because you're interested in what's going to happen the next day and your partner is an interesting person to share it with.

O: Also, the people with the best relationships often have some kind of practice. It can be religious practice, love practice, nature practice, whatever, but they have something that's so

essentially helpful in their growth that it keeps the relationship going.

S: People who get into a relationship who don't already have something that's more important to them than themselves—generally spiritual practice and growth, or maybe service work—are less liable to stay with the process when the relationship doesn't give them exactly what their desire system wishes for.

N: Someone wrote that 35 percent of his relationship comes from the fact that he brings his wife a cup of coffee in bed every morning.

S: What a weak relationship! Boy, that's a miserable relationship. This guy better get himself another hobby!

O: I was just thinking how very thoughtful that is. Serving each other is exceptionally important.

S: Growth. Growth is also important.

O: Yes, various levels of growth, but certainly heart expansion. Everybody would define growth so differently, but love has to grow, your heart has to open more, you have to get clearer about your intentions, clearer about what you really want out of this very short life.

And it's so individual; it depends so much on life experience. Love and simple human kindness are of huge value to me, and I find that I'm drawn to people who are thoughtful and kind. I used to be drawn to people who were only wise.

N: It seems like the bottom line is the level of consciousness and openheartedness that we bring to a long-term relationship.

S: In a relationship, we're working on a mystical union. That's a term that came from the Christian tradition, but it's part of almost all devotional traditions. And it means uniting at a level way beyond our separation. After 26 years, the line between Ondrea and the Beloved is very, very blurred. In that context, you may ask what happens when two people's goals change. Well, if they're working on becoming whole human beings, they'll change in a whole way, whether it means being together or separate.

N: Growth and service and practice are important. But what happens if you have those intentions but there are kids and hectic lives and petty annoyances and betrayals? How does mystical union accommodate that?

S: But that's what everybody has to work with. I mean, if you can't get through that stuff, there is no mystical union. If only mystical union were so easy—if people could just lean into each other's soul space, as it were. In fact, people think they're doing that, and it's actually lust, generally. We say that love is as close as you get to God without really trying. When people live together, maybe they do feel each other's soul, maybe they do feel the Beloved, maybe they both enter the Beloved. But mind arises, preference arises, attitude arises, inclination arises.

O: We raised three kids, and we certainly had our share of times when our hearts were closed to each other and we felt separate, but our commitment was to work on that and to work with it by trying to stay open, trying to understand the other person's conditioning, because our conditionings were so different.

For instance, what you might think of as betrayal I might not think is betrayal, so all of that has to be defined in a relationship. How I might work with betrayal, you might not be willing to, and that's part of what you have to work out with your partner. Some levels of betrayal are workable, and some are not worth putting in the energy for some relationships. There's no right way other than your way.

S: And *betrayal* is a loaded word. A lot of people naturally feel resentment in a relationship because there are two people with two desire systems. Sometimes they're complementary and sometimes contradictory. And when someone doesn't get what he or she wants—it can be something so simple, like not enough gas in the car, little things—the feeling of betrayal may arise. Now, sexual betrayal, that's something else entirely.

N: What do you think about the possibility of open marriages?

S: Raging bullshit. Well, it's fine for young people who don't want a committed relationship. But you might as well kiss your relationship good-bye once you open it. I don't think there is such a thing. People who open their relationships open them at both ends. The relationship becomes something you're just passing through. There's no place for real trust. There's no place where you're concerned about the other person's well-being more than your own, which is what relationship is, which is what love is. I've never, ever seen it work, and we've known some extremely conscious people.

N: But when I look at the carnage in so many marriages, I think maybe we need to step back and look at the whole agreement. There are many, many different kinds of love, and maybe we're just being too narrow.

O: We've known a couple of people who have had multiple relationships within their marriage and it's worked out for them, but it takes a certain inner strength and a depth of self-trust. Part of why marriage has been set up is because of trust, and keeping track of lineage and money and paternity and all that stuff. I think it's all based on trust, and we don't seem to have the capacity to trust deeply unless it's just one other person.

S: Then again, for some, sexual betrayal is like an active catapult. It can throw them right into God. It can clarify their priorities.

N: So you're saying that an open arrangement undercuts intimacy?

O: So many people nowadays run to divorce court because it's easier than trying to work it through. And it's so exciting to go on to that next new relationship, where someone really loves you and doesn't know your frailties. I know many people who keep going from relationship to relationship because it's easier. Although they wouldn't say that. They wouldn't even think of the children. They would only think of themselves, and that's okay too, but I don't think you get as much growth.

S: That sex thing, that's way overrated. Way, way overrated. Because if two people love each other, the part that becomes most interesting in sex is the part that may be the least interesting in the beginning. It's the quality of taking another person internally. I don't think people realize, with our loose sexual energy, the enormity of letting someone inside your aura, so to speak. To let someone closer to you than a foot and a half, you are already doing something that is touching on universal wonders and terrors.

As the intimacy becomes more intimate, though the sex may not be as hot, the intimacy becomes much hotter. Much more fulfilling. Sexual relationships actually become more fulfilling the longer they go on if you start getting by all the hindrances to intimacy—all your fears, your doubts, your distrust. Sex has an exquisite quality to support a relationship, not because of the skin sensory level, but because of heart sensory level.

N: What significance is there in the formality of marriage? The contract?

O: That depends on your conditioning. For us, marriage meant that we were going to work as hard as we could. But we both said that if the other person wanted to go another way or had a major epiphany or wanted a change in life, we would honor that.

The contract gives you a sense of security that both people are willing to work as hard as they can. I certainly don't know that the marriage contract is for everyone, although I think it can be helpful with kids. Then again, I'm 60, and that's an old style of thinking. That's why I think nowadays maybe a six-month marriage contract might be more skillful. The most important thing is to be honest about how you see your relationship: Do you see it as 'til death do you part, do you see it as until you just can't stand each other, do you see it as until the kids are 18? Anything is workable.

N: I'm thinking about children, this container we call family. For me, there's a certain mystical union in

families. Sometimes "staying together for the sake of the children" is actually about honoring this idea of family.

O: Of course we didn't stay together for the children, because we're both divorced and had children.

S: It's only my third marriage . . . I'm working at it!

O: I got married for the old reason that many women in my generation did. I was pregnant. I didn't really want to get married, but I would've been a *puta*, a prostitute—looked at as a lesser woman in those days.

I think that it mostly is an empty relationship when you're staying together for the kids, but we have known some people whose love for their kids was so great that they became more brotherly and sisterly, and it worked very well for them, but that's pretty rare.

S: And usually when people are in that kind of disarray, the children do not benefit from their staying together.

N: Are there other options than the train wreck to divorce?

S: Depends on the individuals. It depends on their spiritual practice. I think it has a lot to do with their toilet training.

O: Oh, we're screwed.

S: What I mean is that our earliest self-esteem and self-image comes into play. The most beautiful thing about love—and the most difficult—is that it makes us go back to our unfinished places and relationships and, maybe, finish them. Your partner is the person who helps you do that, not by serving you, but by serving as a mirror for you, by his or her own honesty. By observing our partners' struggle to be honest we learn to be honest ourselves.

N: I just see so many people who are either rushing to divorce or living in dead marriages. They seem afraid to ask these deep kinds of questions and have these kinds of conversations.

O: I have worked with thousands of people who are dying, and I have heard several common complaints on the deathbed. The first was: "I wish I had got a divorce." Mostly it was fear: They didn't want to start all over again with someone else. Oh, some people were happy. They said marriage was the most wonderful ride of their lives. But many were unhappy. They wished that they hadn't let fear get in the way. But, you know, to wait until you're on your deathbed to start reflecting on what your needs are—it's not too late, but it's awfully late.

N: That's a lot of procrastination.

To learn more about the ideas of counselors, teachers, and writers **STEPHEN** and **ONDREA LEVINE**, visit their website at www.warmrocktapes.com.

The Merry-Go-Round of Desire

An interview with Mark Epstein

A contemporary psychiatrist uses ancient Buddhist wisdom to make sense of desire in our every day lives.

Mark Matousek

I n the nine years since publishing his first book, *Thoughts Without a Thinker*, Mark Epstein, M.D. has done more to pioneer the meeting of Buddhist and Western psychologies than any doctor in this country. Now turning this cross-cultural gift to the polarizing topic of Eros, Epstein continues to break new ground in his forthcoming book, *Open to Desire*, envisioning a middle path where lust for life—questioned in some dharma circles—is no longer seen as the enemy.

Trained at Harvard, Epstein, whose other books include *Going to Pieces Without Falling Apart* and *Going On Being*, is a longtime meditator who lives in New York City with his wife of twenty years, Arlene Schechet, and their two teenage children. One chilly afternoon last fall, attired in a black T-shirt and khakis, he met with me in his basement office to talk about this thorny issue of desire.

—MARK MATOUSEK

You're working on a book about desire. Why desire? After studying Buddhism for thirty years, I realized that people have this idea that Buddhism is about getting rid of desire. I don't think that's true, so the book is a defense of desire, really—an exploration of the Middle Way, trying to chart out an approach to desire that isn't about indulging, necessarily, or repressing.

Why does desire need defending? From the Western, Puritan point of view, it's always been seen as dangerous, devilish, the enemy. From the Eastern spiritual point of view—as adopted by many Western practitioners, at least—it has the connotation of something to be avoided, a poison. As a psychotherapist, I've been trained not to avoid the so-called "real stuff"—anger, fear, anxiety—and this certainly includes desire. Desire is the juice. It's how we discover who we are, what makes a person themselves. I wanted to try to explore how to work with it more creatively.

Many of the ancient stories of the Indian subcontinent, like the *Ramayana*, the epic tale of separation and reunification of the lovers Sita and Rama, explore desire in an expansive, imaginative way. In the *Ramayana*, Sita is kidnapped by the demon Ravana and separated from her lover, Rama. Ravana wants to possess Sita totally. He is enthralled by her but can only see her as an object. Sita resists this, and in her isolation and imprisonment she deepens her own desire for Rama. The separation that Ravana brings about helps her to get more in touch with the nature of her own desire. I was intrigued by the way desire and separation are intertwined in the tale, as if you can't have one without the other. There seems to be a teaching there about what constitutes a true union. I've been reading over these stories to try to bring back some of this ancient wisdom.

What we really want is for the object to be more satisfying than it ever can be.

We should probably define our terms. Are we talking about sexual desire? Carnal desire? I'm taking the psychodynamic view that all desire is really sexual at some level. Freud once said that he wanted to show that not only was everything spirit, but it was also instinct. One of the wonderful things about the Indian perspective is that it doesn't make the same distinctions between lower and higher that we are used to. Lower and higher are one. There is a much more unified view, so that there is no question but that the sensual contains within it the seeds of the divine. The view in the West, at best, is that things are organized in a hierarchical way, with sensual pleasure being a lower rung on a ladder that reaches toward the sublime. In the Indian view, it's not a rung, it's the entire ladder. So I'm trying to keep a focus on sexual desire throughout.

With the same general implications of clinging and attachment? The question is whether clinging and attachment are an intrinsic part of desire. Sometimes in Buddhist scripture they really seem to be talking about desire in a more celebratory way. When I make my defense, I like to make that distinction. The Buddha warned against the clinging and craving that arise when we try to make the object of desire more of an "object" than it really is. If we stay with our desire, however, instead of rejecting it, it takes us to the recognition that what we *really* want is for the object to be more satisfying than it ever can be.

The Buddha's teachings emphasize that because the object is always unsatisfying to some degree, it is our insistence on its being otherwise that causes suffering. Not that desiring is negative in itself. We can learn to linger in the space between desire and its satisfaction, explore that space a bit more. In my interpretation, this is the space that Sita was in during her separation from Rama. When we spend more time there, desire can emerge as something other than clinging.

Or addiction? Yes. Desire becomes addiction after you have that first little taste of something—alcohol, great sex, getting stoned—that comes so close to complete satisfaction … then you start chasing it. The same thing happens in meditation: having that first bit of bliss, then it's gone. You want the perfection back. But you're chasing something you've already lost. If you stay with that widening dissatisfaction and think, "Oh, yeah, of course," then insight can begin to happen. In that gap.

So our relationship to desire is the problem. That's the point I'm trying to make. Different teachers have different approaches to this: some recommend avoidance of temptation or renunciation, while others talk about meeting desire with compassion. Another strategy is to recognize the impermanence of the object of desire—for instance, by countering lust with images of how disgusting the body really is.

Other teachers say that desire is really just energy that we have to learn how to use without getting caught by it. This is traditionally found under the rubric of Tantra, but it appears throughout the Buddhist canon. There's the famous Zen story in which the Buddha holds up a flower, and only one disciple grasps his meaning and smiles. There are many interpretations of this story, and mine is perhaps unorthodox. But the flower, in Indian mythology, seems to be the symbol of desire. Mara, the tempter, shoots arrows of desire at the Buddha, and the Buddha turns them into a rain of flowers. Kama, the god of Eros, shoots five flowered arrows from his bow. When the Buddha holds up the flower, he might be saying, "No big deal." Desire is something that can be met with a smile.

As a therapist, do you believe that it's possible to reject desire in a healthy way? Of course. There's something very useful about the capacity for renunciation. I think that renunciation actually deepens desire. That's one of its main purposes. By renouncing clinging, or addiction, we deepen desire.

Think of Shiva. In the Indian myths, Shiva is the great meditator, the supreme renunciant. He was so absorbed in his meditation that the gods once tried to rouse him to come to their aid in a battle by sending Kama to wake him. But Shiva reduced Kama to ashes with one glance from his third eye. He was so powerful, he could incinerate desire with one look. But the world could not survive without Eros. The gods pleaded with

Shiva, and he resurrected Kama as easily as he had destroyed him. He then left his meditative absorption and turned toward his lover, Parvati. They had sex for the next thousand years. The bliss of their lovemaking was the same as the bliss of his solitary meditation. This is the essential teaching of Shiva: that *tapas*, the heat of renunciation, is the same as *kama*, the heat of passion. One deepens the other. The Buddha's point, I think, was that by renouncing clinging we actually deepen desire. Clinging keeps desire in a frozen, or fixated, state. When we renounce efforts to control or possess that which we desire, we free desire itself.

So it's selective renunciation. I think so. Because you don't want to snuff out the love. They say that the Buddha taught each of his disciples differently. He could look at each of us and see where the clinging was.

It may not be so much that we *have* desire as that we *are* desire. Trying to renounce desire is like trying to renounce yourself. This isn't the way to see the emptiness inside. But clinging is different. We can renounce clinging without estranging ourselves from desire.

Selective renunciation deepens desire because you separate out what's addictive. You free up the erotic? The question would be, What is the truly erotic?

Enlighten us. I think it has something to do with playing with separateness: trying to erase it while at the same time knowing that we cannot. There is a tension between the control we wish we had and the freedom that is naturally present. There were great religious debates in seventeenth-century India about which would bring you closer to divine desire: being in a committed relationship or having an adulterous one. And the adulterous relationship won out because of the quality of separateness, of otherness, that the illicit relationship had. The relationship between husband and wife in those days was more about property. The woman was completely objectified; everything was scripted. There was no room in that relationship for the quality of hiddenness that makes something erotic—or of teasing.

In Japanese garden design there is a principle called "Hide and Reveal." They make a path near a waterfall so that you can never see the waterfall entirely from any one vantage point. You can only get glimpses of it—there's something in that that relates to the erotic. In psychodynamic language, this is the ability to have a relationship between two subjects, instead of a subject and an object. Can you give your lover the freedom of their subjectivity and otherness? Admit that they are outside of your control?

Which in turn could help us remain unattached …

Any attempt to attach too much will only lead to frustration and disappointment. But attachment is a tendency that is endemic to our minds. We can't just pretend it's not there, but if you can keep coming back to the truth—that what we desire is not *ours* in that sense—we can confront our own grasping nature, which, if seen clearly, self-liberates.

What are some of the practices, skills, that someone caught on the merry-go-round of desire can use to find the Middle Way? Meditation is the basic tool for that. In training the mind in bare attention, not holding on to pleasurable experiences and not pushing away unpleasant ones, we can learn to stay more in touch with ourselves. When we practice in this way, pretty quickly we can find out where we are stuck. The mind keeps coming around to the same basic themes. One of my first Buddhist teachers, Jack Kornfield, writes very movingly in his book *A Path with Heart* about his early experiences in long-term meditation at a monastery in Thailand. His mind was just filled with lust. He was freaking out about it, but his teacher just told him to note it. Despairing that it would never change, he tried his best to follow his teacher's instructions. And what he found was that, after a long period of time, his lust turned to loneliness. And it was a familiar loneliness, one that he recognized from childhood and that spoke of his feeling of not being good enough, not deserving enough of his parents' love. I think he said something like, "There's something wrong with me, and I will never be loved." Something like that. But his teacher told him to stay with those feelings, too; just to note them. The point wasn't to recover the childhood pain, it was to go through it. And eventually the loneliness turned into empty space. While it didn't go away permanently, Jack's insight into something beyond the unmet needs of childhood was crucial. This is one way to unhook ourselves from repetitive, destructive, addictive desire. It lets us go in a new direction—it frees desire up.

Sexual relation is as close as one can come to experiencing the mingling of bliss and emptiness.

The way we try to extort love or affection from people can be very subtle. Or we may use food or drugs or television or whatever else to try to get that extra something. When we don't get it, we wonder what's wrong with *us*. And the layers of addiction are never-ending. An alcoholic can stop drinking, but that doesn't mean he's not using sex to the same end, you understand. These layers extend all the way down to someone in a monastery, who can still be addicted to some pleasant feeling in meditation. In Buddhism they say that the most difficult addiction to break is the one to self.

The other tendency in meditation is to push away what we don't want, but aversion constitutes self as much as desire. This can lead to the anti-erotic, anti-celebratory, anti-emotional tendency among some Buddhists. This keeps them feeling more cut off than they want to be.

In a culture of addiction—with overavailability of nearly everything—isn't the learning curve especially steep when it comes to confronting desire? One thing that has helped me think about this is the psychoanalyst Jessica Benjamin's theory that there are two kinds of desire. A male desire (present in both sexes), which knows what it wants and is going after it, which is all about trying to obtain satisfaction.

And a female desire, not just in women, which is more about interpersonal, and intrapersonal, space. The male desire is about doing and being done to, while the feminine desire is about being. Think of a baby at the breast. In one version, the breast is trying to feed the baby—it's forcing itself into the baby's consciousness, or the baby's mouth. In the other version, the breast just is. The baby has to find it, discover it, for herself. It's almost like our culture is hip to "male" desire, assaulting us constantly with "you want this, you want that." It's so much in the object mode that it doesn't yield the room for what she's calling a feminine desire, which is "Give me some space to know what I really want."

We can learn to linger in the space between desire and its satisfaction.

What do you think about transcendence of bodily desire as a healthy path? Transitionally, it might be valuable for people at certain times. So much of our conditioned experience is spent in the lower part of our body. And it's certainly helpful for the sick body. You want to know that your mind is more powerful than any of that, that you're not *only* that but exist psychically, emotionally—on many levels all at once. I remember when I would take classes with Ram Dass, and he would only teach from the heart up. He would lead guided meditations where the energy would only circulate from the fourth through the seventh chakras. It was always implicit, though, that we would bring the energy back down to the lower chakras eventually.

But transcendence as the ultimate thing, I haven't found that to be helpful. It seems like the only idea that really makes sense to me is this one: samsara and nirvana are one. Dissociating yourself from any aspect of who you really are is only a setup for future trouble. The ultimate thing has to be a complete integration of all aspects of the self.

In your own evolution as a lover and practitioner, has your relationship to desire changed, hit walls—have there been tangles? Not to get too intimate ... It's always been a question for me. When I first started to practice, I was mostly aware of my anxiety. But as my mind started to calm down, I began to notice my own desire more. As if desire and anxiety are two sides of the same coin. I've always had a basic view, I suppose, that the Middle Path was the only way to go. Getting to know my first meditation teachers helped. I remember after one of my first Vipassana retreats with Joseph Goldstein and Jack Kornfield, I went into town with them to eat in a restaurant. I think they must have ordered meat or something—they had no pretension about them. It was such a relief. I didn't need to idealize them; their humanness was very obvious and very touching. For me it meant that I didn't have to try to be something other than what I was.

That's one of the main things that encouraged me to become a therapist—the relief I felt at not trying to be other than I was. Suzuki Roshi used to talk about using the manure of the mind as the fertilization for enlightenment. That's how I felt about accepting who I was. I understood that I had to make use of whatever I actually was—not pushing it away was as important as not holding on to it.

I'm interested in this question of transformation. Can laypeople actually transform desire? How much of this is imagination? Tantra is all about the capacity to imagine. Once you understand the emptiness of phenomena, you have the freedom to imagine another reality—superimpose another reality on this one. It's just as real as this one, which you've already understood is empty.

So the energy isn't actually changing? The energy isn't actually changing, no.

"Transformation" is a misnomer, then. Is imagination as important in connecting sex and love, do you think? I think sexual desire is the physical attempt to reach the other, coupled with the intuition that they are forever out of reach. A famous psychoanalyst named Otto Kernberg speaks of sexual union as the experience of a lover revealing himself or herself as a body that can be penetrated and a mind that is impenetrable. You feel these two things simultaneously. Sexual desire has both the male and the female element: the attempt to possess or take over the other, coupled with the impossibility of ever really grasping them. And it's out of that combination that love, empathy, compassion— all those other feelings—emerge. Through realizing the lover's otherness.

That's the basis of love? I don't think that's the basis of love, but that's what happens when you're in love. Being able to appreciate, feel compelled by, the infinite unknowability of the other. It's a mystery you want to get closer to, where there's a yielding but not an ultimate merger. Both of you remain free.

Sex is a real vehicle for experiencing this. Which is why, in Tibetan Tantra, they use sexual relation as a metaphor for what is realizable through advanced practices. Sexual relation is as close as one can come in worldly life to experiencing the mingling of bliss and emptiness that is also understandable through solitary meditation practice.

Yet sex and mindfulness are not necessarily great bedfellows. Lots of us use, or have used, sex as a great way to get unconscious. Yet even with the senses overwhelming us, there's still some awareness there. And it

may be that very sort of awareness, of mind at the brink of going under, that's most powerful. The moment of orgasm is classically seen as a doorway to higher consciousness, but most of us don't stay there for very long. In fact, we run away from it, a little bit afraid of how overwhelming it is. As I understand it, Tantra is about staying within that doorway longer, to rest in the bliss. That's what you train yourself to do. The nonconceptual bliss that you can only really taste through intimate sex, or spiritual practice.

Which is obviously very easy to become addicted to. Yes.

How does pleasure differ from joy, do you think? Buddhist psychology says that every moment of consciousness has pleasurable, unpleasurable, and neutral qualities. Even after enlightenment, these feelings persist. They don't go away. But joy—the Pali word is *sukkka*, the opposite of *dukkba*, or unsatisfactoriness—is a fruit of realization. The capacity for joy increases as the attachment to the self diminishes. In the end, everything becomes sukkha. You know, even dukkha becomes sukkha. So I think it all becomes pleasure.

Yet pleasure has such a bad rep in the Buddhist world. And that's unfortunate. Because the Buddha taught not only about suffering, but about the end of suffering. Desire is only a problem when we mistake what's ephemeral for an object, something we can permanently grasp. It's only suffering because *we don't understand.* You know, this knowledge is encoded in the great Buddhist monuments, or *stupas*, that were built at the height of Buddhism's flowering in India. Surrounding the central mound of the stupa—where the ashes or bones of the Buddha or another enlightened being were stored—was a processional area where visitors to the stupa could circumambulate in a kind of devotional walking meditation. But enclosing the processional area was a great circular railing carved with all kinds of sculptures. These sculptures were often of all of the pleasures of worldly life, and they often included erotic scenes, couples in all forms of embrace, goddesses with trees growing out of their vaginas, these kinds of things. And you had to pass through these scenes, or under them, to reach the processional area. The pleasures of worldly life were the gateways, or portals, to the Buddha's understanding, as symbolized by the central mound. They are blessings that lead us further toward the Buddha's joy.

Index

Index

gay-straight alliances (GSAs), 68
gender quotient test, 32–33
genetics, homosexuality and, 59–67; sex
    differences and, 36–37
genital herpes, 91
genital warts, 91
genomic imprinting, of the chromosome, 36
"gestational" surrogacies, 130
*Getting It Right the First Time: How to Build
    a Healthy Marriage* (McCarthy), 83
Giannetti, Charlene C., 138, 140
Giedd, Jay, 29
gladiatorial games, as entertainment, in
    Rome, 5
Glass, Shirley, 38, 39
Global Campaign for Microbicides, 125
God, homosexuality and, 61
*Going to Pieces Without Falling Apart and
    Going On Being* (Epstein), 197
Gottlieb, Michael, 18
Gottman, John, 83, 96
Government Accountability Office (GAO), 125
gray matter, of the brain, 37
*Great Sex for Moms: Ten Steps to Nurturing
    Passion While Raising Kids* (Raskin),
    103, 128
Greenberg, Les, 96
Grimes, David, 108–109
Gur, Ruben, 37
Gurian Institute, 27
Gurian, Michael, 27, 28, 30

H

Hail, Jacquelyn Dowd, 20
Halford, W. Kim, 101
Hamer, Dean, 60, 61
Heard, Michael, 41
Hepatitis C epidemic, in prisons, 48–51
hepatitis, 91
Higgins, William, 146
high-risk sex, AIDS and, 42
Historia Naturalis (Pliney the Elder), 3
HIV. *See* AIDS
Hodge, Trevor, 6
Hofmann, Regan, on HIV positive, 45–47
homosexuality, 55–58, 74–79; genetics
    and, 59–67; teenagers and, 68–73
homosexuals, 21; AIDS and, 17
honesty, marriage and, 101–102
"honor killings," 166
Hope's Voice, 44
Hopkins, Keith, 4
hormone replacement therapy, 41
*How Can I Get Through to You: Closing the
    Intimacy Gap Between Men and Women*
    (Real), 83
How Sex Changed (Meyerowitz), 55
human papillomavirus (HPV), 125, 126

I

identities, sexuality and, 56
India, sex and love in, 12
infertility, 40–41
Inqueery, 70
Internet: dating on, 148; romances on, 176;
    sex offenders registered on, 157, 158
interstitial cystitis (IC), as possible cause of
    pain during sex, 53
"intimacy disorder," 171

intimacy, sex and, 86
Invention of Heterosexuality, The (Katz), 55
Isaacs, Rebecca, on homosexuality, 65
Isay, Richard, 63
Italy, sex and love in, 10
IV drug use, AIDS and, 42

J

Jamaica, physical appearance of women in, 8
Japan, sex and love in, 13
Johanson, Sue, 152–153
Johnson, Ann, 146
Johnson, David, 56
Johnson, Scott, 102
Johnson, Susan, on couples therapy, 96–100
Jones-Nosacek, Cynthia, 110, 111
Jordan, Beth, 110
Journal of Cross-Cultural Psychology, 8
junior high school, sexual revolution in,
    138–140

K

Katz, Elana, 175
Katz, Jonathan, 55
Kefauver-Harris amendments, 118
Kenya, physical appearance of women in, 9
King, Martin Luther, Jr., 20
Klein, Marty, 176
Koop, C. Everett, 124
Kornfield, Jack, 199
Kort, Joe, on mixed marriages, 181–185
Kortemeyer, Linda Smith, 146–147
Kramer, Peter, 83, 84, 174

L

laparoscopy, as treatment for endometrio-
    sis, 52
later-term abortions, 121–123
Lavender Scare, The (Johnson), 56
Lee, Sing, 7
Legato, Marianne J., 36
lesbians. *See* homosexuality
LeVay, Simon, 59, 60, 62, 63
Levine, Ondrea, on lust, marriage and inti-
    macy, 194–196
Levine, Stephen, on lust, marriage and inti-
    macy, 194–196
Levitra, erectile dysfunction and, 95
levonorgestrol, 115, 116
Lewis, C. S., 4
Love in Action, of Memphis, Tennessee, 69
love, 179–180; and sex, 88–90
Loving Homosexuals as Jesus Would (Th-
    ompson), 70
low self-esteem, AIDS and, 43

M

Maasai tribe, women of, 9
Magdalene, Mary, stories of, 23–24
male desire, 199
manileness, of men, 25–26
March on Washington, 20
marital counseling, 96
Markman, Howard, 101
Marriage and Family Therapy, 102
marriage education, 101–102
marriage, 82; civil, in Massachusetts, 78
    See also mixed-orientation marriage

Martiin, Mary, 109
Massachusetts, civil marriages in, 78
massage, passion and, pregnancy and, 128
Matousek, Mark, interview of Mark Epstein
    by, on desire, 197–200
Maude, abortion and, 113
McCarthy, Barry, 83; on variant arousal pat-
    terns, 170–173
McFadden, Dennis, 62
McSherry, Susan, 52
Meeker, Martin, 56
Megan's Law, 156–158; requirements of, 157
mentoring program, boys and, 30
Mexico, sex and love in, 11
Meyerowitz, Joanne, 55
mifepristone, 117
"Minds of Boys, The" (Gurian), 28
miniature brothels, among wealthy families,
    in Rome, 4
mixed-orientation marriage, 181–185
Mommsen, Theodor, 3
Mongolia, physical appearance of women
    in, 8
"Monogamy Myth, The" (Vaughan), 176
Montgomery bus boycott, 20
morality, versus public health, controversy
    over birth control ills and, 109–110
Murray, Sandra, 96

N

National Institutes of Health (NIH), 49, 50
natural family planning method (NFP), 111
Ndebele tribe, women of, 8
Nelson, Lawrence N., 40
New Gay Teenager, The (Savin-Williams),
    68, 69
"no fault" divorce laws, 177
nomadic tribeswomen, physical appearance
    of, in Mongolia, 8
nonoxynol-9, condoms and contraceptives
    and, 124–127

O

online romances, 176
Open to Desire (Epstein), 197
oral sex, in junior high school, 138, 139;
    pregnancy and, 128
over-the-counter availability, of Plan P, 115
over-the-counter lubricants, as treatment for
    vaginal dryness, 53
oxytocin, women and, 187, 188

P

Partial-Birth Abortion Ban Act, 111
"Passion for More: Wives Reveal the Affairs
    That Make or Break Their Marriages, A"
    (Barash), 178
passion, sex and, 128–129
Path with Heart, A (Kornfield), 199
*Patience of a Saint: How Faith Can Sustain
    You During the Tough Times of Parent-
    ing, The* (Sagarese and Giannetti), 138
pelvic congestion syndrome (PCS), as pos-
    sible cause of pain during sex, 54
Perel, Esther, on erotic intelligence, 85–87
Perry, Bruce, 27
Pharmacists for Life International, 108
Pillard, Richard, 60, 61, 63

Test Your Knowledge Form

We encourage you to photocopy and use this page as a tool to assess how the articles in *Annual Editions* expand on the information in your textbook. By reflecting on the articles you will gain enhanced text information. You can also access this useful form on a product's book support Web site at *http://www.mhcls.com/online/*.

NAME: DATE:

_____

TITLE AND NUMBER OF ARTICLE:

_____

BRIEFLY STATE THE MAIN IDEA OF THIS ARTICLE:

_____

LIST THREE IMPORTANT FACTS THAT THE AUTHOR USES TO SUPPORT THE MAIN IDEA:

_____

WHAT INFORMATION OR IDEAS DISCUSSED IN THIS ARTICLE ARE ALSO DISCUSSED IN YOUR TEXTBOOK OR OTHER READINGS THAT YOU HAVE DONE? LIST THE TEXTBOOK CHAPTERS AND PAGE NUMBERS:

_____

LIST ANY EXAMPLES OF BIAS OR FAULTY REASONING THAT YOU FOUND IN THE ARTICLE:

_____

LIST ANY NEW TERMS/CONCEPTS THAT WERE DISCUSSED IN THE ARTICLE, AND WRITE A SHORT DEFINITION:

We Want Your Advice

ANNUAL EDITIONS revisions depend on two major opinion sources: one is our Advisory Board, listed in the front of this volume, which works with us in scanning the thousands of articles published in the public press each year; the other is you—the person actually using the book. Please help us and the users of the next edition by completing the prepaid article rating form on this page and returning it to us. Thank you for your help!

ANNUAL EDITIONS: Human Sexuality, 30/e

ARTICLE RATING FORM

Here is an opportunity for you to have direct input into the next revision of this volume.
We would like you to rate each of the articles listed below, using the following scale:

1. **Excellent: should definitely be retained**
2. **Above average: should probably be retained**
3. **Below average: should probably be deleted**
4. **Poor: should definitely be deleted**

Your ratings will play a vital part in the next revision.
Please mail this prepaid form to us as soon as possible.
Thanks for your help!

RATING	ARTICLE	RATING	ARTICLE
	1. Vox Populi: Sex, Lies, and Blood Sport		28. How to Talk About Sex
	2. Women's Ideal Bodies Then and Now		29. Access Denied
	3. Sex Around the World		30. You Can't Do That on Television
	4. The Beauty Pageant Prevails		31. Sex, Politics, and Morality at the FDA: Reflections on the Plan B Decision
	5. How AIDS Changed America		
	6. Remembering Bayard Rustin		32. A Late Decision, a Lasting Anguish
	7. The Magdalene Mystique: Why Her Archetype Matters		33. Condoms, Contraceptives and Nonoxynol-9: Complex Issues Obscured by Ideology
	8. The Manliness of Men		34. Sex Without Sex? Keeping Passion Alive
	9. The Trouble with Boys		35. A Tale of Two Mothers
	10. The Gender Quotient Test		36. The Birds and the Bees and Curious Kids
	11. The New Sex Scorecard		37. The Sexual Revolution Hits Junior High
	12. Sudden Infertility		38. The Cuddle Puddle of Stuyvesant High School
	13. Battling a Black Epidemic		39. Your Turn: Give Students the Knowledge to Make Wise Choices About Sex
	14. Positive Thinking		
	15. Prison Outbreak: An Epidemic of Hepatitis C		40. Sex and Love: The New World
	16. When Sex Hurts		41. Staying Up Late with Sue
	17. Everyone's Queer		42. The Sex Offender Next Door
	18. Why Are We Gay?		43. Silent No More
	19. The Battle over Gay Teens		44. Where Girls Marry Rapists for Honor
	20. The End of Gay Culture		45. A Cruel Edge
	21. Great Expectations		46. Sexual Heroin
	22. In Search of Erotic Intelligence		47. The Secret Lives of Wives
	23. 24 Things Love and Sex Experts Are Dying to Tell You		48. My Cheatin' Heart
			49. The New "Mixed" Marriage
	24. How to Tell Your Potential Love About Your Chronic STD		50. Good Sex: Why We Need More of It and a Lot Less of the Bad Stuff
	25. The Viagra Dialogues		51. Pillow Talk
	26. Save Your Relationship		52. The Merry-Go-Round of Desire
	27. Be a Better Couple		

(Continued on next page)

BUSINESS REPLY MAIL
FIRST CLASS MAIL PERMIT NO. 551 DUBUQUE IA

POSTAGE WILL BE PAID BY ADDRESEE

McGraw-Hill Contemporary Learning Series
2460 KERPER BLVD
DUBUQUE, IA 52001-9902

ABOUT YOU

Name   Date

Are you a teacher? ❐   A student? ❐
Your school's name

Department

Address   City   State   Zip

School telephone #

YOUR COMMENTS ARE IMPORTANT TO US!

Please fill in the following information:
For which course did you use this book?

Did you use a text with this ANNUAL EDITION? ❐ yes ❐ no
What was the title of the text?

What are your general reactions to the *Annual Editions* concept?

Have you read any pertinent articles recently that you think should be included in the next edition? Explain.

Are there any articles that you feel should be replaced in the next edition? Why?

Are there any World Wide Web sites that you feel should be included in the next edition? Please annotate.

May we contact you for editorial input? ❐ yes ❐ no
May we quote your comments? ❐ yes ❐ no